Unsolicited Comment.. ....
Targum Isaiah Message:

I had not heard of the Targum before. What a great resource to verify how people believed in the first century.-AL

HEBREW SCRIPTURES ALL THE WAY!! This is a FAN-TASTIC in depth study of The Isaiah Targum.-DC

I was astounded when I noticed that Isaiah 64:24 does not exist in my NASB version. The Targum makes a difference. WOW!-CD

I am so excited! You've already supplemented our study & you didn't even know it – Praise YHVH!!!-DE

It was so nice to find an excellent teaching on this subject. I can now share this teaching with others. –EM

[A Divine Messiah] is a Jewish & Hebraic teaching to begin with, & this originates in the Hebrew Scriptures. Great teaching. Thank you.-RS

I have studied the Scriptures in Isaiah and have been very confused. It's nice to understand what YHWH was really saying through His prophet.-LA

The wisdom of Scripture that Yahweh reveals in the Targum is phenomenal!! Thanks for the insight!! -DD

YHWH speaks to His servants through the WORD of Isaiah. Thank you for sacrificing your time for me and for guiding me out of darkness through this work. Blessings to you.-RF

I really appreciate Eliyahu bringing to light some of the more obscure elements of the passages of Isaiah.-BL

This has been a very encouraging and enlightening study of Immanuel through Isaiah. Shalom, -GD

This was one of the most exciting teachings ever! Thanks Eliyahu for blessing **me** with this message! -BR

Thank you for further increasing my understanding of the full WORD of Yah.-KB

Such a beautiful teaching and once again so overwhelming! Praise YHWH!-JG

Thank you for explaining all of this by laying out the translations. It is very clear that Yeshua our Messiah was born of a virgin birth. Excellent teaching.-SR

TSIYON EDITION

TARGUM ISAIAH IN ENGLISH

With **Parallel *Jewish*** And ***Christian* Texts**

Special Features by
Eliyahu ben David & Dawn
& the Tsiyon Team

Author Online!

For audio CDs, radio programs, news,
and more visit Eliyahu ben David at:

www.Tsiyon.org

Published by
Zarach
College Station, Texas

ISBN-10: 0-9679471-2-X
ISBN-13: 978-0-9679471-2-9

Concept, Cover Design and Copywriting
by Eliyahu ben David

Publishing, Volunteer Coordination and Layout
by Dawn ben David

Scanning, OCR, Transcription, Proofing and Editing
by the Tsiyon Volunteer Team

Acknowledgments

This work is, of course, indebted to Isaiah the faithful prophet for writing down the fountain of living hope filling the book called by his name, to Jonathan ben Uzziel, who authored *Targum Isaiah* some twenty centuries ago, and Tzvi Nassi a/k/a Christian William Henry Pauli, who, two centuries ago was so moved by the message conveyed by these foregoing servants of YHWH that he translated *Targum Isaiah* into English as an act of love for his generation. We are inspired by their example.

We are thankful to the Eternal WORD that Tzvi Nassi's translation of *Targum Isaiah* found its way to us. The particular challenge we faced in producing the *Tsiyon Edition* of *Targum Isaiah* was in the gigantic scope of the text transferal, editing and layout project. Countless hours of scanning, OCR conversion, transcribing, proofreading, layout, editing and other preparatory work, were lovingly given by our Tsiyon volunteers, working right along with us, toward the completion of this volume. It was admittedly a set-back for all of us when just before publication, most of that effort literally went up in flames as our Tsiyon Ministry headquarters was destroyed by fire.

Not to be deterred, with the help of the whole Tsiyon Team, we have done it all again, and this time, with Yah's help, have managed to get this volume all the way to you. We at Tsiyon Ministry would like to thank and acknowledge the whole Tsiyon Team—family, friends, listeners, partners, and ministry volunteers – whose labors of love helped make this book possible–both the first and second time it was completed!

The Great Isaiah Scroll
Column VIII (eight)

Isaiah 8:8 to 9:11

[Figure Left]

The Great Isaiah Scroll
Column XLIV (forty-four)

Isaiah 52:13 to 54:4

[Figure Right]

i

About The Cover Graphics

With every book I work on I feel impelled to make the whole book, including the cover, part of the unified story that needs to be told. In this case I found that very easy to do, especially in the selection of cover background art. I have a connection, a fond memory that influenced that graphic choice. In 1988 I visited Israel and took time to visit the ruins of the Qumran community near the Dead Sea. There I saw a cave with my own eyes that is much more than a cave, it is the site of a modern miracle. In 1947, a young Bedouin shepherd boy chased his wayward goat to that cave, which led to the first of the Dead Sea Scroll discoveries. The boy threw in a rock that struck a ceramic pot containing leather and papyrus scrolls that were twenty centuries old! Thanks to God, a goat, and a shepherd boy, eleven caves around the Dead Sea were eventually found, containing tens of thousands of scroll fragments dating as early as the third century BCE.

220 biblical scrolls were found in the area, confirming the amazing accuracy of the Hebrew Scriptures that have come down to us today. Of these, arguably the very best is the Great Isaiah Scroll. It is one of the best preserved and contains the entire Biblical book of Isaiah in Hebrew.

While in Israel I was blessed to visit the Shrine of the Book, where I was able to view a large section of the Great Isaiah Scroll. I still retain the sense of awe I felt as I saw that ancient message written down on that scroll as much as 200 years before my Messiah walked the dusty roads of Israel. As I looked at the scroll the signature of YHWH Himself kept jumping out at me from its ancient leather panels, filling me with a worshipful fear of the Ancient One.

Scholars told me that scroll is some one thousand years older than the oldest manuscripts of the Hebrew Scriptures known to us before the scroll's discovery. Yet, The text is amazingly close to the Masoretic text of medieval codices that generations of Scripture readers have depended upon. All of this is hard evidence that YHWH has preserved His message to Israel and to mankind. I can't help but think the timing of that discovery was providential, just one year before Israel, fulfilling prophecies from Isaiah, was reborn back in her own Land.

Front Cover Graphic

That brings me back to the cover of this book. The front cover graphic is taken from The Great Isaiah Scroll, Column VIII (eight), containing Isaiah 8:8 to 9:11. The name *Immanuel* appears in this column at the end of line 1 and the end of line 3. In every occurrence of *Immanuel* in the text it is written as one word, indicating a proper name. By contrast, in the Masoretic text, it is written as two words meaning "God with us." This personal name *Immanuel* in the ancient Great Isaiah Scroll demonstrates ancient theological agreement with *Targum Isaiah,* in the belief in a Divine Messiah. Here is an English translation of excerpts from that section of the scroll. (*Immanuel* appears in 7:14; 8:8,10)

> Continue 8:8 and pass over and shall reach Tsor and he shall stretch out his wings filling the wideness of your land O Immanuel. (9) Join together peoples but you shall be broken, and {give} ear to all far off lands, and prepare yourselves but you shall be broken. (10) Counsel advice but it shall be annulled, make speeches but it will not stand for Immanuel has spoken. (12) Say ye not, a conspiracy, to all this people who say a conspiracy and do not fear their fear nor shall you be in dread of YHWH of Hosts (13) And He is a sanctuary, and He is your fear and he is your dread (14) and for sanctification but for a rock of stumbling and he is a rock cliff of offence to both houses of Israel for a snare and for a trap to the inhabitants of Jerusalem. (15) And many among them shall stumble and they shall fall and they shall be broken, snared and captured. (16) Make strait the testimony and seal up the Torah among the learner. (17) And I will wait for YHWH who is hiding his face from the house of Jacob and I will hope for him. (18) Look I and the children whom YHWH has given to me are for a sign and wonders in Israel, from YHWH of Hosts who is dwelling in Mount Tsiyon.
>
> Chapter 9:5 Because a child shall be born to us and a son is given to us and the government shall be upon his shoulders and he shall be called wonderful, counsellor, mighty God, everlasting father the prince of peace. (6) Of the increase of his government and his peace there shall be no end. upon the throne of David and over his kingdom to order it and to establish it in judgement and in righteousness from and until eternity, The zeal of YHWH of Hosts will perform this. [Fred P. Miller Translation]

Back Cover Graphic

The back cover graphic is taken from The Great Isaiah Scroll, Column XLIV (forty-four), containing Isaiah 52:13 to 54:4.

Also, this section includes the controversial Isaiah 53, wherein the Synagogue maintains the suffering servant is the nation, Israel, while believers in Y'shua the Nazarean as Messiah understand the passages to be prophesying about Him. No further comment about this is necessary. We shall let these excerpts from the scroll speak for themselves.

Chapter 53:1 Who has believed our report and the arm of YHWH to whom has it been revealed (2) And he shall come up like a suckling before us and as a root from dry ground there is no form to him and no beauty to him and in his being seen and there is no appearance that we should desire him. (3) He is despised and rejected of men, a man of sorrows and knowing grief and as though hiding faces from him he was despised and we did not esteem him. (4) Surely our griefs he is bearing and our sorrows he carried them and we esteemed him beaten and struck by God and afflicted. (5) and he is wounded for our transgressions, and crushed for our iniquities, the correction of our peace was upon him and by his wounds he has healed us. (6) All of us like sheep have wandered each man to his own way we have turned and YHWH has caused to light on him the iniquity of all of us (7) He was oppressed and he was afflicted and he did not open his mouth, as a lamb to the slaughter he is brought and as a ewe before her shearers is made dumb he did not open his mouth. (8) From prison and from judgement he was taken and his generation who shall discuss it because he was cut off from the land of the living. Because from the transgressions of his people a wound was to him (9) And they gave wicked ones to be his grave and [a scribbled word probably accusative sign "eth"] rich ones in his death although he worked no violence neither deceit in his mouth (10) And YHWH was pleased to crush him and He has caused him grief. If you will appoint his soul a sin offering he will see his seed and he will lengthen his days and the pleasure of YHWH in his hand will advance. (11) Of the toil of his soul he shall see {+light+} and he shall be satisfied and by his knowledge shall he make righteous even my righteous servant for many and their iniquities he will bear. (12) Therefore I will apportion to him among the great ones and with the mighty ones he shall divide the spoil because he laid bare to death his soul and with the transgressors he was numbered, and he, the sins of many, he bore, and for their transgressions he entreated. [Fred P. Miller Translation]

Forward: Targum Isaiah Reveals the Word

By **Eliyahu ben David**

Dawn and I, and our entire Tsiyon Team, are proud to bring you: *Tsiyon Edition Targum Isaiah In English With Parallel Jewish and Christian Texts,* which may be abbreviated as *Tsiyon Targum Isaiah* (TTI).

TTI was created to make *Targum Isaiah* accessible, at an affordable price, to all English speakers. While scholars will find this to be a useful edition of *Targum Isaiah*, this volume was created with the ordinary person in mind. For that reason this forward assumes you know nothing at all about this or any *Targum*, and builds from there. If you know more, feel free to skim until you get to something that catches your attention.

What Are Targumim?

Targumim is technically the correct plural form of *Targum*, but English speakers commonly use *Targums* as the English plural, so we shall as well. *Targums* designate the Aramaic translations, paraphrases really, of the *Tanakh* (a/k/a/ "Old Testament"). When the remnant Jews returned to Israel from the Babylonian Exile, Aramaic gradually became dominant as the colloquial language, while Hebrew declined, eventually becoming the language of the schools and of worship. To aid understanding of the predominantly Aramaic listeners, when a portion of the Hebrew Scriptures was read on the Sabbath an explanatory paraphrase – a Targum – was offered with it. The Targums thus arose to make the Scriptures more understandable to the Aramaic speaking Jews just before and after the turn of the first century.

The Targums paraphrase the Scriptures. A paraphrase expresses what is believed by the translator to be the meaning of the passage. This meaning can vary considerably from the literal word-for-word translation of the verses. A paraphrase is often more readable, and understandable, than a literal translation, if the translator has a deep and correct understanding of the source material. However, one must always remember that the translator may not be getting it right in some verses. If the translator does not understand a verse correctly, then his paraphrase could mislead you, but in any case it will show you what the translator took the verse to mean.

Here is a modern example. In English, we have lots of paraphrase Bibles. Probably the most well-known is the *Good News Bible*. When you read the *Good News Bible*, it is eminently easier to read than, say, the *King James Version*. The advantage is, it is written in modern English, is very fluid and understandable, and so is easy to follow. However, if you want to do a serious word study in the Bible you will need to use a more literal translation. That's because the *Good News Bible* does not literally translate every word. It expresses the understanding of the translator of what the passage means. That understanding could be, and probably is, colored in some passages by theological training and religious dogma.

That example may help you to understand the advantage that the Targums offer to us today. Think about it. The Targums paraphrase the Hebrew Scriptures in Aramaic as it was spoken at the turn of the first century. The Targums were widely used by the Aramaic-speaking Jews in Judea when Y'shua walked the earth. The Targums, because they paraphrase rather than simply translate, tell us how the Jews of that day interpreted the Scriptures back then – what *they* understood the Scriptures to mean. You may be surprised by what they believed.

Who Was Jonathan ben Uzziel?

Targum Isaiah was authored by *Jonathan ben Uzziel* (not the same as Pseudo-Jonathan). According to the *Jewish Encyclopedia* Jonathan ben Uzziel was "Hillel's most distinguished pupil (Suk. 28a; B. B. 134a)." (*Jewish Encyclopedia* - Jonathan ben Uzziel)

In the realm of Jewish thought, none were more accepted than "Hillel's most distinguished pupil." His theology was molded according to the Hillel School that dominated the thinking of the Pharisees of first century Judea.

Demonstrating the high esteem in which Jonathan ben Uzziel is held, we have these excerpts from the *Preface* of the original edition of Pauli's *Targum Isaiah*:

> The Synagogue maintains, that the Prophets Haggai, Zechariah, and Malachi gave Jonathan Ben Uzziel the Paraphrases written upon a roll spread over his head. (Shalsheleth Hakkabala, p. 20.)
>
> We read in the Talmud: (Succah, p.28, f. l.) "Jo. Ben Uzziel was worthy of the Shekina (the Holy Spirit) which rested upon him, as he did upon our teacher Moses. He was such a holy man, that when he studied in the

law, the birds flying over him were burnt to death." (Tract. Megilla, cap. Iii. col 1.)

Such legends, fabulous as they are, express the high veneration in which this writer is held, and his authority in matters of faith.

Jonathan ben Uzziel composed *Targum Isaiah* about 30 BCE. His Targums were held to be inspired by the Holy Spirit and were regularly used in the Synagogue. Jonathan ben Uzziel's *Targum Isaiah* is not the *Book of Isaiah* as Isaiah wrote it. Rather, in it's pages we find the *Book of Isaiah* as Jonathan ben Uzziel, and the mainstream Jewish world of the first century, understood it. Pauli's *Preface* reveals the core of that ancient mystery:

His paraphrases shew us, that the ancient Jewish Church believed in the Divinity of the Messiah then to come, and that that Messiah was to bring in everlasting righteousness by his fulfilling the law, by which righteousness all Israel shall be justified. (Isa. 9:5, Engl. 6; 65. 25.)

Yes, that is a very different belief than is held as mainstream Jewish thought today, and startling by comparison. Nevertheless, it is manifestly the belief of first century Jews as revealed by *Targum Isaiah*.

Who Was Tzivi Nassi?

Tzvi Nassi, like a number of our esteemed forefathers, was a man of several names. Zebi Nasi Hirsch Prinz (Hebrew Tzvi Nassi) in German Heinrich Prinz, and later Christian William Henry Pauli (Breslau 11 August 1800 - Amsterdam 4 May 1877) was a distinguished Hebrew grammarian, translator, lecturer, and author. We consider him here because he is the translator of the *Targum Isaiah* reprinted in this volume.

Youngest of six children, Tzivi Nassi was born the son of an Orthodox Rabbi in Breslau, Silesia (Poland), on August 11, 1800. Young Tzivi found himself orphaned at the early age of fourteen. At that young age his direction was already set in his father's footsteps so that he too became a Rabbi. Zealous for his people and his God, in 1824 he published his *Sermons for Pious Israelites* in German. His studies in Jewish literature, especially the Targums, opened up his life to a hidden Jewish truth. What he learned in those pages paved the way for a conclusion that, before then would have been unthinkable. Namely, that Y'shua the Nazarean is the Jewish Messiah prophesied in Scripture. He shared what he had learned with others and even began teaching his congregation from the *Renewed Covenant Scriptures* (NT). This sadly but inevitably led to persecution and separation from the Synagogue. There was no organized Messianic Jewish presence in those days, so the good Rabbi soon found himself regarded as a Hebrew Christian and he became a Lecturer in Hebrew at Oxford University.

In England, known as Rev. Christian William Henry Pauli, he became a missionary for the *London Society for Promoting Christianity Amongst the Jews,* which was an Anglican missionary society founded in 1809. Today that mission organization is known as the *Church's Ministry Among Jewish People (CMJ).*

The original agenda of the society, in their own words, was:

- Declaring the Messiahship of Jesus to the Jew first and also to the non-Jew
- Endeavoring to teach the Church its Jewish roots
- Encouraging the physical restoration of the Jewish people to Eretz Israel - the Land of Israel
- Encouraging the Hebrew Christian/Messianic Jewish movement

The society's work began among the poor Jewish immigrants in the East End of London and soon spread to Europe, South America, Africa and Palestine. The *London Jews Society,* as it was sometimes called, was the first such society to work on a global basis. Pauli naturally served with that outreach, which was unique back in those early days, in bringing the Good News to Jewish people.

In 1844, as Rev. Christiaan Wilhelm Hirsch Pauli, he moved to Holland, where he continued his work for 30 years and finally finished his race, victorious in his life-long trust in Messiah.

Known works of Nassi/Prinz/Pauli include:
- 1824 Heinrich Prinz *Predigten für fromme Israeliten zur Erbauung und zur wahren Aufklärung in Sachen Gottes.* in Jahrbücher der Theologie und theologischer Nachrichten, Volume 2 Friedrich Heinrich Christian Schwarz
- 1839 Christian William Henry Pauli *Analecta Hebraica* Oxford 1839
- 1863 *The Great Mystery, or How can Three be One* (London, 1863) – Teachings from the Zohar on the plurality in the one God.
- 1871 *The Chaldee Paraphrase on the Prophet Isaiah* of Jonathan ben Uzziel translated by C.W.H. Pauli. - Targum Isaiah reprinted in this volume.

Pauli's love for his Jewish brethren was not unlike that of his namesake, Paul a/k/a Rav Shaul, who insisted, "the Jew first and also the Gentile." Pauli's life-long passion was to reach his Jewish brethren with the message that had so deeply changed his life and filled his heart. Through the efforts of the mission team with which he and his fellows labored, thousands of Jewish people learned the ancient but hidden Jewish truth that led them to Y'shua as their Jewish Messiah. It is our hope that Pauli's *Targum Isaiah*, republished in this *Tsiyon Edition*, will, in like manner, bless many more of our Jewish brethren and many other people as well.

Pauli's English Translation of Targum Isaiah

Pauli took great care to produce a reliable English translation of *Targum Isaiah*. Although by now it is well aged, it's still very readable while also being affordable.

Pauli's target reader was Jewish. This influenced his selection of texts, as he notes in his *Preface*.

> I have followed the text of the *Biblia Magna Hebraica*, the authorized and accepted text of the Synagogue, though I prefer the text of the *Royal Polyglot*, and that of Buxtorff, as given in *Bishop Walton's Polyglot*. Any objection which the Jews would have brought against me, if I had translated from a Christian text, must therefore fall to the ground.

That is not to say that any sincere student of Scripture, of whatever persuasion, will not be blessed in the use of Pauli's *Targum Isaiah*. As he states:

> The Biblical and the theological student will find in this Paraphrase a welcome help in many difficult passages in this Evangelical Prophet; and for the study of the New Testament, this, as well as all other paraphrases of Jonathan Ben Uzziel, are invaluable.

Parallel Texts With This Tsiyon Edition of Targum Isaiah

Common usage of *Targum Isaiah* involves comparison with other Isaiah texts. This can be awkward, juggling Bibles. Hopefully, this *Tsiyon Edition* can make such comparisons a bit less cumbersome. To that end, we have included an accepted Jewish text of Isaiah in the far right column, and a modern English "Christian" text of Isaiah in the far left column, with Targum Isaiah taking up the lion's share in the middle of the open book. You will note that Dawn and the Tsiyon editing team accomplished this rather amazing feat, publishing three versions side by side, by increasing page size, even allowing some room for notes in the margins. This allowed for increased font size of the Targum font, with reduction of font size of the parallel texts. Alas, the smaller font size of the parallel texts is a necessary tradeoff required to accomplish this minor layout miracle, but over all, we feel you will find the parallel texts helpful and enlightening in many passages.

Comparing all three texts to one another makes for a very interesting study. It is a bit of a revelation to find *Targum Isaiah* often in better agreement with the non-Jewish version, revealing how much Jewish thought has changed since the first century. While this work demonstrates this to be so, it is beyond the scope of this work to demonstrate why it is so. For that you will need to consult other sources. We suggest the WORD.

Jewish Isaiah Text - Our Jewish Isaiah text is from the *Jewish Publication Society of America Version* (JPS). The following quote explains more about this version.

> The **Jewish Publication Society of America Version** (JPS) of the Tanakh (the Hebrew Bible) was the first Bible translation published by the *Jewish Publication Society* of America and the first translation of the Tanakh into English by a committee of Jews (though there had been earlier solo efforts, such as that of Isaac Leeser). The full publication title is *The Holy Scriptures According to the Masoretic Text: A New Translation with the Aid of Previous Versions and with Constant Consultation of Jewish Authorities* ..The translation, which appeared in 1917, is heavily indebted to the *Revised Version* and *American Standard Version*. It differs from them in many passages where Jewish and Christian interpretations differ. ..This translation was superseded by the JPS *Tanakh*, which appeared in a complete form in 1985. However, the 1917 version is still widely disseminated through its appearance in the commentaries of the Soncino Books of the Bible and the Torah commentary edited by Joseph H. Hertz. Further, it has influenced many subsequent 20th century translations by drawing attention to the Jewish view of many passages. (Wikipedia – Jewish Publication Society of America Version)

Modern English Isaiah Text - Our modern English Isaiah text is from the *World English Bible,* based on the *American Standard Version*. WEB should work well for comparisons with JPS since both versions are, at least in part, based on the *American Standard Version*. The following quote explains more about the *World English Bible*.

> The **World English Bible** (also known as WEB) is a public domain translation of the Bible that is currently in draft form. Work on the World English Bible began in 1997 and was known as the *American*

Standard Version 1997. The New Testament is considered complete and is available in print. The World English Bible project was started to produce a modern English Bible version that is not copyrighted, does not use archaic English (such as the KJV), or is not translated in Basic English (such as the *Bible In Basic English*). The World English Bible follows the American Standard Version's decision to transliterate the Tetragrammaton, but updates "Jehovah" to be "Yahweh". The British and Messianic Names editions use the traditional forms (e.g., the LORD). (Wikipedia – World English Bible)

The Memra – The Logos – The WORD

A principle and distinguishing feature of the Targums is their use of the Aramaic term: *Memra.* Here is a short introduction to that topic.

We begin with this fact: No man can see the invisible God face-to-face and live.

> ".. man shall not see Me and live." Exodus 33:20 (JPS)

Yet, we have a number of places in Scripture wherein men have seen YHWH, i.e., the LORD. Such appearances of God to men are called *theophanies.* There are many theophanies in Scripture. Theophanies indicated to the ancient sages that another personal expression of YHWH exists Who appears to man. In Aramaic they called Him the *Memra,* or *WORD,* Who shares the very nature of God, while also being God's Messenger. In the Targums, *Memra* is used in the case of each and all theophanies.

This ancient Jewish insight regarding the WORD first arose from Psalm 33:6:

> By the word of the LORD were the heavens made; and all the host of them by the breath of His mouth. Psalm 33:6 (JPS)

The root Hebrew for *word* here is *dabar.* The inflected *word* in the text is *bidabar,* meaning "by the word." The Divine Agent of creation is thus seen to be the WORD. Since the WORD is *Creator* He cannot be a *creation.* He therefore must be eternal, and if eternal, then Divine.

Memra is the Aramaic for this Divine WORD, which corresponds to *Logos* in the Greek. In this English translation of *Targum Isaiah, Memra* is distinctively rendered, as Pauli states in his *Preface*:

> I beg the reader will bear in mind, that the uncreated and essential WORD (St. John i. 1, &c., &c.) is written with capitals, to distinguish it from a *created* word.

In this edition of Pauli's translation we have endeavored to change nothing but page numbers, retaining Pauli's exact translation of the text. In keeping with that, we have retained WORD written with capitals to distinguish the Divine *Memra* from instances of "word" used in the ordinary sense, exactly as Pauli translated it in the original edition.

Attributes of the Memra

First century Jewish theologians ascribed six attributes to the *Memra,* The WORD.

The attributes of the Memra are:

1. The WORD is distinct and yet the same as God.

2. The WORD was the instrument of creation, so the Creator.

3. The WORD was the instrument of salvation, so the Savior.

4. The WORD was the visible presence of God, so the Theophany.

5. The WORD was the covenant maker.

6. The WORD was the revealer of God.

Notice these attributes of the *Memra,* the WORD , as you investigate *Targum Isaiah.*

Sample Verses From Targum Isaiah Revealing the WORD

In preparing this section I compiled nine pages of examples, so I know you will have no trouble finding your own examples as you peruse this volume.

Here are seven examples of the *Memra,* the WORD, found in *Targum Isaiah.*

Example #1 - Isaiah 1:14

> Your new moons and your appointed feasts **my WORD hates;** They are an abomination before me.

"Your feasts" stand in contrast with "the feasts of the Lord" of the Torah. "My WORD hates" refers to a Divine Person, since a mere spoken word can't hate anything. In this case Jonathan ben Uzziel used the word *Memra* personifying the WORD as the One who hates these feasts.

Example #2 - Isaiah 5:24

Therefore they shall be devoured as stubble in the fire, and like dry hay in the flame; they are multiplying their strength, it shall be like an ulcer, and the money of their oppression, as the dust that flyeth away: because they despised the law of the Lord of Hosts, and rejected **the Word, the Holy One of Israel**.

"The Holy One of Israel" is a phrase reserved for none other than *Elohim* - God. Here the Word is called "The Holy One of Israel" - the second Person, if you will, of the plural *Elohim*.

Example #3 - Isaiah 6:8

And I heard the voice of the Word of the Lord, which said, "Whom shall I send to prophecy? and who will go to teach?" Then said I, "Here am I, send me."

"The voice" is that of the Word as Theophany, speaking to Isaiah.

Example #4 - Isaiah 8:5

And the Word of the Lord spake again to me...

This is one of many instances of the Word as Theophany and Revealer.

Example #5 - Isaiah 9:6 & 7

The prophet said to the house of David, "For unto us a Child is born, unto us a Son is given, and He has taken the law upon Himself to keep it. **His name is called from eternity,** Wonderful, T**he mighty God, who liveth to eternity, the Messiah,** whose peace shall be great upon us in His days. The greatness of those who do the law shall be magnified, and to those, that preserve peace. There shall be no end to the throne of David, and of his kingdom, to establish it and to build it in judgment and in righteousness from henceforth, even for ever. By the **Word of the Lord** of hosts this shall be done.

Here the then-coming *Messiah* and the W<small>ORD</small> are brought together in the same passage. Presented as "the mighty God who liveth to eternity," this terminology leaves no doubt as to the Divinity of Messiah. Realize again, this is the orthodox Jewish position on Messiah, thirty years before Y'shua the Nazarean was born.

Example #6 - Isaiah 10:20

> And it shall come to pass in that time, that **the remnant of Israel,** and such as are escaped of the house of Jacob, shall no more again lean on the people whom they served; but they shall lean upon **the W<small>ORD</small> of the Lord, the Holy One of Israel,** in truth.

Here is an encouraging promise for the "remnant of Israel" who "lean upon the W<small>ORD</small>" in truth.

Example #7 - Isaiah 21:16 & 17

> For thus hath the Lord said unto me: **at the end of the years**, as the years of an hireling, **all the glory of the Arabians shall come to an end**. And the strength of the warriors, the mighty, the sons of the Arabians, shall be lessened, because **by the W<small>ORD</small>** of the Lord, the **God of Israel**, **it is thus decreed.**

Here "the W<small>ORD</small> of the Lord" is called "the God of Israel." This is an amazing prophecy for our time at "the end of the years," foretelling as it does, the coming defeat of Arab Islamic might, which has long since been scheduled on the Divine prophetic calendar.

These few examples only scratch the surface of the many treasures to be gleaned from this *Targum Isaiah*. In closing, I leave you with this blessing from it's pages; a blessed promise for the remnant of Israel who expectantly await Messiah's Kingdom:

> *For thus saith the Lord, behold, I bring unto her (Jerusalem) peace, as the floods of the river Euphrates, and the glory of the nations, as an over-whelming stream, and ye shall delight yourselves: ye shall be born upon the sides, and ye shall be nourished upon the knees. As a man whom his mother comforts, so my W<small>ORD</small> shall comfort you; and ye shall be comforted in Jerusalem.* Isaiah 66:12&13 (TTI)

First Index

Passages in which the term *Messiah* occurs.

4:2	11:6	16:5	43:10
9:6	14:29	28:5	52:13
10:27	16:1	42:1	53:2
11:1			

Second Index

Passages in which the term *Shekina* occurs,
Expressing sometimes the Holy Spirit,
and sometimes the Messiah.

1:15	17:2	37:16	60:2
2:3	18:7	38:11	60:13
4:5	26:21	38:14	63:17
5:5	28:10	40:22	64:5
6:3	30:20	45:15	64:6
6:5	32:15	49:14	66:1
6:6	33:5	52:8	
8:17	33:11	54:6	
8:18	33:14	56:5	
12:6	33:17	57:17	
14:2	33:24	59:2	

Third Index

Passages In Which The Essential WORD Is Mentioned

TARGUM TABLE OF CONTENTS
Book of Isaiah/Yisheyah

WORLD ENGLISH BIBLE

1:1 The vision of Isaiah the son of Amoz, which he saw concerning Judah and Jerusalem, in the days of Uzziah, Jotham, Ahaz, and Hezekiah, kings of Judah.

1:2 Hear, heavens, and listen, earth; for Yahweh has spoken: "I have nourished and brought up children, and they have rebelled against me.

1:3 The ox knows his owner, and the donkey his master's crib; but Israel doesn't know, my people don't consider."

1:4 Ah sinful nation, a people loaded with iniquity, a seed of evildoers, children who deal corruptly! They have forsaken Yahweh. They have despised the Holy One of Israel. They are estranged and backward.

1:5 Why should you be beaten more, that you revolt more and more? The whole head is sick, and the whole heart faint.

1:6 From the sole of the foot even to the head there is no soundness in it: wounds, welts, and open sores. They haven't been closed, neither bandaged, neither soothed with oil.

1:7 Your country is desolate. Your cities are burned with fire. Strangers devour your land in your presence, and it is desolate, as overthrown by strangers.

1:8 The daughter of Zion is left like a shelter in a vineyard, like a hut in a field of melons, like a besieged city.

1:9 Unless Yahweh of Armies had left to us a very small remnant, we would have been as Sodom; we would have been like Gomorrah.

TARGUM ISAIAH

1:1 THE PROPHECY OF ISAIAH, THE SON OF AMOZ, WHICH IS PROPHESIED CONCERNING THE MEN OF JUDAH AND THE INHABITANTS OF JERUSALEM, IN THE DAYS OF UZZIAH, JOTHAM, AHAZ, AND HEZEKIAH, THE KINGS OF THE HOUSE OF JUDAH.

1:2 Hear, O heavens, which trembled when I gave my law to my people, and give ear, O earth, which was agitated on account of my words, for the Lord has spoken. My people, the house of Israel, whom I called sons, I loved them, I made them glorious; but they have rebelled against my WORD.

1:3 The ox knoweth his purchaser, and the ass his master's crib; *but* Israel has not learned to know my fear, my people doth not consider to return to my law.

1:4 Woe to those who are called a holy people, because they have sinned; a chosen congregation, but they have multiplied sins; they are surnamed a beloved seed, but they have done evil; they are called beloved sons, but they have corrupted their paths; they have forsaken the worship of the Lord; they abhorred the fear of the Holy One of Israel, and because their

TARGUM ISAIAH

works are evil they are turned away, and they are turned back.

1:5 They do not consider so *as to* say, Wherefore has He smitten us? They continue in sin; they do not say, Why is all the head sick, and the whole heart faint?

1:6 From the lowest of my people even unto the chief of them, there is not one amongst them who is perfect in my fear: all of them are disobedient and rebellious; they are polluted with sins, they are like an ulcerous wound; they have not forsaken their pride, neither long for repentance; they have also no righteousness to protect them.

1:7 Your land is desolate, your cities each burnt with fire; in your presence the nations possess it. On account of their sins it is laid desolate: from you it is transferred, and it belongs to aliens.

1:8 The congregation of Zion is left as a booth in a vineyard after they have gathered the grapes; as a lodge for passing the night in, in a garden of cucumbers after they have gleaned it; as a city against which they lay siege.

1:9 Except the exceeding goodness of the Lord of hosts had caused

JEWISH PUBLICATION SOCIETY 1917

1:1 THE VISION of Isaiah the son of Amoz, which he saw concerning Judah and Jerusalem, in the days of Uzziah, Jotham, Ahaz, and Hezekiah, kings of Judah.

1:2 Hear, O heavens, and give ear, O earth, for the LORD hath spoken: Children I have reared, and brought up, and they have rebelled against Me.

1:3 The ox knoweth his owner, and the ass his master's crib; but Israel doth not know, My people doth not consider.

1:4 Ah sinful nation, a people laden with iniquity, a seed of evil-doers, children that deal corruptly; they have forsaken the LORD, they have contemned the Holy One of Israel, they are turned away backward.

1:5 On what part will ye yet be stricken, seeing ye stray away more and more? The whole head is sick, and the whole heart faint;

1:6 From the sole of the foot even unto the head there is no soundness in it; but wounds, and bruises, and festering sores: they have not been pressed, neither bound up, neither mollified with oil.

1:7 Your country is desolate; your cities are burned with fire; your land, strangers devour it in your presence, and it is desolate, as overthrown by floods.

1:8 And the daughter of Zion is left as a booth in a vineyard, as a lodge in a garden of cucumbers, as a besieged city.

1:9 Except the LORD of hosts had left unto us a very small remnant, we should have been as Sodom, we should have been like unto Gomorrah.

WORLD ENGLISH BIBLE

1:10 Hear the word of Yahweh, you rulers of Sodom! Listen to the law of our God, you people of Gomorrah!

1:11 "What are the multitude of your sacrifices to me?," says Yahweh. "I have had enough of the burnt offerings of rams, and the fat of fed animals. I don't delight in the blood of bulls, or of lambs, or of male goats.

1:12 When you come to appear before me, who has required this at your hand, to trample my courts?

1:13 Bring no more vain offerings. Incense is an abomination to me; new moons, Sabbaths, and convocations: I can't bear with evil assemblies.

1:14 My soul hates your New Moons and your appointed feasts. They are a burden to me. I am weary of bearing them.

1:15 When you spread forth your hands, I will hide my eyes from you. Yes, when you make many prayers, I will not hear. Your hands are full of blood.

1:16 Wash yourselves, make yourself clean. Put away the evil of your doings from before my eyes. Cease to do evil.

1:17 Learn to do well. Seek justice. Relieve the oppressed. Judge the fatherless. Plead for the widow."

1:18 "Come now, and let us reason together," says Yahweh: "Though your sins be as scarlet, they shall be as white as snow. Though they be red like crimson, they shall be as wool.

1:19 If you are willing and obedient, you shall eat the good of the land;

TARGUM ISAIAH

to remain unto us in His mercy a deliverance, we had sins, on account of which we certainly had perished as the men of Sodom, and as the inhabitants of Gomorrah we would have been consumed.

1:10 Hear ye the word of the Lord, ye rulers, whose works are evil, as of the rulers of Sodom; give ear to the law of our God, O people, whose works are evil like those of the people of Gomorrah.

1:11 I have no pleasure in the multitude of your holy sacrifices, saith the Lord: I am full *with* the abundance of the burnt offerings of rams, and the fat of fed beasts, and the blood of bullocks, and of lambs, and of he-goats; for in such I have no pleasure.

1:12 When ye come to appear before me, who has required this at your hand, and that ye should come? Tread not my courts;

1:13 Bring no more the oblation obtained by oppression; sacrifice is an abomination before me; the new moons and Sabbaths, the assembly ye are congregating, your sins shall not be forgiven, *nor shall I hear* your prayer at the time of your congregating yourselves together.

1:14 Your new moons and your

TARGUM ISAIAH

appointed feasts my WORD hates; they are an abomination before me. I have often forgiven you.

1:15 When your priests are spreading out their hands to pray for you, I shall make to ascend the presence of my Shekinah from you; and when you are multiplying prayer, it is not my pleasure to accept your prayer at your hands, they being full of the blood of the innocent.

1:16 Return to the law; make you clean from your sins; put away the evil of your doings from before the presence of my WORD; cease to do evil;

1:17 Learn to do well; seek judgment; judge ye justice for him who is suffering violence; do justice to the orphan; hear ye the cry of the widow.

1:18 Then, when ye return to the law, ye shall pray before me, and I will grant your petition, saith the Lord. Though your sins be stained as with dye, they shall be white as snow; though they be red like crimson, they shall be pure as wool.

1:19 If ye be willing and obedient to my WORD, ye shall eat the good of the land.

JEWISH PUBLICATION SOCIETY 1917

1:10 Hear the word of the LORD, ye rulers of Sodom; give ear unto the law of our God, ye people of Gomorrah.

1:11 To what purpose is the multitude of your sacrifices unto Me? saith the LORD; I am full of the burnt-offerings of rams, and the fat of fed beasts; and I delight not in the blood of bullocks, or of lambs, or of he-goats.

1:12 When ye come to appear before Me, who hath required this at your hand, to trample My courts?

1:13 Bring no more vain oblations; it is an offering of abomination unto Me; new moon and sabbath, the holding of convocations—I cannot endure iniquity along with the solemn assembly.

1:14 Your new moons and your appointed seasons My soul hateth; they are a burden unto Me; I am weary to bear them.

1:15 And when ye spread forth your hands, I will hide Mine eyes from you; yea, when ye make many prayers, I will not hear; your hands are full of blood.

1:16 Wash you, make you clean, put away the evil of your doings from before Mine eyes, cease to do evil;

1:17 Learn to do well; seek justice, relieve the oppressed, judge the fatherless, plead for the widow.

1:18 Come now, and let us reason together, saith the LORD; though your sins be as scarlet, they shall be as white as snow; though they be red like crimson, they shall be as wool.

1:19 If ye be willing and obedient, ye shall eat the good of the land;

WORLD ENGLISH BIBLE

1:20 but if you refuse and rebel, you shall be devoured with the sword; for the mouth of Yahweh has spoken it."

1:21 How the faithful city has become a prostitute! She was full of justice; righteousness lodged in her, but now murderers.

1:22 Your silver has become dross, your wine mixed with water.

1:23 Your princes are rebellious, and companions of thieves. Everyone loves bribes, and follows after rewards. They don't judge the fatherless, neither does the cause of the widow come to them.

1:24 Therefore the Lord, Yahweh of Armies, the Mighty One of Israel, says: "Ah, I will get relief from my adversaries, and avenge myself of my enemies;

1:25 and I will turn my hand on you, thoroughly purge away your dross, and will take away all your tin.

1:26 I will restore your judges as at the first, and your counselors as at the beginning. Afterward you shall be called 'The city of righteousness, a faithful town.'

1:27 Zion shall be redeemed with justice, and her converts with righteousness.

1:28 But the destruction of transgressors and sinners shall be together, and those who forsake Yahweh shall be consumed.

1:29 For they shall be ashamed of the oaks which you have desired, and you shall be confounded for the gardens that you have chosen.

1:30 For you shall be as an oak whose leaf fades, and as a garden that has no water.

1:31 The strong will be like tinder, and his work like a spark. They will both burn together, and no one will quench them."

TARGUM ISAIAH

1:20 But if ye refuse, and will not be obedient to my WORD, ye shall be slain with the sword of the enemy; for the WORD of the Lord has decreed it thus.

1:21 How are the works of the faithful city become like those of an harlot! she was full of those who did judgment, truth was wrought in her; but now they are murderers!

1:22 Thy silver is become dross, thy wine mixed with water.

1:23 Thy princes are rebellious, and companions of thieves: all of them love gifts. One saith to the other, Show me kindness in my cause, and I will repay thee in thy cause. The fatherless they judge not, and the cry of the widow does not come before them.

1:24 Therefore saith the Lord of the world, the Lord of hosts, the Mighty One of Israel, The city of Jerusalem, I will comfort her; but woe to the wicked, when I shall reveal myself, to render just recompense to the enemies of my people, and render vengeance to my enemies.

1:25 And I will turn the blow of my might upon thee; and I will scour away all the wicked, as he

TARGUM ISAIAH

that is scouring with soap, and take away all thy sin.

1:26 And I will appoint in thee judges of truth, upright ones, as at the first, and thy counsellors, as at the beginning: afterward thou shalt be called the holy city, the faithful city.

1:27 As for Zion, when justice shall be practised in her, she shall be redeemed; and those that do the law shall return to her in righteousness.

1:28 The rebels and the sinners shall be broken together; and those that forsake the law of the Lord shall be destroyed.

1:29 For ye shall be confounded of the oaks of idolatry which ye have desired; and ye shall be ashamed of the gardens of idolatry in which ye were seeking help.

1:30 For ye shall be as an oak whose leaf fadeth, and as a watered garden that hath no water.

1:31 The strength of the wicked shall be as tow of flax, and the work of their hand as a spark of fire, when one approaches to the side of the other, both are burning together: thus the wicked shall be consumed, they and their evil works, and none shall have

JEWISH PUBLICATION SOCIETY 1917

1:20 But if ye refuse and rebel, ye shall be devoured with the sword; for the mouth of the LORD hath spoken.

1:21 How is the faithful city become a harlot! She that was full of justice, righteousness lodged in her, but now murderers.

1:22 Thy silver is become dross, thy wine mixed with water.

1:23 Thy princes are rebellious, and companions of thieves; every one loveth bribes, and followeth after rewards; they judge not the fatherless, neither doth the cause of the widow come unto them.

1:24 Therefore saith the Lord, the LORD of hosts, the Mighty One of Israel: Ah, I will ease Me of Mine adversaries, and avenge Me of Mine enemies;

1:25 And I will turn My hand upon thee, and purge away thy dross as with lye, and will take away all thine alloy;

1:26 And I will restore thy judges as at the first, and thy counsellors as at the beginning; afterward thou shalt be called The city of righteousness, the faithful city.

1:27 Zion shall be redeemed with justice, and they that return of her with righteousness.

1:28 But the destruction of the transgressors and the sinners shall be together, and they that forsake the LORD shall be consumed.

1:29 For they shall be ashamed of the terebinths which ye have desired, and ye shall be confounded for the gardens that ye have chosen.

1:30 For ye shall be as a terebinth whose leaf fadeth, and as a garden that hath no water.

1:31 And the strong shall be as tow, and his work as a spark; and they shall both burn together, and none shall quench them.

WORLD ENGLISH BIBLE

2:1 This is what Isaiah the son of Amoz saw concerning Judah and Jerusalem.

2:2 It shall happen in the latter days, that the mountain of Yahweh's house shall be established on the top of the mountains, and shall be raised above the hills; and all nations shall flow to it.

2:3 Many peoples shall go and say, "Come, let's go up to the mountain of Yahweh, to the house of the God of Jacob; and he will teach us of his ways, and we will walk in his paths." For out of Zion the law shall go forth, and the word of Yahweh from Jerusalem.

2:4 He will judge between the nations, and will decide concerning many peoples; and they shall beat their swords into plowshares, and their spears into pruning hooks. Nation shall not lift up sword against nation, neither shall they learn war any more.

2:5 House of Jacob, come, and let us walk in the light of Yahweh.

2:6 For you have forsaken your people, the house of Jacob, because they are filled from the east, with those who practice divination like the Philistines, and they clasp hands with the children of foreigners.

2:7 Their land is full of silver and gold, neither is there any end of their treasures. Their land also is full of horses, neither is there any end of their chariots.

2:8 Their land also is full of idols. They worship the work of their own hands, that which their own fingers have made.

2:9 Man is brought low, and mankind is humbled; therefore don't forgive them.

2:10 Enter into the rock, and hide in the dust, from before the terror of Yahweh, and from the glory of his majesty.

2:11 The lofty looks of man will be brought low, the haughtiness of men will be bowed down, and Yahweh alone will be exalted in that day.

TARGUM ISAIAH

pity upon them.

2:1 THE WORD OF PROPHECY, WHICH ISAIAH THE SON OF AMOZ PROPHESIED CONCERNING THE MEN OF JUDAH AND THE INHABITANTS OF JERUSALEM.

2:2 And it shall come to pass in the end of days, that the mountain of the house of the sanctuary of the Lord shall be established in the top of the mountains, and it shall be exalted above the hills; and all the kingdoms shall be turned to worship upon it.

2:3 And many people shall go and say, Come ye, and let us go up to the mountain of the house of the sanctuary of the Lord, to the house of the Shekinah of the God of Jacob; and He will teach us of His ways, which are right before Him, and we will walk in the instruction of His law; for out of Zion shall go forth the law, and the instruction of the word of the Lord from Jerusalem.

2:4 And He shall judge among the kingdoms, and rebuke many people: and they shall beat their swords into plowshares, and their spears into sickles: nation against nation shall not lift up any weapon, neither shall they learn war any more.

TARGUM ISAIAH

2:5 Those of the house of Jacob shall say, Come ye, and let us walk in the instruction of the law of the Lord.

2:6 Because ye have forsaken the terrible, the mighty One, who has redeemed you of the house of Jacob, therefore your land is full of idols, as from the beginning; and they have become prognosticators by the clouds, like the Philistines; and they are walking in the laws of the nations.

2:7 Also their land is full of silver and gold, and there is no end of their treasures; their land is also full of horses, and there is no end of their chariots.

2:8 Their land is also full of idols; they prostrate themselves to the work of their own hands, to that which is shaped by their own fingers.

2:9 The common man shall be humbled, and the strength of the great men shall become weak; and Thou shalt not pardon them.

2:10 They shall enter into the rock in order to flee with a flight, and to be hidden in the dust, for fear of the Lord, and for the brightness of His glory.

2:11 The lofty looks of the common

JEWISH PUBLICATION SOCIETY 1917

2:1 The word that Isaiah the son of Amoz saw concerning Judah and Jerusalem.

2:2 And it shall come to pass in the end of days, that the mountain of the LORD'S house shall be established as the top of the mountains, and shall be exalted above the hills; and all nations shall flow unto it.

2:3 And many peoples shall go and say: 'Come ye, and let us go up to the mountain of the LORD, to the house of the God of Jacob; and He will teach us of His ways, and we will walk in His paths.' For out of Zion shall go forth the law, and the word of the LORD from Jerusalem.

2:4 And He shall judge between the nations, and shall decide for many peoples; and they shall beat their swords into plowshares, and their spears into pruninghooks; nation shall not lift up sword against nation, neither shall they learn war any more.

2:5 O house of Jacob, come ye, and let us walk in the light of the LORD.

2:6 For Thou hast forsaken Thy people the house of Jacob; for they are replenished from the east, and with soothsayers like the Philistines, and they please themselves in the brood of aliens.

2:7 Their land also is full of silver and gold, neither is there any end of their treasures; their land also is full of horses, neither is there any end of their chariots.

2:8 Their land also is full of idols; every one worshippeth the work of his own hands, that which his own fingers have made.

2:9 And man boweth down, and man lowereth himself; and Thou canst not bear with them.

2:10 Enter into the rock, and hide thee in the dust, from before the terror of the LORD, and from the glory of His majesty.

2:11 The lofty looks of man shall be brought low, and the haughtiness of men shall be bowed down, and the LORD alone shall be exalted in that day.

WORLD ENGLISH BIBLE

2:12 For there will be a day of Yahweh of Armies for all that is proud and haughty, and for all that is lifted up; and it shall be brought low:

2:13 For all the cedars of Lebanon, that are high and lifted up, for all the oaks of Bashan,

2:14 For all the high mountains, for all the hills that are lifted up,

2:15 For every lofty tower, for every fortified wall,

2:16 For all the ships of Tarshish, and for all pleasant imagery.

2:17 The loftiness of man shall be bowed down, and the haughtiness of men shall be brought low; and Yahweh alone shall be exalted in that day.

2:18 The idols shall utterly pass away.

2:19 Men shall go into the caves of the rocks, and into the holes of the earth, from before the terror of Yahweh, and from the glory of his majesty, when he arises to shake the earth mightily.

2:20 In that day, men shall cast away their idols of silver, and their idols of gold, which have been made for themselves to worship, to the moles and to the bats;

2:21 To go into the caverns of the rocks, and into the clefts of the ragged rocks, from before the terror of Yahweh, and from the glory of his majesty, when he arises to shake the earth mightily.

2:22 Stop trusting in man, whose breath is in his nostrils; for of what account is he?

3:1 For, behold, the Lord, Yahweh of Armies, takes away from Jerusalem and from Judah supply and support, the whole supply of bread, and the whole supply of water;

3:2 the mighty man, the man of war, the judge, the prophet, the diviner, the elder,

TARGUM ISAIAH

man shall be humbled, and the strength of the great men shall become weak, and the Lord alone shall be mighty in that time.

2:12 For the day shall come from the Lord of hosts upon all the proud, and upon those who are highminded, and upon all the mighty, yea, they shall be humbled.

2:13 And upon all the kings of the nations, the strong and the mighty; and upon all the princes of the provinces;

2:14 And upon all the high mountains, and upon all the hills that are lifted up;

2:15 And upon all that dwell in a high tower; and upon all who dwell within fortified walls;

2:16 And upon all that dwell in the islands of the sea; and upon all that dwell in beautiful palaces.

2:17 The pride of the common man shall be humbled, and the strength of the great men shall become weak, and the Lord alone shall be mighty in that time.

2:18 And the idols shall utterly come to an end.

2:19 And they shall go into the caves of the rocks, and into the caverns of the earth, for the fear

TARGUM ISAIAH

of the Lord, and for the brightness of His glory, when He shall be revealed to destroy the wicked of the earth.

2:20 At that time the sons of men shall abominate the idols of their silver, and the idols of their gold, which they have made for themselves to prostrate themselves to idols and to images.

2:21 To go into the caves of the rocks, and into the holes of the rocks, for the fear of the Lord and for the brightness of His glory, when He shall be revealed to destroy the wicked of the earth.

2:22 Cease ye to make yourselves servile to man, because he is working terror; the breath of the spirit of life is in his nostrils, for to-day he is alive, but to-morrow he is not, and he is counted as nothing.

3:1 For, behold, the Lord of the world, the Lord of hosts, doth take away from Jerusalem and from Judah the stay and the staff, the whole stay of food, and the whole stay of water.

3:2 The mighty man, and the man that maketh war, the judge, and the prophet, and the scribe, and the diviner, and the ancient,

JEWISH PUBLICATION SOCIETY 1917

2:12 For the LORD of hosts hath a day upon all that is proud and lofty, and upon all that is lifted up, and it shall be brought low;

2:13 And upon all the cedars of Lebanon that are high and lifted up, and upon all the oaks of Bashan;

2:14 And upon all the high mountains, and upon all the hills that are lifted up;

2:15 And upon every lofty tower, and upon every fortified wall;

2:16 And upon all the ships of Tarshish, and upon all delightful imagery.

2:17 And the loftiness of man shall be bowed down, and the haughtiness of men shall be brought low; and the LORD alone shall be exalted in that day.

2:18 And the idols shall utterly pass away.

2:19 And men shall go into the caves of the rocks, and into the holes of the earth, from before the terror of the LORD, and from the glory of His majesty, when He ariseth to shake mightily the earth.

2:20 In that day a man shall cast away his idols of silver, and his idols of gold, which they made for themselves to worship, to the moles and to the bats;

2:21 To go into the clefts of the rocks, and into the crevices of the crags, from before the terror of the LORD, and from the glory of His majesty, when he ariseth to shake mightily the earth.

2:22 Cease ye from man, in whose nostrils is a breath; for how little is he to be accounted!

3:1 For, behold, the Lord, the LORD of hosts, doth take away from Jerusalem and from Judah stay and staff, every stay of bread, and every stay of water;

3:2 The mighty man, and the man of war; the judge, and the prophet, and the diviner, and the elder;

WORLD ENGLISH BIBLE

3:3 the captain of fifty, the honorable man, the counselor, the skilled craftsman, and the clever enchanter.

3:4 I will give boys to be their princes, and children shall rule over them.

3:5 The people will be oppressed, everyone by another, and everyone by his neighbor. The child will behave himself proudly against the old man, and the base against the honorable.

3:6 Indeed a man shall take hold of his brother in the house of his father, saying, "You have clothing, you be our ruler, and let this ruin be under your hand."

3:7 In that day he will cry out, saying, "I will not be a healer; for in my house is neither bread nor clothing. You shall not make me ruler of the people."

3:8 For Jerusalem is ruined, and Judah is fallen; because their tongue and their doings are against Yahweh, to provoke the eyes of his glory.

3:9 The look of their faces testify against them. They parade their sin like Sodom. They don't hide it. Woe to their soul! For they have brought disaster upon themselves.

3:10 Tell the righteous "Good!" For they shall eat the fruit of their deeds.

3:11 Woe to the wicked! Disaster is upon them; for the deeds of his hands will be paid back to him.

3:12 As for my people, children are their oppressors, and women rule over them. My people, those who lead you cause you to err, and destroy the way of your paths.

3:13 Yahweh stands up to contend, and stands to judge the peoples.

3:14 Yahweh will enter into judgment with the elders of his people, and their leaders: "It is you who have eaten up the vineyard. The spoil of the poor is in your houses.

TARGUM ISAIAH

3:3 The captain of fifty, and the honourable man, and the counsellor, and he that commands, and he that obeyeth, and the wise in counsel.

3:4 And I will appoint sucklings *to be* their governors, and the weak shall rule over them.

3:5 The nations shall wage war, man against man, and a man against his neighbour; children shall rule over the ancient, and the base over the honourable.

3:6 For a man shall take hold of his brother, of the family of his father's house, saying, Thou hast clothing, be thou a ruler over us, and this ruin shall be under thy government.

3:7 He shall answer in that time, saying, I am not a proper person to become a chief, and in my house I have nothing that I could eat, and nothing wherewith I could clothe myself; appoint me not a chief over all this people.

3:8 Because the inhabitants of Jerusalem have stumbled, therefore the men of Judah shall go into captivity; surely the speech of their mouth and the wages of their works are revealed before the Lord, and they have provoked

TARGUM ISAIAH

to anger His glory.

3:9 The shew of their faces in judgment bears testimony against them, and they declare their sins as the Sodomites, and they restrain not. Woe unto them! for they have caused that evil should come upon them.

3:10 Say ye to the righteous, that it shall be well with you, for the fruits of their work shall be recompensed.

3:11 Woe to the wicked, whose works are evil; because the reward of their hands shall be returned to them.

3:12 As for my people, their oppressors plunder them, as those who glean the vineyard; and as usurers they rule over them. O my people, those that call thee blessed cause thee to err; and the way of thy path they have perverted.

3:13 The Lord is ready to judge, and to reveal Himself to take vengeance of judgment of the nations.

3:14 The Lord will enter into judgment with the elders of His people, and with their oppressors; because ye have robbed my people, the spoil of the poor *is* in

JEWISH PUBLICATION SOCIETY 1917

3:3 The captain of fifty, and the man of rank, and the counsellor, and the cunning charmer, and the skilful enchanter.

3:4 And I will give children to be their princes, and babes shall rule over them.

3:5 And the people shall oppress one another, every man his fellow, and every man his neighbour; the child shall behave insolently against the aged, and the base against the honourable,

3:6 For a man shall take hold of his brother of the house of his father: 'Thou hast a mantle, be thou our ruler, and let this ruin be under thy hand.'

3:7 In that day shall he swear, saying: 'I will not be a healer; for in my house is neither bread nor a mantle; ye shall not make me ruler of a people.'

3:8 For Jerusalem is ruined, and Judah is fallen; because their tongue and their doings are against the LORD, to provoke the eyes of His glory.

3:9 The show of their countenance doth witness against them; and they declare their sin as Sodom, they hide it not. Woe unto their soul! for they have wrought evil unto themselves.

3:10 Say ye of the righteous, that it shall be well with him; for they shall eat the fruit of their doings.

3:11 Woe unto the wicked! it shall be ill with him; for the work of his hands shall be done to him.

3:12 As for My people, a babe is their master, and women rule over them. O My people, they that lead thee cause thee to err, and destroy the way of thy paths.

3:13 The LORD standeth up to plead, and standeth to judge the peoples.

3:14 The LORD will enter into judgment with the elders of His people, and the princes thereof: 'It is ye that have eaten up the vineyard; the spoil of the poor is in your houses;

WORLD ENGLISH BIBLE

3:15 What do you mean that you crush my people, and grind the face of the poor?" says the Lord, Yahweh of Armies.

3:16 Moreover Yahweh said, "Because the daughters of Zion are haughty, and walk with outstretched necks and flirting eyes, walking to trip as they go, jingling ornaments on their feet;

3:17 therefore the Lord brings sores on the crown of the head of the women of Zion, and Yahweh will make their scalps bald."

3:18 In that day the Lord will take away the beauty of their anklets, the headbands, the crescent necklaces,

3:19 the earrings, the bracelets, the veils,

3:20 the headdresses, the ankle chains, the sashes, the perfume bottles, the charms,

3:21 the signet rings, the nose rings,

3:22 the fine robes, the capes, the cloaks, the purses,

3:23 the hand mirrors, the fine linen garments, the tiaras, and the shawls.

3:24 It shall happen that instead of sweet spices, there shall be rottenness; instead of a belt, a rope; instead of well set hair, baldness; instead of a robe, a wearing of sackcloth; and branding instead of beauty.

3:25 Your men shall fall by the sword, and your mighty in the war.

3:26 Her gates shall lament and mourn; and she shall be desolate and sit on the ground.

4:1 Seven women shall take hold of one man in that day, saying, "We will eat our own bread, and wear our own clothing: only let us be called by your name. Take away our reproach."

4:2 In that day, Yahweh's branch will be beautiful and glorious, and the fruit of the land will be the beauty and glory of the survivors of Israel.

4:3 It will happen, that he who is left in Zion, and he who remains in Jerusalem, shall be called holy, even everyone who is written among the living in Jerusalem;

TARGUM ISAIAH

your houses.

3:15 What mean ye, *that* ye impoverish my people and grind the faces of the poor? They are perishing in their contentions, saith the Lord, the God of hosts.

3:16 And the Lord said, Because the daughters of Zion are haughty, and they are walking with stretched-forth necks, and they walk with their eyes painted, with their hair rolled up, and with their feet they excite *lust*.

3:17 And the Lord shall make servile the glory of the daughters of Zion, and the Lord shall remove their dignity.

3:18 In that day the Lord will take away the ornament of *their* sandals and *their* cauls and head-nets.

3:19 The necklaces, and the bracelets for the hands, and the long robes.

3:20 The crowns, the bracelets for the feet, the crisping-pin, and the ear-rings, and the ornament;

3:21 And the finger-rings, and the jewels;

3:22 The tunics, and the cloaks, and the wimples, and the stays.

3:23 The mirrors, and the fine linen, and the crowns, and the veils.

3:24 It shall come to pass, that

TARGUM ISAIAH

in the place where they were giving forth sweet smells, there shall be putrefaction; and in the place where they were binding the girdles, shall be marks of smiting; and instead of plaited locks, baldness; and instead of their walking in pride, they shall bind on sackcloth; this vengeance shall be taken on them because they have committed fornication in their beauty.

3:25 Thy beautiful men shall be killed by the sword, and thy heroes in the war.

3:26 And the gates of her city shall be laid desolate, and shall come to an end; and the land shall be laid waste, and shall be destroyed.

4:1 And in that time seven women shall take hold of one man, saying, Of that which is ours we will eat, and of that which is ours we will cover ourselves: only let us be called by thy name, to take away our reproach.

4:2 At that time shall the Messiah of the Lord be for joy and for glory to those that are escaped, and those that keep the law shall be for greatness and for praise.

4:3 And it shall come to pass, that he that shall return to Zion, and

JEWISH PUBLICATION SOCIETY 1917

3:15 What mean ye that ye crush My people, and grind the face of the poor?' saith the Lord, the GOD of hosts.

3:16 Moreover the LORD said: because the daughters of Zion are haughty, and walk with stretched-forth necks and wanton eyes, walking and mincing as they go, and making a tinkling with their feet;

3:17 Therefore the Lord will smite with a scab the crown of the head of the daughters of Zion, and the LORD will lay bare their secret parts.

3:18 In that day the Lord will take away the bravery of their anklets, and the fillets, and the crescents;

3:19 the pendants, and the bracelets, and the veils;

3:20 the headtires, and the armlets, and the sashes, and the corselets, and the amulets;

3:21 the rings, and the nose-jewels;

3:22 the aprons, and the mantelets, and the cloaks, and the girdles;

3:23 and the gauze robes, and the fine linen, and the turbans, and the mantles.

3:24 And it shall come to pass, that instead of sweet spices there shall be rottenness; and instead of a girdle rags; and instead of curled hair baldness; and instead of a stomacher a girding of sackcloth; branding instead of beauty.

3:25 Thy men shall fall by the sword, and thy mighty in the war.

3:26 And her gates shall lament and mourn; and utterly bereft she shall sit upon the ground.

4:1 And seven women shall take hold of one man in that day, saying: 'We will eat our own bread, and wear our own apparel; only let us be called by thy name; take thou away our reproach.'

4:2 In that day shall the growth of the LORD be beautiful and glorious, and the fruit of the land excellent and comely for them that are escaped of Israel.

4:3 And it shall come to pass, that he that is left in Zion, and he that remaineth in Jerusalem, shall be called holy, even every one that is written unto life in Jerusalem;

WORLD ENGLISH BIBLE

4:4 when the Lord shall have washed away the filth of the daughters of Zion, and shall have purged the blood of Jerusalem from its midst, by the spirit of justice, and by the spirit of burning.

4:5 Yahweh will create over the whole habitation of Mount Zion, and over her assemblies, a cloud and smoke by day, and the shining of a flaming fire by night; for over all the glory will be a canopy.

4:6 There will be a pavilion for a shade in the daytime from the heat, and for a refuge and for a shelter from storm and from rain.

5:1 Let me sing for my well beloved a song of my beloved about his vineyard. My beloved had a vineyard on a very fruitful hill.

5:2 He dug it up, gathered out its stones, planted it with the choicest vine, built a tower in its midst, and also cut out a winepress therein. He looked for it to yield grapes, but it yielded wild grapes.

5:3 "Now, inhabitants of Jerusalem and men of Judah, please judge between me and my vineyard.

5:4 What could have been done more to my vineyard, that I have not done in it? Why, when I looked for it to yield grapes, did it yield wild grapes?

5:5 Now I will tell you what I will do to my vineyard. I will take away its hedge, and it will be eaten up. I will break down its wall of it, and it will be trampled down.

TARGUM ISAIAH

he that is doing the law, shall be established in Jerusalem, he shall be called holy; every one that is written for eternal life shall see the consolation of Jerusalem.

4:4 When the Lord shall have put away the filth of the daughters of Zion, and when He shall have removed from her midst those that are shedding the innocent blood, which is in Jerusalem, by the word of judgment, and by the word of consummation.

4:5 And the Lord will create upon every holy place of the mountain of Zion, and upon the place of the house of His Shekinah a cloud of glory; which shall be shadowing over it by day, and a thick cloud and a brightness as of flaming fire by night; because of the excellency of the glory which He has promised to bring upon it, the Shekinah shall be protecting it with a protection.

4:6 And over Jerusalem shall be a tabernacle of clouds, to overshadow it by day from the scorching heat, and for a place of refuge from storm and from rain.

5:1 The prophet said, Now I will sing unto Israel, who *is* like unto a vineyard, the seed of Abraham,

TARGUM ISAIAH

my beloved, a song of my beloved, concerning his vineyard. My people, my beloved Israel, I gave to them an inheritance in a high mountain, in a fat land.

5:2 I sanctified them, and I made them glorious, I propped them up as a precious vine; and I built my sanctuary in the midst of them; and I gave also mine altar to make an atonement for their sins; and I thought that they should do good works before me, but they did evil works.

5:3 The prophet said unto them: They have revolted from the law, and are not willing to return. Now, O inhabitants of Jerusalem, and men of Judah, judge now a judgment between me and my people.

5:4 What more good could I have thought to do to them, which I have not done to them? And what is this? I have thought that they should do good; but they have done evil.

5:5 And now, now I will tell you what I will do to my people; I will cause my Shekinah to remove from them, and they shall be for a spoil; I will break down the house of their sanctuary, and

JEWISH PUBLICATION SOCIETY 1917

4:4 when the Lord shall have washed away the filth of the daughters of Zion, and shall have purged the blood of Jerusalem from the midst thereof, by the spirit of judgment, and by the spirit of destruction.

4:5 And the LORD will create over the whole habitation of mount Zion, and over her assemblies, a cloud and smoke by day, and the shining of a flaming fire by night; for over all the glory shall be a canopy.

4:6 And there shall be a pavilion for a shadow in the day-time from the heat, and for a refuge and for a covert from storm and from rain.

5:1 Let me sing of my well-beloved, a song of my beloved touching his vineyard. my well-beloved had a vineyard in a very fruitful hill;

5:2 And he digged it, and cleared it of stones, and planted it with the choicest vine, and built a tower in the midst of it, and also hewed out a vat therein; and he looked that it should bring forth grapes, and it brought forth wild grapes.

5:3 And now, O inhabitants of Jerusalem and men of Judah, judge, I pray you, betwixt me and my vineyard.

5:4 What could have been done more to my vineyard, that I have not done in it? Wherefore, when I looked that it should bring forth grapes, brought it forth wild grapes?

5:5 And now come, I will tell you what I will do to my vineyard: I will take away the hedge thereof, and it shall be eaten up; I will break down the fence thereof, and it shall be trodden down;

WORLD ENGLISH BIBLE

5:6 I will lay it a wasteland. It won't be pruned nor hoed, but it will grow briers and thorns. I will also command the clouds that they rain no rain on it."

5:7 For the vineyard of Yahweh of Armies is the house of Israel, and the men of Judah his pleasant plant: and he looked for justice, but, behold, oppression; for righteousness, but, behold, a cry of distress.

5:8 Woe to those who join house to house, who lay field to field, until there is no room, and you are made to dwell alone in the midst of the land!

5:9 In my ears, Yahweh of Armies says: "Surely many houses will be desolate, even great and beautiful, unoccupied.

5:10 For ten acres of vineyard shall yield one bath, and a homer of seed shall yield an ephah."

5:11 Woe to those who rise up early in the morning, that they may follow strong drink; who stay late into the night, until wine inflames them!

5:12 The harp, lyre, tambourine, and flute, with wine, are at their feasts; but they don't respect the work of Yahweh, neither have they considered the operation of his hands.

5:13 Therefore my people go into captivity for lack of knowledge. Their honorable men are famished, and their multitudes are parched with thirst.

5:14 Therefore Sheol has enlarged its desire, and opened its mouth without measure; and their glory, their multitude, their pomp, and he who rejoices among them, descend into it.

5:15 So man is brought low, mankind is humbled, and the eyes of the arrogant ones are humbled;

5:16 but Yahweh of Armies is exalted in justice, and God the Holy One is sanctified in righteousness.

TARGUM ISAIAH

they shall be for a treading down.

5:6 I will make them abandoned ones; they shall not be visited, neither shall they be supported; and they shall be cast out and forsaken. I will command the prophets that they do not prophesy to them prophecy.

5:7 For the people of the Lord of hosts is the house of Israel, and the men of Judah his pleasant plant. And I thought that they should do judgment, but, behold, they are oppressors; I thought that they should do righteousness, but, behold, they are multiplying sins.

5:8 Woe unto them that join house to house; the field of violence they bring nigh to their fields, saying, Until we possess every place; and they think they shall dwell alone in the midst of the land.

5:9 The prophet said, With mine ears I have heard when this was decreed from before the Lord of hosts, Of a truth many houses shall be desolate, *even* the great and the fair, without inhabitant.

5:10 Because of the sin of not giving tithes, the place of ten acres of vineyard shall produce one bath; and the place where a

TARGUM ISAIAH

cor *of seed was sown* shall produce three measures.

5:11 Woe unto them that rise up early in the morning, chasing after drink of old wine, delaying to separate; tarrying upon their couches till the dawn of the morning. The wine of oppression inflames them!

5:12 And in their feasts are the harp, and the viol, the cithara, the organ, and the wine: and the law of the Lord they regard not, neither consider the work of His power.

5:13 Therefore my people are gone into captivity unawares, and their honourable men have died through famine, and their multitude through dryness and thirst.

5:14 Therefore hell hath enlarged herself, and opened her mouth without measure, and their nobles, and their multitudes, and their tumultuous assemblies, and he that is strong among them, shall descend *into it.*

5:15 And the mean man shall be humbled, and the strength of the strong shall be weakened, and the eyes of the lofty shall be humbled.

5:16 And the Lord of hosts shall be mighty in judgment, and the

JEWISH PUBLICATION SOCIETY 1917

5:6 And I will lay it waste: it shall not be pruned nor hoed, but there shall come up briers and thorns; I will also command the clouds that they rain no rain upon it.

5:7 For the vineyard of the LORD of hosts is the house of Israel, and the men of Judah the plant of His delight; and He looked for justice, but behold violence; for righteousness, but behold a cry.

5:8 Woe unto them that join house to house, that lay field to field, till there be no room, and ye be made to dwell alone in the midst of the land!

5:9 In mine ears said the LORD of hosts: of a truth many houses shall be desolate, even great and fair, without inhabitant.

5:10 For ten acres of vineyard shall yield one bath, and the seed of a homer shall yield an ephah.

5:11 Woe unto them that rise up early in the morning, that they may follow strong drink; that tarry late into the night, till wine inflame them!

5:12 And the harp and the psaltery, the tabret and the pipe, and wine, are in their feasts; but they regard not the work of the LORD, neither have they considered the operation of His hands.

5:13 Therefore My people are gone into captivity, for want of knowledge; and their honourable men are famished, and their multitude are parched with thirst.

5:14 Therefore the nether-world hath enlarged her desire, and opened her mouth without measure; and down goeth their glory, and their tumult, and their uproar, and he that rejoiceth among them.

5:15 And man is bowed down, and man is humbled, and the eyes of the lofty are humbled;

5:16 But the LORD of hosts is exalted through justice, and God the Holy One is sanctified through righteousness.

WORLD ENGLISH BIBLE

5:17 Then the lambs will graze as in their pasture, and strangers will eat the ruins of the rich.

5:18 Woe to those who draw iniquity with cords of falsehood, and wickedness as with cart rope;

5:19 Who say, "Let him make speed, let him hasten his work, that we may see it; and let the counsel of the Holy One of Israel draw near and come, that we may know it!"

5:20 Woe to those who call evil good, and good evil; who put darkness for light, and light for darkness; who put bitter for sweet, and sweet for bitter!

5:21 Woe to those who are wise in their own eyes, and prudent in their own sight!

5:22 Woe to those who are mighty to drink wine, and champions at mixing strong drink;

5:23 who acquit the guilty for a bribe, but deny justice for the innocent!

5:24 Therefore as the tongue of fire devours the stubble, and as the dry grass sinks down in the flame, so their root shall be as rottenness, and their blossom shall go up as dust; because they have rejected the law of Yahweh of Armies, and despised the word of the Holy One of Israel.

5:25 Therefore Yahweh's anger burns against his people, and he has stretched out his hand against them, and has struck them. The mountains tremble, and their dead bodies are as refuse in the midst of the streets. For all this, his anger is not turned away, but his hand is still stretched out.

TARGUM ISAIAH

holy God shall be sanctified in righteousness.

5:17 And the righteous shall be fed, as it is promised concerning them, and they shall multiply; and the substance of the ungodly shall the righteous possess.

5:18 Woe to them that begin to sin by little, drawing sins with the ropes of vanity, and they go on and increase until that they are strong, and *their* sins *are* as a cartrope.

5:19 That say, When will He hasten and reveal His miracle, that we may see *it*: and let the counsel of the Holy One of Israel draw nigh and come, that we may know it!

5:20 Woe to them that say to the wicked who prosper in this world, Ye are good; and say to the meek, Ye are wicked. What, is it not so? When light cometh to the righteous, shall it not be dark with the wicked? And the words of the law shall be sweet to them that do them; but bitterness shall come to the wicked, and they shall know that in the end sin is bitter to them that commit it.

5:21 Woe unto them that are wise in their own eyes, and prudent in their own sight!

TARGUM ISAIAH

5:22 Woe unto them that are mighty to drink wine, and mighty lords of riches, to make themselves drunk with old wine.

5:23 Who justify the guilty in order to receive from him the mammon of falsehood, and wickedly take away the righteousness of the righteous from him.

5:24 Therefore they shall be devoured as stubble in the fire, and like dry hay in the flame; they are multiplying their strength, it shall be like an ulcer, and the money of their oppression, as the dust that flieth away: because they despised the law of the Lord of hosts, and rejected the WORD, the Holy One of Israel.

5:25 Therefore is the anger of the Lord of hosts mighty against His people, and He has lifted the stroke of His power upon them. When He smote them, then the mountains moved, and their carcases were cast out as dung into the midst of the streets. By all this they turn not away from their sins, that His fury may turn away from them; but until now their rebellion groweth stronger, and His stroke is again to take vengeance on them.

JEWISH PUBLICATION SOCIETY 1917

5:17 Then shall the lambs feed as in their pasture, and the waste places of the fat ones shall wanderers eat.

5:18 Woe unto them that draw iniquity with cords of vanity, and sin as it were with a cart rope,

5:19 That say: 'Let Him make speed, let Him hasten His work, that we may see it; and let the counsel of the Holy One of Israel draw nigh and come, that we may know it!'

5:20 Woe unto them that call evil good, and good evil; that change darkness into light, and light into darkness; that change bitter into sweet, and sweet into bitter!

5:21 Woe unto them that are wise in their own eyes, and prudent in their own sight!

5:22 Woe unto them that are mighty to drink wine, and men of strength to mingle strong drink;

5:23 That justify the wicked for a reward, and take away the righteousness of the righteous from him!

5:24 Therefore as the tongue of fire devoureth the stubble, and as the chaff is consumed in the flame, so their root shall be as rottenness, and their blossom shall go up as dust; because they have rejected the law of the LORD of hosts, and contemned the word of the Holy One of Israel.

5:25 Therefore is the anger of the LORD kindled against His people, and He hath stretched forth His hand against them, and hath smitten them, and the hills did tremble, and their carcases were as refuse in the midst of the streets. For all this His anger is not turned away, but His hand is stretched out still.

WORLD ENGLISH BIBLE

5:26 He will lift up a banner to the nations from far, and he will whistle for them from the end of the earth. Behold, they will come speedily and swiftly.

5:27 None shall be weary nor stumble among them; none shall slumber nor sleep; neither shall the belt of their waist be untied, nor the latchet of their shoes be broken:

5:28 whose arrows are sharp, and all their bows bent. Their horses' hoofs will be like flint, and their wheels like a whirlwind.

5:29 Their roaring will be like a lioness. They will roar like young lions. Yes, they shall roar, and seize their prey and carry it off, and there will be no one to deliver.

5:30 They will roar against them in that day like the roaring of the sea. If one looks to the land behold, darkness and distress. The light is darkened in its clouds.

6:1 In the year that king Uzziah died, I saw the Lord sitting on a throne, high and lifted up; and his train filled the temple.

6:2 Above him stood the seraphim. Each one had six wings. With two he covered his face. With two he covered his feet. With two he flew.

6:3 One called to another, and said, "Holy, holy, holy, is Yahweh of Armies! The whole earth is full of his glory!"

6:4 The foundations of the thresholds shook at the voice of him who called, and the house was filled with smoke.

6:5 Then I said, "Woe is me! For I am undone, because I am a man of unclean lips, and I dwell in the midst of a people of unclean lips: for my eyes have seen the King, Yahweh of Armies!"

TARGUM ISAIAH

5:26 And He will lift up an ensign to the nations from far, and he will call him from the end of the earth: and, behold, a king with his army shall come swiftly, as light clouds.

5:27 None shall be weary nor stumble among them; none shall slumber nor sleep; neither shall the girdle of their loins be loosed, nor the latchet of their sandals be broken.

5:28 Whose arrows are sharp, and their bows bent, their horses' hoofs strong like flint, and their wheels swift, behold, like a whirlwind.

5:29 His roaring shall be like a lion, and he shall roar like a young lion, yea, he shall roar, and lay hold of the prey, and shall carry it away safe, and none shall deliver it.

5:30 And in that time he shall roar against them like the roaring of the sea: so that if the wicked should seek support from the inhabitants of the earth, he will bring upon them oppression and destruction; but the righteous which shall be in that hour shall be protected on account of the evil.

6:1 In the year in which King Uzziah was smitten with the leprosy the prophet said, I saw the glory of

TARGUM ISAIAH

the Lord sitting upon His throne, high, and lifted up unto the highest heavens, and the temple was filled with the brightness of His glory.

6:2 Holy ministers *on* high *stood* before him: each one had six wings; with twain he covered his face, that it should not see; and with twain he covered his body, that it should not be seen; and with twain he was ministering.

6:3 And one cried unto another, and they were saying, Holy in the highest and exalted heavens is the house of His Shekinah, holy upon the earth is the work of His might, holy for ever, world without end, is the Lord of hosts, the whole earth is full of the brightness of His glory.

6:4 And the posts of the threshold of the temple moved at the voice of him that cried, and the house of the sanctuary was filled with cloudy darkness.

6:5 Then said I, Woe is me, for I have sinned, for I am a guilty man to reprove, and I dwell in the midst of a people polluted with sin: for mine eyes have seen the glory of the Shekinah of the King of the worlds, the Lord of

JEWISH PUBLICATION SOCIETY 1917

5:26 And He will lift up an ensign to the nations from far, and will hiss unto them from the end of the earth; and, behold, they shall come with speed swiftly;

5:27 None shall be weary nor stumble among them; none shall slumber nor sleep; neither shall the girdle of their loins be loosed, nor the latchet of their shoes be broken;

5:28 Whose arrows are sharp, and all their bows bent; their horses' hoofs shall be counted like flint, and their wheels like a whirlwind;

5:29 Their roaring shall be like a lion, they shall roar like young lions, yea, they shall roar, and lay hold of the prey, and carry it away safe, and there shall be none to deliver.

5:30 And they shall roar against them in that day like the roaring of the sea; and if one look unto the land, behold darkness and distress, and the light is darkened in the skies thereof.

6:1 In the year that king Uzziah died I saw the Lord sitting upon a throne high and lifted up, and His train filled the temple.

6:2 Above Him stood the seraphim; each one had six wings: with twain he covered his face and with twain he covered his feet, and with twain he did fly.

6:3 And one called unto another, and said: Holy, holy, holy, is the LORD of hosts; the whole earth is full of His glory.

6:4 And the posts of the door were moved at the voice of them that called, and the house was filled with smoke.

6:5 Then said I: Woe is me! for I am undone; because I am a man of unclean lips, and I dwell in the midst of a people of unclean lips; for mine eyes have seen the King, the LORD of hosts.

WORLD ENGLISH BIBLE

6:6 Then one of the seraphim flew to me, having a live coal in his hand, which he had taken with the tongs from off the altar.

6:7 He touched my mouth with it, and said, "Behold, this has touched your lips; and your iniquity is taken away, and your sin forgiven."

6:8 I heard the Lord's voice, saying, "Whom shall I send, and who will go for us?" Then I said, "Here I am. Send me!"

6:9 He said, "Go, and tell this people, 'You hear indeed, but don't understand; and you see indeed, but don't perceive.'

6:10 Make the heart of this people fat. Make their ears heavy, and shut their eyes; lest they see with their eyes, and hear with their ears, and understand with their heart, and turn again, and be healed."

6:11 Then I said, "Lord, how long?" He answered, "Until cities are waste without inhabitant, and houses without man, and the land becomes utterly waste,

6:12 And Yahweh has removed men far away, and the forsaken places are many in the midst of the land.

6:13 If there is a tenth left in it, that also will in turn be consumed: as a terebinth, and as an oak, whose stock remains when they are felled; so the holy seed is its stock."

7:1 It happened in the days of Ahaz the son of Jotham, the son of Uzziah, king of Judah, that Rezin the king of Syria, and Pekah the son of Remaliah, king of Israel, went up to Jerusalem to war against it, but could not prevail against it.

7:2 It was told the house of David, saying, "Syria is allied with Ephraim." His heart trembled, and the heart of his people, as the trees of the forest tremble with the wind.

TARGUM ISAIAH

hosts.

6:6 Then flew one of the ministers unto me, and in his mouth was a word, which he received from the Shekinah of Him who sat upon the throne of glory in the highest heavens, above the altar.

6:7 And he placed it in my mouth, and said, Behold, I have put the words of my prophecies in thy mouth, and thy iniquities are put away, and thy sins are expiated.

6:8 And I heard the voice of the WORD of the Lord, which said, Whom shall I send to prophesy? and who will go to teach? Then said I, Here am I, send me.

6:9 And He said, Go, and tell this people, who are diligently hearing, but understand not, and see diligently, but know not.

6:10 Make the heart of this people fat, and make their ears heavy, and darken their eyes; lest they see with their eyes, and hear with their ears, and understand with their heart, and repent, and it shall be forgiven them.

6:11 Then said I, Lord, how long? And He answered, Until the cities be wasted without an inhabitant, and the houses without man, and the land be laid desolate and

TARGUM ISAIAH

wasted.

6:12 And the Lord have removed the children of men far away, and the desolation be great in the midst of the land.

6:13 And there shall be left in it righteous men, one out of ten: they shall return, and they shall be for poverty, as the terebynth and the oak when their leaves fall, they are like to dry *trees*, nevertheless, they are moist to raise up seed from them; thus the captivity of Israel shall be gathered, and shall return to their land, for the seed which is holy is their plantation.

7:1 And it came to pass in the days of Ahaz the son of Jotham, the son of Uzziah, the king of the tribe of the house of Judah, *that* Rezin the king of Syria, and Pekah the son of Remaliah, king of Israel, went up toward Jerusalem to wage war against it, but he was not able to fight against it.

7:2 And it was told the house of David, saying, Syria is joined with the king of Israel to come upon him. And his heart and the heart of his people moved as the moving of the trees of the wood with the wind.

JEWISH PUBLICATION SOCIETY 1917

6:6 Then flew unto me one of the seraphim, with a glowing stone in his hand, which he had taken with the tongs from off the altar;

6:7 and he touched my mouth with it, and said: Lo, this hath touched thy lips; and thine iniquity is taken away, and thy sin expiated.

6:8 And I heard the voice of the Lord, saying: Whom shall I send, and who will go for us? Then I said: 'Here am I; send me.'

6:9 And He said: 'Go, and tell this people: hear ye indeed, but understand not; and see ye indeed, but perceive not.

6:10 Make the heart of this people fat, and make their ears heavy, and shut their eyes; lest they, seeing with their eyes, and hearing with their ears, and understanding with their heart, return, and be healed.'

6:11 Then said I: 'Lord, how long?' And He answered: 'Until cities be waste without inhabitant, and houses without man, and the land become utterly waste,

6:12 And the LORD have removed men far away, and the forsaken places be many in the midst of the land.

6:13 And if there be yet a tenth in it, it shall again be eaten up; as a terebinth, and as an oak, whose stock remaineth, when they cast their leaves, so the holy seed shall be the stock thereof.'

7:1 And it came to pass in the days of Ahaz the son of Jotham, the son of Uzziah, king of Judah, that Rezin the king of Aram, and Pekah the son of Remaliah, king of Israel, went up to Jerusalem to war against it; but could not prevail against it.

7:2 And it was told the house of David, saying: 'Aram is confederate with Ephraim.' And his heart was moved, and the heart of his people, as the trees of the forest are moved with the wind.

WORLD ENGLISH BIBLE

7:3 Then Yahweh said to Isaiah, "Go out now to meet Ahaz, you, and Shearjashub your son, at the end of the conduit of the upper pool, on the highway of the fuller's field.

7:4 Tell him, 'Be careful, and keep calm. Don't be afraid, neither let your heart be faint because of these two tails of smoking torches, for the fierce anger of Rezin and Syria, and of the son of Remaliah.

7:5 Because Syria, Ephraim, and the son of Remaliah, have plotted evil against you, saying,

7:6 "Let's go up against Judah, and tear it apart, and let's divide it among ourselves, and set up a king in its midst, even the son of Tabeel."

7:7 This is what the Lord Yahweh says: "It shall not stand, neither shall it happen."

7:8 For the head of Syria is Damascus, and the head of Damascus is Rezin; and within sixty-five years Ephraim shall be broken in pieces, so that it shall not be a people;

7:9 and the head of Ephraim is Samaria, and the head of Samaria is Remaliah's son. If you will not believe, surely you shall not be established.'"

7:10 Yahweh spoke again to Ahaz, saying,

7:11 "Ask a sign of Yahweh your God; ask it either in the depth, or in the height above."

7:12 But Ahaz said, "I will not ask, neither will I tempt Yahweh."

7:13 He said, "Listen now, house of David. Is it not enough for you to try the patience of men, that you will try the patience of my God also?

7:14 Therefore the Lord himself will give you a sign. Behold, the virgin will conceive, and bear a son, and shall call his name Immanuel.

7:15 He shall eat butter and honey when he knows to refuse the evil, and choose the good.

7:16 For before the child knows to refuse the evil, and choose the good, the land whose two kings you abhor shall be forsaken.

TARGUM ISAIAH

7:3 Then said the Lord unto Isaiah, Go forth now to meet Ahaz, thou and the rest of thy disciples, who have not sinned, and who are turned away from sin, at the end of the conduit of the upper pool, which is by the way of the field of the spreading of the fullers,

7:4 And say unto him, Take heed, and be quiet; fear not, and let not thy heart be moved for the two kings, which are as smoking firebrands, for the strength of the anger of Rezin with Syria, and of the son of Remaliah.

7:5 Because Syria, Ephraim, and the son of Remaliah, have taken evil counsel against thee, saying,

7:6 We will go up into the land of the house of Judah, and let us be united together, and make them profitable unto us. We will make a king in it whom we shall think proper.

7:7 Thus saith the Lord God, It shall not stand, neither shall it come to pass.

7:8 For the head of Syria is Damascus, and the head of Damascus is Rezin, and at the end of threescore and five years the house of Israel shall cease from being a kingdom.

TARGUM ISAIAH

7:9 And the head of Ephraim *is* Samaria, and the head of Samaria *is* the son of Remaliah. If ye will not believe the words of the prophet, surely ye shall not be established,

7:10 Moreover the prophet of the Lord spake again unto Ahaz, saying,

7:11 Ask thee a sign from before the presence of the Lord, that a miracle may be done for thee upon the earth, or that a sign may be shewn thee in heaven.

7:12 But Ahaz said, I will not ask, neither will I tempt the Lord.

7:13 And he said, Hear ye now, O house of David; is it a small thing to you that ye are troublesome to the prophets, that ye refuse also the words of my God?

7:14 Therefore the Lord Himself shall give you a sign; Behold, a virgin shall conceive, and bear a son, and she shall call His name Immanuel.

7:15 Butter and honey a child eats before he knows to reject the evil and to choose the good;

7:16 But before a child shall know to reject the evil and to choose the good, the land shall be laid desolate, on account of which

JEWISH PUBLICATION SOCIETY 1917

7:3 Then said the LORD unto Isaiah: 'Go forth now to meet Ahaz, thou, and Shear-jashub thy son, at the end of the conduit of the upper pool, in the highway of the fullers' field;

7:4 and say unto him: Keep calm, and be quiet; fear not, neither let thy heart be faint, because of these two tails of smoking firebrands, for the fierce anger of Rezin and Aram, and of the son of Remaliah.

7:5 Because Aram hath counselled evil against thee, Ephraim also, and the son of Remaliah, saying:

7:6 Let us go up against Judah, and vex it, and let us make a breach therein for us, and set up a king in the midst of it, even the son of Tabeel;

7:7 thus saith the Lord GOD: it shall not stand, neither shall it come to pass.

7:8 For the head of Aram is Damascus, and the head of Damascus is Rezin; and within threescore and five years shall Ephraim be broken, that it be not a people;

7:9 And the head of Ephraim is Samaria, and the head of Samaria is Remaliah's son. If ye will not have faith, surely ye shall not be established.'

7:10 And the LORD spoke again unto Ahaz, saying:

7:11 'Ask thee a sign of the LORD thy God: ask it either in the depth, or in the height above.'

7:12 But Ahaz said: 'I will not ask, neither will I try the LORD.'

7:13 And he said: 'Hear ye now, O house of David: Is it a small thing for you to weary men, that ye will weary my God also?

7:14 Therefore the Lord Himself shall give you a sign: behold, the young woman shall conceive, and bear a son, and shall call his name Immanuel.

7:15 Curd and honey shall he eat, when he knoweth to refuse the evil, and choose the good.

7:16 Yea, before the child shall know to refuse the evil, and choose the good, the land whose two kings thou hast a horror of shall be forsaken.

WORLD ENGLISH BIBLE

7:17 Yahweh will bring on you, on your people, and on your father's house, days that have not come, from the day that Ephraim departed from Judah; even the king of Assyria.

7:18 It will happen in that day that Yahweh will whistle for the fly that is in the uttermost part of the rivers of Egypt, and for the bee that is in the land of Assyria.

7:19 They shall come, and shall all rest in the desolate valleys, in the clefts of the rocks, on all thorn hedges, and on all pastures.

7:20 In that day the Lord will shave with a razor that is hired in the parts beyond the River, even with the king of Assyria, the head and the hair of the feet; and it shall also consume the beard.

7:21 It shall happen in that day that a man shall keep alive a young cow, and two sheep;

7:22 and it shall happen, that because of the abundance of milk which they shall give he shall eat butter: for everyone will eat butter and honey that is left in the midst of the land.

7:23 It will happen in that day that every place where there were a thousand vines at a thousand silver shekels, shall be for briers and thorns.

7:24 People will go there with arrows and with bow, because all the land will be briers and thorns.

7:25 All the hills that were cultivated with the hoe, you shall not come there for fear of briers and thorns; but it shall be for the sending forth of oxen, and for the treading of sheep."

8:1 Yahweh said to me, "Take a large tablet, and write on it with a man's pen, 'For Maher Shalal Hash Baz;'

8:2 and I will take for myself faithful witnesses to testify: Uriah the priest, and Zechariah the son of Jeberechiah."

TARGUM ISAIAH

thou art in a strait, because of these two kings.

7:17 The Lord shall bring upon thee, and upon thy people, and upon thy father's house, days that have not come from the day of the separation of the house of Ephraim from the house of Judah; *even* the king of Assyria.

7:18 And it shall come to pass at that time that the Lord shall call to a people, to bands of armies, mighty men, who are numerous as flies, and shall bring them from the ends of the land of Egypt; and to mighty armies, who are powerful as bees, and shall bring them from the uttermost parts of the land of Assyria.

7:19 And they shall all of them come and dwell in the streets of the cities, and in the clefts of the rocks, and in all deserts *full* of thorn-hedges, and in all houses of praise.

7:20 In that time the Lord shall slay them as one is slain by a sharp sword, by clubs, and by saws, by those beyond the river, and by the king of Assyria; the king and his army, and even also his rulers, together shall he destroy.

7:21 And it shall come to pass in

TARGUM ISAIAH

that time, that a man shall nourish a young cow and two sheep.

7:22 And it shall come to pass on account of the abundance of the goodness of fatness, one shall eat oil; because with oil and honey shall all the righteous be fed, who are left in the midst of the land.

7:23 And it shall come to pass in that time, *that* every place shall be, where there were a thousand vines for a thousand silverlings, it shall *even* be for briers and thorns.

7:24 With arrows and with bows shall *men* come thither; because all the land shall become briers and thorns.

7:25 And all the hills of the house of Judah, which shall be digged with the mattock, there shall not come thither the fear of briers and thorns: but it shall be for a place of crouching down of oxen, and for a place of dwelling of flocks and of sheep.

8:1 And the Lord said unto me, Take thee a great tablet, and write upon it a clear writing, Hasten to seize the prey, and to take away the spoil.

8:2 And call to witness before me *as* faithful witnesses, the curses,

JEWISH PUBLICATION SOCIETY 1917

7:17 The LORD shall bring upon thee, and upon thy people, and upon thy father's house, days that have not come, from the day that Ephraim departed from Judah; even the king of Assyria.'

7:18 And it shall come to pass in that day, that the LORD shall hiss for the fly that is in the uttermost part of the rivers of Egypt, and for the bee that is in the land of Assyria.

7:19 And they shall come, and shall rest all of them in the rugged valleys, and in the holes of the rocks, and upon all thorns, and upon all brambles.

7:20 In that day shall the Lord shave with a razor that is hired in the parts beyond the River, even with the king of Assyria, the head and the hair of the feet; and it shall also sweep away the beard.

7:21 And it shall come to pass in that day, that a man shall rear a young cow, and two sheep;

7:22 and it shall come to pass, for the abundance of milk that they shall give, he shall eat curd; for curd and honey shall every one eat that is left in the midst of the land.

7:23 And it shall come to pass in that day, that every place, where there were a thousand vines at a thousand silverlings, shall even be for briers and thorns.

7:24 With arrows and with bow shall one come thither; because all the land shall become briers and thorns.

7:25 And all the hills that were digged with the mattock, thou shalt not come thither for fear of briers and thorns, but it shall be for the sending forth of oxen, and for the treading of sheep.

8:1 And the LORD said unto me: 'Take thee a great tablet, and write upon it in common script: The spoil speedeth, the prey hasteth;

8:2 and I will take unto Me faithful witnesses to record, Uriah the priest, and Zechariah the son of Jeberechiah.'

WORLD ENGLISH BIBLE

8:3 I went to the prophetess, and she conceived, and bore a son. Then Yahweh said to me, "Call his name 'Maher Shalal Hash Baz.'

8:4 For before the child knows how to say, 'My father,' and, 'My mother,' the riches of Damascus and the spoil of Samaria will be carried away by the king of Assyria."

8:5 Yahweh spoke to me yet again, saying,

8:6 "Because this people have refused the waters of Shiloah that go softly, and rejoice in Rezin and Remaliah's son;

8:7 now therefore, behold, the Lord brings upon them the mighty flood waters of the River: the king of Assyria and all his glory. It will come up over all its channels, and go over all its banks.

8:8 It will sweep onward into Judah. It will overflow and pass through; it will reach even to the neck; and the stretching out of its wings will fill the breadth of your land, Immanuel.

8:9 Make an uproar, you peoples, and be broken in pieces! Listen, all you from far countries: dress for battle, and be shattered! Dress for battle, and be shattered!

8:10 Take counsel together, and it will be brought to nothing; speak the word, and it will not stand: for God is with us."

8:11 For Yahweh spoke thus to me with a strong hand, and instructed me not to walk in the way of this people, saying,

8:12 "Don't say, 'A conspiracy!' concerning all about which this people say, 'A conspiracy!' neither fear their threats, nor be terrorized.

8:13 Yahweh of Armies is who you must respect as holy. He is the one you must fear. He is the one you must dread.

TARGUM ISAIAH

which I have threatened to bring by the prophecy of Uriah the priest, and, behold, they have come. And also the consolations, which I promised to bring by the prophecy of Zechariah the son of Jeberechiah, I am about to bring.

8:3 And I went to the prophetess; and she conceived, and bare a son. Then said the Lord unto me, Call his name Hasten to seize the prey, and to take away the spoil.

8:4 For before the child shall have knowledge to cry, My father, and my mother, the riches of Damascus and the spoil of Samaria shall be led into captivity before the king of Assyria.

8:5 And the WORD of the Lord spake again to me, saying,

8:6 Forasmuch as this people refuseth the kingdom of the house of David, which guides them in quietness, like the waters of Shiloah, which flow softly, and delight themselves in Rezin and Remaliah's son;

8:7 Therefore, behold, the Lord is bringing, and is causing to ascend upon them, the army of the people, who are many, as the waters of a river, strong and mighty, the king of Assyria, and

TARGUM ISAIAH

his army; and he shall come up over all his channels, and go over all his banks.

8:8 And he shall pass through the land of the house of Judah as an overflowing torrent, unto Jerusalem shall he come; and the people of his army shall fill the breadth of thy land, O Israel.

8:9 Associate yourselves, O ye people, yet ye shall be broken; and give ear all who are at the ends of the earth, strengthen yourselves, yet ye shall be broken, strengthen yourselves, yet ye shall be broken.

8:10 Take counsel together, yet it shall pass away; speak the word, and it shall not be established, because God is our help.

8:11 For the Lord spake thus to me by the power of prophecy, and instructed me that I should not walk in the way of this people, saying,

8:12 Say ye not a rebellion to all that this people shall say a rebellion; neither fear ye their fear; and concerning their strength say ye not strength.

8:13 The Lord of hosts Him shall ye call holy; and let Him *be* your fear, and *let* Him *be* your strength.

8:14 And if ye will not obey, His

JEWISH PUBLICATION SOCIETY 1917

8:3 And I went unto the prophetess; and she conceived, and bore a son. Then said the LORD unto me: 'Call his name Maher-shalal-hashbaz.

8:4 For before the child shall have knowledge to cry: My father, and: My mother, the riches of Damascus and the spoil of Samaria shall be carried away before the king of Assyria.'

8:5 And the LORD spoke unto me yet again, saying:

8:6 Forasmuch as this people hath refused the waters of Shiloah that go softly, and rejoiceth with Rezin and Remaliah's son;

8:7 Now therefore, behold, the Lord bringeth up upon them the waters of the River, mighty and many, even the king of Assyria and all his glory; and he shall come up over all his channels, and go over all his banks;

8:8 And he shall sweep through Judah overflowing as he passeth through he shall reach even to the neck; and the stretching out of his wings shall fill the breadth of thy land, O Immanuel.

8:9 Make an uproar, O ye peoples, and ye shall be broken in pieces; and give ear, all ye of far countries; gird yourselves, and ye shall be broken in pieces; gird yourselves, and ye shall be broken in pieces.

8:10 Take counsel together, and it shall be brought to nought; speak the word, and it shall not stand; for God is with us.

8:11 For the LORD spoke thus to me with a strong hand, admonishing me that I should not walk in the way of this people, saying:

8:12 'Say ye not: A conspiracy, concerning all whereof this people do say: A conspiracy; neither fear ye their fear, nor account it dreadful.

8:13 The LORD of hosts, Him shall ye sanctify; and let Him be your fear, and let Him be your dread.

WORLD ENGLISH BIBLE

8:14 He will be a sanctuary, but for both houses of Israel, he will be a trap and a snare for the inhabitants of Jerusalem.

8:15 Many will stumble over it, fall, be broken, be snared, and be captured."

8:16 Wrap up the testimony. Seal the law among my disciples.

8:17 I will wait for Yahweh, who hides his face from the house of Jacob, and I will look for him.

8:18 Behold, I and the children whom Yahweh has given me are for signs and for wonders in Israel from Yahweh of Armies, who dwells in Mount Zion.

8:19 When they tell you, "Consult with those who have familiar spirits and with the wizards, who chirp and who mutter:" shouldn't a people consult with their God? Should they consult the dead on behalf of the living?

8:20 Turn to the law and to the testimony! If they don't speak according to this word, surely there is no morning for them.

8:21 They will pass through it, very distressed and hungry; and it will happen that when they are hungry, they will worry, and curse by their king and by their God. They will turn their faces upward, **8:22** and look to the earth, and see distress, darkness, and the gloom of anguish. They will be driven into thick darkness.

TARGUM ISAIAH

WORD shall be amongst you for revenge, and for a stone of stumbling, and for a rock of offence to both of the houses of the princes of Israel, for destruction and for a snare, because they contend against those of the house of Judah, who are dwelling in Jerusalem.

8:15 And many among them shall stumble, and fall, and be broken, and be snared, and be taken.

8:16 O prophet, keep the testimony, testify not the testimony among them, because they do not obey; seal and hide the law, they are not willing to learn it.

8:17 The prophet said, On account of this I prayed before the Lord, who has said that he would take away His Shekinah from the house of Jacob, and I intreated before Him.

8:18 Behold, whilst I live with the children, which the Lord has given me, the signs and the wonders, which are promised to come upon Israel shall be established among us. But if they would see and repent, the decree should be annulled, which He decreed against them, that they should go into captivity, and that they should not appear

TARGUM ISAIAH

before the Lord of hosts, whose Shekinah is in the mountain of Zion.

8:19 And when the nations amongst whom you shall be shall say to you, Seek of necromancers, and of the wizards, that peep, and that mutter. Is not this the way of nations, the worshippers of idols? A people seek from their idol, the living from the dead.

8:20 Thus ye shall say unto them: We will listen to the law which has been given to us, and to the testimony: yet ye shall go into captivity amongst the nations, and they shall speak to you according to this word. Now there is none amongst them, who would search and seek after it.

8:21 And one shall pass through the land, stumbling along, and there shall be oppression and famine. And it shall come to pass, when he shall see famine and affliction, he shall curse and despise the name of his Moloch and his idolatry: and he shall look upwards to seek deliverance after the decree has been sealed, and he shall not be able *to obtain it*.

8:22 And he shall seek help from the inhabitants of the earth,

JEWISH PUBLICATION SOCIETY 1917

8:14 And He shall be for a sanctuary; but for a stone of stumbling and for a rock of offence to both the houses of Israel, for a gin and for a snare to the inhabitants of Jerusalem.

8:15 And many among them shall stumble, and fall, and be broken, and be snared, and be taken.'

8:16 'Bind up the testimony, seal the instruction among My disciples.'

8:17 And I will wait for the LORD, that hideth His face from the house of Jacob, and I will look for Him.

8:18 Behold, I and the children whom the LORD hath given me shall be for signs and for wonders in Israel from the LORD of hosts, who dwelleth in mount Zion.

8:19 And when they shall say unto you: 'Seek unto the ghosts and the familiar spirits, that chirp and that mutter; should not a people seek unto their God? on behalf of the living unto the dead

8:20 for instruction and for testimony?' —Surely they will speak according to this word, wherein there is no light.—

8:21 And they shall pass this way that are sore bestead and hungry; and it shall come to pass that, when they shall be hungry, they shall fret themselves, and curse by their king and by their God, and, whether they turn their faces upward,

8:22 or look unto the earth, behold distress and darkness, the gloom of anguish, and outspread thick darkness.

WORLD ENGLISH BIBLE

9:1 But there shall be no more gloom for her who was in anguish. In the former time, he brought into contempt the land of Zebulun and the land of Naphtali; but in the latter time he has made it glorious, by the way of the sea, beyond the Jordan, Galilee of the nations.

9:2 The people who walked in darkness have seen a great light. Those who lived in the land of the shadow of death, on them the light has shined.

9:3 You have multiplied the nation. You have increased their joy. They rejoice before you according to the joy in harvest, as men rejoice when they divide the spoil.

9:4 For the yoke of his burden, and the staff of his shoulder, the rod of his oppressor, you have broken as in the day of Midian.

9:5 For all the armor of the armed man in the noisy battle, and the garments rolled in blood, will be for burning, fuel for the fire.

9:6 For to us a child is born. To us a son is given; and the government will be on his shoulders. His name will be called Wonderful, Counselor, Mighty God, Everlasting Father, Prince of Peace.

9:7 Of the increase of his government and of peace there shall be no end, on the throne of David, and on his kingdom, to establish it, and to uphold it with justice and with righteousness from that time on, even forever. The zeal of Yahweh of Armies will perform this.

9:8 The Lord sent a word into Jacob, and it falls on Israel.

TARGUM ISAIAH

because there shall come upon him oppression, famine, weariness of oppression, darkness, and dispersion.

9:1 For none shall be weary who shall come to oppress them, as at the former time, *when* the people of the land of Zebulun, and the people of the land of Naphtali went into captivity: and those that were left, a mighty king led into captivity, because they did not remember the power of the *Red Sea*, neither the wonders of the Jordan, the war of the fortifications of the nations.

9:2 The people, the house of Israel, which walked in Egypt as in the darkness, went forth to see a great light. They that dwelt in the land of the shadow of death, upon them hath the light shined.

9:3 Thou hast multiplied the people, the house of Israel, unto them Thou hast multiplied the joy: they joy before Thee as the joy of the conquerors of battle, as *men* rejoice when they divide the spoil.

9:4 For Thou hast taken away the yoke of his dominion, and the government of oppression, the government wherewith he enslaved him is broken as in the day of

TARGUM ISAIAH

Midian.

9:5 All their transactions are in wickedness; they are polluted with sins, as a garment dipped in blood, the marks of its filth cannot be purified; thus it is like something, in which there is no use, but to be burned in fire: thus He shall bring forth against them nations, who *are* mighty as fire, and they shall slay them.

9:6 The prophet said to the house of David, For unto us a Child is born, unto us a Son is given, and He has taken the law upon Himself to keep it. His name is called from eternity, Wonderful, The Mighty God, who liveth to eternity, The Messiah, whose peace shall be great upon us in His days.

9:7 The greatness of those who do the law shall be magnified, and to those, that preserve peace. There shall be no end to the throne of David, and of his kingdom, to establish it and to build it in judgment and in righteousness from henceforth, even for ever. By the WORD of the Lord of hosts this shall be done.

9:8 The Lord sent a word into the house of Jacob, and it was heard

JEWISH PUBLICATION SOCIETY 1917

9:1 (8:23) For is there no gloom to her that was stedfast? Now the former hath lightly afflicted the land of Zebulun and the land of Naphtali, but the latter hath dealt a more grievous blow by the way of the sea, beyond the Jordan, in the district of the nations.

9:2 (9:1) The people that walked in darkness have seen a great light; they that dwelt in the land of the shadow of death, upon them hath the light shined.

9:3 (9:2) Thou hast multiplied the nation, Thou hast increased their joy; they joy before Thee according to the joy in harvest, as men rejoice when they divide the spoil.

9:4 (9:3) For the yoke of his burden, and the staff of his shoulder, the rod of his oppressor, Thou hast broken as in the day of Midian.

9:5 (9:4) For every boot stamped with fierceness, and every cloak rolled in blood, shall even be for burning, for fuel of fire.

9:6 (9:5) For a child is born unto us, a son is given unto us; and the government is upon his shoulder; and his name is called Pele-joez-el-gibbor-Abi-ad-sar-shalom;

9:7 (9:6) That the government may be increased, and of peace there be no end, upon the throne of David, and upon his kingdom, to establish it, and to uphold it through justice and through righteousness from henceforth even for ever. The zeal of the LORD of hosts doth perform this.

9:8 (9:7) The Lord sent a word into Jacob, and it hath lighted upon Israel.

9:9 (9:8) And all the people shall know, even Ephraim and the inhabitant of Samaria, that say in pride and in arrogancy of heart:

WORLD ENGLISH BIBLE

9:9 All the people will know, including Ephraim and the inhabitants of Samaria, who say in pride and in arrogance of heart,

9:10 "The bricks have fallen, but we will build with cut stone. The sycamore fig trees have been cut down, but we will put cedars in their place."

9:11 Therefore Yahweh will set up on high against him the adversaries of Rezin, and will stir up his enemies,

9:12 The Syrians in front, and the Philistines behind; and they will devour Israel with open mouth. For all this, his anger is not turned away, but his hand is stretched out still.

9:13 Yet the people have not turned to him who struck them, neither have they sought Yahweh of Armies.

9:14 Therefore Yahweh will cut off from Israel head and tail, palm branch and reed, in one day.

9:15 The elder and the honorable man is the head, and the prophet who teaches lies is the tail.

9:16 For those who lead this people lead them astray; and those who are led by them are destroyed.

9:17 Therefore the Lord will not rejoice over their young men, neither will he have compassion on their fatherless and widows; for everyone is profane and an evildoer, and every mouth speaks folly. For all this his anger is not turned away, but his hand is stretched out still.

9:18 For wickedness burns like a fire. It devours the briers and thorns; yes, it kindles in the thickets of the forest, and they roll upward in a column of smoke.

9:19 Through the wrath of Yahweh of Armies, the land is burnt up; and the people are the fuel for the fire. No one spares his brother.

TARGUM ISAIAH

in Israel.

9:9 The people, all of them have become great; Ephraim and the inhabitants of Samaria, that say in greatness and stoutness of heart,

9:10 The princes are carried captive; but we will appoint better ones than they. Treasures are plundered, but we will purchase more beautiful ones than they.

9:11 Therefore the Lord shall make strong the hatred of Rezin against him, and he will stir up his adversaries.

9:12 The Syrians from the east, and the Philistines from the west; and they shall spoil the treasures of Israel in every place. For all this they do not turn away from their sins, that His anger might turn away from them; but still they hold fast their rebellion, and yet His stroke will be to take vengeance on them.

9:13 And the people have not returned to the worship *of God*, from the time that He brought upon them the stroke; and they do not seek the instruction of the Lord of hosts.

9:14 And the Lord will destroy from Israel the prince, the captain, the ruler, and the governor, in one

36

TARGUM ISAIAH

day.

9:15 The ancient and honourable one, he *is* the head, and the scribe that teaches lies, he is the feeble one.

9:16 And those that praise this people cause them to err, and their princes swallow *them* up.

9:17 Therefore the Lord shall have no joy in their young men, neither shall have mercy on their fatherless and widows: for all of them are hypocrites and evildoers, and all their mouths speak lies. For all this they do not turn away from their sins, that His anger might turn away from them; but still they hold fast their rebellion, and yet His stroke is ready to take vengeance on them.

9:18 The punishment of their sins shall burn like fire; it shall consume the sinners and the wicked, and shall rule over the rest of the people, and shall make an end of a great host.

9:19 Through the wrath from before the presence of the Lord of hosts the earth shall be burnt up, and the people shall be like the burning fuel of fire: no man shall spare his brother.

9:20 And he shall spoil on the

JEWISH PUBLICATION SOCIETY 1917

9:10 (9:9) 'The bricks are fallen, but we will build with hewn stones; the sycamores are cut down, but cedars will we put in their place.'

9:11 (9:10) Therefore the LORD doth set upon high the adversaries of Rezin against him, and spur his enemies;

9:12 (9:11) The Arameans on the east, and the Philistines on the west; and they devour Israel with open mouth. For all this His anger is not turned away, but His hand is stretched out still.

9:13 (9:12) Yet the people turneth not unto Him that smiteth them, neither do they seek the LORD of hosts.

9:14 (9:13) Therefore the LORD doth cut off from Israel head and tail, palm-branch and rush, in one day.

9:15 (9:14) The elder and the man of rank, he is the head; and the prophet that teacheth lies, he is the tail.

9:16 (9:15) For they that lead this people cause them to err; and they that are led of them are destroyed.

9:17 (9:16) Therefore the Lord shall have no joy in their young men, neither shall He have compassion on their fatherless and widows; for every one is ungodly and an evil-doer, and every mouth speaketh wantonness. For all this His anger is not turned away, but His hand is stretched out still.

9:18 (9:17) For wickedness burneth as the fire; it devoureth the briers and thorns; yea, it kindleth in the thickets of the forest, and they roll upward in thick clouds of smoke.

9:19 (9:18) Through the wrath of the LORD of hosts is the land burnt up; the people also are as the fuel of fire; no man spareth his brother.

9:20 (9:19) And one snatcheth on the right hand, and is hungry; and he eateth on the left hand, and is not satisfied; they eat every man the flesh of his own arm:

WORLD ENGLISH BIBLE

9:20 One will devour on the right hand, and be hungry; and he will eat on the left hand, and they will not be satisfied. Everyone will eat the flesh of his own arm:

9:21 Manasseh, Ephraim; and Ephraim, Manasseh; and they together shall be against Judah. For all this his anger is not turned away, but his hand is stretched out still.

10:1 Woe to those who decree unrighteous decrees, and to the writers who write oppressive decrees;

10:2 to deprive the needy from justice, and to rob the poor among my people of their rights, that widows may be their spoil, and that they may make the fatherless their prey!

10:3 What will you do in the day of visitation, and in the desolation which will come from afar? To whom will you flee for help? Where will you leave your wealth?

10:4 They will only bow down under the prisoners, and will fall under the slain. For all this his anger is not turned away, but his hand is stretched out still.

10:5 Alas Assyrian, the rod of my anger, the staff in whose hand is my indignation!

10:6 I will send him against a profane nation, and against the people who anger me will I give him a command to take the spoil and to take the prey, and to tread them down like the mire of the streets.

10:7 However he doesn't mean so, neither does his heart think so; but it is in his heart to destroy, and to cut off not a few nations.

10:8 For he says, "Aren't all of my princes kings?

10:9 Isn't Calno like Carchemish? Isn't Hamath like Arpad? Isn't Samaria like Damascus?"

TARGUM ISAIAH

south, and be hungry; and he shall destroy on the north, and not be satisfied: they shall spoil the substance, every man the substance of his neighbour.

9:21 Those of the house of Manasseh, with those of the house of Ephraim, and they of the house of Ephraim, with those of the house of Manasseh, shall be joined together as one, to come against them of the house of Judah. For all this they do not turn away from their sins, that His anger might turn away from them; but still they hold fast their rebellion, and yet His stroke is ready to take vengeance on them.

10:1 Woe unto them that sign oppressive decrees, and to those *who* write a grievous enactment.

10:2 To turn aside the needy from judgment, and to rob whatever the poor of my people desire in judgment, that widows may be their prey, and that they may rob the wealth of the orphans.

10:3 What will ye do in the day that your sins shall be visited upon you? when the tumult of oppression shall come from far? whither will ye flee for help? and where will ye leave your glory?

TARGUM ISAIAH

10:4 Therefore out of your land ye shall be fettered amongst the captives; and out of your cities ye shall be cast out slain. For all this they do not turn away from their sins, that His anger might turn away from them; but still they hold fast their rebellion, and yet His stroke will be to take vengeance on them.

10:5 Woe to the Assyrian, the government of my fury, an angel is sent from me against them for a curse!

10:6 I will send him against an hypocritical assembly, and against a people that have transgressed my law will I give him a charge, to take the spoil, and to take the prey, and to place him for a treading under foot like the mire of the streets.

10:7 Howbeit he did not purpose so, neither doth his heart think so; but to destroy he hath said in his heart, and to make an end of nations without compassion.

10:8 For he saith, Are not all my rulers altogether as kings considered before me?

10:9 Is it not so? As Carchemish is subdued before me, shall not Calno be so? Surely, as Arphad is

JEWISH PUBLICATION SOCIETY 1917

9:21 (9:20) Manasseh, Ephraim; and Ephraim, Manasseh; and they together are against Judah. For all this His anger is not turned away, but His hand is stretched out still.

10:1 Woe unto them that decree unrighteous decrees, and to the writers that write iniquity;

10:2 To turn aside the needy from judgment, and to take away the right of the poor of My people, that widows may be their spoil, and that they may make the fatherless their prey!

10:3 And what will ye do in the day of visitation, and in the ruin which shall come from far? To whom will ye flee for help? And where will ye leave your glory?

10:4 They can do nought except crouch under the captives, and fall under the slain. For all this His anger is not turned away, but His hand is stretched out still.

10:5 O Asshur, the rod of Mine anger, in whose hand as a staff is Mine indignation!

10:6 I do send him against an ungodly nation, and against the people of My wrath do I give him a charge, to take the spoil, and to take the prey, and to tread them down like the mire of the streets.

10:7 Howbeit he meaneth not so, neither doth his heart think so; but it is in his heart to destroy, and to cut off nations not a few.

10:8 For he saith: 'Are not my princes all of them kings?

10:9 Is not Calno as Carchemish? Is not Hamath as Arpad? Is not Samaria as Damascus?

WORLD ENGLISH BIBLE

10:10 As my hand has found the kingdoms of the idols, whose engraved images exceeded those of Jerusalem and of Samaria;

10:11 shall I not, as I have done to Samaria and her idols, so do to Jerusalem and her idols?

10:12 Therefore it will happen that, when the Lord has performed his whole work on Mount Zion and on Jerusalem, I will punish the fruit of the willful proud heart of the king of Assyria, and the insolence of his haughty looks.

10:13 For he has said, "By the strength of my hand I have done it, and by my wisdom; for I have understanding: and I have removed the boundaries of the peoples, and have robbed their treasures. Like a valiant man I have brought down their rulers.

10:14 My hand has found the riches of the peoples like a nest, and like one gathers eggs that are abandoned, have I gathered all the earth. There was no one who moved their wing, or that opened their mouth, or chirped."

10:15 Should an axe brag against him who chops with it? Should a saw exalt itself above him who saws with it? As if a rod should lift those who lift it up, or as if a staff should lift up someone who is not wood.

10:16 Therefore the Lord, Yahweh of Armies, will send among his fat ones leanness; and under his glory a burning will be kindled like the burning of fire.

10:17 The light of Israel will be for a fire, and his Holy One for a flame; and it will burn and devour his thorns and his briers in one day.

10:18 He will consume the glory of his forest, and of his fruitful field, both soul and body. It will be as when a standard bearer faints.

TARGUM ISAIAH

delivered into my hands, shall not Hamath be so? As I have done to Damascus, so will I do to Samaria.

10:10 As my hand hath found the kingdoms which worship idols, although their images were more than those of Jerusalem, and their statues more than those of Samaria;

10:11 Shall I not, as I have done to Samaria and to her idols, so do to Jerusalem and to her idols?

10:12 And it shall come to pass, when the Lord hath finished to do all he hath said in Mount Zion, and in Jerusalem, I will visit upon the works of the loftiness of the heart of the king of Assyria, and the glory of his high looks.

10:13 For he saith, By the strength of my hand I have done it, and by my wisdom; for I am prudent: and I have led nations into captivity from province to province; and the cities of their glory I have plundered: and I have brought down with strength those that dwell in fortified places.

10:14 And my hand hath found as a nest the riches of the people: and as one gathereth eggs *that are* left, I have gathered all the inhabitants of the earth; and there

TARGUM ISAIAH

was none that moved from thence and flew thither, that opened his mouth and spoke a word.

10:15 What, is it possible that the axe should boast itself against him that heweth therewith, saying, Behold, I have cut! Or shall the saw magnify itself against him that draweth it, saying, Do I not draw? When a rod is lifted up to smite, it is not the rod that smites, but he that smites with it.

10:16 Because the king of Assyria magnifies himself, therefore the Lord of the world, the Lord of hosts, shall send among his princes a blow; and beneath the vessels of their glory they are utterly burned up like the burning of a fire.

10:17 And there shall be the Lord, the Light of Israel, and His Holy One, His WORD, strong as fire, and His word as a flame; and it shall slay, and make an end of his rulers and of his governors in one day.

10:18 And it shall consume the glory of the multitude of his army, and their souls with their bodies, and he shall be broken, and be a fugitive.

10:19 And the rest of his warriors

JEWISH PUBLICATION SOCIETY 1917

10:10 As my hand hath reached the kingdoms of the idols, whose graven images did exceed them of Jerusalem and of Samaria;

10:11 Shall I not, as I have done unto Samaria and her idols, so do to Jerusalem and her idols?

10:12 Wherefore it shall come to pass, that when the Lord hath performed His whole work upon mount Zion and on Jerusalem, I will punish the fruit of the arrogant heart of the king of Assyria, and the glory of his haughty looks.

10:13 For he hath said: by the strength of my hand I have done it, and by my wisdom, for I am prudent; in that I have removed the bounds of the peoples, and have robbed their treasures, and have brought down as one mighty the inhabitants;

10:14 And my hand hath found as a nest the riches of the peoples; and as one gathereth eggs that are forsaken, have I gathered all the earth; and there was none that moved the wing, or that opened mouth, or chirped.

10:15 Should the axe boast itself against him that heweth therewith? Should the saw magnify itself against him that moveth it? as if a rod should move them that lift it up, or as if a staff should lift up him that is not wood.

10:16 Therefore will the Lord, the LORD of hosts, send among his fat ones leanness; and under his glory there shall be kindled a burning like the burning of fire.

10:17 And the light of Israel shall be for a fire, and his Holy One for a flame; and it shall burn and devour his thorns and his briers in one day.

10:18 And the glory of his forest and of his fruitful field, he will consume both soul and body; and it shall be as when a sick man wasteth away.

WORLD ENGLISH BIBLE

10:19 The remnant of the trees of his forest shall be few, so that a child could write their number.

10:20 It will come to pass in that day that the remnant of Israel, and those who have escaped from the house of Jacob will no more again lean on him who struck them, but shall lean on Yahweh, the Holy One of Israel, in truth.

10:21 A remnant will return, even the remnant of Jacob, to the mighty God.

10:22 For though your people, Israel, are like the sand of the sea, only a remnant of them will return. A destruction is determined, overflowing with righteousness.

10:23 For the Lord, Yahweh of Armies, will make a full end, and that determined, in the midst of all the earth.

10:24 Therefore the Lord, Yahweh of Armies, says "My people who dwell in Zion, don't be afraid of the Assyrian, though he strike you with the rod, and lift up his staff against you, as Egypt did.

10:25 For yet a very little while, and the indignation against you will be accomplished, and my anger will be directed to his destruction."

10:26 Yahweh of Armies will stir up a scourge against him, as in the slaughter of Midian at the rock of Oreb. His rod will be over the sea, and he will lift it up like he did against Egypt.

10:27 It will happen in that day, that his burden will depart from off your shoulder, and his yoke from off your neck, and the yoke shall be destroyed because of the anointing oil.

10:28 He has come to Aiath. He has passed through Migron. At Michmash he stores his baggage.

10:29 They have gone over the pass. They have taken up their lodging at Geba. Ramah trembles. Gibeah of Saul has fled.

10:30 Cry aloud with your voice, daughter of Gallim! Listen, Laishah! You poor Anathoth!

TARGUM ISAIAH

shall come to an end, that the people shall be a small number, and they shall be reckoned a weak kingdom.

10:20 And it shall come to pass in that time, that the remnant of Israel, and such as are escaped of the house of Jacob, shall no more again lean on the people whom they served; but they shall lean upon the WORD of the Lord, the Holy One of Israel, in truth.

10:21 The remnant which have not sinned, and have turned away from sin, the remnant of the house of Jacob, shall return to worship before the mighty God.

10:22 Though thy people Israel be as the sand of the sea, a remnant which hath not sinned, but hath turned away from sin, for them mighty things shall be done, which shall prevail, *even* those which speak in righteousness.

10:23 For a completion, and an end, the Lord, the God of hosts is making with all the wicked in the midst of the earth.

10:24 Therefore, thus saith the Lord, the God of hosts, O my people, that dwellest in Zion, be not afraid of the Assyrian: he shall smite thee with his government,

TARGUM ISAIAH

and his dominion he shall lift up upon thee, after the manner of Egypt.

10:25 For yet a little while, and the curses shall cease from you of the house of Jacob; and mine anger shall be upon the people that work iniquity, to destroy them.

10:26 And the Lord of hosts shall bring upon him a stroke, as the stroke of Midian at the rock of Oreb: and his dominion shall depart from you, as the dominion of Pharaoh departed by the sea, and mighty works shall be done for you after the manner of Egypt.

10:27 And it shall come to pass at that time, *that* his dominion shall depart from you, and his yoke from off thy neck, and the nations shall be broken from before the Messiah.

10:28 He is come to Aiath, he has passed through Migron; at Micmash he shall appoint the princes of his army.

10:29 They waded, they passed through the Jordan: at Geba they passed the night; the inhabitants of Ramah are broken; the men of Gibeah of Saul have fled.

10:30 Lift up your voice, men of the daughter of Gallim: give ear,

JEWISH PUBLICATION SOCIETY 1917

10:19 And the remnant of the trees of his forest shall be few, that a child may write them down.

10:20 And it shall come to pass in that day, that the remnant of Israel, and they that are escaped of the house of Jacob, shall no more again stay upon him that smote them; but shall stay upon the LORD, the Holy One of Israel, in truth.

10:21 A remnant shall return, even the remnant of Jacob, unto God the Mighty.

10:22 For though thy people, O Israel, be as the sand of the sea, only a remnant of them shall return; an extermination is determined, overflowing with righteousness.

10:23 For an extermination wholly determined shall the Lord, the GOD of hosts, make in the midst of all the earth.

10:24 Therefore thus saith the Lord, the GOD of hosts: O My people that dwellest in Zion, be not afraid of Asshur, though he smite thee with the rod, and lift up his staff against thee, after the manner of Egypt.

10:25 For yet a very little while, and the indignation shall be accomplished, and Mine anger shall be to their destruction.

10:26 And the LORD of hosts shall stir up against him a scourge, as in the slaughter of Midian at the Rock of Oreb; and as His rod was over the sea, so shall He lift it up after the manner of Egypt.

10:27 And it shall come to pass in that day, that his burden shall depart from off thy shoulder, and his yoke from off thy neck, and the yoke shall be destroyed by reason of fatness.

10:28 He is come to Aiath, he is passed through Migron; at Michmas he layeth up his baggage;

10:29 They are gone over the pass; they have taken up their lodging at Geba; Ramah trembleth; Gibeath-shaul is fled.

10:30 Cry thou with a shrill voice, O daughter of Gallim! Hearken, O Laish! O thou poor Anathoth!

WORLD ENGLISH BIBLE

10:31 Madmenah is a fugitive. The inhabitants of Gebim flee for safety.

10:32 This very day he will halt at Nob. He shakes his hand at the mountain of the daughter of Zion, the hill of Jerusalem.

10:33 Behold, the Lord, Yahweh of Armies, will lop the boughs with terror. The tall will be cut down, and the lofty will be brought low.

10:34 He will cut down the thickets of the forest with iron, and Lebanon will fall by the Mighty One.

11:1 A shoot will come out of the stock of Jesse, and a branch out of his roots will bear fruit.

11:2 The Spirit of Yahweh will rest on him: the spirit of wisdom and understanding, the spirit of counsel and might, the spirit of knowledge and of the fear of Yahweh.

11:3 His delight will be in the fear of Yahweh. He will not judge by the sight of his eyes, neither decide by the hearing of his ears;

11:4 but with righteousness he will judge the poor, and decide with equity for the humble of the earth. He will strike the earth with the rod of his mouth; and with the breath of his lips he will kill the wicked.

11:5 Righteousness will be the belt of his waist, and faithfulness the belt of his waist.

11:6 The wolf will live with the lamb, and the leopard will lie down with the young goat; The calf, the young lion, and the fattened calf together; and a little child will lead them.

TARGUM ISAIAH

ye who are dwelling in Laish, who are dwelling in poor Anathoth.

10:31 The men of Madmenah are broken; the inhabitants of Gebim are fled.

10:32 As yet the day is still high, and he has much time to come. Behold, Sennacherib the king of Assyria shall come, and shall stand in Nob, the city of the priests, before the wall of Jerusalem; he answered and said to his army, Is not this the city of Jerusalem, against which I have tumultuously brought together all my camps? Behold, she is weaker than all the fortified cities of the nations which I have subdued by the strength of my hand. He came up, he stood and shook his head; he stretched out and moved his hand against the mount of the house of the sanctuary which is in Zion, and against the court which is in Jerusalem.

10:33 Behold, the Lord of the world, the Lord of hosts, shall cast forth slaughter into his camp, as grapes that are trod in a winepress: and the high ones of stature shall be hewn down, and the mighty shall be humbled.

10:34 And He shall slay the mighty

TARGUM ISAIAH

men of his camp, who are strong as iron. And those that make war upon the earth shall be cast down.

11:1 And a King shall come forth from the sons of Jesse, and from his children's children the Messiah shall be anointed.

11:2 And there shall dwell upon Him the Spirit of prophecy from before the Lord: the Spirit of wisdom and understanding, the Spirit of counsel and might, the Spirit of knowledge and of the fear of the Lord.

11:3 He shall bring him to the fear of the Lord: and He shall not judge according to the sight of His eyes, neither reprove after the hearing of His ears.

11:4 But with righteousness shall He judge the poor, and reprove with faithfulness the needy of the earth; and He shall smite the sinners of the earth with the word of His mouth, and with the speech of His lips He shall slay the wicked.

11:5 And the righteous shall be round about Him, and those that work *in* faith shall draw nigh unto Him.

11:6 In the days of the Messiah of Israel peace shall be multiplied

JEWISH PUBLICATION SOCIETY 1917

10:31 Madmenah is in mad flight; the inhabitants of Gebim flee to cover.

10:32 This very day shall he halt at Nob, shaking his hand at the mount of the daughter of Zion, the hill of Jerusalem.

10:33 Behold, the Lord, the LORD of hosts, shall lop the boughs with terror; and the high ones of stature shall be hewn down, and the lofty shall be laid low.

10:34 And He shall cut down the thickets of the forest with iron, and Lebanon shall fall by a mighty one.

11:1 And there shall come forth a shoot out of the stock of Jesse, and a twig shall grow forth out of his roots.

11:2 And the spirit of the LORD shall rest upon him, the spirit of wisdom and understanding, the spirit of counsel and might, the spirit of knowledge and of the fear of the LORD.

11:3 And his delight shall be in the fear of the LORD; and he shall not judge after the sight of his eyes, neither decide after the hearing of his ears;

11:4 But with righteousness shall he judge the poor, and decide with equity for the meek of the land; and he shall smite the land with the rod of his mouth, and with the breath of his lips shall he slay the wicked.

11:5 And righteousness shall be the girdle of his loins, and faithfulness the girdle of his reins.

11:6 And the wolf shall dwell with the lamb, and the leopard shall lie down with the kid; and the calf and the young lion and the fatling together; and a little child shall lead them.

WORLD ENGLISH BIBLE

11:7 The cow and the bear will graze. Their young ones will lie down together. The lion will eat straw like the ox.

11:8 The nursing child will play near a cobra's hole, and the weaned child will put his hand on the viper's den.

11:9 They will not hurt nor destroy in all my holy mountain; for the earth will be full of the knowledge of Yahweh, as the waters cover the sea.

11:10 It will happen in that day that the nations will seek the root of Jesse, who stands as a banner of the peoples; and his resting place will be glorious.

11:11 It will happen in that day that the Lord will set his hand again the second time to recover the remnant that is left of his people from Assyria, from Egypt, from Pathros, from Cush, from Elam, from Shinar, from Hamath, and from the islands of the sea.

11:12 He will set up a banner for the nations, and will assemble the outcasts of Israel, and gather together the dispersed of Judah from the four corners of the earth.

11:13 The envy also of Ephraim will depart, and those who persecute Judah will be cut off. Ephraim won't envy Judah, and Judah won't persecute Ephraim.

11:14 They will fly down on the shoulders of the Philistines on the west. Together they will plunder the children of the east. They will extend their power over Edom and Moab, and the children of Ammon will obey them.

11:15 Yahweh will utterly destroy the tongue of the Egyptian sea; and with his scorching wind he will wave his hand over the River, and will split it into seven streams, and cause men to march over in sandals.

11:16 There will be a highway for the remnant that is left of his people from Assyria, like there was for Israel in the day that he came up out of the land of Egypt.

TARGUM ISAIAH

in the earth. The wolf shall dwell with the lamb, and the leopard shall dwell with the kid; and the calf, and the lion, and the fatling together; and a little sucking child shall be leading them.

11:7 And the cow and the bear shall feed together, their young ones shall lie down together; and the lion shall eat straw like the ox.

11:8 And the sucking child shall play on the hole of the asp, and the weaned child shall put forth his hand on the glistering pupil of the eyes of the cockatrice.

11:9 They shall not hurt nor destroy in all my holy mountain, for the earth shall be full of the knowledge of the fear of the Lord, as the waters cover the sea.

11:10 And there shall be at that time a son of the son of Jesse, who shall stand for an ensign of the people; kings shall obey Him, and the place of His dwelling shall be in glory.

11:11 And it shall come to pass at that time, that the Lord shall use a second time His might to redeem the remnant of His people, which shall be left, from Assyria, and from Egypt, and from Pattros, and from India, and from Elam,

TARGUM ISAIAH

and from Babylon, and from Hamath, and from the islands of the sea.

11:12 And He shall lift up an ensign for the nations, and shall assemble the scattered of Israel, and the captivity of Judah He shall gather together from the four winds of the earth.

11:13 The envy of the house of Ephraim shall depart, and those that oppress the house of Judah shall come to an end: those of the house of Ephraim shall not envy the house of Judah; and those of the house of Judah shall not oppress the house of Ephraim.

11:14 They shall be united in one mind to smite the Philistines towards the west: they shall spoil the children of the east. Against Edom and Moab they shall stretch out their hands, and the children of Ammon shall obey them.

11:15 And the Lord shall dry up the tongue of the Egyptian sea, and shall lift the stroke of His strength upon Euphrates by the word of His prophets, and shall smite it in seven streams, and *men* shall walk through it dryshod.

11:16 And there shall be a paved way for the remnant of His

JEWISH PUBLICATION SOCIETY 1917

11:7 And the cow and the bear feed; their young ones shall lie down together; and the lion shall eat straw like the ox.

11:8 And the sucking child shall play on the hole of the asp, and the weaned child shall put his hand on the basilisk's den.

11:9 They shall not hurt nor destroy in all My holy mountain; for the earth shall be full of the knowledge of the LORD, as the waters cover the sea.

11:10 And it shall come to pass in that day, that the root of Jesse, that standeth for an ensign of the peoples, unto him shall the nations seek; and his resting-place shall be glorious.

11:11 And it shall come to pass in that day, that the Lord will set His hand again the second time to recover the remnant of His people, that shall remain from Assyria, and from Egypt, and from Pathros, and from Cush, and from Elam, and from Shinar, and from Hamath, and from the islands of the sea.

11:12 And He will set up an ensign for the nations, and will assemble the dispersed of Israel, and gather together the scattered of Judah from the four corners of the earth.

11:13 The envy also of Ephraim shall depart, and they that harass Judah shall be cut off; Ephraim shall not envy Judah, and Judah shall not vex Ephraim.

11:14 And they shall fly down upon the shoulder of the Philistines on the west; together shall they spoil the children of the east; they shall put forth their hand upon Edom and Moab; and the children of Ammon shall obey them.

11:15 And the LORD will utterly destroy the tongue of the Egyptian sea; and with His scorching wind will He shake His hand over the River, and will smite it into seven streams, and cause men to march over dry-shod.

11:16 And there shall be a highway for the remnant of His people, that shall remain from Assyria, like as there was for Israel in the day that he came up out of the land of Egypt.

WORLD ENGLISH BIBLE

12:1 In that day you will say, "I will give thanks to you, Yahweh; for though you were angry with me, your anger has turned away and you comfort me.

12:2 Behold, God is my salvation. I will trust, and will not be afraid; for Yah, Yahweh, is my strength and song; and he has become my salvation."

12:3 Therefore with joy you will draw water out of the wells of salvation.

12:4 In that day you will say, "Give thanks to Yahweh! Call on his name. Declare his doings among the peoples. Proclaim that his name is exalted!

12:5 Sing to Yahweh, for he has done excellent things! Let this be known in all the earth!

12:6 Cry aloud and shout, you inhabitant of Zion; for the Holy One of Israel is great in the midst of you!"

13:1 The burden of Babylon, which Isaiah the son of Amoz saw:

13:2 Set up a banner on the bare mountain! Lift up your voice to them! Wave your hand, that they may go into the gates of the nobles.

13:3 I have commanded my consecrated ones; yes, I have called my mighty men for my anger, even my proudly exulting ones.

13:4 The noise of a multitude is in the mountains, as of a great people; the noise of an uproar of the kingdoms of the nations gathered together! Yahweh of Armies is mustering the army for the battle.

13:5 They come from a far country, from the uttermost part of heaven, even Yahweh, and the weapons of his indignation, to destroy the whole land.

13:6 Wail; for the day of Yahweh is at hand! It will come as destruction from the Almighty.

TARGUM ISAIAH

people, which shall be left, from Assyria, like as it was to Israel in the day of their coming up from the land of Egypt.

12:1 And thou shalt say at that time, I will confess before Thee, O Lord, for that I have sinned before Thee, Thine anger is upon me; but when I return to the law, Thine anger will turn from me, and Thou wilt have mercy on me.

12:2 Behold, in the WORD of God is my salvation; I am trusting, and shall not be moved, because my strength and my praise is the fear of the Lord: He hath spoken by His WORD, and He is become my Saviour.

12:3 And ye shall receive a new doctrine with joy from the chosen of the righteous.

12:4 And at that time shall ye say, Praise the Lord, pray in His name, declare His doings among the people, remember ye that powerful is His name.

12:5 Praise the Lord, for He has done mighty works; this is revealed in all the earth.

12:6 Cry out and shout, O congregation of Zion, because He is great that promised to cause His Shekinah to dwell in the midst of thee, the Holy One of Israel.

13:1 THE BURDEN OF THE CUP OF CURSING TO GIVE TO BABYLON TO DRINK, WHICH ISAIAH THE SON OF AMOZ DID PROPHESY.

13:2 Against the fortified city that dwells securely lift up the ensign, exalt the voice unto them, shake the hand, that they may go into the gates of the nobles.

13:3 I have commanded those that are prepared by me, I have also called together my mighty ones, that they may avenge my wrath upon them, my strength, and my praise.

13:4 There *is* a voice of a multitude in the mountains, like as of a great people: the voice of the tumultuous assembly of kings, of nations being assembled, the Lord of hosts is mustering the armies for battle.

13:5 They are coming from a far country, from the ends of the earth: the Lord and the vessels of the cup of cursing before Him, to destroy all the wicked of the earth.

13:6 Howl ye, for nigh is the day, ready to come from before the Lord; like spoil from before the Almighty it shall come.

12:1 And in that day thou shalt say: 'I will give thanks unto Thee, O LORD; for though Thou was angry with me, Thine anger is turned away, and Thou comfortest me.

12:2 Behold, God is my salvation; I will trust, and will not be afraid; for GOD the LORD is my strength and song; and He is become my salvation.'

12:3 Therefore with joy shall ye draw water out of the wells of salvation.

12:4 And in that day shall ye say: 'Give thanks unto the LORD, proclaim His name, declare His doings among the peoples, make mention that His name is exalted.

12:5 Sing unto the LORD; for He hath done gloriously; this is made known in all the earth.

12:6 Cry aloud and shout, thou inhabitant of Zion, for great is the Holy One of Israel in the midst of thee.'

13:1 The burden of Babylon, which Isaiah the son of Amoz did see.

13:2 Set ye up an ensign upon the high mountain, lift up the voice unto them, wave the hand, that they may go into the gates of the nobles.

13:3 I have commanded My consecrated ones, yea, I have called My mighty ones for mine anger, even My proudly exulting ones.

13:4 Hark, a tumult in the mountains, like as of a great people! Hark, the uproar of the kingdoms of the nations gathered together! The LORD of hosts mustereth the host of the battle.

13:5 They come from a far country, from the end of heaven, even the LORD, and the weapons of His indignation, to destroy the whole earth.

13:6 Howl ye; for the day of the LORD is at hand; as destruction from the Almighty shall it come.

WORLD ENGLISH BIBLE

13:7 Therefore all hands will be feeble, and everyone's heart will melt.

13:8 They will be dismayed. Pangs and sorrows will seize them. They will be in pain like a woman in labor. They will look in amazement one at another. Their faces will be faces of flame.

13:9 Behold, the day of Yahweh comes, cruel, with wrath and fierce anger; to make the land a desolation, and to destroy its sinners out of it.

13:10 For the stars of the sky and its constellations will not give their light. The sun will be darkened in its going forth, and the moon will not cause its light to shine.

13:11 I will punish the world for their evil, and the wicked for their iniquity. I will cause the arrogance of the proud to cease, and will humble the haughtiness of the terrible.

13:12 I will make people more rare than fine gold, even a person than the pure gold of Ophir.

13:13 Therefore I will make the heavens tremble, and the earth will be shaken out of its place in the wrath of Yahweh of Armies, and in the day of his fierce anger.

13:14 It will happen that like a hunted gazelle, and like sheep that no one gathers, they will each turn to their own people, and will each flee to their own land.

13:15 Everyone who is found will be thrust through. Everyone who is captured will fall by the sword.

13:16 Their infants also will be dashed in pieces before their eyes. Their houses will be ransacked, and their wives raped.

13:17 Behold, I will stir up the Medes against them, who will not value silver, and as for gold, they will not delight in it.

13:18 Their bows will dash the young men in pieces; and they shall have no pity on the fruit of the womb. Their eyes will not spare children.

TARGUM ISAIAH

13:7 Therefore shall all hands be slackened, and every man's heart shall melt.

13:8 They shall be struck with consternation; distress and pangs shall take hold of them; they shall tremble as with the trembling of a woman that travaileth: they shall be amazed one at another; their countenances shall be like flames of fire.

13:9 Behold, the day from before the presence of the Lord cometh, cruel both with wrath and fierce anger, to lay the land desolate: and He shall destroy the sinners out of it.

13:10 For the stars of heaven and their constellations shall not give their light: the sun shall be darkened in his going forth; and the moon shall not cause her light to shine.

13:11 And I will visit the inhabitants of the world with the punishment for evil, and the wicked *for* their iniquity: and I will put an end to the greatness of the wicked, and the strength of the mighty I will humble.

13:12 And I will love them that fear me more than gold, in which the sons of men glory; and those that

TARGUM ISAIAH

keep the law more than the fine gold of Ophir.

13:13 Therefore I will shake the heavens, and the earth shall remove out of her place, from before the presence of the Lord of hosts, and in the day of the fierceness of His anger.

13:14 And he shall be as a roe chased, and as sheep when there is none to gather them together: they shall every man turn to his own people, and flee every one into his own land.

13:15 Every one that shall be found in her shall be slain, and every one that shall enter into the fortified cities shall be slain by the sword.

13:16 And their children shall be dashed before their eyes; their houses shall be plundered, and their wives ravished.

13:17 Behold, I am bringing upon them the Medes, who are not impelled by silver; and *as for* gold, they delight not in it.

13:18 And their bows shall strike through the young men; and they shall not compassionate the child of the womb; their eye shall not spare the children.

13:19 And Babylon shall become,

JEWISH PUBLICATION SOCIETY 1917

13:7 Therefore shall all hands be slack, and every heart of man shall melt.

13:8 And they shall be affrighted; pangs and throes shall take hold them; they shall be in pain as a woman in travail; they shall look aghast one at another; their faces shall be faces of flame.

13:9 Behold, the day of the LORD cometh, cruel, and full of wrath and fierce anger; to make the earth a desolation, and to destroy the sinners thereof out of it,

13:10 For the stars of heaven and the constellations thereof shall not give their light; the sun shall be darkened in his going forth, and the moon shall not cause her light to shine.

13:11 And I will visit upon the world their evil, and upon the wicked their iniquity; and I will cause the arrogancy of the proud to cease, and will lay low the haughtiness of the tyrants.

13:12 I will make man more rare than fine gold, even man than the pure gold of Ophir.

13:13 Therefore I will make the heavens to tremble, and the earth shall be shaken out of her place, for the wrath of the LORD of hosts, and for the day of His fierce anger.

13:14 And it shall come to pass, that as the chased gazelle, and as sheep that no man gathereth, they shall turn every man to his own people, and shall flee every man to his own land.

13:15 Every one that is found shall be thrust through; and every one that is caught shall fall by the sword.

13:16 Their babes also shall be dashed in pieces before their eyes; their houses shall be spoiled, and their wives ravished.

13:17 Behold, I will stir up the Medes against them, who shall not regard silver, and as for gold, they shall not delight in it.

13:18 And their bows shall dash the young men in pieces; and they shall have no pity on the fruit of the womb; their eye shall not spare children.

WORLD ENGLISH BIBLE

13:19 Babylon, the glory of kingdoms, the beauty of the Chaldeans' pride, will be like when God overthrew Sodom and Gomorrah.

13:20 It will never be inhabited, neither will it be lived in from generation to generation. The Arabian will not pitch a tent there, neither will shepherds make their flocks lie down there.

13:21 But wild animals of the desert will lie there, and their houses will be full of jackals. Ostriches will dwell there, and wild goats will frolic there.

13:22 Wolves will cry in their castles, and jackals in the pleasant palaces. Her time is near to come, and her days will not be prolonged.

14:1 For Yahweh will have compassion on Jacob, and will yet choose Israel, and set them in their own land. The foreigner will join himself with them, and they will unite with the house of Jacob.

14:2 The peoples will take them, and bring them to their place. The house of Israel will possess them in Yahweh's land for servants and for handmaids. They will take as captives those whose captives they were; and they shall rule over their oppressors.

14:3 It will happen in the day that Yahweh will give you rest from your sorrow, from your trouble, and from the hard service in which you were made to serve,

14:4 that you will take up this parable against the king of Babylon, and say, "How the oppressor has ceased! The golden city has ceased!"

14:5 Yahweh has broken the staff of the wicked, the scepter of the rulers,

14:6 who struck the peoples in wrath with a continual stroke, who ruled the nations in anger, with a persecution that none restrained.

14:7 The whole earth is at rest, and is quiet. They break out song.

14:8 Yes, the fir trees rejoice with you, with the cedars of Lebanon, saying, "Since you are humbled, no lumberjack has come up against us."

TARGUM ISAIAH

she that was aforetimes the joy of kings, the beauty of the Chaldeens' excellency, as the overthrow wherewith the Lord overthrew Sodom and Gomorrah.

13:20 It shall not be inhabited for ever; nor shall it be dwelt in from generation to generation: neither shall the Arabian pitch his tent there, neither shall the shepherds dwell there.

13:21 But the martens shall lodge there; and their houses shall be filled with howling monsters: and there shall the ostriches dwell; and devils shall delight themselves there.

13:22 The wild cats shall shriek in their palaces; and dragons in the place of the abodes of their luxuries. And nigh to come is the time of the destruction of Babylon, and her days shall not be prolonged.

14:1 For the Lord will have compassion upon the house of Jacob, and will delight again in Israel, and shall make them to dwell in their land; and proselytes shall be joined unto them, and they shall be united unto the house of Jacob.

14:2 And the nations shall take them, and shall bring them to their

TARGUM ISAIAH

land; and the house of Israel shall possess them in the land of the Shekinah of the Lord for servants and handmaids: and they shall take them captives, whose captivcs they were; those who had made them their servants shall *now* serve them.

14:3 And it shall come to pass in that day, that the Lord shall give thee rest from thy distress, from thy bondage, and from the hard servitude which was served upon thee,

14:4 That thou shalt take up this proverb against the king of Babylon, and say, How hath the dominion that made us servile ceased! *How* is come to an end the strength of the sinner!

14:5 The Lord hath broken the strength of the wicked, the government of sinners,

14:6 Of him who was smiting the people in fury, with a perpetual stroke, *of him who was* ruling the nations in anger, ruling and none hindered.

14:7 The whole earth is at rest, is quiet, they rejoice with a song.

14:8 Rulers also rejoiced over thee; the rich in treasures said, Since thou art laid down, the destroyer

JEWISH PUBLICATION SOCIETY 1917

13:19 And Babylon, the glory of kingdoms, the beauty of the Chaldeans' pride, shall be as when God overthrew Sodom and Gomorrah.

13:20 It shall never be inhabited, neither shall it be dwelt in from generation to gencration; neither shall the Arabian pitch tent there; neither shall the shepherds make their fold there.

13:21 But wild-cats shall lie there; and their houses shall be full of ferrets; and ostriches shall dwell there, and satyrs shall dance there.

13:22 And jackals shall howl in their castles, and wild-dogs in the pleasant palaces; and her time is near to come, and her days shall not be prolonged.

14:1 For the LORD will have compassion on Jacob, and will yet choose Israel, and set them in their own land; and the stranger shall join himself with them, and they shall cleave to the house of Jacob.

14:2 And the peoples shall take them, and bring them to their place; and the house of Israel shall possess them in the land of the LORD for servants and for handmaids; and they shall take them captive, whose captives they were; and they shall rule over their oppressors.

14:3 And it shall come to pass in the day that the LORD shall give thee rest from thy travail, and from thy trouble, and from the hard service wherein thou wast made to serve,

14:4 that thou shalt take up this parable against the king of Babylon, and say: How hath the oppressor ceased! the ex-actress of gold ceased!

14:5 The LORD hath broken the staff of the wicked, the sceptre of the rulers,

14:6 That smote the peoples in wrath with an incessant stroke, that ruled the nations in anger, with a persecution that none restrained.

14:7 The whole earth is at rest, and is quiet; they break forth into singing.

14:8 Yea, the cypresses rejoice at thee, and the cedars of Lebanon: 'Since thou art laid down, no feller is come up against us.'

WORLD ENGLISH BIBLE

14:9 Sheol from beneath has moved for you to meet you at your coming. It stirs up the dead for you, even all the rulers of the earth. It has raised up from their thrones all the kings of the nations.

14:10 They all will answer and ask you, "Have you also become as weak as we are? Have you become like us?"

14:11 Your pomp is brought down to Sheol, with the sound of your stringed instruments. Maggots are spread out under you, and worms cover you.

14:12 How you have fallen from heaven, morning star, son of the dawn! How you are cut down to the ground, who laid the nations low!

14:13 You said in your heart, "I will ascend into heaven! I will exalt my throne above the stars of God! I will sit on the mountain of assembly, in the far north!

14:14 I will ascend above the heights of the clouds! I will make myself like the Most High!"

14:15 Yet you shall be brought down to Sheol, to the depths of the pit.

14:16 Those who see you will stare at you. They will ponder you, saying, "Is this the man who made the earth to tremble, who shook kingdoms;

14:17 who made the world like a wilderness, and overthrew its cities; who didn't release his prisoners to their home?"

14:18 All the kings of the nations, sleep in glory, everyone in his own house.

14:19 But you are cast away from your tomb like an abominable branch, clothed with the slain, who are thrust through with the sword, who go down to the stones of the pit; like a dead body trodden under foot.

14:20 You will not join them in burial, because you have destroyed your land. You have killed your people. The seed of evildoers will not be named forever.

14:21 Prepare for slaughter of his children because of the iniquity of their fathers, that they not rise up and possess the earth, and fill the surface of the world with cities.

TARGUM ISAIAH

is not come up upon us.

14:9 Hell from beneath is moved for thee, to meet thee at thy coming; she rouseth for thee the mighty: all the rich in treasures, all the kings of the nations rise from their thrones.

14:10 All of them shall answer and say unto thee, Art thou become sick as we? Unto us thou hast become like.

14:11 Thy glory is brought down to the grave, the rattling noise of the songs of thy musical instruments: the worm is spread under thee, and upon thee vermin.

14:12 How art thou cast down from on high, who wast shining among the sons of men as the star Venus among the stars: thou art dashed down to the earth, who wast a slaughterer among the nations.

14:13 And thou, thou hast said in thy heart, I will climb up the heavens; I will place the throne of my kingdom above the people of God, and I will sit upon the mountain of the solemn assembly upon the ends of the north;

14:14 I will have the ascendency over all people; I will be higher than all of them.

14:15 But to the grave thou shalt

TARGUM ISAIAH

be brought down, to the ends of the pit of the place of perdition.

14:16 Those that see thee shall look attentively at thee, they shall consider thee, and say, Is this the man that made the earth to tremble, that laid waste kingdoms?

14:17 *That* made the world as a wilderness, that laid waste its cities, and did not open the gate to his prisoners.

14:18 All the kings of the nations, all of them, lie down in glory, each in his eternal abode.

14:19 But thou art cast out of thy grave as a hidden abortion, *as* those hidden among the slain, as those pierced by the sword, *as* those that are descending the lowest pit of the place of destruction, as a carcase trodden under foot.

14:20 Thou shalt not be like one of them in burial; because thou hast destroyed thy country, thou hast slain thy people: the seed of evildoers shall not be established for ever.

14:21 Prepare ye slaughter for his children, for the iniquity of their fathers; lest they rise and possess the earth, and the faces of the world be filled with enemies.

14:9 The nether-world from beneath is moved for thee to meet thee at thy coming; the shades are stirred up for thee, even all the chief ones of the earth; all the kings of the nations are raised up from their thrones.

14:10 All they do answer and say unto thee: 'Art thou also become weak as we? Art thou become like unto us?

14:11 Thy pomp is brought down to the nether-world, and the noise of thy psalteries; the maggot is spread under thee, and the worms cover thee.'

14:12 How art thou fallen from heaven, O day-star, son of the morning! How art thou cut down to the ground, that didst cast lots over the nations!

14:13 And thou saidst in thy heart: 'I will ascend into heaven, above the stars of God will I exalt my throne, and I will sit upon the mount of meeting, in the uttermost parts of the north;

14:14 I will ascend above the heights of the clouds; I will be like the Most High.'

14:15 Yet thou shalt be brought down to the nether-world, to the uttermost parts of the pit.

14:16 They that saw thee do narrowly look upon thee, they gaze earnestly at thee: 'Is this the man that made the earth to tremble, that did shake kingdoms;

14:17 That made the world as a wilderness, and destroyed the cities thereof; that opened not the house of his prisoners?'

14:18 All the kings of the nations, all of them, sleep in glory, every one in his own house.

14:19 But thou art cast forth away from thy grave like an abhorred offshoot, in the raiment of the slain, that are thrust through with the sword, that go down to the pavement of the pit, as a carcass trodden under foot.

14:20 Thou shalt not be joined with them in burial, because thou hast destroyed thy land, thou hast slain thy people; the seed of evil-doers shall not be named for ever.

14:21 Prepare ye slaughter for his children for the iniquity of their fathers; that they rise not up, and possess the earth, and fill the face of the world with cities.

WORLD ENGLISH BIBLE

14:22 "I will rise up against them," says Yahweh of Armies, "and cut off from Babylon name and remnant, and son and son's son," says Yahweh.

14:23 "I will also make it a possession for the porcupine, and pools of water. I will sweep it with the broom of destruction," says Yahweh of Armies.

14:24 Yahweh of Armies has sworn, saying, "Surely, as I have thought, so shall it happen; and as I have purposed, so shall it stand:

14:25 that I will break the Assyrian in my land, and tread him under foot on my mountains. Then his yoke will leave them, and his burden leave their shoulders.

14:26 This is the plan that is determined for the whole earth. This is the hand that is stretched out over all the nations.

14:27 For Yahweh of Armies has planned, and who can stop it? His hand is stretched out, and who can turn it back?"

14:28 This burden was in the year that king Ahaz died.

14:29 Don't rejoice, O Philistia, all of you, because the rod that struck you is broken; for out of the serpent's root an adder will emerge, and his fruit will be a fiery flying serpent.

14:30 The firstborn of the poor will eat, and the needy will lie down in safety; and I will kill your root with famine, and your remnant will be killed.

14:31 Howl, gate! Cry, city! You are melted away, Philistia, all of you; for smoke comes out of the north, and there is no straggler in his ranks.

14:32 What will they answer the messengers of the nation? That Yahweh has founded Zion, and in her the afflicted of his people will take refuge.

15:1 The burden of Moab: for in a night, Ar of Moab is laid waste, and brought to nothing; for in a night Kir of Moab is laid waste, and brought to nothing.

TARGUM ISAIAH

14:22 And I will reveal myself to take vengeance of them, saith the Lord of hosts; and I will destroy of Babylon the name, and the remnant, and the son, and the son's son, saith the Lord of hosts.

14:23 And I will make it an inheritance for the hedgehog, a place of desolation, pools of water: and I will sweep her as they are sweeping with a besom: and I will throw her down to destroy her, saith the Lord of hosts.

14:24 The Lord of hosts hath sworn, saying, Surely as I have thought, so shall it be; and as I have purposed, *so* shall it stand.

14:25 To break the Assyrian in my land, and upon the mountains of my people I will tread him under foot; then there shall depart from them his dominion, and his yoke off from their necks shall cease.

14:26 This is the purpose that is purposed upon all the inhabitants of the earth; and this is the might of the ruler which is lifted up over all the kingdoms.

14:27 For the Lord of hosts has purposed, and who can remove it? yea, His power is exalted, and who can withstand it?

14:28 In the year that king Ahaz

TARGUM ISAIAH

died was the burden of this prophecy.

14:29 Rejoice not, O Philistia, all of ye, because the government that hath made you servile is broken; because from the children of Jesse shall come forth the Messiah, and His works among you shall be as a flying serpent.

14:30 And the poor of my people shall be fed, and the meek in His days shall dwell in safety; and He shall slay with famine thy children, and the remnant of thy people He shall kill.

14:31 Howl, on account of thy gate, cry on account of thy city, ye, O Philistines, all of you; ye shall be broken: because from the north vengeance is coming, and is not delaying its appointed time.

14:32 And what good news will they tell the messengers of the nations? That the Lord hath founded Zion, and the poor of His people shall trust in it.

15:1 THE BURDEN OF THE CUP OF CURSING TO GIVE MOAB TO DRINK. Because in the night Leheyath-Moab is destroyed, and they were asleep. Yea, in the night the fortified city of Moab was subdued,

JEWISH PUBLICATION SOCIETY 1917

14:22 And I will rise up against them, saith the LORD of hosts, and cut off from Babylon name and remnant, and offshoot and offspring, saith the LORD.

14:23 I will also make it a possession for the bittern, and pools of water; and I will sweep it with the besom of destruction, saith the LORD of hosts.

14:24 The LORD of hosts hath sworn, saying: Surely as I have thought, so shall it come to pass; and as I have purposed, so shall it stand,

14:25 That I will break Asshur in My land, and upon My mountains tread him under foot; then shall his yoke depart from off them, and his burden depart from off their shoulder.

14:26 This is the purpose that is purposed upon the whole earth; and this is the hand that is stretched out upon all the nations.

14:27 For the LORD of hosts hath purposed, and who shall disannul it? And His hand is stretched out, and who shall turn it back?

14:28 In the year that king Ahaz died was this burden.

14:29 Rejoice not, O Philistia, all of thee, because the rod that smote thee is broken: for out of the serpent's root shall come forth a basilisk, and his fruit shall be a flying serpent.

14:30 And the first-born of the poor shall feed, and the needy shall lie down in safety; and I will kill thy root with famine, and thy remnant shall be slain.

14:31 Howl, O gate; cry, O city; melt away, O Philistia, all of thee; for there cometh a smoke out of the north, and there is no straggler in his ranks.

14:32 What then shall one answer the messengers of the nation? That the LORD hath founded Zion, and in her shall the afflicted of His people take refuge.

15:1 The burden of Moab. For in the night that Ar of Moab is laid waste, he is brought to ruin; for in the night that Kir of Moab is laid waste, he is brought to ruin.

WORLD ENGLISH BIBLE

15:2 They have gone up to Bayith, and to Dibon, to the high places, to weep. Moab wails over Nebo and over Medeba. Baldness is on all of their heads. Every beard is cut off.

15:3 In their streets, they clothe themselves in sackcloth. In their streets and on their housetops, everyone wails, weeping abundantly.

15:4 Heshbon cries out with Elealeh. Their voice is heard even to Jahaz. Therefore the armed men of Moab cry aloud. Their souls tremble within them.

15:5 My heart cries out for Moab! Her nobles flee to Zoar, to Eglath Shelishiyah; for they go up by the ascent of Luhith with weeping; for in the way of Horonaim, they raise up a cry of destruction.

15:6 For the waters of Nimrim will be desolate; for the grass has withered away, the tender grass fails, there is no green thing.

15:7 Therefore they will carry away the abundance they have gotten, and that which they have stored up, over the brook of the willows.

15:8 For the cry has gone around the borders of Moab; its wailing to Eglaim, and its wailing to Beer Elim.

15:9 For the waters of Dimon are full of blood; for I will bring yet more on Dimon, a lion on those of Moab who escape, and on the remnant of the land.

16:1 Send the lambs for the ruler of the land from Selah to the wilderness, to the mountain of the daughter of Zion.

16:2 For it will be that as wandering birds, as a scattered nest, so will the daughters of Moab be at the fords of the Arnon.

16:3 Give counsel! Execute justice! Make your shade like the night in the midst of the noonday! Hide the outcasts! Don't betray the fugitive!

16:4 Let my outcasts dwell with you! As for Moab, be a hiding place for him from the face of the destroyer. For the extortioner is brought to nothing. Destruction ceases. The oppressors are consumed out of the land.

TARGUM ISAIAH

and they were in deep slumber.

15:2 They went up to the houses in Dibon, to the high place, to weep. Over Nebo, and over Medeba the Moabites are howling: on every head is baldness; every beard is shorn.

15:3 In their streets they shall gird themselves with sackcloth: on their house-tops, and in their broadplaces all of them shall howl, crying and weeping.

15:4 And the inhabitants of Heshbon and Elealeh shall cry out aloud; unto Jahats is their voice heard: therefore the armed of Moab are howling, and crying out aloud for their souls.

15:5 The Moabites shall think to flee to Zoar, unto Eglath Tiltum Rabb'tha; for the ascent of Luhith they shall ascend it as with weeping; because in the descent of Horonaim they shall declare the cry of the broken in battle.

15:6 For the waters of Nimrim shall become desolate; for the herbage is withered away; the grass faileth, there is no green herb.

15:7 Therefore the remnant of their riches, shall be plundered; and their border, which is by the western sea, shall be taken from

TARGUM ISAIAH

them.

15:8 For the cry encompasseth the border of Moab; unto Eglaim are they howling, and unto Beer-Elim they are crying aloud.

15:9 For the waters of Dimon shall be full of blood: for I will appoint upon Dimon an assembly of armies. Upon the escaped of Moab, a king with his army shall ascend; yea, to spoil the remainder of their land.

16:1 They shall bring tributes to the Messiah of Israel, who shall prevail over those who are in the wilderness, *unto* the mountain of the congregation of Zion.

16:2 Otherwise it shall come to pass, as a bird which *men* have driven away, being cast out of its nest, the daughters of Moab shall be led round about, made to wade Arnon.

16:3 Take counsel, execute counsel. Make thy shadow as the night in the day, in the midst of the noonday: hide the outcasts; touch not the dispersed.

16:4 Let my outcasts dwell with thee, O kingdom of Moab! be thou a covert to them on account of the spoilers: for the extortioner is at an end, the spoiler ceaseth,

JEWISH PUBLICATION SOCIETY 1917

15:2 He is gone up to Baith, and to Dibon, to the high places, to weep; upon Nebo, and upon Medeba, Moab howleth; on all their heads is baldness, every beard is shaven.

15:3 In their streets they gird themselves with sackcloth; on their housetops, and in their broad places, every one howleth, weeping profusely.

15:4 And Heshbon crieth out, and Elealeh; their voice is heard even unto Jahaz; therefore the armed men of Moab cry aloud; his soul is faint within him.

15:5 My heart crieth out for Moab; her fugitives reach unto Zoar, a heifer of three years old; for by the ascent of Luhith with weeping they go up; for in the way of Horonaim they raise up a cry of destruction.

15:6 For the Waters of Nimrim shall be desolate; for the grass is withered away, the herbage faileth, there is no green thing.

15:7 Therefore the abundance they have gotten, and that which they have laid up, shall they carry away to the brook of the willows.

15:8 For the cry is gone round about the borders of Moab; the howling thereof unto Eglaim, and the howling thereof unto Beer-elim.

15:9 For the waters of Dimon are full of blood; for I will bring yet more upon Dimon, a lion upon him that escapeth of Moab, and upon the remnant of the land.

16:1 Send ye the lambs for the ruler of the land from the crags that are toward the wilderness, unto the mount of the daughter of Zion.

16:2 For it shall be that, as wandering birds, as a scattered nest, so shall the daughters of Moab be at the fords of Arnon.

16:3 'Give counsel, execute justice; make thy shadow as the night in the midst of the noonday; hide the outcasts; betray not the fugitive.

16:4 Let mine outcasts dwell with thee; as for Moab, be thou a covert to him from the face of the spoiler.' For the extortion is at an end, spoiling ceaseth, they that trampled down are consumed out of the land;

WORLD ENGLISH BIBLE

16:5 A throne will be established in loving kindness. One will sit on it in truth, in the tent of David, judging, seeking justice, and swift to do righteousness.

16:6 We have heard of the pride of Moab, that he is very proud; even of his arrogance, his pride, and his wrath. His boastings are nothing.

16:7 Therefore Moab will wail for Moab. Everyone will wail. You will mourn for the raisin cakes of Kir Hareseth, utterly stricken.

16:8 For the fields of Heshbon languish with the vine of Sibmah. The lords of the nations have broken down its choice branches, which reached even to Jazer, which wandered into the wilderness. Its shoots were spread abroad. They passed over the sea.

16:9 Therefore I will weep with the weeping of Jazer for the vine of Sibmah. I will water you with my tears, Heshbon, and Elealeh: for on your summer fruits and on your harvest the battle shout has fallen.

16:10 Gladness is taken away, and joy out of the fruitful field; and in the vineyards there will be no singing, neither joyful noise. Nobody will tread out wine in the presses. I have made the shouting stop.

16:11 Therefore my heart sounds like a harp for Moab, and my inward parts for Kir Heres.

16:12 It will happen that when Moab presents himself, when he wearies himself on the high place, and comes to his sanctuary to pray, that he will not prevail.

16:13 This is the word that Yahweh spoke concerning Moab in time past.

16:14 But now Yahweh has spoken, saying, "Within three years, as a worker bound by contract would count them, the glory of Moab shall be brought into contempt, with all his great multitude; and the remnant will be very small and feeble."

TARGUM ISAIAH

all that trampled under foot have come to an end.

16:5 Then the throne of the Messiah of Israel shall be established in goodness, and He shall sit upon it in truth in the city of David, judging and seeking justice, and executing truth.

16:6 We have heard of the princes of Moab; who are very proud; their nobles, and their delicate ones, and their pride shall not profit them, when their punishment comes.

16:7 Therefore the Moabites shall howl: over the Moabites all of them shall cry aloud; and they shall howl over the men of the city of their strength; they, mourning, shall say, surely they are conquered.

16:8 Because the armies of Heshbon are spoiled, the multitude of Sebama are killed, the kings of the people have killed their rulers; they reached unto Jazer; they strayed to the desert; their fugitives passed by, they crossed the sea.

16:9 Therefore, as I have brought armies against Jazer, so will I bring slayers against Sibmah; I will water thee with my tears, O

Heshbon and Elealeh! for upon thy harvest, and upon thy vintage the robbers have fallen.

16:10 And joy is taken away and gladness out of the fruitful field, and in the vineyards they shall not rejoice, neither shall they play sport; in the vats the treaders shall not tread out the wine; the treading of grapes I have made to cease.

16:11 Wherefore the bowels of the Moabites shall sound as a harp, and their heart shall mourn over the men of the city of their strength.

16:12 And it shall come to pass, that one shall see, that when Moab is wearied out upon his high place, he shall enter his idol-temple to pray, yet he shall not prevail.

16:13 This is the word which the Lord spake concerning the Moabites long ago:

16:14 But now the Lord hath spoken, saying: Within three years, as the years of an hireling, the glory of the Moabites shall come to an end, with all *that* great multitude; and the remnant shall be small, a few; all their glory shall come to an end.

17:1 THE BURDEN OF THE CUP OF

16:5 And a throne is established through mercy, and there sitteth thereon in truth, in the tent of David, one that judgeth, and seeketh justice, and is ready in righteousness.

16:6 We have heard of the pride of Moab; he is very proud; even of his haughtiness, and his pride, and his arrogancy, his ill-founded boastings.

16:7 Therefore shall Moab wail for Moab, every one shall wail; for the sweet cakes of Kir-hareseth shall ye mourn, sorely stricken.

16:8 For the fields of Heshbon languish, and the vine of Sibmah, whose choice plants did overcome the lords of nations; they reached even unto Jazer, they wandered into the wilderness; her branches were spread abroad, they passed over the sea.

16:9 Therefore I will weep with the weeping of Jazer for the vine of Sibmah; I will water thee with my tears, O Heshbon, and Elealeh; for upon thy summer fruits and upon thy harvest the battle shout is fallen.

16:10 And gladness and joy are taken away out of the fruitful field; and in the vineyards there shall be no singing, neither shall there be shouting; no treader shall tread out wine in the presses; I have made the vintage shout to cease.

16:11 Wherefore my heart moaneth like a harp for Moab, and mine inward parts for Kir-heres.

16:12 And it shall come to pass, when it is seen that Moab hath wearied himself upon the high place, that he shall come to his sanctuary to pray; but he shall not prevail

16:13 This is the word that the LORD spoke concerning Moab in time past.

16:14 But now the LORD hath spoken, saying: 'Within three years, as the years of a hireling, and the glory of Moab shall wax contemptible for all his great multitude; and the remnant shall be very small and without strength.'

WORLD ENGLISH BIBLE

17:1 The burden of Damascus: "Behold, Damascus is taken away from being a city, and it will be a ruinous heap.

17:2 The cities of Aroer are forsaken. They will be for flocks, which shall lie down, and none shall make them afraid.

17:3 The fortress shall cease from Ephraim, and the kingdom from Damascus, and the remnant of Syria. They will be as the glory of the children of Israel," says Yahweh of Armies.

17:4 "It will happen in that day that the glory of Jacob will be made thin, and the fatness of his flesh will become lean.

17:5 It will be like when the harvester gathers the wheat, and his arm reaps the grain. Yes, it will be like when one gleans grain in the valley of Rephaim.

17:6 Yet gleanings will be left there, like the shaking of an olive tree, two or three olives in the top of the uppermost bough, four or five in the outermost branches of a fruitful tree," says Yahweh, the God of Israel.

17:7 In that day, people will look to their Maker, and their eyes will have respect for the Holy One of Israel.

17:8 They will not look to the altars, the work of their hands; neither shall they respect that which their fingers have made, either the Asherim, or the incense altars.

17:9 In that day, their strong cities will be like the forsaken places in the woods and on the mountain top, which were forsaken from before the children of Israel; and it will be a desolation.

17:10 For you have forgotten the God of your salvation, and have not remembered the rock of your strength. Therefore you plant pleasant plants, and set out foreign seedlings.

17:11 In the day of your planting, you hedge it in. In the morning, you make your seed blossom, but the harvest flees away in the day of grief and of desperate sorrow.

TARGUM ISAIAH

CURSING TO GIVE DAMASCUS TO DRINK. Behold, Damascus is removed, so as to be no more a kingdom: and it shall be as a city laid waste.

17:2 Their cities are deserted, they are laid waste; they shall be for dwelling-places for flocks of sheep; they shall lie down, and none shall make them to move away.

17:3 The government shall cease from Ephraim, and the kingdom from Damascus, and the remnant of the solitary ones from Syria, and their glory shall be as the glory of the children of Israel, saith the Lord of hosts.

17:4 And it shall come to pass at that time, that the glory of Jacob shall be humbled, and the riches of his glory shall be carried away.

17:5 And it shall be, as when one gathereth the standing harvest, and reapeth the ears with his arm; and it shall be as one that is gathering ears in the valley of giants.

17:6 Yet a gleaning shall be left in it, as *in* the shaking of the olive tree, two *or* three berries on the top of the uppermost branch; so shall the righteous be left lonely in the midst of the world, among the kingdoms, saith the Lord, the God of Israel.

TARGUM ISAIAH

17:7 At that time a man shall stay himself upon the service of his Maker, and his eyes shall hopefully look for the WORD, the Holy One of Israel.

17:8 He shall not rest upon the altars, the work of his hands, or stay himself upon that which his fingers have prepared, neither upon the groves nor upon the sun-images.

17:9 At that time the cities of their strength shall be as a fortification that was laid desolate and waste from before the children of Israel, and each shall be a desolation.

17:10 Because thou hast forsaken the God of thy salvation, and thou hast not remembered the fear of the Mighty One, whose WORD was thy support; therefore thou hast planted a choice plant, and hast multiplied despicable works.

17:11 After that ye were sanctified to be a people, there ye made your works despicable; and also when ye came to the land, the place of my Shekinah, there it was your duty to worship me; ye forsook my worship, and ye served idols: ye abhorred repentance till the day of your destruction came, then your sorrow was

JEWISH PUBLICATION SOCIETY 1917

17:1 The burden of Damascus. Behold, Damascus is taken away from being a city, and it shall be a ruinous heap.

17:2 The cities of Aroer are forsaken; they shall be for flocks, which shall lie down, and none shall make them afraid.

17:3 The fortress also shall cease from Ephraim, and the kingdom from Damascus; and the remnant of Aram shall be as the glory of the children of Israel, saith the LORD of hosts.

17:4 And it shall come to pass in that day, that the glory of Jacob shall be made thin, and the fatness of his flesh shall wax lean.

17:5 And it shall be as when the harvestman gathereth the standing corn, and reapeth the ears with his arm; yea, it shall be as when one gleaneth ears in the valley of Rephaim.

17:6 Yet there shall be left therein gleanings, as at the beating of an olive-tree, two or three berries in the top of the uppermost bough, four or five in the branches of the fruitful tree, saith the LORD, the God of Israel.

17:7 In that day shall a man regard his Maker, and his eyes shall look to the Holy One of Israel.

17:8 And he shall not regard the altars, the work of his hands, neither shall he look to that which his fingers have made, either the Asherim, or the sun-images.

17:9 In that day shall his strong cities be as the forsaken places, which were forsaken from before the children of Israel, after the manner of woods and lofty forests; and it shall be a desolation.

17:10 For thou hast forgotten the God of thy salvation, and thou hast not been mindful of the Rock of thy stronghold; therefore thou didst plant plants of pleasantness, and didst set it with slips of a stranger;

17:11 In the day of thy planting thou didst make it to grow, and in the morning thou didst make thy seed to blossom—a heap of boughs in the day of grief and of desperate pain.

WORLD ENGLISH BIBLE

17:12 Ah, the uproar of many peoples, who roar like the roaring of the seas; and the rushing of nations, that rush like the rushing of mighty waters!

17:13 The nations will rush like the rushing of many waters: but he will rebuke them, and they will flee far off, and will be chased like the chaff of the mountains before the wind, and like the whirling dust before the storm.

17:14 At evening, behold, terror! Before the morning, they are no more. This is the portion of those who plunder us, and the lot of those who rob us.

18:1 Ah, the land of the rustling of wings, which is beyond the rivers of Ethiopia;

18:2 that sends ambassadors by the sea, even in vessels of papyrus on the waters, saying, "Go, you swift messengers, to a nation tall and smooth, to a people awesome from their beginning onward, a nation that measures out and treads down, whose land the rivers divide!"

18:3 All you inhabitants of the world, and you dwellers on the earth, when a banner is lifted up on the mountains, look! When the trumpet is blown, listen!

18:4 For Yahweh said to me, "I will be still, and I will see in my dwelling place, like clear heat in sunshine, like a cloud of dew in the heat of harvest."

18:5 For before the harvest, when the blossom is over, and the flower becomes a ripening grape, he will cut off the sprigs with pruning hooks, and he will cut down and take away the spreading branches.

18:6 They will be left together for the ravenous birds of the mountains, and for the animals of the earth. The ravenous birds will summer on them, and all the animals of the earth will winter on them.

TARGUM ISAIAH

a breathing out of soul.

17:12 Woe to the multitude of many people, which make a noise like the noise of the sea, and to the tumultuous assembly of kings, which roar like the roaring of mighty waters.

17:13 The kings roar like the roaring of many waters, and he shall rebuke him, and he shall flee far off, and shall be driven as the chaff of the hills before the wind, and like a rolling thing before the whirlwind.

17:14 And at eveningtide behold, as if he had not been; and before the morning behold, as if he had not been. This is the portion of those that hate us, and the lot of those who spoil us.

18:1 Ho! the land which is beyond the rivers of India, to which they come in ships from a far country, whose sails are spread as an eagle flieth with its wings.

18:2 That sendeth ambassadors by the sea, even in ships on the face of the waters, *saying*, Go, ye swift messengers, unto a people oppressed and plundered, unto a people *that was* mighty in times past, *and shall be so* in time to come: a people oppressed and

TARGUM ISAIAH

robbed, whose land the nations have spoiled.

18:3 All ye inhabitants of the world, and ye dwellers on the earth, when the standard is lifted up on the mountains, ye shall see the standard, and the trumpet shall sound, ye shall hear of redemption.

18:4 For thus hath the Lord said unto me: I will give rest to my people, yea, I will make them to rest, and I will delight in my holy habitation to do them good: blessings and consolations I will bring upon them quickly, when the heat is intense through the heat of the sun, then *I will be to them* a cloud of dew *as* in the heat of harvest.

18:5 Before the time of harvest cometh the tree is ready to bud, and the unripe grape bursts forth into a flower: He shall slay the rulers of the nations with the sword, and their mighty ones He shall remove, and cause to pass away.

18:6 They shall be left together unto the fowl of the mountains, and to the beasts of the earth: all the fowls of the heavens shall dwell upon them in the summer, and all the beasts of the earth

JEWISH PUBLICATION SOCIETY 1917

17:12 Ah, the uproar of many peoples, that roar like the roaring of the seas; and the rushing of nations, that rush like the rushing of mighty waters!

17:13 The nations shall rush like the rushing of many waters; but He shall rebuke them, and they shall flee far off, and shall be chased as the chaff of the mountains before the wind, and like the whirling dust before the storm.

17:14 At eventide behold terror; and before the morning they are not. This is the portion of them that spoil us, and the lot of them that rob us.

18:1 Ah, land of the buzzing of wings, which is beyond the rivers of Ethiopia;

18:2 That sendeth ambassadors by the sea, even in vessels of papyrus upon the waters! Go, ye swift messengers, to a nation tall and of glossy skin, to a people terrible from their beginning onward; a nation that is sturdy and treadeth down, whose land the rivers divide!

18:3 All ye inhabitants of the world, and ye dwellers on the earth, when an ensign is lifted up on the mountains, see ye; and when the horn is blown, hear ye.

18:4 For thus hath the LORD said unto me: I will hold Me still, and I will look on in My dwelling-place, like clear heat in sunshine, like a cloud of dew in the heat of harvest.

18:5 For before the harvest, when the blossom is over, and the bud becometh a ripening grape, He will cut off the sprigs with pruning-hooks, and the shoots will He take away and lop off.

18:6 They shall be left together unto the ravenous birds of the mountains, and to the beasts of the earth; and the ravenous birds shall summer upon them, and all the beasts of the earth shall winter upon them.

WORLD ENGLISH BIBLE

18:7 In that time, a present will be brought to Yahweh of Armies from a people tall and smooth, even from a people awesome from their beginning onward, a nation that measures out and treads down, whose land the rivers divide, to the place of the name of Yahweh of Armies, Mount Zion.

19:1 The burden of Egypt: "Behold, Yahweh rides on a swift cloud, and comes to Egypt. The idols of Egypt will tremble at his presence; and the heart of Egypt will melt in its midst.

19:2 I will stir up the Egyptians against the Egyptians, and they will fight everyone against his brother, and everyone against his neighbor; city against city, and kingdom against kingdom.

19:3 The spirit of Egypt will fail in its midst. I will destroy its counsel. They will seek the idols, the charmers, those who have familiar spirits, and the wizards.

19:4 I will give over the Egyptians into the hand of a cruel lord. A fierce king will rule over them," says the Lord, Yahweh of Armies.

19:5 The waters will fail from the sea, and the river will be wasted and become dry.

19:6 The rivers will become foul. The streams of Egypt will be diminished and dried up. The reeds and flags will wither away.

19:7 The meadows by the Nile, by the brink of the Nile, and all the sown fields of the Nile, will become dry, be driven away, and be no more.

19:8 The fishermen will lament, and all those who fish in the Nile will mourn, and those who spread nets on the waters will languish.

19:9 Moreover those who work in combed flax, and those who weave white cloth, will be confounded.

19:10 The pillars will be broken in pieces. All those who work for hire will be grieved in soul.

19:11 The princes of Zoan are utterly foolish. The counsel of the wisest counselors of Pharaoh has become stupid. How do you say to Pharaoh, "I am the son of the wise, the son of ancient kings?"

TARGUM ISAIAH

shall winter upon them.

18:7 At that time shall one bring an offering unto the Lord of hosts, to a people oppressed and spoiled, to a people that was mighty in times past, *and shall be so* in time to come, a people oppressed and robbed, whose land the nations have spoiled, unto the place which is called by the name of the Lord of hosts, whose Shekinah is in the mountain of Zion.

19:1 THE BURDEN OF THE CUP OF CURSING TO MAKE THE EGYPTIANS TO DRINK. Behold, the Lord is revealed in the cloud of His glory, to take vengeance of the Egyptians; and the idols of the Egyptians shall be broken before His face, and the heart of the Egyptians shall be melted within them.

19:2 And I will excite Egyptians against Egyptians, and they shall wage war, every man against his brother, and every man against his neighbour: city against city, kingdom against kingdom.

19:3 And the spirit of the Egyptians shall melt within them, and their wise men I will destroy: and they shall seek to the idols, and to the charmers, to the deceitful, and to the diviners.

TARGUM ISAIAH

19:4 And I will deliver the Egyptians into the hand of a cruel lord; and a fierce king shall rule over them, saith the Lord of the world, the Lord of hosts.

19:5 And the waters of the sea shall be laid desolate, and their river shall be wasted and dried up.

19:6 And their rivers shall be laid waste, and their deep streams shall be dried up and wasted: the reeds and flags shall not grow.

19:7 And the greatest part of the river shall wither, and that which is on its bank, and every sown place of their rivers shall wither, and shall be dried up, and nothing shall grow.

19:8 The fishermen shall be laid desolate, and all they that cast angle into the brook, and they that spread nets upon the faces of the waters shall be destroyed.

19:9 They shall be confounded which work combed flax, and weave nets of it.

19:10 And there shall be trodden under foot the well watered place, where they have been making pits, waterpools each for himself.

19:11 Surely the princes of Tanes have become foolish; the wise, the counsellors of Pharaoh have

JEWISH PUBLICATION SOCIETY 1917

18:7 In that time shall a present be brought unto the LORD of hosts of a people tall and of glossy skin, and from a people terrible from their beginning onward; a nation that is sturdy and treadeth down, whose land the rivers divide, to the place of the name of the LORD of hosts, the mount Zion.

19:1 The burden of Egypt. Behold, the LORD rideth upon a swift cloud, and cometh unto Egypt; and the idols of Egypt shall be moved at His presence, and the heart of Egypt shall melt within it.

19:2 And I will spur Egypt against Egypt; and they shall fight every one against his brother, and everyone against his neighbour; city against city, and kingdom against kingdom.

19:3 And the spirit of Egypt shall be made empty within it; and I will make void the counsel thereof; and they shall seek unto the idols, and to the whisperers, and to the ghosts, and to the familiar spirits.

19:4 And I will give over the Egyptians into the hand of a cruel lord; and a fierce king shall rule over them, saith the Lord, the LORD of hosts.

19:5 And the waters shall fail from the sea, and the river shall be drained dry,

19:6 And the rivers shall become foul; the streams of Egypt shall be minished and dried up; the reeds and flags shall wither.

19:7 The mosses by the Nile, by the brink of the Nile, and all that is sown by the Nile, shall become dry, be driven away, and be no more.

19:8 The fishers also shall lament, and all they that cast angle into the Nile shall mourn, and they that spread nets upon the waters shall languish.

19:9 Moreover they that work in combed flax, and they that weave cotton, shall be ashamed.

19:10 And her foundations shall be crushed, all they that make dams shall be grieved in soul.

19:11 The princes of Zoan are utter fools; the wisest counsellors of Pharaoh are a senseless counsel; how can ye say unto Pharaoh: 'I am the son of the wise, the son of ancient kings'?

WORLD ENGLISH BIBLE

19:12 Where then are your wise men? Let them tell you now; and let them know what Yahweh of Armies has purposed concerning Egypt.

19:13 The princes of Zoan have become fools. The princes of Memphis are deceived. They have caused Egypt to go astray, who are the cornerstone of her tribes.

19:14 Yahweh has mixed a spirit of perverseness in the midst of her; and they have caused Egypt to go astray in all of its works, like a drunken man staggers in his vomit.

19:15 Neither shall there be any work for Egypt, which head or tail, palm branch or rush, may do.

19:16 In that day the Egyptians will be like women. They will tremble and fear because of the shaking of the hand of Yahweh of Armies, which he shakes over them.

19:17 The land of Judah will become a terror to Egypt. Everyone to whom mention is made of it will be afraid, because of the plans of Yahweh of Armies, which he determines against it.

19:18 In that day, there will be five cities in the land of Egypt that speak the language of Canaan, and swear to Yahweh of Armies. One will be called "The city of destruction."

19:19 In that day, there will be an altar to Yahweh in the midst of the land of Egypt, and a pillar to Yahweh at its border.

19:20 It will be for a sign and for a witness to Yahweh of Armies in the land of Egypt; for they will cry to Yahweh because of oppressors, and he will send them a savior and a defender, and he will deliver them.

19:21 Yahweh will be known to Egypt, and the Egyptians will know Yahweh in that day. Yes, they will worship with sacrifice and offering, and will vow a vow to Yahweh, and will perform it.

19:22 Yahweh will strike Egypt, striking and healing. They will return to Yahweh, and he will be entreated by them, and will heal them.

TARGUM ISAIAH

counselled an erroneous counsel; how will ye say to Pharaoh, We are the sons of the wise, and thou art the son of ancient kings.

19:12 Where are thy wise men? Let them tell thee now, and let them know what the Lord of hosts has counselled against Egypt.

19:13 The princes of Tanes have become foolish, the men of Memphis have erred; they caused the Egyptians, the lords of the provinces, to err.

19:14 The Lord hath sent among them a spirit of error, and they have caused the Egyptians to err in all their works, as a drunkard staggereth, and tramples in his vomit.

19:15 And the Egyptians shall have no king to reign, no prince, noble, governor, or ruler.

19:16 At that time the Egyptians shall be weak, they shall be afraid, and fear on account of the exultation of the power of the Lord of hosts, which He is lifting up against them.

19:17 And the land of the house of Judah shall be a terror unto Egypt; if any one mention it unto them, they shall tremble; because of the counsel of the Lord of

TARGUM ISAIAH

hosts, which he hath counselled against them.

19:18 At that time, there shall be five cities in the land of Egypt, speaking the language of Canaan, and swearing by the name of the Lord of hosts. The city of Beth-Shemesh, which is to be destroyed, shall be called one of them.

19:19 At that time there shall be prepared an altar before the Lord in the midst of the land of Egypt: and a pillar by the border thereof before the Lord.

19:20 And it shall be for a sign, and for a witness before the Lord of hosts in the land of Egypt, when they shall pray before the Lord because of their oppressors, and He shall send unto them a Saviour, and a Judge, and He shall deliver them.

19:21 And the power of the Lord shall be revealed to do good to the Egyptians, and the Egyptians shall know the fear of the Lord at that time, and they shall worship with holy sacrifices and offerings; yea, they shall vow vows before the Lord, and shall perform them.

19:22 And the Lord shall smite Egypt with a stroke, and shall

JEWISH PUBLICATION SOCIETY 1917

19:12 Where are they, then, thy wise men? And let them tell thee now; and let them know what the LORD of hosts hath purposed concerning Egypt.
19:13 The princes of Zoan are become fools, the princes of Noph are deceived; they have caused Egypt to go astray, that are the corner-stone of her tribes.
19:14 The LORD hath mingled within her a spirit of dizziness; and they have caused Egypt to stagger in every work thereof, as a drunken man staggereth in his vomit.
19:15 Neither shall there be for Egypt any work, which head or tail, palm-branch or rush, may do.
19:16 In that day shall Egypt be like unto women; and it shall tremble and fear because of the shaking of the hand of the LORD of hosts, which He shaketh over it.
19:17 And the land of Judah shall become a terror unto Egypt, whensoever one maketh mention thereof to it; it shall be afraid, because of the purpose of the LORD of hosts, which He purposeth against it.
19:18 In that day there shall be five cities in the land of Egypt that speak the language of Canaan, and swear to the LORD of hosts; one shall be called The city of destruction.
19:19 In that day shall there be an altar to the LORD in the midst of the land of Egypt, and a pillar at the border thereof to the LORD.
19:20 And it shall be for a sign and for a witness unto the LORD of hosts in the land of Egypt; for they shall cry unto the LORD because of the oppressors, and He will send them a saviour, and a defender, who will deliver them.
19:21 And the LORD shall make Himself known to Egypt, and the Egyptians shall know the LORD in that day; yea, they shall worship with sacrifice and offering, and shall vow a vow unto the LORD, and shall perform it.
19:22 And the LORD will smite Egypt, smiting and healing; and they shall return unto the LORD, and He will be entreated of them, and will heal them.

WORLD ENGLISH BIBLE

19:23 In that day there will be a highway out of Egypt to Assyria, and the Assyrian shall come into Egypt, and the Egyptian into Assyria; and the Egyptians will worship with the Assyrians.

19:24 In that day, Israel will be the third with Egypt and with Assyria, a blessing in the midst of the earth;

19:25 because Yahweh of Armies has blessed them, saying, "Blessed be Egypt my people, Assyria the work of my hands, and Israel my inheritance."

20:1 In the year that Tartan came to Ashdod, when Sargon the king of Assyria sent him, and he fought against Ashdod and took it;

20:2 at that time Yahweh spoke by Isaiah the son of Amoz, saying, "Go, and loosen the sackcloth from off your waist, and take your shoes from off your feet." He did so, walking naked and barefoot.

20:3 Yahweh said, "As my servant Isaiah has walked naked and barefoot three years for a sign and a wonder concerning Egypt and concerning Ethiopia,

20:4 so the king of Assyria will lead away the captives of Egypt and the exiles of Ethiopia, young and old, naked and barefoot, and with buttocks uncovered, to the shame of Egypt.

20:5 They will be dismayed and confounded, because of Ethiopia their expectation, and of Egypt their glory.

20:6 The inhabitants of this coast land will say in that day, 'Behold, this is our expectation, where we fled for help to be delivered from the king of Assyria. And we, how will we escape?'"

21:1 The burden of the wilderness of the sea. As whirlwinds in the South sweep through, it comes from the wilderness, from an awesome land.

TARGUM ISAIAH

heal them, and they shall return to the worship of the Lord, and He shall hear their prayers, and shall heal them.

19:23 And at that time there shall be a highway from Egypt to Assyria; and the Assyrians shall fight against the Egyptians, and the Egyptians against the Assyrians, and the Egyptians shall serve the Assyrians.

19:24 And at that time Israel shall be a third party to the Egyptians and to the Assyrians, a blessing in the midst of the land.

19:25 Whom the Lord of hosts hath blessed, saying, Blessed be my people, whom I have brought out of Egypt; and because they sinned before me, I carried them captive into Assyria; but when they repent, they are called my people, and Israel mine inheritance.

20:1 In the year that Tharthan marched to Ashdod, (when Sargon, the king of Assyria, sent him,) and he waged battle against Ashdod, and subdued it;

20:2 At that time the Lord decreed by Isaiah, the son of Amoz, saying, Go and remove the sackcloth which is on thy loins, and put off thy sandals from off thy feet: and

TARGUM ISAIAH

he did so, walking naked and barefoot.

20:3 And the Lord said, Like as my servant Isaiah hath walked naked and barefoot three years *for* a sign and wonder upon Egypt and Cush:

20:4 So shall the king of Assyria lead the captives, and the captivity of Cush, the young and old, naked and barefoot, even *with their* shame uncovered, to the disgrace of Egypt.

20:5 And they shall be afraid and confounded because of Cush, the place of their confidence, and because of Egypt, their boasting.

20:6 At that time the inhabitant of this island shall say: Such is become the place of our trust, to which we were hoping to flee for help to be delivered from before the king of Assyria, if hitherto they could not deliver themselves, how shall we be delivered?

21:1 The burden of the armies which are coming from the wilderness, as the waters of the sea, rushing along as the tempests: yea, they are coming by the way of the south, hurrying along; yea, they are coming from the wilderness, from the land, in which terrible

JEWISH PUBLICATION SOCIETY 1917

19:23 In that day shall there be a highway out of Egypt to Assyria, and the Assyrian shall come into Egypt, and the Egyptian into Assyria; and the Egyptians shall worship with the Assyrians.

19:24 In that day shall Israel be the third with Egypt and with Assyria, a blessing in the midst of the earth;

19:25 for that the LORD of hosts hath blessed him, saying: 'Blessed be Egypt My people and Assyria the work of My hands, and Israel Mine inheritance.'

20:1 In the year that Tartan came into Ashdod, when Sargon the king of Assyria sent him, and he fought against Ashdod and took it;

20:2 at that time the LORD spoke by Isaiah the son of Amoz, saying: 'Go, and loose the sackcloth from off thy loins, and put thy shoe from off thy foot.' And he did so, walking naked and barefoot.

20:3 And the LORD said: 'Like as My servant Isaiah hath walked naked and barefoot to be for three years a sign and a wonder upon Egypt and upon Ethiopia,

20:4 so shall the king of Assyria lead away the captives of Egypt, and the exiles of Ethiopia, young and old, naked and barefoot, and with buttocks uncovered, to the shame of Egypt.

20:5 And they shall be dismayed and ashamed, because of Ethiopia their expectation, and of Egypt their glory.

20:6 And the inhabitant of this coastland shall say in that day: Behold, such is our expectation, whither we fled for help to be delivered from the king of Assyria; and how shall we escape?'

21:1 The burden of the wilderness of the sea. As whirlwinds in the South sweeping on, it cometh from the wilderness, from a dreadful land.

WORLD ENGLISH BIBLE

21:2 A grievous vision is declared to me. The treacherous man deals treacherously, and the destroyer destroys. Go up, Elam; attack! I have stopped all of Media's sighing.

21:3 Therefore my thighs are filled with anguish. Pains have taken hold on me, like the pains of a woman in labor. I am in so much pain that I can't hear. I so am dismayed that I can't see.

21:4 My heart flutters. Horror has frightened me. The twilight that I desired has been turned into trembling for me.

21:5 They prepare the table. They set the watch. They eat. They drink. Rise up, you princes, oil the shield!

21:6 For the Lord said to me, "Go, set a watchman. Let him declare what he sees.

21:7 When he sees a troop, horsemen in pairs, a troop of donkeys, a troop of camels, he shall listen diligently with great attentiveness."

21:8 He cried like a lion: "Lord, I stand continually on the watchtower in the daytime, and every night I stay at my post.

21:9 Behold, here comes a troop of men, horsemen in pairs." He answered, "Fallen, fallen is Babylon; and all the engraved images of her gods are broken to the ground.

21:10 You are my threshing, and the grain of my floor!" That which I have heard from Yahweh of Armies, the God of Israel, I have declared to you.

21:11 The burden of Dumah. One calls to me out of Seir, "Watchman, what of the night? Watchman, what of the night?"

21:12 The watchman said, "The morning comes, and also the night. If you will inquire, inquire. Come back again."

TARGUM ISAIAH

things are done.

21:2 The prophet said: a dreadful vision has been declared unto me. The violent deal violently, and the spoilers spoil. Come up, ye Elamites; encompass, ye Media! I will give rest to all who sigh on account of the king of Babylon.

21:3 Therefore their loins shall be full of terror: behold, fear shall seize them, like the pangs of a woman that travaileth. They are become foolish, so that they cannot hear; they have erred, so that they cannot see.

21:4 Their heart is bewildered; distress and terrors have seized them, because the place of their confidence hath become destruction unto them.

21:5 Prepare the table, place the watchmen, eat ye, drink ye; rise, ye princes, polish, and make bright the arms!

21:6 For thus hath the Lord said unto me: Go, set a watchman, let him report what he seeth.

21:7 And he saw a chariot, a man, and with him a couple of horsemen: a rider on an ass, a rider on a camel. The prophet said, I listened diligently, and, behold, I saw mighty armies!

TARGUM ISAIAH

21:8 The prophet said, the voice of armies, coming with coats of mail, is as a lion; and I stand continually upon the watchtower before the Lord in the day, and as a guard I stand all the night. **21:9** And, behold, this was coming: A chariot! a man! and with him a couple of horsemen. He answered, and said, She is fallen! Yea, it shall come to pass, that Babylon shall fall, and all the images of her idols shall be dashed to pieces to the ground. **21:10** Kings, who are skilful to wage war, shall come against her to plunder her, like a husbandman who is skilful to thrash the floor. The prophet said, The voice of the WORD of the Lord of Hosts, the God of Israel, which I have heard, I have declared unto you. **21:11** THE BURDEN OF THE CUP OF CURSING TO GIVE DUMA TO DRINK. He thundered unto me from the heavens, Prophet! explain unto them the prophecy; prophet! explain unto them what shall hereafter come to pass. **21:12** The prophet said, there is a reward to the righteous, and there is punishment to the wicked: if ye will repent, repent ye, whilst ye

JEWISH PUBLICATION SOCIETY 1917

21:2 A grievous vision is declared unto me: 'The treacherous dealer dealeth treacherously, and the spoiler spoileth. Go up, O Elam! besiege, O Media! All the sighing thereof have I made to cease.' **21:3** Therefore are my loins filled with convulsion; pangs have taken hold upon me, as the pangs of a woman in travail; I am bent so that I cannot hear; I am affrighted so that I cannot see. **21:4** My heart is bewildered, terror hath overwhelmed me; the twilight that I longed for hath been turned for me into trembling. **21:5** They prepare the table, they light the lamps, they eat, they drink—' Rise up, ye princes, anoint the shield.' **21:6** For thus hath the Lord said unto me: Go, set a watchman; let him declare what he seeth! **21:7** And when he seeth a troop, horsemen by pairs, a troop of asses, a troop of camels, he shall hearken diligently with much heed. **21:8** And he cried as a lion: 'Upon the watch-tower, O Lord, I stand continually in the daytime, and I am set in my ward all the nights.' **21:9** And, behold, there came a troop of men, horsemen by pairs. And he spoke and said: 'Fallen, fallen is Babylon; and all the graven images of her gods are broken unto the ground.' **21:10** O thou my threshing, and the winnowing of my floor, that which I have heard from the LORD of hosts, the God of Israel, have I declared unto you. **21:11** The burden of Dumah. One calleth unto me out of Seir: 'Watchman, what of the night? Watchman, what of the night?' **21:12** The watchman said: 'The morning cometh, and also the night—if ye will inquire, inquire ye; return, come.'

WORLD ENGLISH BIBLE

21:13 The burden on Arabia. In the forest in Arabia you will lodge, you caravans of Dedanites.

21:14 They brought water to him who was thirsty. The inhabitants of the land of Tema met the fugitives with their bread.

21:15 For they fled away from the swords, from the drawn sword, from the bent bow, and from the heat of battle.

21:16 For the Lord said to me, "Within a year, as a worker bound by contract would count it, all the glory of Kedar will fail,

21:17 and the residue of the number of the archers, the mighty men of the children of Kedar, will be few; for Yahweh, the God of Israel, has spoken it."

22:1 The burden of the valley of vision. What ails you now, that you have all gone up to the housetops?

22:2 You that are full of shouting, a tumultuous city, a joyous town; your slain are not slain with the sword, neither are they dead in battle.

22:3 All your rulers fled away together. They were bound by the archers. All who were found by you were bound together. They fled far away.

22:4 Therefore I said, "Look away from me. I will weep bitterly. Don't labor to comfort me for the destruction of the daughter of my people.

22:5 For it is a day of confusion, and of treading down, and of perplexity, from the Lord, Yahweh of Armies, in the valley of vision; a breaking down of the walls, and a crying to the mountains."

22:6 Elam carried his quiver, with chariots of men and horsemen; and Kir uncovered the shield.

22:7 It happened that your choicest valleys were full of chariots, and the horsemen set themselves in array at the gate.

TARGUM ISAIAH

are able to repent.

21:13 THE BURDEN OF THE CUP OF CURSING TO GIVE THE ARABIANS TO DRINK. In the forest, at even, the caravan of the sons of Dedan shall remain for the night.

21:14 Bring bottles of water before the thirsty, who dwell in land of the south; prepare for the fugitives the daily food which ye eat.

21:15 Because, on account of the slaughter they have fled: from the face of the drawn sword; and from the face of the bent bow; and from the face of the strength of the battle.

21:16 For thus hath the Lord said unto me: at the end of the years, as the years of an hireling, all the glory of the Arabians shall come to an end.

21:17 And the strength of the warriors, the mighty, the sons of the Arabians, shall be lessened, because by the WORD of the Lord, the God of Israel, it is thus decreed.

22:1 THE BURDEN OF THE PROPHECY CONCERNING THE CITY THAT DWELLETH IN THE VALLEY, OF WHICH THE PROPHETS PROPHESIED. What aileth you here, that all of you are gone up to the house-tops?

22:2 On account of the tumult

TARGUM ISAIAH

wherewith the praiseworthy, the fortified, the joyous city is filled. Thy slain were not slain by the sword, neither did they die in battle.

22:3 All thy rulers have been led forth; from before the bent bow, they are gone into captivity together: all that were found in thee have been slain, together they have fled afar.

22:4 Wherefore I said: Leave off from me, I will weep bitterly, seek ye not to comfort me for the desolation of the congregation of my people.

22:5 For it is a day of tumult, and of treading under foot, and of slaughter before the Lord, the God of hosts, against the city that dwelleth in the valley, against which the prophets prophesied. Thy search the houses, they encompass the towers *which are* on the tops of the mountains.

22:6 And the Elamites have taken arms in the chariot of a man, and with him *are* a couple of horsemen, and on the wall they hang the shields.

22:7 And it shall come to pass that the most beautiful of thy valleys shall be filled with chariots; and

JEWISH PUBLICATION SOCIETY 1917

21:13 The burden upon Arabia. In the thickets in Arabia shall ye lodge, O ye caravans of Dedanites.

21:14 Unto him that is thirsty bring ye water! The inhabitants of the land of Tema did meet the fugitive with his bread.

21:15 For they fled away from the swords, from the drawn sword, and from the bent bow, and from the grievousness of war.

21:16 For thus hath the Lord said unto me: 'Within a year, according to the years of a hireling, and all the glory of Kedar shall fail;

21:17 and the residue of the number of the archers, the mighty men of the children of Kedar, shall be diminished; for the LORD, the God of Israel, hath spoken it.'

22:1 The burden concerning the Valley of Vision. What aileth thee now, that thou art wholly gone up to the housetops,

22:2 Thou that art full of uproar, a tumultuous city, a joyous town? Thy slain are not slain with the sword, nor dead in battle.

22:3 All thy rulers are fled together, without the bow they are bound; all that are found of thee are bound together, they are fled afar off.

22:4 Therefore said I: 'Look away from me, I will weep bitterly; strain not to comfort me, for the destruction of the daughter of my people.'

22:5 For it is a day of trouble, and of trampling, and of perplexity, from the Lord, the GOD of hosts, in the Valley of Vision; Kir shouting, and Shoa at the mount.

22:6 And Elam bore the quiver, with troops of men, even horsemen; and Kir uncovered the shield.

22:7 And it came to pass, when thy choicest valleys were full of chariots, and the horsemen set themselves in array at the gate,

WORLD ENGLISH BIBLE

22:8 He took away the covering of Judah; and you looked in that day to the armor in the house of the forest.

22:9 You saw the breaches of the city of David, that they were many; and you gathered together the waters of the lower pool.

22:10 You numbered the houses of Jerusalem, and you broke down the houses to fortify the wall.

22:11 You also made a reservoir between the two walls for the water of the old pool. But you didn't look to him who had done this, neither did you have respect for him who purposed it long ago.

22:12 In that day, the Lord, Yahweh of Armies, called to weeping, and to mourning, and to baldness, and to dressing in sackcloth:

22:13 and behold, joy and gladness, killing cattle and killing sheep, eating flesh and drinking wine: "Let us eat and drink, for tomorrow we will die."

22:14 Yahweh of Armies revealed himself in my ears, "Surely this iniquity will not be forgiven you until you die," says the Lord, Yahweh of Armies.

22:15 Thus says the Lord, Yahweh of Armies, "Go, get yourself to this treasurer, even to Shebna, who is over the house, and say,

22:16 'What are you doing here? Who has you here, that you have dug out a tomb here?' Cutting himself out a tomb on high, chiseling a habitation for himself in the rock!"

22:17 Behold, Yahweh will overcome you and hurl you away violently. Yes, he will grasp you firmly.

22:18 He will surely wind you around and around, and throw you like a ball into a large country. There you will die, and there the chariots of your glory will be, you shame of your lord's house.

TARGUM ISAIAH

the horsemen shall be set against the gates.

22:8 And he shall discover the covering of Judah, and he shall look at that time upon the arms of the house of the treasury of the sanctuary.

22:9 And the breaches of the city of David ye shall see, because they are many; and ye shall gather together the people to the lower pool.

22:10 And ye shall number the houses of Jerusalem, and ye shall break down the houses to fortify the wall.

22:11 And ye shall make a lake between the walls of the water of the old pool: but ye have not looked unto the maker thereof, neither had respect unto him that created it of old.

22:12 And the prophet of the Lord, the God, *the God* of hosts, called in that day to weeping, and to mourning, and to baldness, and to girding with sackcloth:

22:13 But, behold, joy and gladness; they say, Let us slay oxen, and kill sheep, we will eat flesh, we will drink wine; let us eat, and drink, since we shall die, and not live.

TARGUM ISAIAH

22:14 The prophet said, with mine ears I was hearing when this was decreed from before the Lord of hosts, *namely*, that this your iniquity shall not be forgiven you till you die the second death, said the Lord, the God, *the God* of hosts.

22:15 Thus said the Lord, the God, *the God* of hosts, Come, go to this ruler, *even* to Shebna, who is appointed over the house.

22:16 And thou shalt say to him, What hast thou here? and what hast thou here, that thou hast prepared for thyself here a place?— He hath prepared on high his place! he hath put in the rock the place of his habitation!

22:17 Behold, the Lord will cast thee out with a mighty casting out, and confusion shall cover thee.

22:18 He shall take away from thee thy tiara, and the enemies shall enclose thee, like a surrounding wall, and they shall lead thee into captivity into a spacious country, there thou shalt die, and thither the chariots of thy glory shall return in disgrace, because thou hast not preserved the honour of thy master's house.

JEWISH PUBLICATION SOCIETY 1917

22:8 And the covering of Judah was laid bare, that thou didst look in that day to the armour in the house of the forest.

22:9 And ye saw the breaches of the city of David, that they were many; and ye gathered together the waters of the lower pool.

22:10 And ye numbered the houses of Jerusalem, and ye broke down the houses to fortify the wall;

22:11 ye made also a basin between the two walls for the water of the old pool—but ye looked not unto Him that had done this, neither had ye respect unto Him that fashioned it long ago.

22:12 And in that day did the Lord, the GOD of hosts, call to weeping, and to lamentation, and to baldness, and to girding with sackcloth;

22:13 And behold joy and gladness, slaying oxen and killing sheep, eating flesh and drinking wine—' Let us eat and drink, for tomorrow we shall die!'

22:14 And the LORD of hosts revealed Himself in mine ears: Surely this iniquity shall not be expiated by you till ye die, saith the Lord, the GOD of hosts.

22:15 Thus saith the Lord, the GOD of hosts: Go, get thee unto this steward, even unto Shebna, who is over the house:

22:16 What hast thou here, and whom hast thou here, that thou hast hewed thee out here a sepulchre, thou that hewest thee out a sepulchre on high, and gravest a habitation for thyself in the rock?

22:17 Behold, the LORD will hurl thee up and down with a man's throw; yea, He will wind thee round and round;

22:18 He will violently roll and toss thee like a ball into a large country; there shalt thou die, and there shall be the chariots of thy glory, thou shame of the lord's house.

WORLD ENGLISH BIBLE

22:19 I will thrust you from your office. You will be pulled down from your station.

22:20 It will happen in that day that I will call my servant Eliakim the son of Hilkiah,

22:21 and I will clothe him with your robe, and strengthen him with your belt. I will commit your government into his hand; and he will be a father to the inhabitants of Jerusalem, and to the house of Judah.

22:22 I will lay the key of the house of David on his shoulder. He will open, and no one will shut. He will shut, and no one will open.

22:23 I will fasten him like a nail in a sure place. He will be for a throne of glory to his father's house.

22:24 They will hang on him all the glory of his father's house, the offspring and the issue, every small vessel, from the cups even to all the pitchers.

22:25 "In that day," says Yahweh of Armies, "the nail that was fastened in a sure place will give way. It will be cut down, and fall. The burden that was on it will be cut off, for Yahweh has spoken it."

23:1 The burden of Tyre. Howl, you ships of Tarshish! For it is laid waste, so that there is no house, no entering in. From the land of Kittim it is revealed to them.

23:2 Be still, you inhabitants of the coast, you whom the merchants of Sidon, that pass over the sea, have replenished.

23:3 On great waters, the seed of the Shihor, the harvest of the Nile, was her revenue. She was the market of nations.

23:4 Be ashamed, Sidon; for the sea has spoken, the stronghold of the sea, saying, "I have not travailed, nor brought forth, neither have I nourished young men, nor brought up virgins."

TARGUM ISAIAH

22:19 And I will thrust thee down from thy station, and I will divest thee of thy office.

22:20 And it shall come to pass at that time, that I will make my servant Eliakim great, the son of Hilkiah.

22:21 And I will clothe him with thy robe, and with thy girdle I will gird him, and I will commit thy government into his hand, and he shall be a prince to the inhabitants of Jerusalem, and to the house of Judah.

22:22 And I will place the key of the house of the sanctuary, and the government of the house of David, in his hand; and he shall open, and none shall shut; and he shall shut, and none shall open.

22:23 And I will appoint him a faithful chief-governor, *an* officer in a firm place, and he shall be for a glorious throne to his father's house.

22:24 All the nobles of his father's house shall rest themselves upon him, children, and children's children, from young men to little ones, from the priests clothed with the ephod to the Levites that are holding the lyres.

22:25 At that time, saith the Lord

78

TARGUM ISAIAH

of hosts, there shall be removed the faithful chief governor, who ministered in a firm place, and he shall be cut off, and he shall fall: and there shall be accomplished the burden of prophecy, which was concerning him; because the WORD of the Lord hath so decreed it.

23:1 THE BURDEN OF THE CUP OF CURSING, TO GIVE TYRE TO DRINK. Howl, O ye that are embarking in ships of the sea, because their havens are spoiled, so that none can enter in. From the land of Chittim it is coming upon them.

23:2 The inhabitants of the island are destroyed, the merchants that pass over the sea they used to replenish thee.

23:3 She was the plentiful mart for many nations; the harvest of the increase of the river was her revenue, and she became the mart of the nations.

23:4 The Sidonians are confounded, because the west hath spoken, which dwells in the strength of the sea, saying, O that I had never travailed, never conceived, and never nourished up young men, never brought up virgins delicately!

JEWISH PUBLICATION SOCIETY 1917

22:19 And I will thrust thee from thy post, and from thy station shalt thou be pulled down.

22:20 And it shall come to pass in that day, that I will call my servant Eliakim the son of Hilkiah;

22:21 And I will clothe him with thy robe, and bind him with thy girdle, and I will commit thy government into his hand; and he shall be a father to the inhabitants of Jerusalem, and to the house of Judah.

22:22 And the key of the house of David will I lay upon his shoulder; and he shall open, and none shall shut; and he shall shut, and none shall open.

22:23 And I will fasten him as a peg in a sure place; and he shall be for a throne of honour to his father's house.

22:24 And they shall hang upon him all the glory of his father's house, the offspring and the issue, all vessels of small quantity, from the vessels of cups even to all the vessels of flagons.

22:25 In that day, saith the LORD of hosts, shall the peg that was fastened in a sure place give way; and it shall be hewn down, and fall, and the burden that was upon it shall be cut off; for the LORD hath spoken it.

23:1 The burden of Tyre. Howl, ye ships of Tarshish, for it is laid waste, so that there is no house, no entering in; from the land of Kittim it is revealed to them.

23:2 Be still, ye inhabitants of the coastland; thou whom the merchants of Zidon, that pass over the sea, have replenished.

23:3 And on great waters the seed of Shihor, the harvest of the Nile, was her revenue; and she was the mart of nations.

23:4 Be thou ashamed, O Zidon; for the sea hath spoken, the stronghold of the sea, saying: 'I have not travailed, nor brought forth, neither have I reared young men, nor brought up virgins.'

WORLD ENGLISH BIBLE

23:5 When the report comes to Egypt, they will be in anguish at the report of Tyre.

23:6 Pass over to Tarshish! Wail, you inhabitants of the coast!

23:7 Is this your joyous city, whose antiquity is of ancient days, whose feet carried her far away to travel?

23:8 Who has planned this against Tyre, the giver of crowns, whose merchants are princes, whose traffickers are the honorable of the earth?

23:9 Yahweh of Armies has planned it, to stain the pride of all glory, to bring into contempt all the honorable of the earth.

23:10 Pass through your land like the Nile, daughter of Tarshish. There is no restraint any more.

23:11 He has stretched out his hand over the sea. He has shaken the kingdoms. Yahweh has ordered the destruction of Canaan's strongholds.

23:12 He said, "You shall rejoice no more, you oppressed virgin daughter of Sidon. Arise, pass over to Kittim. Even there you will have no rest."

23:13 Behold, the land of the Chaldeans. This people was not. The Assyrians founded it for those who dwell in the wilderness. They set up their towers. They overthrew its palaces. They made it a ruin.

23:14 Howl, you ships of Tarshish, for your stronghold is laid waste!

23:15 It will come to pass in that day that Tyre will be forgotten seventy years, according to the days of one king. After the end of seventy years it will be to Tyre like in the song of the prostitute.

23:16 Take a harp; go about the city, you prostitute that has been forgotten. Make sweet melody. Sing many songs, that you may be remembered.

23:17 It will happen after the end of seventy years that Yahweh will visit Tyre, and she shall return to her wages, and will play the prostitute with all the kingdoms of the world on the surface of the earth.

TARGUM ISAIAH

23:5 When they heard of the stroke wherewith the Egyptians were smitten, the Tyrians quaked when they heard it.

23:6 They have gone to a province of the sea. Howl, O inhabitants of the island!

23:7 Is this your strong *city*, Tyre, of ancient days? In olden time they were bringing her gifts from a distant land; behold, now she is removed to sojourn *afar off*!

23:8 Who hath taken this counsel against Tyre, *against her* that was giving advice? whose merchants *are* princes, and whose rulers the nobles of the land.

23:9 The Lord of hosts is the counsellor against her to defile the glory of all the objects of rejoicing, and make contemptible all the nobles of the land.

23:10 Remove from thy land, as the waters of a river; flee to a province of the sea: there is no more strength.

23:11 His power is lifted up against the sea, to make the kingdom to tremble; the Lord has given the command concerning the merchant *city*, to make an end of her strength.

23:12 And he said, ye shall no more

TARGUM ISAIAH

be strong, ye that did violence to the people which are in Zidon. Arise, pass over to Chittim; even there ye shall have no rest.

23:13 Behold the land of the Chaldeans, this is the people that formerly did not exist; the Assyrians founded it in the islands; they raised up her beacons, they destroyed her palaces, they have made her a ruinous heap.

23:14 Howl, ye that are embarking in ships of the sea, for the sea-coast of your strength is spoiled.

23:15 And it shall come to pass at that time, that Tyre shall be put by for seventy years, according to the days of one king: at the end of seventy years, it shall be unto Tyre as the song of an harlot.

23:16 Thy glory is changed: wander *to another* country, O city, who hast been as an harlot, thou art doomed to oblivion: thy harp is turned into mourning, and thy song to lamentation; perhaps, thou mayest be remembered.

23:17 And it shall come to pass after the end of seventy years that Tyre shall be remembered before the Lord; and she shall return to her place, and her mart shall be plentiful for all the kingdoms of

JEWISH PUBLICATION SOCIETY 1917

23:5 When the report cometh to Egypt, they shall be sorely pained at the report of Tyre.

23:6 Pass ye over to Tarshish; howl, ye inhabitants of the coast-land.

23:7 Is this your joyous city, whose feet in antiquity, in ancient days, carried her afar off to sojourn?

23:8 Who hath devised this against Tyre, the crowning city, whose merchants are princes, whose traffickers are the honourable of the earth?

23:9 The LORD of hosts hath devised it, to pollute the pride of all glory, to bring into contempt all the honourable of the earth.

23:10 Overflow thy land as the Nile, O daughter of Tarshish! there is no girdle any more.

23:11 He hath stretched out His hand over the sea, He hath shaken the kingdoms; the LORD hath given commandment concerning Canaan, to destroy the strongholds thereof;

23:12 And He said: 'Thou shalt no more rejoice.' O thou oppressed virgin daughter of Zidon, arise, pass over to Kittim; even there shalt thou have no rest.

23:13 Behold, the land of the Chaldeans—this is the people that was not, when Asshur founded it for shipmen—they set up their towers, they overthrew the palaces thereof; it is made a ruin.

23:14 Howl, ye ships of Tarshish, for your stronghold is laid waste.

23:15 And it shall come to pass in that day, that Tyre shall be forgotten seventy years, according to the days of one king; after the end of seventy years it shall fare with Tyre as in the song of the harlot:

23:16 Take a harp, go about the city, thou harlot long forgotten; make sweet melody, sing many songs, that thou mayest be remembered.

23:17 And it shall come to pass after the end of seventy years, that the LORD will remember Tyre, and she shall return to her hire, and shall have commerce with all the kingdoms of the world upon the face of the earth.

WORLD ENGLISH BIBLE

23:18 Her merchandise and her wages will be holiness to Yahweh. It will not be treasured nor laid up; for her merchandise will be for those who dwell before Yahweh, to eat sufficiently, and for durable clothing.

24:1 Behold, Yahweh makes the earth empty, makes it waste, turns it upside down, and scatters its inhabitants.

24:2 It will be as with the people, so with the priest; as with the servant, so with his master; as with the maid, so with her mistress; as with the buyer, so with the seller; as with the creditor, so with the debtor; as with the taker of interest, so with the giver of interest.

24:3 The earth will be utterly emptied and utterly laid waste; for Yahweh has spoken this word.

24:4 The earth mourns and fades away. The world languishes and fades away. The lofty people of the earth languish.

24:5 The earth also is polluted under its inhabitants, because they have transgressed the laws, violated the statutes, and broken the everlasting covenant.

24:6 Therefore the curse has devoured the earth, and those who dwell therein are found guilty. Therefore the inhabitants of the earth are burned, and few men left.

24:7 The new wine mourns. The vine languishes. All the merry-hearted sigh.

24:8 The mirth of tambourines ceases. The sound of those who rejoice ends. The joy of the harp ceases.

24:9 They will not drink wine with a song. Strong drink will be bitter to those who drink it.

24:10 The confused city is broken down. Every house is shut up, that no man may come in.

24:11 There is a crying in the streets because of the wine. All joy is darkened. The mirth of the land is gone.

24:12 The city is left in desolation, and the gate is struck with destruction.

24:13 For it will be so in the midst of the earth among the peoples, as the shaking of an olive tree, as the gleanings when the vintage is done.

TARGUM ISAIAH

the nations, which are upon the face of the earth.

23:18 And her merchandise and her gain shall be holy before the Lord, it shall not be treasured nor laid up; for it shall be for them that are serving before the Lord; her gain shall be for food sufficient, and for vestments of glory.

24:1 Behold, the Lord shall spoil the land and deliver it over to the enemy; and confusion shall cover the faces of the princes, because they have transgressed the law, and scattered its inhabitants.

24:2 And it shall be, as with the laity, so with the priest; as with the servant, so with his master; as with the handmaid, so with her mistress; as with the buyer, so with the seller; as with the borrower, so with the lender: as with the giver of usury, so with the usurer.

24:3 The land shall be utterly destroyed, it shall be utterly trampled under foot; for the Lord hath spoken this word.

24:4 The land mourneth, it is laid desolate; the world is laid waste, it is laid desolate: the strength of the people of the land hath come to an end.

24:5 The land hath become guilty

TARGUM ISAIAH

beneath her inhabitants, because they have transgressed the law, and they have made the festivals to cease, they have changed the everlasting covenant.

24:6 Because of perjury the land hath become a desert, and all the inhabitants in it are laid desolate: therefore are the inhabitants of the land destroyed, and the men that are left are but few.

24:7 All that drink wine mourn, because the vines are broken down, all the merry-hearted sigh.

24:8 The mirth of tabrets ceaseth; the tumultuous assembly of the mighty is restrained, the joy of the harp ceaseth.

24:9 They shall no more drink wine with songs; strong drink shall be bitter to them that drink it.

24:10 Their city is broken down, *and* laid desolate: all their houses are shut up, so that no one can enter.

24:11 They cry for wine in the streets; all joy is ended: all gladness is removed from the land.

24:12 Desolation is left in the city, and there is a tumult in the destruction of the gates.

24:13 When thus the righteous shall be left alone in the midst of the

JEWISH PUBLICATION SOCIETY 1917

23:18 And her gain and her hire shall be holiness to the LORD; it shall not be treasured nor laid up; for her gain shall be for them that dwell before the LORD, to eat their fill, and for stately clothing.

24:1 Behold, the LORD maketh the earth empty and maketh it waste, and turneth it upside down, and scattereth abroad the inhabitants thereof.

24:2 And it shall be, as with the people, so with the priest; as with the servant, so with his master; as with the maid, so with her mistress; as with the buyer, so with the seller; as with the lender, so with the borrower; as with the creditor, so with the debtor.

24:3 The earth shall be utterly emptied, and clean despoiled; for the LORD hath spoken this word.

24:4 The earth fainteth and fadeth away, the world faileth and fadeth away, the lofty people of the earth do fail.

24:5 The earth also is defiled under the inhabitants thereof; because they have transgressed the laws, violated the statute, broken the everlasting covenant.

24:6 Therefore hath a curse devoured the earth, and they that dwell therein are found guilty; therefore the inhabitants of the earth waste away, and men are left few.

24:7 The new wine faileth, the vine fadeth; all the merry-hearted do sigh.

24:8 The mirth of tabrets ceaseth, the noise of them that rejoice endeth, the joy of the harp ceaseth.

24:9 They drink not wine with a song; strong drink is bitter to them that drink it.

24:10 Broken down is the city of wasteness; every house is shut up, that none may come in.

24:11 There is a crying in the streets amidst the wine; all joy is darkened, the mirth of the land is gone.

24:12 In the city is left desolation, and the gate is smitten unto ruin.

24:13 For thus shall it be in the midst of the earth, among the peoples, as at the beating of an olive-tree, as at the gleanings when the vintage is done.

WORLD ENGLISH BIBLE

24:14 These shall lift up their voice. They will shout for the majesty of Yahweh. They cry aloud from the sea.

24:15 Therefore glorify Yahweh in the east, even the name of Yahweh, the God of Israel, in the islands of the sea!

24:16 From the uttermost part of the earth have we heard songs. Glory to the righteous! But I said, "I pine away! I pine away! woe is me!" The treacherous have dealt treacherously. Yes, the treacherous have dealt very treacherously.

24:17 Fear, the pit, and the snare, are on you who inhabitant the earth.

24:18 It will happen that he who flees from the noise of the fear will fall into the pit; and he who comes up out of the midst of the pit will be taken in the snare; for the windows on high are opened, and the foundations of the earth tremble.

24:19 The earth is utterly broken. The earth is torn apart. The earth is shaken violently.

24:20 The earth will stagger like a drunken man, and will sway back and forth like a hammock. Its disobedience will be heavy on it, and it will fall and not rise again.

24:21 It shall happen in that day that Yahweh will punish the army of the high ones on high, and the kings of the earth on the earth.

24:22 They shall be gathered together, as prisoners are gathered in the pit, and shall be shut up in the prison; and after many days shall they be visited.

24:23 Then the moon shall be confounded, and the sun ashamed; for Yahweh of Armies will reign on Mount Zion, and in Jerusalem; and before his elders will be glory.

25:1 Yahweh, you are my God. I will exalt you! I will praise your name, for you have done wonderful things, things planned long ago, in complete faithfulness and truth.

TARGUM ISAIAH

earth, among the kingdoms, as the shaking of olives, as the gleaning of grapes after the vintage.

24:14 They shall lift up their voice, they shall praise on account of the WORD of the Lord: they shall rejoice as they rejoiced on account of the mighty works which were done for them by the sea.

24:15 When light shall come to the righteous, they shall glorify the Lord: in the islands of the sea they shall laud and bless the name of the Lord, the God of Israel.

24:16 From the house of the sanctuary, *yea*, from thence joy shall go forth to all the inhabitants of the earth, for we have heard the praise of the righteous! The prophet said, a secret! A reward to the righteous is shown to me, a secret! A punishment for the wicked is revealed to me. Woe to the oppressors, for they shall be oppressed; and to those who spoil, for, behold, they shall be spoiled.

24:17 The terror, the pit, and the snare, are upon thee, O inhabitant of the land.

24:18 And it shall come to pass, that he who fleeth from before the terror, he shall fall into the midst of the pit; and he that cometh up

TARGUM ISAIAH

out of the midst of the pit shall be taken in the snare: for mighty works are done in the heavens, therefore the foundations of the earth quake.

24:19 The land is terribly shaken, the land terribly reeleth to and fro, the land is utterly broken.

24:20 The land is utterly cast down like a drunkard, she is tottering like a couch: and her sins are heavy upon her: she shall fall, and rise no more.

24:21 And it shall come to pass at that time, *that* the Lord shall punish the mighty host that is dwelling in power, and the kings, the sons of men, who are dwelling upon the earth.

24:22 And they shall be utterly gathered for the prison, and they shall be shut up in the dungeon, and after many days they shall be remembered.

24:23 And they shall be confounded that worship the moon, and they shall be ashamed that worship the sun; because the power of the Lord of hosts shall be revealed in mount Sion, and before the elders of his people in glory.

25:1 O Lord, thou art my God: I will exalt thee; I will praise thy

JEWISH PUBLICATION SOCIETY 1917

24:14 Those yonder lift up their voice, they sing for joy; for the majesty of the LORD they shout from the sea:

24:15 'Therefore glorify ye the LORD in the regions of light, even the name of the LORD, the God of Israel, in the isles of the sea.'

24:16 From the uttermost part of the earth have we heard songs: 'Glory to the righteous.' But I say: I waste away, I waste away, woe is me! The treacherous deal treacherously; yea, the treacherous deal very treacherously.

24:17 Terror, and the pit, and the trap, are upon thee, O inhabitant of the earth.

24:18 And it shall come to pass, that he who fleeth from the noise of the terror shall fall into the pit; and he that cometh up out of the midst of the pit shall be taken in the trap; for the windows on high are opened, and the foundations of the earth do shake;

24:19 The earth is broken, broken down, the earth is crumbled in pieces, the earth trembleth and tottereth;

24:20 The earth reeleth to and fro like a drunken man, and swayeth to and fro as a lodge; and the transgression thereof is heavy upon it, and it shall fall, and not rise again.

24:21 And it shall come to pass in that day, that the LORD will punish the host of the high heaven on high, and the kings of the earth upon the earth.

24:22 And they shall be gathered together, as prisoners are gathered in the dungeon, and shall be shut up in the prison, and after many days shall they be punished.

24:23 Then the moon shall be confounded, and the sun ashamed; for the LORD of hosts will reign in mount Zion, and in Jerusalem, and before His elders shall be Glory.

25:1 O LORD, Thou art my God, I will exalt Thee, I will praise Thy name, for Thou hast done wonderful things; even counsels of old, in faithfulness and truth.

WORLD ENGLISH BIBLE

25:2 For you have made a city into a heap, a fortified city into a ruin, a palace of strangers to be no city. It will never be built.

25:3 Therefore a strong people will glorify you. A city of awesome nations will fear you.

25:4 For you have been a stronghold to the poor, a stronghold to the needy in his distress, a refuge from the storm, a shade from the heat, when the blast of the dreaded ones is like a storm against the wall.

25:5 As the heat in a dry place will you bring down the noise of strangers; as the heat by the shade of a cloud, the song of the dreaded ones will be brought low.

25:6 In this mountain, Yahweh of Armies will make all peoples a feast of fat things, a feast of choice wines, of fat things full of marrow, of well refined choice wines.

25:7 He will destroy in this mountain the surface of the covering that covers all peoples, and the veil that is spread over all nations.

25:8 He has swallowed up death forever! The Lord Yahweh will wipe away tears from off all faces. He will take the reproach of his people away from off all the earth, for Yahweh has spoken it.

25:9 It shall be said in that day, "Behold, this is our God! We have waited for him, and he will save us! This is Yahweh! We have waited for him. We will be glad and rejoice in his salvation!"

25:10 For in this mountain the hand of Yahweh will rest. Moab will be trodden down in his place, even like straw is trodden down in the water of the dunghill.

25:11 He will spread out his hands in its midst, like one who swims spreads out hands to swim, but his pride will be humbled together with the craft of his hands.

TARGUM ISAIAH

name; for thou hast done wonderful things; surely thou hast brought to pass and hast established the counsels which thou hadst promised of old to bring to pass.

25:2 For thou hast made the unfortified cities heaps; the fortified city is a ruin; the idolatrous house of the nations in the city of Jerusalem, shall never be built up again.

25:3 Therefore shall the strong people glorify thee, the city of terrible nations shall fear thee.

25:4 For thou hast been a strength to the poor, a help to the needy in the time of distress; as those who are protected from before a storm, *or who* are protected as in a shade from the scorching heat; thus the words of the wicked against the righteous are as a storm that beats against the wall.

25:5 As the scorching heat in a dry land thou shalt bring low the tumult of the mighty: as the shade of a cooling rock in a parched land, thus peace of mind shall be to the righteous, when the wicked shall be humbled.

25:6 And in this mountain shall the Lord of hosts make a feast and a banquet; they think that it shall be *for their* glory; but it shall be to

TARGUM ISAIAH

them for disgrace and for mighty afflictions, from which they shall not deliver themselves, afflictions through which they shall come to an end.

25:7 The face of the prince, of the prince of all the people shall be destroyed; and the face of the king, of the ruler of all the kingdoms.

25:8 Death shall be forgotten for ever; and the Lord God shall wipe away tears from off all the faces, and the reproach of his people he shall remove from off all the earth, because it hath been decreed thus by the WORD of the Lord.

25:9 And one shall say at that time: Behold, this is our God; this is he for whom we have hoped, and he shall save us: this is the Lord, for His WORD we have hoped; we will rejoice, and be glad in his salvation.

25:10 For the power of the Lord of hosts shall be revealed in this mountain; and the Moabites shall be trodden under foot even as straw is in the clay.

25:11 And he shall extend the stroke of his power among them, as the swimmer extends himself

25:2 For Thou hast made of a city a heap, of a fortified city a ruin; a castle of strangers to be no city, it shall never be built.

25:3 Therefore shall the strong people glorify Thee, the city of the terrible nations shall fear Thee.

25:4 For Thou hast been a stronghold to the poor, a stronghold to the needy in his distress, a refuge from the storm, a shadow from the heat; for the blast of the terrible ones was as a storm against the wall.

25:5 As the heat in a dry place, Thou didst subdue the noise of strangers; as the heat by the shadow of a cloud, the song of the terrible ones was brought low.

25:6 And in this mountain will the LORD of hosts make unto all peoples a feast of fat things, a feast of wines on the lees, of fat things full of marrow, of wines on the lees well refined.

25:7 And He will destroy in this mountain the face of the covering that is cast over all peoples, and the veil that is spread over all nations.

25:8 He will swallow up death for ever; and the Lord GOD will wipe away tears from off all faces; and the reproach of His people will He take away from off all the earth; for the LORD hath spoken it.

25:9 And it shall be said in that day: 'Lo, this is our God, for whom we waited, that He might save us; this is the LORD, for whom we waited, we will be glad and rejoice in His salvation.'

25:10 For in this mountain will the hand of the LORD rest, and Moab shall be trodden down in his place, even as straw is trodden down in the dunghill.

25:11 And when he shall spread forth his hands in the midst thereof, as he that swimmeth spreadeth forth his hands to swim, his pride shall be brought down together with the cunning of his hands.

WORLD ENGLISH BIBLE

25:12 He has brought the high fortress of your walls down, laid low, and brought to the ground, even to the dust.

26:1 In that day, this song will be sung in the land of Judah: "We have a strong city. God appoints salvation for walls and bulwarks.

26:2 Open the gates, that the righteous nation may enter: the one which keeps faith.

26:3 You will keep whoever's mind is steadfast in perfect peace, because he trusts in you.

26:4 Trust in Yahweh forever; for in Yah, Yahweh, is an everlasting Rock.

26:5 For he has brought down those who dwell on high, the lofty city. He lays it low. He lays it low even to the ground. He brings it even to the dust.

26:6 The foot shall tread it down; Even the feet of the poor, and the steps of the needy."

26:7 The way of the just is uprightness. You who are upright make the path of the righteous level.

26:8 Yes, in the way of your judgments, Yahweh, have we waited for you. Your name and your renown are the desire of our soul.

26:9 With my soul have I desired you in the night. Yes, with my spirit within me will I seek you earnestly; for when your judgments are in the earth, the inhabitants of the world learn righteousness.

26:10 Let favor be shown to the wicked, yet he will not learn righteousness. In the land of uprightness he will deal wrongfully, and will not see Yahweh's majesty.

26:11 Yahweh, your hand is lifted up, yet they don't see; but they will see your zeal for the people, and be disappointed. Yes, fire will consume your adversaries.

TARGUM ISAIAH

to swim; and he shall humble his glory, together with the wiles of his hands.

25:12 He shall cast down the fortified city, the great city; he shall thrust *it* down, it shall come to the earth, *even* to the dust.

26:1 AT THAT TIME THEY SHALL SING A NEW SONG IN THE LAND OF THE HOUSE OF JUDAH: We have a strong city, salvation and mercy shall be established upon *her* walls.

26:2 Open ye the gates, and let the righteous nation enter, which have kept the law with a perfect heart.

26:3 In a perfect heart they shall preserve peace: peace shall be wrought for them, because they have trusted in thy WORD.

26:4 Trust ye in the WORD of the Lord for ever and ever: thus ye shall be saved by the WORD, who is the fear of the Lord, the mighty One to eternity.

26:5 For he will humble the inhabitants of the high and strong city; he will humble her, he will cast her unto the ground, he will bring her *even* to the dust.

26:6 The feet shall tread her down, the feet of the just, the sole of the foot of the poor, of the needy of

TARGUM ISAIAH

the people.

26:7 The paths of the righteous are right: thou wilt establish the works of the ways of the just,

26:8 Yea, for the way of thy judgment, O Lord, have we hoped; to thy name and to the remembrance of thee is the desire of our soul.

26:9 My soul desireth to pray before thee in the night; yea, my spirit within me is blessing thee: when thy judgments are prepared for the earth, those that dwell in the world shall be taught to practise truth.

26:10 Thou hast granted unto the wicked continuance, that verily they should return to the law; but they did not return, all the days that they lived;—that they should practise truth in the earth, but they dealt falsely: yea, they will not regard the praise of thy glory, O Lord!

26:11 O Lord, when thou shalt be revealed in thy power to do good to them that fear thee, there will be no light to the enemies of thy people: the wicked shall see it, and shall be confounded. The vengeance of *thy* people shall cover them; yea, fire shall consume

JEWISH PUBLICATION SOCIETY 1917

25:12 And the high fortress of thy walls will He bring down, lay low, and bring to the ground, even to the dust.

26:1 In that day shall this song be sung in the land of Judah: We have a strong city; walls and bulwarks doth He appoint for salvation.

26:2 Open ye the gates, that the righteous nation that keepeth faithfulness may enter in.

26:3 The mind stayed on Thee Thou keepest in perfect peace; because it trusteth in Thee.

26:4 Trust ye in the LORD for ever, for the LORD is GOD, an everlasting Rock.

26:5 For He hath brought down them that dwell on high, the lofty city, laying it low, laying it low even to the ground, bringing it even to the dust.

26:6 The foot shall tread it down, even the feet of the poor, and the steps of the needy.

26:7 The way of the just is straight; Thou, Most Upright, makest plain the path of the just.

26:8 Yea, in the way of Thy judgments, O LORD, have we waited for Thee; to Thy name and to Thy memorial is the desire of our soul.

26:9 With my soul have I desired Thee in the night; yea, with my spirit within me have I sought Thee earnestly; for when Thy judgments are in the earth, the inhabitants of the world learn righteousness.

26:10 Let favour be shown to the wicked, yet will he not learn righteousness; in the land of uprightness will he deal wrongfully, and will not behold the majesty of the LORD.

26:11 LORD, Thy hand was lifted up, yet they see not; they shall see with shame Thy zeal for the people; yea, fire shall devour Thine adversaries.

WORLD ENGLISH BIBLE

26:12 Yahweh, you will ordain peace for us, for you have also worked all our works for us.

26:13 Yahweh our God, other lords besides you have had dominion over us, but by you only will we make mention of your name.

26:14 The dead shall not live. The deceased shall not rise. Therefore have you visited and destroyed them, and caused all memory of them to perish.

26:15 You have increased the nation, O Yahweh. You have increased the nation! You are glorified! You have enlarged all the borders of the land.

26:16 Yahweh, in trouble they have visited you. They poured out a prayer when your chastening was on them.

26:17 Like as a woman with child, who draws near the time of her delivery, is in pain and cries out in her pangs; so we have been before you, Yahweh.

26:18 We have been with child. We have been in pain. We gave birth, it seems, only to wind. We have not worked any deliverance in the earth; neither have the inhabitants of the world fallen.

26:19 Your dead shall live. My dead bodies shall arise. Awake and sing, you who dwell in the dust; for your dew is like the dew of herbs, and the earth will cast forth the dead.

26:20 Come, my people, enter into your rooms, and shut your doors behind you. Hide yourself for a little moment, until the indignation is past.

26:21 For, behold, Yahweh comes forth out of his place to punish the inhabitants of the earth for their iniquity. The earth also will disclose her blood, and will no longer cover her slain.

27:1 In that day, Yahweh with his hard and great and strong sword will punish leviathan, the fleeing serpent, and leviathan the twisted serpent; and he will kill the dragon that is in the sea.

TARGUM ISAIAH

thy enemies.

26:12 O Lord, thou wilt ordain peace for us: for at all times, when we restrained ourselves from our sins, thou wast working for us.

26:13 O Lord our God, the nations have had dominion over us, being lords over us beside thee; but we trust in thy WORD; we praise thy name.

26:14 They worship idols, who do not live, their heroes, who shall not rise; therefore, when thou shalt visit their sins, thou wilt make an end of them, and make all memorial of them to perish.

26:15 Thou shalt reveal thyself to gather the dispersed of thy people, thou wilt bring together their captivity. Thou wilt reveal thyself in thy power to cast all the wicked into hell.

26:16 O Lord, in distress they remembered thy fear: in their trouble they were ardently learning the doctrine of thy law.

26:17 Like as a woman with child, who draweth near the time of her delivery, trembleth, and crieth out in her pangs, so have we been, because we have sinned before thee.

26:18 Distress swift as the wind hath seized us, like a woman with child, who draweth near the time of her delivery; the inhabitants of the world have not brought deliverance: they have not tilled the earth, neither have they been able to perform any miracles.

26:19 Thou art he who dost quicken the dead, the bones of their dead bodies thou dost raise up. They shall live, and offer praise before thee, all that were cast into the dust, because thy dew is the dew of light to them who do thy law; but thou wilt deliver the wicked into hell, to whom thou hast given power, for they have transgressed against thy WORD.

26:20 Come, O My people; produce for thyself good works, which shall protect thee in the time of distress: hide thyself as it were for a little moment, until the curse shall have passed away.

26:21 For, behold, the Lord is revealing himself from the place of his Shekinah, to punish the inhabitants of the earth for their sins; and the earth shall disclose the innocent blood that was shed in her, and shall no more cover her slain.

27:1 At that time the Lord shall punish with his great, mighty,

26:12 LORD, Thou wilt establish peace for us; for Thou hast indeed wrought all our works for us.

26:13 O LORD our God, other lords beside Thee have had dominion over us; but by Thee only do we make mention of Thy name.

26:14 The dead live not, the shades rise not; to that end hast Thou punished and destroyed them, and made all their memory to perish.

26:15 Thou hast gotten Thee honour with the nations, O LORD, yea, exceeding great honour with the nations; Thou art honoured unto the farthest ends of the earth.

26:16 LORD, in trouble have they sought Thee, silently they poured out a prayer when Thy chastening was upon them.

26:17 Like as a woman with child, that draweth near the time of her delivery, is in pain and crieth out in her pangs; so have we been at Thy presence, O LORD.

26:18 We have been with child, we have been in pain, we have as it were brought forth wind; we have not wrought any deliverance in the land; neither are the inhabitants of the world come to life.

26:19 Thy dead shall live, my dead bodies shall arise—awake and sing, ye that dwell in the dust—for Thy dew is as the dew of light, and the earth shall bring to life the shades.

26:20 Come, my people, enter thou into thy chambers, and shut thy doors about thee; hide thyself for a little moment, until the indignation be overpast.

26:21 For, behold, the LORD cometh forth out of His place to visit upon the inhabitants of the earth their iniquity; the earth also shall disclose her blood, and shall no more cover her slain.

27:1 In that day the LORD with His sore and great and strong sword will punish leviathan the slant serpent, and leviathan the tortuous serpent; and He will slay the dragon that is in the sea.

WORLD ENGLISH BIBLE

27:2 In that day, sing to her, "A pleasant vineyard!

27:3 I, Yahweh, am its keeper. I will water it every moment. Lest anyone damage it, I will keep it night and day.

27:4 Wrath is not in me, but if I should find briers and thorns, I would do battle! I would march on them and I would burn them together.

27:5 Or else let him take hold of my strength, that he may make peace with me. Let him make peace with me."

27:6 In days to come, Jacob will take root. Israel will blossom and bud. They will fill the surface of the world with fruit.

27:7 Has he struck them as he struck those who struck them? Or are they killed like those who killed them were killed?

27:8 In measure, when you send them away, you contend with them. He has removed them with his rough blast in the day of the east wind.

27:9 Therefore by this the iniquity of Jacob will be forgiven, and this is all the fruit of taking away his sin: that he makes all the stones of the altar as chalk stones that are beaten in pieces, so that the Asherim and the incense altars shall rise no more.

TARGUM ISAIAH

and strong sword the king, who has magnified himself as Pharaoh the first, and the king who has exalted himself as Sennacherib the second; and he shall slay the king that is strong as the dragon that is in the sea.

27:2 At that time the congregation of Israel, which is like a vineyard planted in a goodly land, shall sing concerning that vineyard:

27:3 I, the Lord, keep the covenant of their fathers with them, that I may not destroy them; but at the time that they provoked me to anger, I gave them the cup of their punishment to drink; but their sins were the cause of their punishment; nevertheless, my WORD shall protect them by day and by night.

27:4 Behold, many mighty works are before me. Is it not so? If the house of Israel would set their face to do my law, I would send my anger and my fury among the nations, who are waging war against them, and I would destroy them, as the fire destroyeth the briers and the thorns together.

27:5 If they would lay hold on the words of my law, peace would be made with them; henceforth peace

TARGUM ISAIAH

would be made with them.

27:6 They shall be gathered from the midst of their captivity, and return to their country; there children shall be born to the house of Jacob; they of the house of Israel shall be fruitful, and they shall multiply; their children's children shall fill the face of the world.

27:7 Hath he smitten him (*Judah and Israel*), as He smote those that smote him? Or is he (*Judah and Israel*) slain according to the slaughter of them that are slain by Him (*by God*).

27:8 With the measure wherewith thou didst measure, they shall measure unto thee, thou didst send forth and oppress them. He meditated a word against them. He prevailed against them in the day of wrath.

27:9 By this, therefore, shall the sins of the house of Jacob be forgiven; and *thus it shall be* with all the works of the perverseness of their sins, *namely*, that they shall make all the stones of the (*idolatrous*) altar like chalk stones that are beaten asunder; the groves and the sun-images shall not be raised up again.

27:10 But the city that was fortified

JEWISH PUBLICATION SOCIETY 1917

27:2 In that day sing ye of her: 'A vineyard of foaming wine!'

27:3 I the LORD do guard it, I water it every moment; lest Mine anger visit it, I guard it night and day.

27:4 Fury is not in Me; would that I were as the briers and thorns in flame! I would with one step burn it altogether.

27:5 Or else let him take hold of My strength, that he may make peace with Me; yea, let him make peace with Me.

27:6 In days to come shall Jacob take root, Israel shall blossom and bud; and the face of the world shall be filled with fruitage.

27:7 Hath He smitten him as He smote those that smote him? Or is he slain according to the slaughter of them that were slain by Him?

27:8 In full measure, when Thou sendest her away, Thou dost contend with her; He hath removed her with His rough blast in the day of the east wind.

27:9 Therefore by this shall the iniquity of Jacob be expiated, and this is all the fruit of taking away his sin: when he maketh all the stones of the altar as chalkstones that are beaten in pieces, so that the Asherim and the sun-images shall rise no more.

WORLD ENGLISH BIBLE

27:10 For the fortified city is solitary, a habitation deserted and forsaken, like the wilderness. The calf will feed there, and there he will lie down, and consume its branches.

27:11 When its boughs are withered, they will be broken off. The women will come and set them on fire, for they are a people of no understanding. Therefore he who made them will not have compassion on them, and he who formed them will show them no favor.

27:12 It will happen in that day, that Yahweh will thresh from the flowing stream of the Euphrates to the brook of Egypt; and you will be gathered one by one, children of Israel.

27:13 It will happen in that day that a great trumpet will be blown; and those who were ready to perish in the land of Assyria, and those who were outcasts in the land of Egypt, shall come; and they will worship Yahweh in the holy mountain at Jerusalem.

28:1 Woe to the crown of pride of the drunkards of Ephraim, and to the fading flower of his glorious beauty, which is on the head of the fertile valley of those who are overcome with wine!

28:2 Behold, the Lord has a mighty and strong one. Like a storm of hail, a destroying storm, and like a storm of mighty waters overflowing, he will cast them down to the earth with his hand.

28:3 The crown of pride of the drunkards of Ephraim will be trodden under foot.

28:4 The fading flower of his glorious beauty, which is on the head of the fertile valley, shall be like the first-ripe fig before the summer; which someone picks and eats as soon as he sees it.

28:5 In that day, Yahweh of Armies will become a crown of glory, and a diadem of beauty, to the residue of his people;

TARGUM ISAIAH

shall sit solitary: she shall totter, and be forsaken like a desert; the just shall wage war against her, and plunder her treasures, and make an end of her hosts, so that none shall go forth.

27:11 Their armies shall be cut off; and they shall be confounded on account of their works, *which* shall be broken: women shall enter the house of their idolatry, and teach them, because they are a people of no understanding: therefore He that made them shall not have mercy on them, and He that created them shall show them no favor.

27:12 And it shall come to pass at that time, that the slain of the Lord shall be cast from the bank of the river Euphrates into the river of Egypt; and ye shall be brought near one to the other, O ye sons of Israel.

27:13 And it shall come to pass at that time, that the great trumpet shall be blown, and they shall come, who had gone into captivity into the land of Assyria, and those who were cast into the land of Egypt, and they shall worship before the Lord, in the holy mountain at Jerusalem.

TARGUM ISAIAH

28:1 Woe that He gave a crown to the proud and foolish prince of Israel, and that He gave a diadem to the wicked of the house of the sanctuary of His praise; they who are at the head of the valley of fatness are smitten with wine.

28:2 Behold, plagues, strong and mighty, are coming from the Lord: like a storm of hail, like a whirlwind, like a storm of mighty waters, overflowing, thus the nations shall come upon them, and shall lead them into captivity to another land on account of the sins which are in their hands.

28:3 The crown of the pride of the foolish prince of Israel shall be trodden down with feet.

28:4 And the diadem, which He gave to the wicked of the house of the sanctuary of His praise, which is on the head of the valley of fatness, shall be as the first ripe fig before the summer, which, when one sees it, no sooner is it in the hand, than one devours it.

28:5 At that time, the Messiah of the Lord of hosts shall be for a crown of rejoicing, and for a crown of praise to the remnant

JEWISH PUBLICATION SOCIETY 1917

27:10 For the fortified city is solitary, a habitation abandoned and forsaken, like the wilderness; there shall the calf feed, and there shall he lie down, and consume the branches thereof

27:11 When the boughs thereof are withered, they shall be broken off; the women shall come, and set them on fire; for it is a people of no understanding; therefore He that made them will not have compassion upon them, and He that formed them will not be gracious unto them.

27:12 And it shall come to pass in that day, that the LORD will beat off His fruit from the flood of the River unto the Brook of Egypt, and ye shall be gathered one by one, O ye children of Israel.

27:13 And it shall come to pass in that day, that a great horn shall be blown; and they shall come that were lost in the land of Assyria, and they that were dispersed in the land of Egypt; and they shall worship the LORD in the holy mountain at Jerusalem.

28:1 Woe to the crown of pride of the drunkards of Ephraim, and to the fading flower of his glorious beauty, which is on the head of the fat valley of them that are smitten down with wine!

28:2 Behold, the Lord hath a mighty and strong one, as a storm of hail, a tempest of destruction, as a storm of mighty waters overflowing, that casteth down to the earth with violence.

28:3 The crown of pride of the drunkards of Ephraim shall be trodden under foot;

28:4 And the fading flower of his glorious beauty, which is on the head of the fat valley, shall be as the first-ripe fig before the summer, which when one looketh upon it, while it is yet in his hand he eateth it up.

28:5 In that day shall the LORD of hosts be for a crown of glory, and for a diadem of beauty, unto the residue of His people;

WORLD ENGLISH BIBLE

28:6 and a spirit of justice to him who sits in judgment, and strength to those who turn back the battle at the gate.

28:7 They also reel with wine, and stagger with strong drink. The priest and the prophet reel with strong drink. They are swallowed up by wine. They stagger with strong drink. They err in vision. They stumble in judgment.

28:8 For all tables are completely full of filthy vomit and filthiness.

28:9 Whom will he teach knowledge? To whom will he explain the message? Those who are weaned from the milk, and drawn from the breasts?

28:10 For it is precept on precept, precept on precept; line on line, line on line; here a little, there a little.

28:11 But he will speak to this nation with stammering lips and in another language;

28:12 to whom he said, "This is the resting place. Give rest to weary"; and "This is the refreshing"; yet they would not hear.

28:13 Therefore the word of Yahweh will be to them precept on precept, precept on precept; line on line, line on line; here a little, there a little; that they may go, fall backward, be broken, be snared, and be taken.

TARGUM ISAIAH

of His people:

28:6 For a word of true judgment to them that sit in the house of justice, in order that they should judge according to truth; and to give victory to them that are going forth into battle, to bring them back in peace to their homes.

28:7 But verily these are drunk with wine, they are swallowed up of old wine: the priest and the scribe are drunk, in old wine they are swallowed up: on account of wine they have erred; they are turned after sweet food; their judges have erred.

28:8 Because all their tables are full of polluted and loathsome food: they have not a spot free from rapine.

28:9 To whom was the law given? and to whom was the command given to understand wisdom? Was it not to the house of Israel, who were beloved above all nations, and beloved above all the kingdoms?

28:10 Surely, they were commanded to do the law; but what they were commanded, they were not willing to do. The prophets prophesied unto them, that if they would repent, it should be forgiven them;

TARGUM ISAIAH

but they did not obey the words of the prophets: they walked after the desire of their soul, neither did they desire to do my law. They hoped to have idolatrous worship established among them, and they did not consider the worship of the house of my sanctuary: to worship in the house of my sanctuary was as a little thing in their eyes, my Shekinah was as a little thing in their eyes.

28:11 Because with feigned speed, and with mocking language, this people mocked the prophets, who prophesies unto them.

28:12 The prophets said unto them, This is the house of the sanctuary, worship ye in it: and this is the possession in which there is rest; but they would not accept instructions.

28:13 This shall be the cup of their punishment, because they have transgressed the word of the Lord, and because they were commanded to do my law, but would not do what they were commanded. Therefore they shall be delivered unto the nations, who do not know the law; because they walked after the desire of their soul, and had no delight to do my

JEWISH PUBLICATION SOCIETY 1917

28:6 And for a spirit of judgment to him that sitteth in judgment, and for strength to them that turn back the battle at the gate.

28:7 But these also reel through wine, and stagger through strong drink; the priest and the prophet reel through strong drink, they are confused because of wine, they stagger because of strong drink; they reel in vision, they totter in judgment.

28:8 For all tables are full of filthy vomit, and no place is clean.

28:9 Whom shall one teach knowledge? And whom shall one make to understand the message? Them that are weaned from the milk, them that are drawn from the breasts?

28:10 For it is precept by precept, precept by precept, line by line, line by line; here a little, there a little.

28:11 For with stammering lips and with a strange tongue shall it be spoken to this people;

28:12 To whom it was said: 'This is the rest, give ye rest to the weary; and this is the refreshing'; yet they would not hear.

28:13 And so the word of the LORD is unto them precept by precept, precept by precept, line by line, line by line; here a little, there a little; that they may go, and fall backward, and be broken, and snared, and taken.

WORLD ENGLISH BIBLE

28:14 Therefore hear the word of Yahweh, you scoffers, that rule this people in Jerusalem:

28:15 "Because you have said, 'We have made a covenant with death, and with Sheol are we in agreement. When the overflowing scourge passes through, it won't come to us; for we have made lies our refuge, and we have hidden ourselves under falsehood.'"

28:16 Therefore thus says the Lord Yahweh, "Behold, I lay in Zion for a foundation a stone, a tried stone, a precious cornerstone of a sure foundation. He who believes shall not act hastily.

28:17 I will make justice the measuring line, and righteousness the plumb line. The hail will sweep away the refuge of lies, and the waters will overflow the hiding place.

28:18 Your covenant with death shall be annulled, and your agreement with Sheol shall not stand. When the overflowing scourge passes through, then you will be trampled down by it.

28:19 As often as it passes through, it will seize you; for morning by morning it will pass through, by day and by night; and it will be nothing but terror to understand the message."

28:20 For the bed is too short to stretch out on, and the blanket is too narrow to wrap oneself in.

TARGUM ISAIAH

will. Therefore they shall hope for help at the time that I shall bring distress upon them; but they shall have no help or support. Because the house of my sanctuary was too little in their eyes to worship there, therefore they shall be left as a little thing in the eyes of the nations, among whom they shall go in captivity, in order that they may walk, and stumble backward, and be broken, and snared, and taken.

28:14 Therefore, hear ye the word of the Lord, O wicked men, rulers of this people that are in Jerusalem:

28:15 Because ye say, "We have made a covenant with death, and have made peace with the destroyer:" ye say, when the blow of the enemy shall come upon you like an overwhelming river, "It shall not come upon us, because we have placed our confidence in a lie, and have hidden ourselves under falsehood."

28:16 Therefore, thus saith the Lord God, Behold, I appoint a King in Zion; a King mighty, powerful, and terrible: I will make Him powerful, and I will strengthen Him, saith the prophet. But the righ-

TARGUM ISAIAH

JEWISH PUBLICATION SOCIETY 1917

teous, who believe these things shall not be moved, when distress shall come.

28:17 And I will make judgment straight as a line of a building, and justice as a plummet, because ye would hide yourselves. And my justice shall burn against the confidence of your lie; and because ye would hide yourselves from the *coming* distress, the nations shall lead you into captivity.

28:18 And your covenant with death shall be destroyed, and your peace with the destroyer shall not stand. When the stroke of the enemy shall come upon you, it shall be like an overwhelming river, and ye shall be unto them for a treading under foot.

28:19 At the time of its passing by, it shall lead you captive, because each morning it shall pass by, by day and by night: and it shall come to pass before the time of the curse shall have come, that ye shall consider the words of the prophets.

28:20 For their strength shall be diminished by reason of mighty slavery; and the government of the oppressor shall increase their subjection.

28:14 Wherefore hear the word of the LORD, ye scoffers, the ballad-mongers of this people which is in Jerusalem:

28:15 Because ye have said: 'We have made a covenant with death, and with the nether-world are we at agreement; when the scouring scourge shall pass through, it shall not come unto us; for we have made lies our refuge, and in falsehood have we hid ourselves';

28:16 Therefore thus saith the Lord GOD: Behold, I lay in Zion for a foundation a stone, a tried stone, a costly corner-stone of sure foundation; he that believeth shall not make haste.

28:17 And I will make justice the line, and righteousness the plummet; and the hail shall sweep away the refuge of lies, and the waters shall overflow the hiding-place.

28:18 And your covenant with death shall be disannulled and your agreement with the nether-world shall not stand; when the scouring scourge shall pass through, then ye shall be trodden down by it,

28:19 As often as it passeth through, it shall take you; for morning by morning shall it pass through, by day and by night; and it shall be sheer terror to understand the message.

28:20 For the bed is too short for a man to stretch himself; and the covering too narrow when he gathereth himself up.

WORLD ENGLISH BIBLE

28:21 For Yahweh will rise up as on Mount Perazim. He will be angry as in the valley of Gibeon; that he may do his work, his unusual work, and bring to pass his act, his extraordinary act.

28:22 Now therefore don't be scoffers, lest your bonds be made strong; for I have heard a decree of destruction from the Lord, Yahweh of Armies, on the whole earth.

28:23 Give ear, and hear my voice! Listen, and hear my speech!

28:24 Does he who plows to sow plow continually? Does he keep turning the soil and breaking the clods?

28:25 When he has leveled its surface, doesn't he plant the dill, and scatter the cumin seed, and put in the wheat in rows, the barley in the appointed place, and the spelt in its place?

28:26 For his God instructs him in right judgment, and teaches him.

28:27 For the dill are not threshed with a sharp instrument, neither is a cart wheel turned over the cumin; but the dill is beaten out with a stick, and the cumin with a rod.

28:28 Bread flour must be ground; so he will not always be threshing it. Although he drives the wheel of his threshing cart over it, his horses don't grind it.

28:29 This also comes forth from Yahweh of Armies, who is wonderful in counsel, and excellent in wisdom.

29:1 Woe to Ariel! Ariel, the city where David encamped! Add year to year; let the feasts come around;

TARGUM ISAIAH

28:21 For as the mountains trembled when the glory of the Lord was revealed in the days of king Uzziah, and in the wonders which He performed for Joshua in the valley of Gibeon, taking vengeance on the wicked, who had transgressed against His WORD: so shall He be revealed to take vengeance on them, who work works, strange works, and on those who worship with idolatrous worship.

28:22 But now deal not wickedly, lest your bands be made strong: for I have heard from the Lord, *the God* of hosts, a consummation, and an end, upon all the inhabitants of the land.

28:23 The prophet said, Listen to, and hear my voice, turn and hear my word.

28:24 The prophets prophesied at all times in order to teach, if peradventure the ears of sinners might be opened, and receive instruction.

28:25 Is it not so? If the house of Israel would set their faces to do the law, and repent, then behold, He would gather them from among the nations, amongst whom they were dispersed, like fitches and cumin that are scattered: and, behold, he would bring their off-spring together according to their tribes, as seed of wheat in the uncultivated field, and barley in the appointed place, and spelt in the borders.

28:26 All these things are instruction of judgment, that they may know, that our God shows them the right path, in which they ought to walk.

28:27 For they do not tread out the fitches with an iron threshing instrument, nor do they turn the wheels of a cart upon the cumin; but they beat out the fitches with a staff, and the cumin with a rod.

28:28 Corn they tread out, yet they will not continue to tread it out for ever; but he will throw it into confusion with the wheel of his wain, and would separate the corn, and blow away the chaff.

28:29 This also cometh forth from the Lord of hosts, who in the vast knowledge of His mind hath established the world; He hath multiplied His works in the beginning by His great wisdom.

29:1 Woe to the altar, the altar which is built in the city in which David dwelt; because of the assembly of the armies which are

28:21 For the LORD will rise up as in mount Perazim, He will be wroth as in the valley of Gibeon; that He may do His work, strange is His work, and bring to pass His act, strange is His act.

28:22 Now therefore be ye not scoffers, lest your bands be made strong; for an extermination wholly determined have I heard from the Lord, the GOD of hosts, upon the whole land.

28:23 Give ye ear, and hear my voice; attend, and hear my speech.

28:24 Is the plowman never done with plowing to sow, with the opening and harrowing of his ground?

28:25 When he hath made plain the face thereof, doth he not cast abroad the black cummin, and scatter the cummin, and put in the wheat in rows and the barley in the appointed place and the spelt in the border thereof?

28:26 For He doth instruct him aright; his God doth teach him.

28:27 For the black cummin is not threshed with a threshing-sledge, neither is a cart-wheel turned about upon the cummin; but the black cummin is beaten out with a staff, and the cummin with a rod.

28:28 Is bread corn crushed? Nay, he will not ever be threshing it; and though the roller of his wagon and its sharp edges move noisily, he doth not crush it.

28:29 This also cometh forth from the LORD of hosts: Wonderful is His counsel, and great His wisdom.

29:1 Ah, Ariel, Ariel, the city where David encamped! Add ye year to year, let the feasts come round!

WORLD ENGLISH BIBLE

29:2 then I will distress Ariel, and there will be mourning and lamentation. She shall be to me as an altar hearth.

29:3 I will encamp against you all around you, and will lay siege against you with posted troops. I will raise siege works against you.

29:4 You will be brought down, and will speak out of the ground. Your speech will mumble out of the dust. Your voice will be as of one who has a familiar spirit, out of the ground, and your speech will whisper out of the dust.

29:5 But the multitude of your foes will be like fine dust, and the multitude of the ruthless ones like chaff that blows away. Yes, it will be in an instant, suddenly.

29:6 She will be visited by Yahweh of Armies with thunder, with earthquake, with great noise, with whirlwind and storm, and with the flame of a devouring fire.

29:7 The multitude of all the nations that fight against Ariel, even all who fight against her and her stronghold, and who distress her, will be like a dream, a vision of the night.

29:8 It will be like when a hungry man dreams, and behold, he eats; but he awakes, and his hunger isn't satisfied; or like when a thirsty man dreams, and behold, he drinks; but he awakes, and behold, he is faint, and he is still thirsty. The multitude of all the nations that fight against Mount Zion will be like that.

29:9 Pause and wonder! Blind yourselves and be blind! They are drunken, but not with wine; they stagger, but not with strong drink.

29:10 For Yahweh has poured out on you a spirit of deep sleep, and has closed your eyes, the prophets; and he has covered your heads, the seers.

29:11 All vision has become to you like the words of a book that is sealed, which men deliver to one who is educated, saying, "Read this, please"; and he says, "I can't, for it is sealed:"

TARGUM ISAIAH

gathering themselves together against her year by year, because the festivals shall cease.

29:2 And I will distress the city, in which the altar is, and she shall be desolate and empty; and she shall be surrounded before me with the blood of the slain, as the altar is surrounded round about with the blood of the holy sacrifices in the day of the festival.

29:3 And I will encamp against thee with armies; and I will build a fortified camp against thee, and I will cast up a mound against thee.

29:4 And thou shalt be brought low, and shalt speak from beneath the earth, thy words shall gibber from the dust; and thy voice shall come like that of a necromancer out of the ground; yea, thy words shall gibber from the dust.

29:5 Moreover the multitude of those scattering thee shall be like small dust, and the tumultuous assembly of the mighty as chaff that passeth away; and there shall be a tumult suddenly.

29:6 Thou shalt be visited with thunder from the Lord of hosts, and with earthquake, and with a great noise; with storm, and tempest, and a flame of devouring

TARGUM ISAIAH

fire.

29:7 And the multitude of all the nations, that are gathered together against the city, and the altar which is in her, and all their camps and their armies, that are oppressing her, shall be like a phantom of the night.

29:8 And it shall be as when a hungry man dreameth, behold, he eateth; but he awakes, and he is in want: or as when a thirsty man dreameth, and behold, he drinketh; but he awaketh, and behold, he is faint, he is spent: so shall the multitude of all the nations be, that gather themselves together against the mountain of Zion.

29:9 Be astounded, wonder, be ye terrified, and muse, and marvel. They are drunk, but not with wine; they stagger, but not with old wine.

29:10 Because the Lord shall cast among you a spirit of error; and He shall hide the prophets from you, and He shall hide the scribes, and the teachers, who teach you the instruction of the law.

29:11 And all the prophecy shall be unto you as the words of a sealed book, which if one gives to a man

JEWISH PUBLICATION SOCIETY 1917

29:2 Then will I distress Ariel, and there shall be mourning and moaning; and she shall be unto Me as a hearth of God.

29:3 And I will encamp against thee round about, and will lay siege against thee with a mound, and I will raise siege works against thee.

29:4 And brought down thou shalt speak out of the ground, and thy speech shall be low out of the dust; and thy voice shall be as of a ghost out of the ground, and thy speech shall chirp out of the dust.

29:5 But the multitude of thy foes shall be like small dust, and the multitude of the terrible ones as chaff that passeth away; yea, it shall be at an instant suddenly—

29:6 There shall be a visitation from the LORD of hosts with thunder, and with earthquake, and great noise, with whirlwind and tempest, and the flame of a devouring fire.

29:7 And the multitude of all the nations that war against Ariel, even all that war against her, and the bulwarks about her, and they that distress her, shall be as a dream, a vision of the night.

29:8 And it shall be as when a hungry man dreameth, and, behold, he eateth, but he awaketh, and his soul is empty; or as when a thirsty man dreameth, and, behold, he drinketh, but he awaketh, and, behold, he is faint, and his soul hath appetite—so shall the multitude of all the nations be, that fight against mount Zion.

29:9 Stupefy yourselves, and be stupid! Blind yourselves, and be blind! ye that are drunken, but not with wine, that stagger, but not with strong drink.

29:10 For the LORD hath poured out upon you the spirit of deep sleep, and hath closed your eyes; the prophets, and your heads, the seers, hath He covered.

29:11 And the vision of all this is become unto you as the words of a writing that is sealed, which men deliver to one that is learned, saying: 'Read this, I pray thee'; and he saith: 'I cannot, for it is sealed';

WORLD ENGLISH BIBLE

29:12 and the book is delivered to one who is not educated, saying, "Read this, please"; and he says, "I can't read."

29:13 The Lord said, "Because this people draws near with their mouth and with their lips to honor me, but they have removed their heart far from me, and their fear of me is a commandment of men which has been taught;

29:14 therefore, behold, I will proceed to do a marvelous work among this people, even a marvelous work and a wonder; and the wisdom of their wise men will perish, and the understanding of their prudent men will be hidden."

29:15 Woe to those who deeply hide their counsel from Yahweh, and whose works are in the dark, and who say, "Who sees us?" and "Who knows us?"

29:16 You turn things upside down! Should the potter be thought to be like clay; that the thing made should say about him who made it, "He didn't make me"; or the thing formed say of him who formed it, "He has no understanding?"

29:17 Isn't it yet a very little while, and Lebanon will be turned into a fruitful field, and the fruitful field will be regarded as a forest?

29:18 In that day, the deaf will hear the words of the book, and the eyes of the blind will see out of obscurity and out of darkness.

29:19 The humble also will increase their joy in Yahweh, and the poor among men will rejoice in the Holy One of Israel.

29:20 For the ruthless is brought to nothing, and the scoffer ceases, and all those who are alert to do evil are cut off—

29:21 who cause a person to be indicted by a word, and lay a snare for the arbiter in the gate, and who deprive the innocent of justice with false testimony.

29:22 Therefore thus says Yahweh, who redeemed Abraham, concerning the house of Jacob: "Jacob shall no longer be ashamed, neither shall his face grow pale.

TARGUM ISAIAH

that is learned, saying, "Read this now;" then he shall answer, "I am not able, because it is sealed."

29:12 Or should the book be given to one that is not learned, saying, "Read this now," then he shall answer, "I am not learned."

29:13 Wherefore the Lord hath said: Because I am magnified by the mouth of this people, and with their lips they do honour me, but their heart is far from my fear, and their fear towards me is as the commandment of men teaching *them*:

29:14 Therefore, behold, I shall again strike this people with wonderful strokes; the wisdom of their wise *men* shall perish, and the understanding of their prudent *men* shall be hidden.

29:15 Woe unto them that purpose to hide counsel from before the Lord, that their works may be in darkness, and they say, None sees us, and none takes cognizance of our works.

29:16 Why do ye seek to pervert your works? Behold, as the clay in the hand of the potter, thus are ye accounted before me. Is it possible that the clay should say to its maker, Thou hast not made

TARGUM ISAIAH

me? or should the creature say to its creator, Thou dost not understand me?

29:17 Is it not yet a very little while, and Lebanon shall turn into a fruitful field, and the fruitful field shall be inhabited by many cities.

29:18 And at that time those that are like the deaf shall hear the words of the book, and the eyes of the blind shall see out of obscurity, and out of darkness.

29:19 And those that have suffered affliction on account of the WORD of the Lord shall increase *their* joy, and the poor of the sons of men shall rejoice in the WORD of the holy One of Israel.

29:20 For the oppressor is come to an end, and the plunderer is made to cease, and all that rose up early to act violently have come to an end;

29:21 All that declare the sons of men guilty on account of their words. The court of justice that is in the gate seeks to ensnare him, who reproves them with the words of the law. They turn aside the just by false judgment.

29:22 Therefore thus hath the Lord said, who hath redeemed Abraham, concerning the house

JEWISH PUBLICATION SOCIETY 1917

29:12 and the writing is delivered to him that is not learned, saying: 'Read this, I pray thee'; and he saith: 'I am not learned.'

29:13 And the Lord said: Forasmuch as this people draw near, and with their mouth and with their lips do honour Me, but have removed their heart far from Me, and their fear of Me is a commandment of men learned by rote;

29:14 Therefore, behold, I will again do a marvellous work among this people, even a marvellous work and a wonder; and the wisdom of their wise men shall perish, and the prudence of their prudent men shall be hid.

29:15 Woe unto them that seek deep to hide their counsel from the LORD, and their works are in the dark, and they say: 'Who seeth us? and who knoweth us?'

29:16 O your perversity! Shall the potter be esteemed as clay; that the thing made should say of him that made it: 'He made me not'; or the thing framed say of him that framed it: 'He hath no understanding?'

29:17 Is it not yet a very little while, and Lebanon shall be turned into a fruitful field, and the fruitful field shall be esteemed as a forest?

29:18 And in that day shall the deaf hear the words of a book, and the eyes of the blind shall see out of obscurity and out of darkness.

29:19 The humble also shall increase their joy in the LORD, and the neediest among men shall exult in the Holy One of Israel.

29:20 For the terrible one is brought to nought, and the scorner ceaseth, and all they that watch for iniquity are cut off;

29:21 That make a man an offender by words, and lay a snare for him that reproveth in the gate, and turn aside the just with a thing of nought.

29:22 Therefore thus saith the LORD, who redeemed Abraham, concerning the house of Jacob: Jacob shall not now be ashamed, neither shall his face now wax pale;

WORLD ENGLISH BIBLE

29:23 But when he sees his children, the work of my hands, in the midst of him, they will sanctify my name. Yes, they will sanctify the Holy One of Jacob, and will stand in awe of the God of Israel.

29:24 They also who err in spirit will come to understanding, and those who grumble will receive instruction."

30:1 "Woe to the rebellious children," says Yahweh, "who take counsel, but not from me; and who make an alliance, but not with my Spirit, that they may add sin to sin,

30:2 who set out to go down into Egypt, and have not asked my advice; to strengthen themselves in the strength of Pharaoh, and to take refuge in the shadow of Egypt!

30:3 Therefore the strength of Pharaoh will be your shame, and the refuge in the shadow of Egypt your confusion.

30:4 For their princes are at Zoan, and their ambassadors have come to Hanes.

30:5 They shall all be ashamed because of a people that can't profit them, that are not a help nor profit, but a shame, and also a reproach."

30:6 The burden of the animals of the South. Through the land of trouble and anguish, of the lioness and the lion, the viper and fiery flying serpent, they carry their riches on the shoulders of young donkeys, and their treasures on the humps of camels, to an unprofitable people.

30:7 For Egypt helps in vain, and to no purpose; therefore have I called her Rahab who sits still.

30:8 Now go, write it before them on a tablet, and inscribe it in a book, that it may be for the time to come forever and ever.

TARGUM ISAIAH

of Jacob: They of the house of Jacob shall not henceforth be confounded, neither shall their faces henceforth look dismayed.

29:23 But when *they of the house of Jacob* shall see the mighty deeds which I shall do for their children, the kindness *which I have promised* Abraham, and his posterity after him in their own land, they shall sanctify my name among them; they shall say, Holy is the holy One of Jacob; and concerning the God of Israel they shall say, He is mighty.

29:24 And they who were not taught by the spirit of understanding shall have knowledge; and they who said, All these things are nothing, shall receive instruction.

30:1 Woe unto the rebellious children, saith the Lord, who take counsel, but not of my WORD, who consult a consultation, but do not ask my prophets, that they may add sin unto the sins of their soul.

30:2 Who go to descend into Egypt, but ask not the words of my prophets: to strengthen themselves with the strength of Pharaoh, and to trust in the shadow of Egypt.

30:3 Therefore the strength of Pharaoh shall be unto you for confu-

TARGUM ISAIAH

sion; and confidence in the shadow of Egypt for disgrace.

30:4 For their princes were in Tanes, and their messengers have reached Taphnes.

30:5 All of them go unto a people to be confounded, *a people* that shall not profit them, who shall be of no help, and of no profit, but for a confusion, and reproaches.

30:6 They carry upon their beasts of burden on the way southward, into a land of oppression and distress, a place of the lion, and the whelps of the lionesses, and serpents, and of the flying basilisks—they carry upon the shoulders of their young cattle their treasures, and they bring upon the bunches of camels whatever is in their treasuries unto a people, that shall not profit them.

30:7 And as for the Egyptians, their help is vanity and emptiness; therefore I shall meet many of them slain: I will bring armed men upon them.

30:8 Now go, write it amongst them upon a tablet, and mark it upon lines of a book, that it may be for a witness before me in the day of judgment for ever:

30:9 That this is a rebellious peo-

JEWISH PUBLICATION SOCIETY 1917

29:23 When he seeth his children, the work of My hands, in the midst of him, that they sanctify My name; yea, they shall sanctify the Holy One of Jacob, and shall stand in awe of the God of Israel.

29:24 They also that err in spirit shall come to understanding, and they that murmur shall learn instruction.

30:1 Woe to the rebellious children, saith the LORD, that take counsel, but not of Me; and that form projects, but not of My spirit, that they may add sin to sin;

30:2 That walk to go down into Egypt, and have not asked at My mouth; to take refuge in the stronghold of Pharaoh, and to take shelter in the shadow of Egypt!

30:3 Therefore shall the stronghold of Pharaoh turn to your shame, and the shelter in the shadow of Egypt to your confusion.

30:4 For his princes are at Zoan, and his ambassadors are come to Hanes.

30:5 They shall all be ashamed of a people that cannot profit them, that are not a help nor profit, but a shame, and also a reproach.

30:6 The burden of the beasts of the South. Through the land of trouble and anguish, from whence come the lioness and the lion, the viper and flying serpent, they carry their riches upon the shoulders of young asses, and their treasures upon the humps of camels, to a people that shall not profit them.

30:7 For Egypt helpeth in vain, and to no purpose; therefore have I called her arrogancy that sitteth still.

30:8 Now go, write it before them on a tablet, and inscribe it in a book, that it may be for the time to come for ever and ever.

WORLD ENGLISH BIBLE

30:9 For it is a rebellious people, lying children, children who will not hear the law of Yahweh;

30:10 who tell the seers, "Don't see!" and to the prophets, "Don't prophesy to us right things. Tell us pleasant things. Prophesy deceits.

30:11 Get out of the way. Turn aside from the path. Cause the Holy One of Israel to cease from before us."

30:12 Therefore thus says the Holy One of Israel, "Because you despise this word, and trust in oppression and perverseness, and rely on it;

30:13 therefore this iniquity shall be to you like a breach ready to fall, swelling out in a high wall, whose breaking comes suddenly in an instant.

30:14 He will break it as a potter's vessel is broken, breaking it in pieces without sparing, so that there won't be found among the broken piece a piece good enough to take fire from the hearth, or to dip up water out of the cistern."

30:15 For thus said the Lord Yahweh, the Holy One of Israel, "You will be saved in returning and rest. Your strength will be in quietness and in confidence." You refused,

30:16 but you said, "No, for we will flee on horses"; therefore you will flee; and, "We will ride on the swift"; therefore those who pursue you will be swift.

30:17 One thousand will flee at the threat of one. At the threat of five, you will flee until you are left like a beacon on the top of a mountain, and like a banner on a hill.

30:18 Therefore Yahweh will wait, that he may be gracious to you; and therefore he will be exalted, that he may have mercy on you, for Yahweh is a God of justice. Blessed are all those who wait for him.

30:19 For the people will dwell in Zion at Jerusalem. You will weep no more. He will surely be gracious to you at the voice of your cry. When he hears you, he will answer you.

30:20 Though the Lord may give you the bread of adversity and the water of affliction, yet your teachers won't be hidden anymore, but your eyes will see your teachers;

TARGUM ISAIAH

ple, lying children, children that will not receive the instruction of the law of the Lord:

30:10 Who say to the prophets, Prophesy ye not: and as for doctrines, teach us not the doctrine of the law: speak ye with us with signs, relate unto us various things:

30:11 Turn us from the right path, make us to cease from tradition; put at a distance from us the WORD of the Holy One of Israel.

30:12 Wherefore thus saith the Holy One of Israel, Because ye have despised this word, and trust in lie and oppression, and stay thereon:

30:13 Therefore this sin shall be unto you as a city laid waste, and made a ruinous heap, as a bending wall, whose breaking cometh very suddenly.

30:14 And its breaking *shall be* as the breaking of a potter's vessel of clay, who is breaking it without compassion, and among its fragments there shall not be found a potsherd to take fire from the hearth, or to draw water from the cistern.

30:15 For thus saith the Lord God, the Holy One of Israel: I have said, If ye return to my law, ye shall have rest, and ye shall be

TARGUM ISAIAH

redeemed, ye shall be quiet, and ye shall dwell in safety, and be mighty; but ye would not.

30:16 And ye said: Nay, but we will flee on horses; therefore shall ye flee; and, We will ride upon the swift; therefore shall they be swift that pursue you.

30:17 One thousand of you shall flee because of the rebuke of one, because of the rebuke of five: till ye be left as a signal-fire on the top of a mountain; and as a beacon on a high hill.

30:18 And therefore the Lord will shew you pity, and He that is mighty will compassionate you; for the Lord is the God who doeth judgment: blessed are the righteous who wait for His salvation.

30:19 For the people of Zion shall dwell in Jerusalem; thou shalt weep no more. He will assuredly shew thee compassion: the voice of thy prayer He will hear, and He will answer thy supplication.

30:20 And the Lord shall give unto you the treasures of the enemy, and the spoil of the oppressor, and He will no more take away His Shekinah from the house of the sanctuary, and thine eyes shall behold my Shekinah in the house

JEWISH PUBLICATION SOCIETY 1917

30:9 For it is a rebellious people, lying children, children that refuse to hear the teaching of the LORD;

30:10 That say to the seers: 'See not,' and to the prophets: 'Prophesy not unto us right things, speak unto us smooth things, prophesy delusions;

30:11 Get you out of the way, turn aside out of the path, cause the Holy One of Israel to cease from before us.'

30:12 Wherefore thus saith the Holy One of Israel: because ye despise this word, and trust in oppression and perverseness, and stay thereon;

30:13 Therefore this iniquity shall be to you as a breach ready to fall, swelling out in a high wall, whose breaking cometh suddenly at an instant.

30:14 And He shall break it as a potter's vessel is broken, breaking it in pieces without sparing; so that there shall not be found among the pieces thereof a sherd to take fire from the hearth, or to take water out of the cistern.

30:15 For thus said the Lord GOD, the Holy One of Israel: in sitting still and rest shall ye be saved, in quietness and in confidence shall be your strength; and ye would not.

30:16 But ye said: 'No, for we will flee upon horses'; therefore shall ye flee; and: 'We will ride upon the swift'; therefore shall they that pursue you be swift.

30:17 One thousand shall flee at the rebuke of one, at the rebuke of five shall ye flee; till ye be left as a beacon upon the top of a mountain, and as an ensign on a hill.

30:18 And therefore will the LORD wait, that He may be gracious unto you, and therefore will He be exalted, that He may have compassion upon you; for the LORD is a God of justice, happy are all they that wait for Him.

30:19 For, O people that dwellest in Zion at Jerusalem, thou shalt weep no more; He will surely be gracious unto thee at the voice of thy cry, when He shall

30:20 And though the Lord give you sparing bread and scant water, yet shall not thy Teacher hide Himself any more, but thine eyes shall see thy Teacher;

WORLD ENGLISH BIBLE

30:21 and when you turn to the right hand, and when you turn to the left, your ears will hear a voice behind you, saying, "This is the way. Walk in it."

30:22 You shall defile the overlaying of your engraved images of silver, and the plating of your molten images of gold. You shall cast them away as an unclean thing. You shall tell it, "Go away!"

30:23 He will give the rain for your seed, with which you will sow the ground; and bread of the increase of the ground will be rich and plentiful. In that day, your livestock will feed in large pastures.

30:24 The oxen likewise and the young donkeys that till the ground will eat savory provender, which has been winnowed with the shovel and with the fork.

30:25 There shall be brooks and streams of water on every lofty mountain and on every high hill in the day of the great slaughter, when the towers fall.

30:26 Moreover the light of the moon will be like the light of the sun, and the light of the sun will be seven times brighter, like the light of seven days, in the day that Yahweh binds up the fracture of his people, and heals the wound they were struck with.

30:27 Behold, the name of Yahweh comes from far away, burning with his anger, and in thick rising smoke. His lips are full of indignation, and his tongue is as a devouring fire.

30:28 His breath is as an overflowing stream that reaches even to the neck, to sift the nations with the sieve of destruction; and a bridle that leads to ruin will be in the jaws of the peoples.

30:29 You will have a song, as in the night when a holy feast is kept; and gladness of heart, as when one goes with a flute to come to Yahweh's mountain, to Israel's Rock.

TARGUM ISAIAH

of the sanctuary.

30:21 And thine ears shall hear a word behind thee, saying, This is the right way, walk ye in it, and turn ye not from it to the right, or to the left.

30:22 And ye shall defile the covering of your idols of silver, and the ornament of thy molten images of gold; ye shall abominate *it*, as they abominate the impurity of a menstruous woman, thus ye shall abominate it.

30:23 Then shall He give rain for thy seed, with which thou shalt sow the ground, and corn and fruit shall increase in the land, and there shall be sustenance and goodness; and at that time, the just shall be nourished from their cattle, with the marrow of the tender and the fat ones.

30:24 And the oxen and the asses, with which they plough the ground, shall eat fattening meslin, which has been winnowed with the shovel and with the fan.

30:25 And there shall be upon every high mountain, and upon every high and lofty *hill*, rivers flowing with water *at the time of* the ruin of the kings and their armies, in the day of the great slaughter, at

TARGUM ISAIAH

the falling of the princes.

30:26 Moreover the light of the moon shall be as the light of the sun, and the light of the sun shall in future shine three hundred and forty-three times more brightly, as the light of seven days, in the day that the Lord shall turn the captivity of His people, and heal the sickness caused by His blow.

30:27 Behold, the Name of the Lord shall be revealed, as the prophets of old have prophesied concerning Him: His wrath is mighty, and too heavy to bear. His curse shall go forth from before Him upon the wicked, and His word as a consuming fire.

30:28 And His word is as an overwhelming river *reaching* unto the neck: He shall slay the mighty; He will assuredly agitate the nations with the agitation of vanity: *and there shall be* a bridle of error in the jaws of the people.

30:29 Ye shall have a song as in the night, as in the night when the festival is sanctified with joy of heart, as when they march with thanksgivings and the pipe, to enter the holy mountain of the Lord, to appear before the mighty One of Israel.

JEWISH PUBLICATION SOCIETY 1917

30:21 And thine ears shall hear a word behind thee, saying: 'This is the way, walk ye in it, when ye turn to the right hand, and when ye turn to the left.'

30:22 And ye shall defile thy graven images overlaid with silver, and thy molten images covered with gold; thou shalt put them far away as one unclean; thou shalt say unto it: 'Get thee hence.'

30:23 And He will give the rain for thy seed, wherewith thou sowest the ground, and bread of the increase of the ground, and it shall be fat and plenteous; in that day shall thy cattle feed in large pastures.

30:24 The oxen likewise and the young asses that till the ground shall eat savoury provender, which hath been winnowed with the shovel and with the fan.

30:25 And there shall be upon every lofty mountain, and upon every high hill streams and watercourses, in the day of the great slaughter, when the towers fall.

30:26 Moreover the light of the moon shall be as the light of the sun, and the light of the sun shall be sevenfold, as the light of the seven days, in the day that the LORD bindeth up the bruise of His people, and healeth the stroke of their wound.

30:27 Behold, the name of the LORD cometh from far, with His anger burning, and in thick uplifting of smoke; His lips are full of indignation, and His tongue is as a devouring fire;

30:28 And His breath is as an overflowing stream, that divideth even unto the neck, to sift the nations with the sieve of destruction; and a bridle that causeth to err shall be in the jaws of the peoples.

30:29 Ye shall have a song as in the night when a feast is hallowed; and gladness of heart, as when one goeth with the pipe to come into the mountain of the LORD, to the Rock of Israel.

WORLD ENGLISH BIBLE

30:30 Yahweh will cause his glorious voice to be heard, and will show the descent of his arm, with the indignation of his anger, and the flame of a devouring fire, with a blast, storm, and hailstones.

30:31 For through the voice of Yahweh the Assyrian will be dismayed. He will strike him with his rod.

30:32 Every stroke of the rod of punishment, which Yahweh will lay on him, will be with the sound of tambourines and harps. He will fight with them in battles, brandishing weapons.

30:33 For his burning place has long been ready. Yes, for the king it is prepared. He has made its pyre deep and large with fire and much wood. Yahweh's breath, like a stream of sulfur, kindles it.

31:1 Woe to those who go down to Egypt for help, and rely on horses, and trust in chariots because they are many, and in horsemen because they are very strong, but they don't look to the Holy One of Israel, and they don't seek Yahweh!

31:2 Yet he also is wise, and will bring disaster, and will not call back his words, but will arise against the house of the evildoers, and against the help of those who work iniquity.

31:3 Now the Egyptians are men, and not God; and their horses flesh, and not spirit. When Yahweh stretches out his hand, both he who helps shall stumble, and he who is helped shall fall, and they all shall be consumed together.

31:4 For thus says Yahweh to me, "As the lion and the young lion growling over his prey, if a multitude of shepherds is called together against him, will not be dismayed at their voice, nor abase himself for their noise, so Yahweh of Armies will come down to fight on Mount Zion and on its heights.

31:5 As birds hovering, so Yahweh of Armies will protect Jerusalem. He will protect and deliver it. He will pass over and preserve it."

TARGUM ISAIAH

30:30 And the Lord shall proclaim the brightness of the voice of His WORD, and He shall reveal the strength of His arm in the fury of His anger, and in flames of fire, destroying the graven images with scattering, and storm, and hailstones.

30:31 For through the voice of the WORD of the Lord the Assyrian shall be broken, he that smote *by his* power.

30:32 And it shall come to pass, that the Lord shall cause to rest the vengeance of His might in every pass of their princes and mighty ones, *even* amongst them. The house of Israel shall praise with tabrets and harps, because of the mighty war which shall be waged for them against the people.

30:33 For hell is made ready from eternity on account of their sins; yea, the eternal King hath prepared it deep and wide: a fiery pyre as of abundance of fuel burns in it: the WORD of the Lord, like an overwhelming torrent of brimstone, shall kindle it.

31:1 Woe to them that go down to Egypt for help, who stay themselves upon horses, and trust in chariots, because they are many:

TARGUM ISAIAH

and in horsemen, because they are very strong; but they stay not themselves upon the WORD of the Holy One of Israel, neither seek instruction from the Lord.

31:2 And also He in His wisdom will bring evil on account of what he is doing; and He will not make to fail His words, but He will arise against the house of evildoers; and against those who help the work of a lie.

31:3 And the Egyptians are men, and *none of them* a mighty one, and their horses *are* flesh, and not spirit: and the Lord shall deal the stroke of His power, and he that helpeth shall stumble, and he that is holpen shall fall, and all of them together shall be destroyed.

31:4 For thus the Lord hath said unto me: Like as the lion and the lion's whelp roar over their prey, when a multitude of shepherds are come together, he will not be afraid of their voice, neither be terrified at their tumult; thus shall the kingdom of the Lord of hosts be revealed encamping upon the mountain of Zion, and upon its hill.

31:5 As a bird by flying, so the power of the Lord of hosts shall

JEWISH PUBLICATION SOCIETY 1917

30:30 And the LORD will cause His glorious voice to be heard, and will show the lighting down of His arm, with furious anger, and the flame of a devouring fire, with a bursting of clouds, and a storm of rain, and hailstones.

30:31 For through the voice of the LORD shall Asshur be dismayed, the rod with which He smote.

30:32 And in every place where the appointed staff shall pass, which the LORD shall lay upon him, it shall be with tabrets and harps; and in battles of wielding will He fight with them.

30:33 For a hearth is ordered of old; yea, for the king it is prepared, deep and large; the pile thereof is fire and much wood; the breath of the LORD, like a stream of brimstone, doth kindle it.

31:1 Woe to them that go down to Egypt for help, and rely on horses, and trust in chariots, because they are many, and in horsemen, because they are exceeding mighty; but they look not unto the Holy One of Israel, neither seek the LORD!

31:2 Yet He also is wise, and bringeth evil, and doth not call back His words; but will arise against the house of the evil-doers, and against the help of them that work iniquity.

31:3 Now the Egyptians are men, and not God, and their horses flesh, and not spirit; so when the LORD shall stretch out His hand, both he that helpeth shall stumble, and he that is helped shall fall, and they all shall perish together.

31:4 For thus saith the LORD unto me: Like as the lion, or the young lion, growling over his prey, though a multitude of shepherds be called forth against him, will not be dismayed at their voice, nor abase himself for the noise of them; so will the LORD of hosts come down to fight upon mount Zion, and upon the hill thereof.

31:5 As birds hovering, so will the LORD of hosts protect Jerusalem; He will deliver it as He protecteth it, He will rescue it as He passeth over.

WORLD ENGLISH BIBLE

31:6 Return to him from whom you have deeply revolted, children of Israel.

31:7 For in that day everyone shall cast away his idols of silver and his idols of gold—sin which your own hands have made for you.

31:8 "The Assyrian will fall by the sword, not of man; and the sword, not of mankind, shall devour him. He will flee from the sword, and his young men will become subject to forced labor.

31:9 His rock will pass away by reason of terror, and his princes will be afraid of the banner," says Yahweh, whose fire is in Zion, and his furnace in Jerusalem.

32:1 Behold, a king shall reign in righteousness, and princes shall rule in justice.

32:2 A man shall be as a hiding place from the wind, and a covert from the storm, as streams of water in a dry place, as the shade of a large rock in a weary land.

32:3 The eyes of those who see will not be dim, and the ears of those who hear will listen.

32:4 The heart of the rash will understand knowledge, and the tongue of the stammerers will be ready to speak plainly.

32:5 The fool will no longer be called noble, nor the scoundrel be highly respected.

32:6 For the fool will speak folly, and his heart will work iniquity, to practice profanity, and to utter error against Yahweh, To make empty the soul of the hungry, and to cause the drink of the thirsty to fail.

32:7 The ways of the scoundrel are evil. He devises wicked devices to destroy the humble with lying words, even when the needy speaks right.

TARGUM ISAIAH

be revealed; He shall protect, He shall deliver, He shall save, and He shall make to pass away.

31:6 Return to the law; for you have multiplied sin, O sons of Israel!

31:7 At that time each man shall abhor the idols of their silver and the idols of their gold, which your hands have made for you for a god.

31:8 Then shall the Assyrian fall by a sword not of man; and the sword not of a man shall destroy him: and he shall betake himself to flight as from before those who slay with the sword, and his heroes shall be for destruction.

31:9 And his princes shall flee through fear, they shall move away; and his princes shall be broken on account of the miracle, saith the Lord, whose splendour is in Zion to them who obey the law, and whose burning furnace of fire is in Jerusalem for them who transgress His word.

32:1 Behold, a King shall reign in truth, and the righteous shall be magnified to execute just vengeance on the people.

32:2 And the just that were hidden because of the wicked, as those

TARGUM ISAIAH

who hide themselves on account of a storm, shall return, and shall be magnified, and their instruction shall be received quickly, like the waters that flow into a dry land, like the shadow of a great rock in a parched land.

32:3 And the eyes of the righteous shall not be shut, and the ears of those who receive instruction shall hear.

32:4 Even the heart of the rash shall understand knowledge, and the tongue of those that was tied shall be ready to speak plainly.

32:5 And the wicked man shall no more be called just, and he that transgresses against His WORD shall not be called mighty.

32:6 For the wicked will talk wickedness, and in their heart they meditate violence, to practise falsehood, and to speak revolt against the Lord, to weary the soul of the righteous, who long after instruction, as the hungry after bread; and after the words of the law, which are like water to him that is athirst, they purpose to make to cease.

32:7 And the wicked, whose works are evil, take counsel with sinners to destroy the poor with ly-

JEWISH PUBLICATION SOCIETY 1917

31:6 Turn ye unto Him against whom ye have deeply rebelled, O children of Israel.

31:7 For in that day they shall cast away every man his idols of silver, and his idols of gold, which your own hands have made unto you for a sin.

31:8 Then shall Asshur fall with the sword, not of man, and the sword, not of men, shall devour him; and he shall flee from the sword, and his young men shall become tributary.

31:9 And his rock shall pass away by reason of terror, and his princes shall be dismayed at the ensign, saith the LORD, whose fire is in Zion, and His furnace in Jerusalem.

32:1 Behold, a king shall reign in righteousness, and as for princes, they shall rule in justice.

32:2 And a man shall be as in a hiding-place from the wind, and a covert from the tempest; as by the watercourses in a dry place, as in the shadow of a great rock in a weary land.

32:3 And the eyes of them that see shall not be closed, and the ears of them that hear shall attend.

32:4 The heart also of the rash shall understand knowledge, and the tongue of the stammerers shall be ready to speak plainly.

32:5 The vile person shall be no more called liberal, nor the churl said to be noble.

32:6 For the vile person will speak villainy, and his heart will work iniquity, to practise ungodliness, and to utter wickedness against the LORD, to make empty the soul of the hungry, and to cause the drink of the thirsty to fail.

32:7 The instruments also of the churl are evil; he deviseth wicked devices to destroy the poor with lying words, and the needy when he speaketh right.

WORLD ENGLISH BIBLE

32:8 But the noble devises noble things; and he will continue in noble things.

32:9 Rise up, you women who are at ease! Hear my voice! You careless daughters, give ear to my speech!

32:10 For days beyond a year you will be troubled, you careless women; for the vintage shall fail. The harvest won't come.

32:11 Tremble, you women who are at ease! Be troubled, you careless ones! Strip yourselves, make yourselves naked, and put sackcloth on your waist.

32:12 Beat your breasts for the pleasant fields, for the fruitful vine.

32:13 Thorns and briars will come up on my people's land; yes, on all the houses of joy in the joyous city.

32:14 For the palace will be forsaken. The populous city will be deserted. The hill and the watchtower will be for dens forever, a delight for wild donkeys, a pasture of flocks;

32:15 Until the Spirit is poured on us from on high, and the wilderness becomes a fruitful field, and the fruitful field is considered a forest.

32:16 Then justice will dwell in the wilderness; and righteousness will remain in the fruitful field.

32:17 The work of righteousness will be peace; and the effect of righteousness, quietness and confidence forever.

32:18 My people will live in a peaceful habitation, in safe dwellings, and in quiet resting places.

32:19 Though hail flattens the forest, and the city is leveled completely.

32:20 Blessed are you who sow beside all waters, who send out the feet of the ox and the donkey.

TARGUM ISAIAH

ing words, and the words of the needy in judgment.

32:8 But the righteous counsel truth, and in their truth they shall be established.

32:9 Ye provinces that dwell at ease: arise, hear my voice. Ye cities that dwell in safety, listen to my word.

32:10 Those who dwell at ease shall be agitated for days and years, because the corn is come to an end, and there is no fruit to gather.

32:11 They that dwell at ease shall be broken, they that dwell in safety shall tremble; strip ye, and make you bare, and gird *sackcloth* upon your loins.

32:12 They beat the breasts for the pleasant fields, for the fruitladen vines.

32:13 Upon the land of my people thorns and thistles shall come up, yea, in all the houses of joy in the fortified city.

32:14 For the house of the sanctuary shall be laid waste; the noisy city shall be desolate, in which they worship: the house of our strength and hiding place shall be searched out, dug up, desolate and waste unto a time. The place which was a house of joy and gladness for kings is now become

TARGUM ISAIAH

a spoil for armies.

32:15 All these things *shall come upon us* until refreshing shall come to us from the face of Him, whose Shekinah is in the highest heavens. The wilderness shall become a fruitful field, and the fruitful field shall be inhabited by many cities.

32:16 Then they that do justice shall dwell in the wilderness, and those that do righteousness shall inhabit the fruitful field.

32:17 And they that do righteousness shall be at peace, and those that adorn righteousness shall be in quietness, and they shall be in safety forever.

32:18 And my people shall dwell in their habitations in peace, and in their land in safety, and in their cities at ease.

32:19 And hail shall descend and shall slay the armies of the nations, and their encampments shall be laid desolate, and come to an end.

32:20 Blessed are ye, O just, ye work out for yourselves good works: because ye are like those, who sow by watered places, sending the oxen to tread out *the corn*, and asses to gather it in.

JEWISH PUBLICATION SOCIETY 1917

32:8 But the liberal deviseth liberal things; and by liberal things shall he stand.

32:9 Rise up, ye women that are at ease, and hear my voice; ye confident daughters, give ear unto my speech.

32:10 After a year and days shall ye be troubled, ye confident women; for the vintage shall fail, the ingathering shall not come.

32:11 Tremble, ye women that are at ease; be troubled, ye confident ones; strip you, and make you bare, and gird sackcloth upon your loins,

32:12 Smiting upon the breasts for the pleasant fields, for the fruitful vine;

32:13 For the land of my people whereon thorns and briers come up; yea, for all the houses of joy and the joyous city.

32:14 For the palace shall be forsaken; the city with its stir shall be deserted; the mound and the tower shall be for dens for ever, a joy of wild asses, a pasture of flocks;

32:15 Until the spirit be poured upon us from on high, and the wilderness become a fruitful field, and the fruitful field be counted for a forest.

32:16 Then justice shall dwell in the wilderness, and righteousness shall abide in the fruitful field.

32:17 And the work of righteousness shall be peace; and the effect of righteousness quietness and confidence for ever.

32:18 And my people shall abide in a peaceable habitation, and in secure dwellings, and in quiet resting-places.

32:19 And it shall hail, in the downfall of the forest; but the city shall descend into the valley.

32:20 Happy are ye that sow beside all waters, that send forth freely the feet of the ox and the ass.

WORLD ENGLISH BIBLE

33:1 Woe to you who destroy, but you weren't destroyed; and who betray, but nobody betrayed you! When you have finished destroying, you will be destroyed; and when you have made an end of betrayal, you will be betrayed.

33:2 Yahweh, be gracious to us. We have waited for you. Be our strength every morning, our salvation also in the time of trouble.

33:3 At the noise of the thunder, the peoples have fled. When you lift yourself up, the nations are scattered.

33:4 Your spoil will be gathered as the caterpillar gathers. Men will leap on it as locusts leap.

33:5 Yahweh is exalted, for he dwells on high. He has filled Zion with justice and righteousness.

33:6 There will be stability in your times, abundance of salvation, wisdom, and knowledge. The fear of Yahweh is your treasure.

33:7 Behold, their valiant ones cry outside; the ambassadors of peace weep bitterly.

33:8 The highways are desolate. The traveling man ceases. The covenant is broken. He has despised the cities. He doesn't respect man.

33:9 The land mourns and languishes. Lebanon is confounded and withers away. Sharon is like a desert, and Bashan and Carmel are stripped bare.

33:10 "Now I will arise," says Yahweh; "Now I will lift myself up. Now I will be exalted.

33:11 You will conceive chaff. You will bring forth stubble. Your breath is a fire that will devour you.

TARGUM ISAIAH

33:1 Woe to him who is coming to spoil thee, and shall they not spoil thee? And *woe to him* that is coming to plunder, and shall they not plunder thee? When thou shalt come to spoil, they shall spoil thee, and when thou shalt be weary of plundering, they shall plunder thee.

33:2 O Lord, be merciful unto us; we have hoped for Thy Word: be Thou our strength every day, our salvation also in the time of distress.

33:3 At the voice of a tumultuous noise the people are afraid, on account of the multitude of mighty actions kingdoms are scattered.

33:4 And the house of Israel shall gather the treasures of the people, their enemies, as they gather the locusts. They shall be armed with the instruments of warfare, as they that are armed with a sling.

33:5 Mighty is the Lord who maketh His Shekinah to dwell in the highest heavens, who hath promised to fill Zion with them that do true justice and righteousness.

33:6 And it shall come to pass, whatever good Thou hast promised to them that fear Thee, Thou wilt bring and establish it in its

TARGUM ISAIAH

time: strength and salvation, wisdom and knowledge. For them that fear the Lord, the treasure of His goodness is prepared.

33:7 When Thou shalt reveal Thyself to them, the messengers of the nations shall cry bitterly in the street; those who had gone forth to proclaim peace, shall return to weep in the bitterness of soul.

33:8 The highways lie desolate, the wayfaring man ceaseth: because they have forgotten the covenant: they shall be removed far from their cities; they have not considered the sons of men, evil shall come upon them.

33:9 The land mourneth, it is laid desolate; Lebanon is withered, it shakes off its leaves: Sharon has become like a desert; Bashan is laid desolate, and Carmel.

33:10 Now I will reveal myself, saith the Lord; now will I lift myself up on high; now will I be exalted.

33:11 Ye, O people! have purposed for yourselves purposes of iniquity; ye have worked for yourselves evil works, because your works are evil; My WORD shall consume you, as a whirlwind consumes

JEWISH PUBLICATION SOCIETY 1917

33:1 Woe to thee that spoilest, and thou wast not spoiled; and dealest treacherously, and they dealt not treacherously with thee! When thou hast ceased to spoil, thou shalt be spoiled; and when thou art weary with dealing treacherously, they shall deal treacherously with thee.

33:2 O LORD, be gracious unto us; we have waited for Thee; be Thou their arm every morning, our salvation also in the time of trouble.

33:3 At the noise of the tumult the peoples are fled; at the lifting up of Thyself the nations are scattered.

33:4 And your spoil is gathered as the caterpillar gathereth; as locusts leap do they leap upon it.

33:5 The LORD is exalted, for He dwelleth on high; He hath filled Zion with justice and righteousness.

33:6 And the stability of thy times shall be a hoard of salvation—wisdom and knowledge, and the fear of the LORD which is His treasurer

33:7 Behold, their valiant ones cry without; the ambassadors of peace weep bitterly.

33:8 The highways lie waste, the wayfaring man ceaseth; he hath broken the covenant, he hath despised the cities, he regardeth not man.

33:9 The land mourneth and languisheth; Lebanon is ashamed, it withereth; Sharon is like a wilderness; and Bashan and Carmel are clean bare.

33:10 Now will I arise, saith the LORD; now will I be exalted; now will I lift Myself up.

33:11 Ye conceive chaff, ye shall bring forth stubble; your breath is a fire that shall devour you.

WORLD ENGLISH BIBLE

33:12 The peoples will be like the burning of lime, like thorns that are cut down and burned in the fire.

33:13 Hear, you who are far off, what I have done; and, you who are near, acknowledge my might."

33:14 The sinners in Zion are afraid. Trembling has seized the godless ones. Who among us can live with the devouring fire? Who among us can live with everlasting burning?

33:15 He who walks righteously, and speaks blamelessly; He who despises the gain of oppressions, who gestures with his hands, refusing to take a bribe, who stops his ears from hearing of blood, and shuts his eyes from looking at evil—

33:16 he will dwell on high. His place of defense will be the fortress of rocks. His bread will be supplied. His waters will be sure.

33:17 Your eyes will see the king in his beauty. They will see a distant land.

33:18 Your heart will meditate on the terror. Where is he who counted? Where is he who weighed? Where is he who counted the towers?

33:19 You will no longer see the fierce people, a people of a deep speech that you can't comprehend, with a strange language that you can't understand.

33:20 Look at Zion, the city of our appointed festivals. Your eyes will see Jerusalem, a quiet habitation, a tent that won't be removed. Its stakes will never be plucked up, nor will any of its cords be broken.

TARGUM ISAIAH

chaff.

33:12 And the people shall be as the burning of fire, as thorns are cut up and burnt in the fire.

33:13 Hear ye, O righteous, that keep the law from of old, what I have done; and know ye, ye sinners that have returned to my law, that my strength is nigh.

33:14 The sinners in Zion are afraid; terror hath seized the wicked, who, when they were committing theft in their ways, said: Who of us shall dwell in Zion, in which the brightness of His Shekinah is like devouring fire? Who of us shall sojourn in Jerusalem, where the wicked shall be judged, to be delivered into hell, into everlasting burning?

33:15 The prophet said, The just shall live in it, every one who walketh in righteousness, and speaketh honest things; removing himself to a distance from the mammon of iniquity; removing himself from oppressions, that restraineth his hands from holding a bribe, that stoppeth his ears from hearing of the shedding of innocent blood, and shutteth his eyes from looking at the workers of iniquity.

33:16 The house of his inhabitation

TARGUM ISAIAH

shall be in a high and exalted place; *in* the house of the sanctuary shall his soul be satisfied; his food shall be sufficient; his waters shall continue; like a fountain of water, whose waters fail not.

33:17 Thine eyes shall see the Shekinah of the king of the worlds in his beauty; thou shalt behold and see those that descend down to hell.

33:18 Thy heart shalt meditate great things: where are the scribes? where are the rulers? where are the mathematicians? let them come, if they are able to count the number of the slain of the chief of the camp of the mighty.

33:19 Thou shalt not be able to see the government of a mighty people, whose language is so unintelligible *that thou canst* not understand it, whose tongue stammereth, because *there is* no understanding in them.

33:20 O Zion, thou shalt see their fall; O city of our festivals, thine eyes shall see the consolation of Jerusalem in her prosperity *and* security, like a tabernacle that is not taken down, and whose pegs are not drawn out for ever, and whose cords shall not be broken.

JEWISH PUBLICATION SOCIETY 1917

33:12 And the peoples shall be as the burnings of lime; as thorns cut down, that are burned in the fire.

33:13 Hear, ye that are far off, what I have done; and, ye that are near, acknowledge My might.

33:14 The sinners in Zion are afraid; trembling hath seized the ungodly: 'Who among us shall dwell with the devouring fire? Who among us shall dwell with everlasting burnings?'

33:15 He that walketh righteously, and speaketh uprightly; he that despiseth the gain of oppressions, that shaketh his hands from holding of bribes, that stoppeth his ears from hearing of blood, and shutteth his eyes from looking upon evil;

33:16 He shall dwell on high; his place of defence shall be the munitions of rocks; his bread shall be given, his waters shall be sure.

33:17 Thine eyes shall see the king in his beauty; they shall behold a land stretching afar.

33:18 Thy heart shall muse on the terror: 'Where is he that counted, where is he that weighed? Where is he that counted the towers?'

33:19 Thou shalt not see the fierce people; a people of a deep speech that thou canst not perceive, of a stammering tongue that thou canst not understand.

33:20 Look upon Zion, the city of our solemn gatherings; thine eyes shall see Jerusalem a peaceful habitation, a tent that shall not be removed, the stakes whereof shall never be plucked up, neither shall any of the cords thereof be broken.

WORLD ENGLISH BIBLE

33:21 But there Yahweh will be with us in majesty, a place of broad rivers and streams, in which no galley with oars will go, neither will any gallant ship pass by there.

33:22 For Yahweh is our judge. Yahweh is our lawgiver. Yahweh is our king. He will save us.

33:23 Your rigging is untied. They couldn't strengthen the foot of their mast. They couldn't spread the sail. Then the prey of a great spoil was divided. The lame took the prey.

33:24 The inhabitant won't say, "I am sick." The people who dwell therein will be forgiven their iniquity.

34:1 Come near, you nations, to hear! Listen, you peoples. Let the earth and all it contains hear; the world, and everything that comes from it.

34:2 For Yahweh is enraged against all the nations, and angry with all their armies. He has utterly destroyed them. He has given them over for slaughter.

34:3 Their slain will also be cast out, and the stench of their dead bodies will come up; and the mountains will melt in their blood.

34:4 All of the army of the sky will be dissolved. The sky will be rolled up like a scroll, and all its armies will fade away, as a leaf fades from off a vine or a fig tree.

34:5 For my sword has drunk its fill in the sky. Behold, it will come down on Edom, and on the people of my curse, for judgment.

TARGUM ISAIAH

33:21 Yea, surely from thence the power of the Lord shall be revealed, to do good unto us from the place whence overflowing rivers of broad span shall flow, through which shall not pass the fishermen's boat, nor the large pinnacle go through it.

33:22 For the Lord is our judge, who by His power brought us out of Egypt; the Lord, who is our teacher, who gave us the doctrine of the law from Sinai; the Lord is our king, He will redeem us, and execute for us vengeance of judgment on the host of Gog,

33:23 At that time the people shall be bereft of their strength, and shall be like a ship, whose ropes are broken; neither shall there be strength in their mast, which is cut down, so that it is not possible to spread a sail upon it; then shall the house of Israel divide the treasures of the people, the abundance of spoil and prey; and although the blind and the lame are left among them, they also shall divide the abundance of spoil and prey.

33:24 Henceforth they shall not say to the people which dwell round about them, I shall return to the

TARGUM ISAIAH

Shekinah. (From you is come upon us the evil plague.) The people, the house of Israel, shall be gathered together, and they shall return to their land, their sins being forgiven.

34:1 Come near, ye nations, to hear; and hearken, ye kingdoms: let the earth hear, and the world's fullness, and all that dwell in her.

34:2 For the wrath from before the presence of the Lord is upon all the nations, and slaughter upon all their hosts: He hath condemned them and delivered them over to the slaughter.

34:3 And their slain shall be cast out; and their stink shall ascend from their carcasses; and the mountains shall be melted with their blood.

34:4 And all the pleasant host of heaven shall be dissolved, and they shall be blotted out from beneath the heavens, as it is said concerning them in this book; and all their armies shall come to an end, as the fading leaf from the vine, and as the withering fig from the fig-tree.

34:5 Because my sword is revealed in heaven; behold, it shall be uncovered upon Edom, and upon

JEWISH PUBLICATION SOCIETY 1917

33:21 But there the LORD will be with us in majesty, in a place of broad rivers and streams; wherein shall go no galley with oars, neither shall gallant ship pass thereby.

33:22 For the LORD is our Judge, the LORD is our Lawgiver, the LORD is our King; He will save us.

33:23 Thy tacklings are loosed; they do not hold the stand of their mast, they do not spread the sail; then is the prey of a great spoil divided; the lame take the prey.

33:24 And the inhabitant shall not say: 'I am sick'; the people that dwell therein shall be forgiven their iniquity.

34:1 Come near, ye nations, to hear, and attend, ye peoples; let the earth hear, and the fulness thereof, the world, and all things that come forth of it.

34:2 For the LORD hath indignation against all the nations, and fury against all their host; He hath utterly destroyed them, He hath delivered them to the slaughter.

34:3 Their slain also shall be cast out, and the stench of their carcasses shall come up, and the mountains shall be melted with their blood.

34:4 And all the host of heaven shall moulder away, and the heavens shall be rolled together as a scroll; and all their host shall fall down, as the leaf falleth off from the vine, and as a falling fig from the fig-tree.

34:5 For My sword hath drunk its fill in heaven; behold, it shall come down upon Edom, and upon the people of My ban, to judgment.

WORLD ENGLISH BIBLE

34:6 Yahweh's sword is filled with blood. It is covered with fat, with the blood of lambs and goats, with the fat of the kidneys of rams; for Yahweh has a sacrifice in Bozrah, And a great slaughter in the land of Edom.

34:7 The wild oxen will come down with them, and the young bulls with the mighty bulls; and their land will be drunken with blood, and their dust made greasy with fat.

34:8 For Yahweh has a day of vengeance, a year of recompense for the cause of Zion.

34:9 Its streams will be turned into pitch, its dust into sulfur, And its land will become burning pitch.

34:10 It won't be quenched night nor day. Its smoke will go up forever. From generation to generation, it will lie waste. No one will pass through it forever and ever.

34:11 But the pelican and the porcupine will possess it. The owl and the raven will dwell in it. He will stretch the line of confusion over it, and the plumb line of emptiness.

34:12 They shall call its nobles to the kingdom, but none shall be there; and all its princes shall be nothing.

34:13 Thorns will come up in its palaces, nettles and thistles in its fortresses; and it will be a habitation of jackals, a court for ostriches.

34:14 The wild animals of the desert will meet with the wolves, and the wild goat will cry to his fellow. Yes, the night creature shall settle there, and shall find herself a place of rest.

34:15 The arrow snake will make her nest there, and lay, hatch, and gather under her shade. Yes, the kites will be gathered there, every one with her mate.

34:16 Search in the book of Yahweh, and read: not one of these will be missing. none will lack her mate. For my mouth has commanded, and his Spirit has gathered them.

TARGUM ISAIAH

the people which I have condemned to judgment.

34:6 The sword before the presence of the Lord is filled with blood, it is fattened, it is fattened with the blood of kings and rulers, it is fattened with the kidneys of princes; because there is a slaughter before the Lord in Bozrah, and a great sacrifice in the land of Edom.

34:7 And the mighty men shall be slain with them, and the rulers, and the princes; and their land shall be drunken with their own blood; and their dust made fat with their own fat.

34:8 For it is the day of vengeance before the presence of the Lord; the year of recompense, to take vengeance of judgment *on* account of the ignominy of Zion.

34:9 And the rivers of Samaria shall be turned into pitch, and her dust into brimstone, and the land shall become burning pitch.

34:10 By night and by day it shall not be extinguished; her smoke shall ascend for ever: from generation to generation she shall lie waste; none shall pass through her to everlasting ages.

34:11 The pelican and the porcupine shall inherit her, and the

TARGUM ISAIAH

owls and the ravens shall dwell in her: and the line of devastation shall be extended over her, and the plummet of desolation.

34:12 They said, we are the sons of free men, and they were not willing to accept over them a kingly government; and all her princes shall come to nothing.

34:13 And in her palaces shall spring up thorns, *and* the nettles, and the brambles in their fortified city: and she shall become a habitation for dragons, a place for the daughter of the ostrich.

34:14 And there shall meet one another, martens and wild cats, and demons, each shall sport with its companion: verily dryads shall dwell there, and they shall find rest for themselves.

34:15 And the hedgehog shall make its nest there, and shall breed there; partridges shall chirp in the shady *boughs*: surely, the vultures shall be gathered thither, every one with her mate.

34:16 Search ye out of the book of the Lord, and seek: no one of them shall fail, none shall tarry for her mate, for by His Word they shall be gathered together, and by His pleasure they shall be

JEWISH PUBLICATION SOCIETY 1917

34:6 The sword of the LORD is filled with blood, it is made fat with fatness, with the blood of lambs and goats, with the fat of the kidneys of rams; for the LORD hath a sacrifice in Bozrah, and a great slaughter in the land of Edom.

34:7 And the wild-oxen shall come down with them, and the bullocks with the bulls; and their land shall be drunken with blood, and their dust made fat with fatness.

34:8 For the LORD hath a day of vengeance, a year of recompense for the controversy of Zion.

34:9 And the streams thereof shall be turned into pitch, and the dust thereof into brimstone, and the land thereof shall become burning pitch.

34:10 It shall not be quenched night nor day, the smoke thereof shall go up for ever; from generation to generation it shall lie waste: none shall pass through it for ever and ever.

34:11 But the pelican and the bittern shall possess it, and the owl and the raven shall dwell therein; and He shall stretch over it the line of confusion, and the plummet of emptiness.

34:12 As for her nobles, none shall be there to be called to the kingdom; and all her princes shall be nothing.

34:13 And thorns shall come up in her palaces, nettles and thistles in the fortresses thereof; and it shall be a habitation of wild-dogs, an enclosure for ostriches.

34:14 And the wild-cats shall meet with the jackals, and the satyr shall cry to his fellow; yea, the night-monster shall repose there, and shall find her a place of rest.

34:15 There shall the arrowsnake make her nest, and lay, and hatch, and brood under her shadow; yea, there shall the kites be gathered, every one with her mate.

34:16 Seek ye out of the book of the LORD, and read; no one of these shall be missing, none shall want her mate; for My mouth it hath commanded, and the breath thereof it hath gathered them.

WORLD ENGLISH BIBLE

34:17 He has cast the lot for them, and his hand has divided it to them with a measuring line. They shall possess it forever. From generation to generation they will dwell in it.

35:1 The wilderness and the dry land will be glad. The desert will rejoice and blossom like a rose.

35:2 It will blossom abundantly, and rejoice even with joy and singing. Lebanon's glory Lebanon will be given to it, the excellence of Carmel and Sharon. They will see Yahweh's glory, the excellence of our God.

35:3 Strengthen the weak hands, and make firm the feeble knees.

35:4 Tell those who have a fearful heart, "Be strong. Don't be afraid. Behold, your God will come with vengeance, God's retribution. He will come and save you.

35:5 Then the eyes of the blind will be opened, and the ears of the deaf will be unstopped.

35:6 Then the lame man will leap like a deer, and the tongue of the mute will sing; for waters will break out in the wilderness, and streams in the desert.

35:7 The burning sand will become a pool, and the thirsty ground springs of water. Grass with reeds and rushes will be in the habitation of jackals, where they lay.

35:8 A highway will be there, a road, and it will be called The Holy Way. The unclean shall not pass over it, but it will be for those who walk in the Way. Wicked fools will not go there.

35:9 No lion will be there, nor will any ravenous animal go up on it. They will not be found there; but the redeemed will walk there.

35:10 The Yahweh's ransomed ones will return, and come with singing to Zion; and everlasting joy will be on their heads. They will obtain gladness and joy, and sorrow and sighing will flee away."

TARGUM ISAIAH

brought together.

34:17 And He by His Word hath cast the lot for them; and by His will He hath divided *it* unto them by line; they shall possess it forever; from generation to generation they shall dwell therein.

35:1 They that dwell in the wilderness, in a thirsty land, shall rejoice; and those that inhabit the desert shall rejoice, and shall shine as the lilies.

35:2 They shall greatly rejoice and be glad, yea, with joy and gladness. The glory of Lebanon shall be given unto them; the splendour of Carmel and of Sharon. The house of Israel to whom these things are promised, they, they shall see the glory of the Lord, the beauty of our God.

35:3 The prophet said: Strengthen ye the weak hands, and confirm ye the feeble knees.

35:4 Say ye to the fearful of heart that they may keep the law, Be ye strong, and fear ye not: behold, your God shall be revealed to take vengeance of judgment: the Lord of retributions, the Lord shall be revealed, and He shall save you.

35:5 Then the eyes of Israel shall be opened, which were blind to the

TARGUM ISAIAH

law, and their ears, which were as of the deaf, shall hear and receive the words of the prophets.

35:6 Then when they shall see the captives of Israel gathered to go up to their own land as the swift harts, and not tarry, they shall sing with their tongue, which has been tied, because then the waters shall gush forth in the wilderness, and rivers in the plain.

35:7 Then the mirage shall become pools of water, and the thirsty place springs of water, *in* the place where the dragons dwell, reeds and rushes shall come up.

35:8 And a trodden way shall be there, and a straight one; and it shall be called the way of holiness; the unclean shall not pass over it, and the wayfaring men shall not cease; the ignorant shall not err.

35:9 There shall not be there a king doing evil, and an oppressive governor shall not pass over it, yea, they shall not be found there; but the redeemed shall walk there.

35:10 And the redeemed of the Lord shall return, because they shall be gathered from the midst of their captivity; and they shall

JEWISH PUBLICATION SOCIETY 1917

34:17 And He hath cast the lot for them, and His hand hath divided it unto them by line; they shall possess it for ever, from generation to generation shall they dwell therein.

35:1 The wilderness and the parched land shall be glad; and the desert shall rejoice, and blossom as the rose.

35:2 It shall blossom abundantly, and rejoice, even with joy and singing; the glory of Lebanon shall be given unto it, the excellency of Carmel and Sharon; they shall see the glory of the LORD, the excellency of our God.

35:3 Strengthen ye the weak hands, and make firm the tottering knees.

35:4 Say to them that are of a fearful heart: 'Be strong, fear not'; behold, your God will come with vengeance, with the recompense of God He will come and save you.

35:5 Then the eyes of the blind shall be opened, and the ears of the deaf shall be unstopped.

35:6 Then shall the lame man leap as a hart, and the tongue of the dumb shall sing; for in the wilderness shall waters break out, and streams in the desert.

35:7 And the parched land shall become a pool, and the thirsty ground springs of water; in the habitation of jackals herds shall lie down, it shall be an enclosure for reeds and rushes.

35:8 And a highway shall be there, and a way, and it shall be called The way of holiness; the unclean shall not pass over it; but it shall be for those; the wayfaring men, yea fools, shall not err therein.

35:9 No lion shall be there, nor shall any ravenous beast go up thereon, they shall not be found there; but the redeemed shall walk there;

35:10 And the ransomed of the LORD shall return, and come with singing unto Zion, and everlasting joy shall be upon their heads; they shall obtain gladness and joy, and sorrow and sighing shall flee away.

WORLD ENGLISH BIBLE

36:1 Now it happened in the fourteenth year of king Hezekiah, that Sennacherib king of Assyria attacked all of the fortified cities of Judah, and captured them.

36:2 The king of Assyria sent Rabshakeh from Lachish to Jerusalem to king Hezekiah with a large army. He stood by the aqueduct from the upper pool in the fuller's field highway.

36:3 Then Eliakim the son of Hilkiah, who was over the household, and Shebna the scribe, and Joah, the son of Asaph, the recorder came out to him.

36:4 Rabshakeh said to them, "Now tell Hezekiah, 'Thus says the great king, the king of Assyria, "What confidence is this in which you trust?

36:5 I say that your counsel and strength for the war are only vain words. Now in whom do you trust, that you have rebelled against me?

36:6 Behold, you trust in the staff of this bruised reed, even in Egypt, which if a man leans on it, it will go into his hand and pierce it. So is Pharaoh king of Egypt to all who trust in him.

36:7 But if you tell me, 'We trust in Yahweh our God,' isn't that he whose high places and whose altars Hezekiah has taken away, and has said to Judah and to Jerusalem, 'You shall worship before this altar?'"

36:8 Now therefore, please make a pledge to my master the king of Assyria, and I will give you two thousand horses, if you are able on your part to set riders on them.

36:9 How then can you turn away the face of one captain of the least of my master's servants, and put your trust on Egypt for chariots and for horsemen?

36:10 Have I come up now without Yahweh against this land to destroy it? Yahweh said to me, "Go up against this land, and destroy it.""

TARGUM ISAIAH

come to Zion with a song, and they shall have everlasting joy, which shall not cease, and a cloud of glory shall overshadow their heads: joy and gladness shall be found, and sorrow and sighing shall cease from them, namely, from the house of Israel.

36:1 Now it came to pass in the fourteenth year of king Hezekiah, that Sennacherib king of Assyria came up against all the fenced cities of the house of Judah, and took them.

36:2 And the king of Assyria sent Rabshakeh from Lachish to Jerusalem unto king Hezekiah with a great army. And he stood by the conduit of the upper pool in the highway of the field of the fullers.

36:3 Then came forth unto him Eliakim, Hilkiah's son, who was appointed over the household, and Shebna, the scribe, and Joah, Asaph's son, who was appointed over the records.

36:4 And Rabshakeh said unto them, say ye now to Hezekiah, Thus saith our great king, the king of Assyria, What confidence *is* this wherein thou trustiest?

36:5 I say (*you speak* but empty words) I make war with counsel

TARGUM ISAIAH

and might: now, in whom dost thou trust, that thou hast rebelled against me?

36:6 Behold, thou trustest in the support of this broken reed, in Pharaoh, the king of Egypt; on which if a man lean, it will enter his hand and wound him: so is Pharaoh the king of Egypt to all that trust in him.

36:7 But if ye say to me, We trust in the WORD of the Lord our God: is it not he, whose high places and whose altars Hezekiah hath taken away, and said to the men of Judah and to the inhabitants of Jerusalem, Ye shall worship before this altar?

36:8 And now, pledge thyself with my master the king of Assyria, and I will give thee two thousand horses, if thou be able on thy part to appoint riders upon them.

36:9 And how dost thou expect to turn back the face of one of the least princes, servants of my master? yet, thou trustest in Egypt for chariots and horsemen.

36:10 Am I now come up without the WORD of the Lord against this land to destroy it? The Lord said unto me, Go up against this land, and destroy it.

JEWISH PUBLICATION SOCIETY 1917

36:1 Now it came to pass in the fourteenth year of king Hezekiah, that Sennacherib king of Assyria came up against all the fortified cities of Judah, and took them.

36:2 And the king of Assyria sent Rab-shakeh from Lachish to Jerusalem unto king Hezekiah with a great army. And he stood by the conduit of the upper pool in the highway of the fullers' field.

36:3 Then came forth unto him Eliakim the son of Hilkiah, that was over the household, and Shebna the scribe, and Joah the son of Asaph the recorder.

36:4 And Rab-shakeh said unto them: 'Say ye now to Hezekiah: Thus saith the great king, the king of Assyria: What confidence is this wherein thou trustest?

36:5 I said: It is but vain words; for counsel and strength are for the war. Now on whom dost thou trust, that thou hast rebelled against me?

36:6 Behold, thou trustest upon the staff of this bruised reed, even upon Egypt; whereon if a man lean, it will go into his hand, and pierce it; so is Pharaoh king of Egypt to all that trust on him.

36:7 But if thou say unto me: We trust in the LORD our God; is not that He, whose high places and whose altars Hezekiah hath taken away, and hath said to Judah and to Jerusalem: Ye shall worship before this altar?

36:8 Now therefore, I pray thee, make a wager with my master, the king of Assyria, and I will give thee two thousand horses, if thou be able on thy part to set riders upon them.

36:9 How then canst thou turn away the face of one captain, even of the least of my master's servants? yet thou puttest thy trust on Egypt for chariots and for horsemen!

36:10 And am I now come up without the LORD against this land to destroy it? The LORD said unto me: Go up against this land, and destroy it.'

WORLD ENGLISH BIBLE

36:11 Then Eliakim, Shebna and Joah said to Rabshakeh, "Please speak to your servants in Aramaic, for we understand it; and don't speak to us in the Jews' language in the hearing of the people who are on the wall."

36:12 But Rabshakeh said, "Has my master sent me only to your master and to you, to speak these words, and not to the men who sit on the wall, who will eat their own dung and drink their own urine with you?"

36:13 Then Rabshakeh stood, and called out with a loud voice in the Jews' language, and said, "Hear the words of the great king, the king of Assyria!

36:14 Thus says the king, 'Don't let Hezekiah deceive you; for he will not be able to deliver you.

36:15 Don't let Hezekiah make you trust in Yahweh, saying, "Yahweh will surely deliver us. This city won't be given into the hand of the king of Assyria."'

36:16 Don't listen to Hezekiah, for thus says the king of Assyria, 'Make your peace with me, and come out to me; and each of you eat from his vine, and each one from his fig tree, and each one of you drink the waters of his own cistern;

36:17 until I come and take you away to a land like your own land, a land of grain and new wine, a land of bread and vineyards.

36:18 Beware lest Hezekiah persuade you, saying, "Yahweh will deliver us." Have any of the gods of the nations delivered their lands from the hand of the king of Assyria?

36:19 Where are the gods of Hamath and Arpad? Where are the gods of Sepharvaim? Have they delivered Samaria from my hand?

36:20 Who are they among all the gods of these countries that have delivered their country out of my hand, that Yahweh should deliver Jerusalem out of my hand?'"

36:21 But they remained silent, and said nothing in reply, for the king's commandment was, "Don't answer him."

36:22 Then Eliakim the son of Hilkiah, who was over the household, and Shebna the scribe, and Joah, the son of Asaph, the recorder, came to Hezekiah with their clothes torn, and told him the words of Rabshakeh.

TARGUM ISAIAH

36:11 Then said Eliakim and Shebna and Joah unto Rabshakeh, Speak, I pray thee, unto thy servants in the Syrian language; for we understand it: and speak not to us in the Jews' language before the people that *are* upon the wall.

36:12 But Rabshakeh said, Hath my master sent me to thy master and to thee to speak these words? *hath he not sent me* to the men that sit upon the wall, that they may eat their own dung, and drink their own piss in the siege with you?

36:13 Then Rabshakeh stood forth, and cried with a loud voice in the Jews' language, and said, Hear ye the words of our great king, the king of Assyria.

36:14 Thus saith the king, Let not Hezekiah cause you to err: for he shall not be able to deliver you.

36:15 Neither let Hezekiah make you trust in the WORD of the Lord, saying, The Lord will surely deliver us: this city shall not be delivered into the hand of the king of Assyria.

36:16 Hearken not to Hezekiah: for thus saith the king of Assyria, Make peace with me, and come out to me: and eat ye every one of the fruit of his vine, and every one of the fruit of his fig tree, and drink ye every one of the waters of his cistern:

36:17 Until I come and take you away to a good land like your own land, a land of corn and wine, a land of fields and vineyards.

36:18 *Beware* lest Hezekiah cause you to err, saying, The Lord shall deliver us. Hath any of the gods of the nations delivered his land from the hand of the king of Assyria?

36:19 Where are the gods of Hamath and Arphad? where are the gods of Sepharvaim? what? have they delivered Samaria out of my hand?

36:20 Who *are they* among all the gods of these lands, that have delivered their land from my hand, that the Lord shall deliver Jerusalem from my hand?

36:21 But they held their peace, and answered him not a word: for the king's commandment was, saying, Answer him not.

36:22 Then came Eliakim, the son of Hilkiah, who was appointed over the household, and Shebna the scribe, and Joah, the son of Asaph, who was appointed over

36:11 Then said Eliakim and Shebna and Joah unto Rab-shakeh: 'Speak, I pray thee, unto thy servants in the Aramean language, for we understand it; and speak not to us in the Jews' language, in the ears of the people that are on the wall.'

36:12 But Rab-shakeh said: 'Hath my master sent me to thy master, and to thee, to speak these words? hath he not sent me to the men that sit upon the wall, to eat their own dung, and to drink their own water with you?'

36:13 Then Rab-shakeh stood, and cried with a loud voice in the Jews' language, and said: 'Hear ye the words of the great king, the king of Assyria.

36:14 Thus saith the king: Let not Hezekiah beguile you, for he will not be able to deliver you;

36:15 neither let Hezekiah make you trust in the LORD, saying: The LORD will surely deliver us; this city shall not be given into the hand of the king of Assyria.

36:16 Hearken not to Hezekiah; for thus saith the king of Assyria: Make your peace with me, and come out to me; and eat ye every one of his vine, and every one of his fig-tree, and drink ye every one the waters of his own cistern;

36:17 until I come and take you away to a land like your own land, a land of corn and wine, a land of bread and vineyards.

36:18 Beware lest Hezekiah persuade you, saying: The LORD will deliver us. Hath any of the gods of the nations delivered his land out of the hand of the king of Assyria?

36:19 Where are the gods of Hamath and Arpad? where are the gods of Sepharvaim? and have they delivered Samaria out of my hand?

36:20 Who are they among all the gods of these countries, that have delivered their country out of my hand, that the LORD should deliver Jerusalem out of my hand?'

36:21 But they held their peace, and answered him not a word; for the king's commandment was, saying: 'Answer him not.'

36:22 Then came Eliakim the son of Hilkiah, that was over the household, and Shebna the scribe, and Joah the son of Asaph the recorder, to Hezekiah with their clothes rent, and told him the words of Rab-shakeh.

WORLD ENGLISH BIBLE

37:1 It happened, when king Hezekiah heard it, that he tore his clothes, covered himself with sackcloth, and went into Yahweh's house.

37:2 He sent Eliakim, who was over the household, and Shebna the scribe, and the elders of the priests, covered with sackcloth, to Isaiah the prophet, the son of Amoz.

37:3 They said to him, "Thus says Hezekiah, 'This day is a day of trouble, and of rebuke, and of rejection; for the children have come to the birth, and there is no strength to bring forth.

37:4 It may be Yahweh your God will hear the words of Rabshakeh, whom the king of Assyria his master has sent to defy the living God, and will rebuke the words which Yahweh your God has heard. Therefore lift up your prayer for the remnant that is left.'"

37:5 So the servants of king Hezekiah came to Isaiah.

37:6 Isaiah said to them, "Tell your master, 'Thus says Yahweh, "Don't be afraid of the words that you have heard, with which the servants of the king of Assyria have blasphemed me.

37:7 Behold, I will put a spirit in him and he will hear news, and will return to his own land. I will cause him to fall by the sword in his own land."'"

37:8 So Rabshakeh returned, and found the king of Assyria warring against Libnah, for he had heard that he was departed from Lachish.

37:9 He heard news concerning Tirhakah king of Ethiopia, "He has come out to fight against you." When he heard it, he sent messengers to Hezekiah, saying,

37:10 "Thus you shall speak to Hezekiah king of Judah, saying, 'Don't let your God in whom you trust deceive you, saying, "Jerusalem won't be given into the hand of the king of Assyria."

37:11 Behold, you have heard what the kings of Assyria have done to all lands, by destroying them utterly. Shall you be delivered?

TARGUM ISAIAH

the records, to Hezekiah, now having their clothes rent, and told him the words of Rabshakeh.

37:1 And it came to pass, when king Hezekiah heard it, he rent his clothes, and covered himself with sackcloth, and went into the house of the sanctuary of the Lord.

37:2 And he sent Eliakim, who was appointed over the household, and Shebna the scribe, and the elders of the priests, thus covered with sackcloth, unto Isaiah the prophet, the son of Amoz.

37:3 And they said unto him, Thus saith Hezekiah: This day is a day of distress, of reproach, and of contumely: for distress hath laid hold on us, as a woman that sitteth upon the stool of a woman in labour, and hath no strength to bring forth.

37:4 Perhaps the words of Rabshakeh may be heard by the Lord thy God, whom the king of Assyria, his master, hath sent to reproach the people of the living God, and he may take vengeance for the words which were heard before thy God, wherefore thou shalt supplicate in prayer for the remnant that is left.

37:5 So the servants of king Heze-

TARGUM ISAIAH

kiah came to Isaiah.

37:6 And Isaiah said unto them, Thus shall ye say unto your master, Thus saith the Lord, Be not afraid on account of the words that thou hast heard, wherewith the servants of the king of Assyria have blasphemed before me.

37:7 Behold, I will put a spirit within him, and he shall hear a rumour, and return to his own land: and I will cause him to fall by the sword in his own land.

37:8 So Rabshakeh returned, and found the king of Assyria waging war against Libnah: for he had heard that he had departed from Lachish.

37:9 And *Sennacherib* heard say concerning Tirhaka king of Ethiopia, he hath gone forth to wage war against thee. And when he heard *it*, he sent messengers to Hezekiah, saying,

37:10 Thus shall ye speak to Hezekiah, king of the tribe of the house of Judah, saying, Let not thy God, in whom thou trustest, cause thee to err, saying, Jerusalem shall not be delivered into the hand of the king of Assyria.

37:11 Behold, thou hast heard what the kings of Assyria have done to

JEWISH PUBLICATION SOCIETY 1917

37:1 And it came to pass, when king Hezekiah heard it, that he rent his clothes, and covered himself with sackcloth, and went into the house of the LORD.

37:2 And he sent Eliakim, who was over the household, and Shebna the scribe, and the elders of the priests, covered with sackcloth, unto Isaiah the prophet the son of Amoz.

37:3 And they said unto him: 'Thus saith Hezekiah: This day is a day of trouble, and of rebuke, and of contumely; for the children are come to the birth, and there is not strength to bring forth.

37:4 It may be the LORD thy God will hear the words of Rab-shakeh, whom the king of Assyria his master hath sent to taunt the living God, and will rebuke the words which the LORD thy God hath heard; wherefore make prayer for the remnant that is left.'

37:5 So the servants of king Hezekiah came to Isaiah.

37:6 And Isaiah said unto them: 'Thus shall ye say to your master: Thus saith the LORD: Be not afraid of the words that thou hast heard, wherewith the servants of the king of Assyria have blasphemed Me.

37:7 Behold, I will put a spirit in him, and he shall hear a rumour, and shall return unto his own land; and I will cause him to fall by the sword in his own land.'

37:8 So Rab-shakeh returned, and found the king of Assyria warring against Libnah; for he had heard that he was departed from Lachish.

37:9 And he heard say concerning Tirhakah king of Ethiopia: 'He is come out to fight against thee.' And when he heard it, he sent messengers to Hezekiah, saying:

37:10 'Thus shall ye speak to Hezekiah king of Judah, saying: Let not thy God in whom thou trustest beguile thee, saying: Jerusalem shall not be given into the hand of the king of Assyria.

37:11 Behold, thou hast heard what the kings of Assyria have done to all lands, by destroying them utterly; and shalt thou be delivered?

WORLD ENGLISH BIBLE

37:12 Have the gods of the nations delivered them, which my fathers have destroyed, Gozan, Haran, Rezeph, and the children of Eden who were in Telassar?

37:13 Where is the king of Hamath, and the king of Arpad, and the king of the city of Sepharvaim, of Hena, and Ivvah?'"

37:14 Hezekiah received the letter from the hand of the messengers and read it. Then Hezekiah went up to Yahweh's house, and spread it before Yahweh.

37:15 Hezekiah prayed to Yahweh, saying,

37:16 "Yahweh of Armies, the God of Israel, who is enthroned among the cherubim, you are the God, even you alone, of all the kingdoms of the earth. You have made heaven and earth.

37:17 Turn your ear, Yahweh, and hear. Open your eyes, Yahweh, and behold. Hear all of the words of Sennacherib, who has sent to defy the living God.

37:18 Truly, Yahweh, the kings of Assyria have destroyed all the countries and their land,

37:19 and have cast their gods into the fire; for they were no gods, but the work of men's hands, wood and stone; therefore they have destroyed them.

37:20 Now therefore, Yahweh our God, save us from his hand, that all the kingdoms of the earth may know that you are Yahweh, even you only."

37:21 Then Isaiah the son of Amoz sent to Hezekiah, saying, "Thus says Yahweh, the God of Israel, 'Because you have prayed to me against Sennacherib king of Assyria,

37:22 this is the word which Yahweh has spoken concerning him. The virgin daughter of Zion has despised you and ridiculed you. The daughter of Jerusalem has shaken her head at you.

37:23 Whom have you defied and blasphemed? Against whom have you exalted your voice and lifted up your eyes on high? Against the Holy One of Israel.

TARGUM ISAIAH

all lands by destroying them utterly; and dost thou imagine that thou wilt be delivered?

37:12 Have the gods of the nations delivered those whom my fathers have destroyed, *as* Gozan, and Haran, and Rezeph, and the inhabitants of Eden which *were* in Telassar?

37:13 Where is the king of Hamath, and the king of Arphad, and the king of the city of Sepharvaim? hath he not removed them, and carried them captive?

37:14 And Hezekiah received letters from the hands of the messengers, and read one of them: and Hezekiah went to the house of the sanctuary of the Lord, and spread it before the Lord.

37:15 And Hezekiah prayed before the Lord, saying,

37:16 O Lord God of hosts, the God of Israel, whose Shekinah dwelleth above the Cherubim! Thou art the Lord, and there is none besides Thee in all the kingdoms of the earth; Thou hast made the heavens and the earth.

37:17 It is manifest to Thee, O Lord, judge therefore; and it hath been heard by Thee, O Lord, avenge therefore! Take vengeance

134

TARGUM ISAIAH

JEWISH PUBLICATION SOCIETY 1917

on account of all the words of Sennacherib, who hath sent to reproach the people of the living God.

37:18 Of a truth, O Lord, the kings of Assyria have laid waste all the provinces and their lands,

37:19 And have burnt their gods in the fire: for they were no gods, they are of no use, but they are the work of men's hands, wood and stone, therefore they have destroyed them.

37:20 And now, O Lord our God, save us from his hand, that all the kingdoms of the earth may know that Thou art the Lord; there is none besides Thee.

37:21 Then Isaiah the son of Amoz sent to Hezekiah, saying, Thus saith the Lord, the God of Israel, whereas thou hast prayed before me concerning Sennacherib, the king of Assyria:

37:22 This is the word which the Lord hath spoken concerning him. The kingdom of the congregation of Zion despises thee, abhors thee; the people which are in Jerusalem shake their head behind thee.

37:23 Whom hast thou reproached, and against whom hast thou ex-

37:12 Have the gods of the nations delivered them, which my fathers have destroyed, Gozan, and Haran, and Rezeph, and the children of Eden that were in Telassar?

37:13 Where is the king of Hamath, and the king of Arpad, and the king of the city of Sepharvaim, of Hena, and Ivvah?'

37:14 And Hezekiah received the letter from the hand of the messengers, and read it; and Hezekiah went up unto the house of the LORD, and spread it before the LORD.

37:15 And Hezekiah prayed unto the LORD, saying:

37:16 'O LORD of hosts, the God of Israel, that sittest upon the cherubim, Thou art the God, even Thou alone, of all the kingdoms of the earth; Thou hast made heaven and earth.

37:17 Incline Thine ear, O LORD, and hear; open Thine eyes, O LORD, and see; and hear all the words of Sennacherib, who hath sent to taunt the living God.

37:18 Of a truth, LORD, the kings of Assyria have laid waste all the countries, and their land,

37:19 and have cast their gods into the fire; for they were no gods, but the work of men's hands, wood and stone; therefore they have destroyed them.

37:20 Now therefore, O LORD our God, save us from his hand, that all the kingdoms of the earth may know that Thou art the LORD, even Thou only.'

37:21 Then Isaiah the son of Amoz sent unto Hezekiah, saying: 'Thus saith the LORD, the God of Israel: Whereas thou hast prayed to Me against Sennacherib king of Assyria,

37:22 this is the word which the LORD hath spoken concerning him: The virgin daughter of Zion hath despised thee and laughed thee to scorn; the daughter of Jerusalem hath shaken her head at thee.

37:23 Whom hast thou taunted and blasphemed? And against whom hast thou exalted thy voice? Yea, thou hast lifted up thine eyes on high, even against the Holy One of Israel!

WORLD ENGLISH BIBLE

37:24 By your servants, have you defied the Lord, and have said, "With the multitude of my chariots I have come up to the height of the mountains, to the innermost parts of Lebanon. I will cut down its tall cedars and its choice fir trees. I will enter into its farthest height, the forest of its fruitful field.

37:25 I have dug and drunk water, and with the sole of my feet I will dry up all the rivers of Egypt."

37:26 Have you not heard how I have done it long ago, and formed it in ancient times? Now I have brought it to pass, that it should be yours to destroy fortified cities, turning them into ruinous heaps.

37:27 Therefore their inhabitants had little power. They were dismayed and confounded. They were like the grass of the field, and like the green herb, like the grass on the housetops, and like a field before its crop has grown.

37:28 But I know your sitting down, your going out, your coming in, and your raging against me.

37:29 Because of your raging against me, and because your arrogance has come up into my ears, therefore will I put my hook in your nose and my bridle in your lips, and I will turn you back by the way by which you came.

37:30 This shall be the sign to you. You will eat this year that which grows of itself, and in the second year that which springs from the same; and in the third year sow and reap and plant vineyards, and eat their fruit.

37:31 The remnant that is escaped of the house of Judah will again take root downward, and bear fruit upward.

TARGUM ISAIAH

alted thyself? and before whom hast thou lifted up thy voice? Yea, thou hast lifted up thine eyes on high; because thou hast spoken words which are not right before the Holy One of Israel.

37:24 By thy servants hast thou reproached the people of the Lord, and hast said, By the multitude of my chariots am I come up against their fortified cities; and moreover, I will seize the house of their sanctuary, and I will slay the most beautiful of their mighty ones, and the choicest of their rulers, and I will subdue the city of their strength, and I will destroy the multitude of their army.

37:25 I have digged cisterns, and I have drunk water, and I have dried up all the waters of the deep rivers with the sole of the people that were with me.

37:26 Hast thou not heard long ago, what I have done to Pharaoh, king of Egypt? Yea, also, the prophets of Israel have prophesied concerning thee; but thou hast not repented. I contemplated doing this unto thee, since the days of old. I have prepared it, now I will bring it to pass, and it shall be ruin unto thee; because it shall be before thee as the raging of waves, which destroy fortified cities.

37:27 Therefore their inhabitants had their strength cut off, they were dismayed and confounded; they were as the grass of the fields, yea, as the green grass, as the herb on the housetops, as corn blasted before it becomes an ear of corn.

37:28 And thy sitting down in counsel, and thy going forth to wage war, and thy coming into the land of Israel is known to me, and that thou art enraged is known to me.

37:29 Because thou art enraged against my WORD, and thy tumultuous noise hath come up before me: therefore I will put a ring in thy nostril, and a bridle in thy lips, and I will turn thee back by the way by which thou camest.

37:30 And this shall be a sign to thee: Eat this year such as groweth of itself; and in the second year, that which springeth of the same; and in the third year, sow ye, and reap, and plant vineyards, and eat the fruit thereof.

37:31 And again the escaped of the house of Judah that are left *shall*

37:24 By thy servants hast thou taunted the Lord, and hast said: With the multitude of my chariots am I come up to the height of the mountains, to the innermost parts of Lebanon; and I have cut down the tall cedars thereof, and the choice cypress-trees thereof; and I have entered into his farthest height, the forest of his fruitful field.

37:25 I have digged and drunk water, and with the sole of my feet have I dried up all the rivers of Egypt.

37:26 Hast thou not heard? Long ago I made it, in ancient times I fashioned it; now have I brought it to pass, yea, it is done; that fortified cities should be laid waste into ruinous heaps.

37:27 Therefore their inhabitants were of small power, they were dismayed and confounded; they were as the grass of the field, and as the green herb, as the grass on the housetops, and as a field of corn before it is grown up.

37:28 But I know thy sitting down, and thy going out, and thy coming in, and thy raging against Me.

37:29 Because of thy raging against Me, and for that thine uproar is come up into Mine ears, therefore will I put My hook in thy nose, and My bridle in thy lips, and I will turn thee back by the way by which thou camest.

37:30 And this shall be the sign unto thee: ye shall eat this year that which groweth of itself, and in the second year that which springeth of the same; and in the third year sow ye, and reap, and plant vineyards, and eat the fruit thereof.

37:31 And the remnant that is escaped of the house of Judah shall again take root downward, and bear fruit upward.

WORLD ENGLISH BIBLE

37:32 For out of Jerusalem a remnant will go forth, and survivors will escape from Mount Zion. The zeal of Yahweh of Armies will perform this.'

37:33 Therefore thus says Yahweh concerning the king of Assyria, 'He will not come to this city, nor shoot an arrow there, neither will he come before it with shield, nor cast up a mound against it.

37:34 By the way that he came, by the same he shall return, and he shall not come to this city,' says Yahweh.

37:35 'For I will defend this city to save it, for my own sake, and for my servant David's sake.'"

37:36 The angel of Yahweh went out and struck one hundred and eighty-five thousand men in the camp of the Assyrians. When men arose early in the morning, behold, these were all dead bodies.

37:37 So Sennacherib king of Assyria departed, went away, returned to Nineveh, and stayed there.

37:38 It happened, as he was worshipping in the house of Nisroch his god, that Adrammelech and Sharezer his sons struck him with the sword; and they escaped into the land of Ararat. Esar Haddon his son reigned in his place.

38:1 In those days was Hezekiah sick and near death. Isaiah the prophet, the son of Amoz, came to him, and said to him, "Thus says Yahweh, 'Set your house in order, for you will die, and not live.'"

38:2 Then Hezekiah turned his face to the wall and prayed to Yahweh,

38:3 and said, "Remember now, Yahweh, I beg you, how I have walked before you in truth and with a perfect heart, and have done that which is good in your sight." Hezekiah wept bitterly.

38:4 Then the word of Yahweh came to Isaiah, saying,

38:5 "Go, and tell Hezekiah, 'Thus says Yahweh, the God of David your father, "I have heard your prayer. I have seen your tears. Behold, I will add fifteen years to your life.

TARGUM ISAIAH

be like a tree which sends forth its roots downwards, and lifts its branches upwards.

37:32 For the remnant of the righteous shall go forth from Jerusalem, and the escaped of them that establish the law from mount Zion: by the WORD of the Lord of hosts shall this be done.

37:33 Therefore thus saith the Lord concerning the king of Assyria, He shall not come into this city, nor shoot an arrow there, nor come before it with shields, nor shall he cast up a mound against it.

37:34 By the way that he came, by the same he shall return, and he shall not come into this city, saith the Lord.

37:35 For I will defend this city to save it, for the sake of my WORD, and for the sake of David my servant.

37:36 Then the angel of the Lord went forth, and slew in the camp of the Assyrians a hundred and four score and five thousand: and when they arose early in the morning, behold, they were all of them dead corpses.

37:37 Then Sennacherib king of Assyria departed, and went away, and returned and dwelt at Nineveh.

TARGUM ISAIAH

37:38 And it came to pass, as he was worshipping in the temple of Nisroch his god, that Adramelech and Sharezer his sons slew him with the sword, and they escaped into the land of Kardu: and Eserhaddon his son reigned in his stead.

38:1 In those days was Hezekiah sick unto death. And Isaiah the prophet, the son of Amoz, came unto him, and said unto him, Thus saith the Lord, Order thy household, for thou art dying, and shalt not live.

38:2 Then Hezekiah turned his face towards the wall of the house of the sanctuary, and prayed before the Lord,

38:3 And said, Hear my prayer, O Lord, remember, I beseech thee, how I have served before Thee in truth, and with a perfect heart, and I have done that which is right in Thy eyes. And Hezekiah wept sore.

38:4 Then the words of prophecy came from before the Lord to Isaiah, saying,

38:5 Go, and say to Hezekiah, Thus saith the Lord, the God of David thy father, Thy prayer hath been heard by me, thy tears are ob-

JEWISH PUBLICATION SOCIETY 1917

37:32 For out of Jerusalem shall go forth a remnant, and out of mount Zion they that shall escape; the zeal of the LORD of hosts shall perform this.

37:33 Therefore thus saith the LORD concerning the king of Assyria: He shall not come unto this city, nor shoot an arrow there, neither shall he come before it with shield, nor cast a mound against it.

37:34 By the way that he came, by the same shall he return, and he shall not come unto this city, saith the LORD.

37:35 For I will defend this city to save it, for Mine own sake, and for My servant David's sake.'

37:36 And the angel of the LORD went forth, and smote in the camp of the Assyrians a hundred and fourscore and five thousand; and when men arose early in the morning, behold, they were all dead corpses.

37:37 So Sennacherib king of Assyria departed, and went, and returned, and dwelt at Nineveh.

37:38 And it came to pass, as he was worshipping in the house of Nisroch his god, that Adrammelech and Sarezer his sons smote him with the sword; and they escaped into the land of Ararat. And Esarhaddon his son reigned in his stead.

38:1 In those days was Hezekiah sick unto death. And Isaiah the prophet the son of Amoz came to him, and said unto him: 'Thus saith the LORD: Set thy house in order; for thou shalt die, and not live.'

38:2 Then Hezekiah turned his face to the wall, and prayed unto the LORD,

38:3 and said: 'Remember now, O LORD, I beseech Thee, how I have walked before Thee in truth and with a whole heart, and have done that which is good in Thy sight.' And Hezekiah wept sore.

38:4 Then came the word of the LORD to Isaiah, saying:

38:5 'Go, and say to Hezekiah: Thus saith the LORD, the God of David thy father: I have heard thy prayer, I have seen thy tears; behold, I will add unto thy days fifteen years.

WORLD ENGLISH BIBLE

38:6 I will deliver you and this city out of the hand of the king of Assyria, and I will defend this city.

38:7 This shall be the sign to you from Yahweh, that Yahweh will do this thing that he has spoken.

38:8 Behold, I will cause the shadow on the sundial, which has gone down on the sundial of Ahaz with the sun, to return backward ten steps. So the sun returned ten steps on the sundial on which it had gone down."""

38:9 The writing of Hezekiah king of Judah, when he had been sick, and had recovered of his sickness.

38:10 I said, "In the middle of my life I go into the gates of Sheol.I am deprived of the residue of my years."

38:11 I said, "I won't see Yah, Yah in the land of the living. I will see man no more with the inhabitants of the world.

38:12 My dwelling is removed, and is carried away from me like a shepherd's tent. I have rolled up, like a weaver, my life. He will cut me off from the loom. From day even to night you will make an end of me.

38:13 I waited patiently until morning. He breaks all my bones like a lion. From day even to night you will make an end of me.

38:14 I chattered like a swallow or a crane. I moaned like a dove. My eyes weaken looking upward. Lord, I am oppressed. Be my security."

38:15 What will I say? He has both spoken to me, and himself has done it. I will walk carefully all my years because of the anguish of my soul.

TARGUM ISAIAH

served by me: behold, I will add to thy days fifteen years;

38:6 And I will deliver thee and this city out of the hand of the king of Assyria: and I will defend this city.

38:7 And this shall be a sign unto thee from before the Lord, that the Lord will do this thing that He hath promised.

38:8 Behold, I will turn back the shadow on the hour-lines by which the sun is gone down on the dial of Ahaz, ten hours backwards. And the sun returned ten hours on the figure of the hourlines, which it had gone down.

38:9 THE WRITING OF THE THANKSGIVING FOR THE MIRACLE, WHICH HAD BEEN DONE FOR HEZEKIAH, THE KING OF THE TRIBE OF THE HOUSE OF JUDAH, WHEN HE HAD BEEN SICK, AND WAS HEALED OF HIS SICKNESS.

38:10 I said in the sorrow of my days, I shall go into the gates of the grave; *but* because He remembered me for good, an addition hath been made to my years.

38:11 I thought, I shall not appear again before the terrible God, in the land of the house of His Shekinah, in which is length of life: and I shall no more serve

TARGUM ISAIAH

before Him in the house of the sanctuary, from whence shall go forth joy unto all the inhabitants of the earth; neither shall I dwell in Jerusalem the holy city; my habitation is cut down.

38:12 From the children of my generation my days are taken away, they are cut off, and gone away from me; they are folded up like a shepherd's tent; my life is cut off like a weaver's web; from the glory of my kingdom I am gone into captivity; my days and my nights are ended,

38:13 I roar until the morning like a lion that roareth when he breaketh the bones of a beast; thus on account of my sorrow all my bones are broken; my days and my nights are come to an end,

38:14 As a swallow chirps which is caught, so I chirped; and I moan like a dove: I lifted up mine eyes, that refreshing might come to me from (before) Him whose Shekinah is in the highest heavens: O Lord, hear my prayer; grant my petition.

38:15 What praise shall I utter and speak unto Him? For He hath multiplied His kindness towards me. With what shall I serve Him,

JEWISH PUBLICATION SOCIETY 1917

38:6 And I will deliver thee and this city out of the hand of the king of Assyria; and I will defend this city.

38:7 And this shall be the sign unto thee from the LORD, that the LORD will do this thing that He hath spoken:

38:8 behold, I will cause the shadow of the dial, which is gone down on the sun-dial of Ahaz, to return backward ten degrees.' So the sun returned ten degrees, by which degrees it was gone down.

38:9 The writing of Hezekiah king of Judah, when he had been sick, and was recovered of his sickness.

38:10 I said: In the noontide of my days I shall go, even to the gates of the nether-world; I am deprived of the residue of my years.

38:11 I said: I shall not see the LORD, even the LORD in the land of the living; I shall behold man no more with the inhabitants of the world.

38:12 My habitation is plucked up and carried away from me as a shepherd's tent; I have rolled up like a weaver my life; He will cut me off from the thrum; from day even to night wilt Thou make an end of me.

38:13 The more I make myself like unto a lion until morning, the more it breaketh all my bones; from day even to night wilt Thou make an end of me.

38:14 Like a swallow or a crane, so do I chatter, I do moan as a dove; mine eyes fail with looking upward. O LORD, I am oppressed, be Thou my surety.

38:15 What shall I say? He hath both spoken unto me, and Himself hath done it; I shall go softly all my years for the bitterness of my soul.

WORLD ENGLISH BIBLE

38:16 Lord, men live by these things; and my spirit finds life in all of them: you restore me, and cause me to live.

38:17 Behold, for peace I had great anguish, but you have in love for my soul delivered it from the pit of corruption; for you have cast all my sins behind your back.

38:18 For Sheol can't praise you. Death can't celebrate you. Those who go down into the pit can't hope for your truth.

38:19 The living, the living, he shall praise you, as I do this day. The father shall make known your truth to the children.

38:20 Yahweh will save me. Therefore we will sing my songs with stringed instruments all the days of our life in the house of Yahweh.

38:21 Now Isaiah had said, "Let them take a cake of figs, and lay it for a poultice on the boil, and he shall recover."

38:22 Hezekiah also had said, "What is the sign that I will go up to the house of Yahweh?"

39:1 At that time, Merodach Baladan the son of Baladan, king of Babylon, sent letters and a present to Hezekiah; for he heard that he had been sick, and had recovered.

39:2 Hezekiah was pleased with them, and showed them the house of his precious things, the silver, and the gold, the spices, and the precious oil, and all the house of his armor, and all that was found in his treasures. There was nothing in his house, nor in all his dominion, that Hezekiah didn't show them.

39:3 Then Isaiah the prophet came to king Hezekiah, and asked him, "What did these men say? Where did they come from to you?" Hezekiah said, "They have come from a country far from me, even from Babylon."

TARGUM ISAIAH

and what shall I render unto Him for all the years He hath added to my life, and delivered my soul from bitterness.

38:16 O Lord, Thou hast said concerning all the dead, that Thou wilt quicken them, and Thou hast quickened my spirit before any of them: Thou hast quickened, Thou hast made me to live.

38:17 Behold, to them that obey the law, peace shall be multiplied before Thee; but Thou wilt bring bitterness to the wicked: therefore, when I knew the day of my death, I poured out my tears in prayer before Thee; my bitterness was great, but Thou hast had pleasure in my life, not to destroy it; for Thou hast cast all my sins far away from Thy presence.

38:18 For they that are in the grave do not praise Thee; neither do the dead celebrate Thee, nor do those that descend into the pit of the place of Abaddon hope for Thy salvation.

38:19 The living, the living shall praise Thee, as I *do* this day: the fathers unto their children shall make known Thy might, and They shall confess, saying, that all these things are truth.

TARGUM ISAIAH

38:20 The Lord has promised to save us: and we will sing the song of His praise all the days of our life in the house of the sanctuary of the Lord.

38:21 For Isaiah had said, Let them take a lump of figs, and lay it on the boil, and he shall recover.

38:22 And Hezekiah said, What is the sign that I shall go up to the house of the sanctuary of the Lord?

39:1 At that time Merodach-Baladan, the son of Baladan, king of Babylon, sent letters and presents to Hezekiah, when he had heard that he had been sick, and was recovered.

39:2 And Hezekiah was glad of them, and showed them the house of his treasures, the silver, and the gold, and the spices, and the precious ointment, and all the house of his vessels, and everything that was found in his treasury: and there was not anything in his house, nor in all his dominion, that Hezekiah showed them not.

39:3 Then came Isaiah the prophet unto king Hezekiah, and said unto him, What said these men? and from whence came they unto

JEWISH PUBLICATION SOCIETY 1917

38:16 O Lord, by these things men live, and altogether therein is the life of my spirit; wherefore recover Thou me, and make me to live.

38:17 Behold, for my peace I had great bitterness; but Thou hast in love to my soul delivered it from the pit of corruption; for Thou hast cast all my sins behind Thy back.

38:18 For the nether-world cannot praise Thee, death cannot celebrate Thee; they that go down into the pit cannot hope for Thy truth.

38:19 The living, the living, he shall praise Thee, as I do this day; the father to the children shall make known Thy truth.

38:20 The LORD is ready to save me; therefore we will sing songs to the stringed instruments all the days of our life in the house of the LORD.

38:21 And Isaiah said: 'Let them take a cake of figs, and lay it for a plaster upon the boil, and he shall recover.'

38:22 And Hezekiah said. 'What is the sign that I shall go up to the house of the LORD?'

39:1 At that time Merodach-baladan the son of Baladan, king of Babylon, sent a letter and a present to Hezekiah; for he heard that he had been sick, and was recovered.

39:2 And Hezekiah was glad of them, and showed them his treasure-house, the silver, and the gold, and the spices, and the precious oil, and all the house of his armour, and all that was found in his treasures; there was nothing in his house, nor in all his dominion, that Hezekiah showed them not.

39:3 Then came Isaiah the prophet unto king Hezekiah, and said unto him: 'What said these men? and from whence came they unto thee?' And Hezekiah said: 'They are come from a far country unto me, even from Babylon.'

WORLD ENGLISH BIBLE

39:4 Then he asked, "What have they seen in your house?" Hezekiah answered, "They have seen all that is in my house. There is nothing among my treasures that I have not shown them."

39:5 Then Isaiah said to Hezekiah, "Hear the word of Yahweh of Armies:

39:6 'Behold, the days are coming when all that is in your house, and that which your fathers have stored up until this day, will be carried to Babylon. Nothing will be left,' says Yahweh.

39:7 'They will take away your sons who will issue from you, whom you shall father, and they will be eunuchs in the king of Babylon's palace.'"

39:8 Then Hezekiah said to Isaiah, "Yahweh's word which you have spoken is good." He said moreover, "For there will be peace and truth in my days."

40:1 "Comfort, comfort my people," says your God.

40:2 "Speak comfortably to Jerusalem; and call out to her that her warfare is accomplished, that her iniquity is pardoned, that she has received of Yahweh's hand double for all her sins."

40:3 The voice of one who calls out," Prepare the way of Yahweh in the wilderness! Make a level highway in the desert for our God.

40:4 Every valley shall be exalted, and every mountain and hill shall be made low. The uneven shall be made level, and the rough places a plain.

40:5 The glory of Yahweh shall be revealed, and all flesh shall see it together; for the mouth of Yahweh has spoken it."

40:6 The voice of one saying, "Cry!" One said, "What shall I cry?" "All flesh is like grass, and all its glory is like the flower of the field.

40:7 The grass withers, the flower fades, because Yahweh's breath blows on it. Surely the people are like grass.

40:8 The grass withers, the flower fades; but the word of our God stands forever."

TARGUM ISAIAH

thee? And Hezekiah said, They are come from a far country unto me, *even* from Babylon.

39:4 Then said he, What have they seen in thine house? And Hezekiah answered, All that *is* in mine house have they seen: there is not anything in my treasures that I have not showed them.

39:5 Then said Isaiah to Hezekiah, Hear the word of the Lord of hosts:

39:6 Behold the days come, that all that is in thy house shall be taken away, and that which thy fathers have treasured up unto this day, yea, it shall be carried to Babylon, nothing shall be left, saith the Lord.

39:7 And thy sons which shall come forth from thee *shall be* in the palace of the king of Babylon.

39:8 Then said Hezekiah to Isaiah, Right is the word of the Lord which thou hast spoken: and he said, for there shall be peace and truth in my days.

40:1 O ye prophets, prophesy comforts to my people, saith your God.

40:2 Speak ye comfortably, to Jerusalem, and prophesy concerning her, that she shall be filled with the people of the captivity,

TARGUM ISAIAH

because her sins are forgiven, for she hath received the cup of consolations from the Lord, as if she had been smitten twice for all her sins.

40:3 A voice of one crying in the wilderness, Prepare ye the way before the people of the Lord; cast up a highway in the plain before the congregation of our God.

40:4 All the valleys shall be exalted, and every mountain and hill shall be made low, and the rugged way shall be a level, and the hilly ground a valley.

40:5 And the glory of the Lord shall be revealed, and all the sons of flesh shall see together, that by the WORD of the Lord it has been decreed thus.

40:6 The voice of one crying, Prophesy! He answered and said, What shall I prophesy? All the wicked *are* as grass, and all their strength as chaff of the field.

40:7 The grass withereth, its flower fadeth: because the spirit of the Lord bloweth upon it: surely the wicked among a people are considered like grass.

40:8 The wicked dieth, and his thoughts perish; but the word of

39:4 Then said he: 'What have they seen in thy house?' And Hezekiah answered: 'All that is in my house have they seen; there is nothing among my treasures that I have not shown them.'

39:5 Then said Isaiah to Hezekiah: 'Hear the word of the LORD of hosts:

39:6 Behold, the days come, that all that is in thy house, and that which thy fathers have laid up in store until this day, shall be carried to Babylon; nothing shall be left, saith the LORD.

39:7 And of thy sons that shall issue from thee, whom thou shalt beget, shall they take away; and they shall be officers in the palace of the king of Babylon.'

39:8 Then said Hezekiah unto Isaiah: 'Good is the word of the LORD which thou hast spoken.' He said moreover: 'If but there shall be peace and truth in my days.'

40:1 Comfort ye, comfort ye My people, saith your God.

40:2 Bid Jerusalem take heart, and proclaim unto her, that her time of service is accomplished, that her guilt is paid off; that she hath received of the LORD'S hand double for all her sins.

40:3 Hark! one calleth: 'Clear ye in the wilderness the way of the LORD, make plain in the desert a highway for our God.

40:4 Every valley shall be lifted up, and every mountain and hill shall be made low; and the rugged shall be made level, and the rough places a plain;

40:5 And the glory of the LORD shall be revealed, and all flesh shall see it together; for the mouth of the LORD hath spoken it.'

40:6 Hark! one saith: 'Proclaim!' And he saith: 'What shall I proclaim?' 'All flesh is grass, and all the goodliness thereof is as the flower of the field;

40:7 The grass withereth, the flower fadeth; because the breath of the LORD bloweth upon it—surely the people is grass.

40:8 The grass withereth, the flower fadeth; but the word of our God shall stand for ever.'

WORLD ENGLISH BIBLE

40:9 You who tell good news to Zion, go up on a high mountain. You who tell good news to Jerusalem, lift up your voice with strength. Lift it up. Don't be afraid. Say to the cities of Judah, "Behold, your God!"

40:10 Behold, the Lord Yahweh will come as a mighty one, and his arm will rule for him. Behold, his reward is with him, and his recompense before him.

40:11 He will feed his flock like a shepherd. He will gather the lambs in his arm, and carry them in his bosom. He will gently lead those who have their young.

40:12 Who has measured the waters in the hollow of his hand, and marked off the sky with his span, and calculated the dust of the earth in a measure, and weighed the mountains in scales, and the hills in a balance?

40:13 Who has directed the Spirit of Yahweh, or has taught him as his counselor?

40:14 Who did he take counsel with, and who instructed him, and taught him in the path of justice, and taught him knowledge, and showed him the way of understanding?

40:15 Behold, the nations are like a drop in a bucket, and are regarded as a speck of dust on a balance. Behold, he lifts up the islands like a very little thing.

40:16 Lebanon is not sufficient to burn, nor its animals sufficient for a burnt offering.

40:17 All the nations are like nothing before him. They are regarded by him as less than nothing, and vanity.

40:18 To whom then will you liken God? Or what likeness will you compare to him?

40:19 A workman has cast an image, and the goldsmith overlays it with gold, and casts silver chains for it.

TARGUM ISAIAH

our God shall stand for ever.

40:9 Upon a high mountain get up, ye prophets, that bring good tidings unto Zion; lift ye up your voice with strength that bring good tidings to Jerusalem; lift *it* up, be not afraid, say to the cities of the house of Judah, The kingdom of your God is revealed.

40:10 Behold, the Lord God shall be revealed, and the strength of the arm of His might shall rule before Him: behold, the reward of those who perform His word is with Him, because their works are manifest to Him.

40:11 He shall feed those that are of His flock like a shepherd: He shall gather the lambs with His arm, and He shall carry the tender ones in His bosom; He shall lead gently those that give suck.

40:12 He who hath promised these things, shall confirm *them*: He hath spoken *it*, *and* He will do *it*; He in whose sight all the waters of the world are accounted as a drop in the hollow of the hand, and the expansion of the heavens as if they had been prepared with the span; and the dust of the earth as if measured in a measure, and the mountains as if weighed in scales,

146

TARGUM ISAIAH

JEWISH PUBLICATION SOCIETY 1917

and the hills in a balance.

40:13 Who hath directed the Holy Spirit in the mouth of all the prophets? Is it not the Lord? He maketh known the words of His will to the righteous, the servants of His WORD.

40:14 I will make known wisdom to them who pray for it from Him, and I will teach them the way of justice; yea, He will give the law to their sons, and He will make known to their sons' sons the path of understanding.

40:15 Behold, the nations *are* as a drop of a bucket, and are counted as the small dust of the balance: behold, the isles are as fine dust that flieth away.

40:16 And the trees of Lebanon are not sufficient for fire, nor the beasts in it sufficient for a holocaust.

40:17 All nations are as nothing, their works are accounted before Him as naught.

40:18 And whom do you think able to contend with God? and what is the likeness that ye can compare with Him?

40:19 Behold, the artificer maketh an image, and the goldsmith overlayeth it with gold, and with silver

40:9 O thou that tellest good tidings to Zion, get thee up into the high mountain; O thou that tellest good tidings to Jerusalem, lift up thy voice with strength; lift it up, be not afraid; say unto the cities of Judah: 'Behold your God!'

40:10 Behold, the Lord GOD will come as a Mighty One, and His arm will rule for Him; behold, His reward is with Him, and His recompense before Him.

40:11 Even as a shepherd that feedeth his flock, that gathereth the lambs in his arm, and carrieth them in his bosom, and gently leadeth those that give suck.

40:12 Who hath measured the waters in the hollow of his hand, and meted out heaven with the span, and comprehended the dust of the earth in a measure, and weighed the mountains in scales, and the hills in a balance?

40:13 Who hath meted out the spirit of the LORD? Or who was His counsellor that he might instruct Him?

40:14 With whom took He counsel, and who instructed Him, and taught Him in the path of right, and taught Him knowledge, and made Him to know the way of discernment?

40:15 Behold, the nations are as a drop of a bucket, and are counted as the small dust of the balance; behold the isles are as a mote in weight.

40:16 And Lebanon is not sufficient fuel, nor the beasts thereof sufficient for burnt-offerings.

40:17 All the nations are as nothing before Him; they are accounted by Him as things of nought, and vanity.

40:18 To whom then will ye liken God? Or what likeness will ye compare unto Him?

40:19 The image perchance, which the craftsman hath melted, and the goldsmith spread over with gold, the silversmith casting silver chains?

WORLD ENGLISH BIBLE

40:20 He who is too impoverished for such an offering chooses a tree that will not rot. He seeks a skillful workman to set up an engraved image for him that will not be moved.

40:21 Haven't you known? Haven't you heard, yet? Haven't you been told from the beginning? Haven't you understood from the foundations of the earth?

40:22 It is he who sits above the circle of the earth, and its inhabitants are like grasshoppers; who stretches out the heavens like a curtain, and spreads them out like a tent to dwell in;

40:23 who brings princes to nothing; who makes the judges of the earth like meaningless.

40:24 They are planted scarcely. They are sown scarcely. Their stock has scarcely taken root in the ground. He merely blows on them, and they wither, and the whirlwind takes them away as stubble.

40:25 "To whom then will you liken me? Who is my equal?" says the Holy One.

40:26 Lift up your eyes on high, and see who has created these, who brings out their army by number. He calls them all by name. by the greatness of his might, and because he is strong in power, Not one is lacking.

40:27 Why do you say, Jacob, and speak, Israel, "My way is hidden from Yahweh, and the justice due me is disregarded by my God?"

40:28 Haven't you known? Haven't you heard? The everlasting God, Yahweh, The Creator of the ends of the earth, doesn't faint. He isn't weary. His understanding is unsearchable.

40:29 He gives power to the weak. He increases the strength of him who has no might.

40:30 Even the youths faint and get weary, and the young men utterly fall;

40:31 But those who wait for Yahweh will renew their strength. They will mount up with wings like eagles. They will run, and not be weary. They will walk, and not faint.

TARGUM ISAIAH

chains the silversmith fasteneth it.

40:20 He cuts a wild ash of the forest, which rottenness will seize; he procures a skilful artist to fix the image, that it be not moved.

40:21 Have ye not known? have ye not heard? hath not the work in the creation been declared unto you in its order from the beginning? Have ye not understood that ye ought to fear Him, who hath created the foundations of the earth?

40:22 Who maketh the Shekinah of His glory to dwell in exalted strength, and all the inhabitants of the earth are in His estimation as locusts; He that stretched out the heavens as a little thing, and spreadeth them out as the tent of the glory of the house of the Shekinah.

40:23 Who gives princes over to weakness; the judges of the earth He bringeth to naught.

40:24 Although they multiply, although they increase, although their children become great in the earth, yet, nevertheless, He will send His wrath among them, and they shall be confounded: and His WORD shall scatter them, as the whirlwind the chaff.

TARGUM ISAIAH

JEWISH PUBLICATION SOCIETY 1917

40:25 To whom, then, will ye liken me? and to *whom* will ye equal *me?* saith the Holy One.

40:26 Lift up your eyes on high, and behold, that ye may fear Him, who hath created these things, who bringeth forth the host of the heavens by number: He calleth them all by their name: on account of the combination of forces and might of power, not one is hindered in its orb.

40:27 Why sayest thou, O Jacob, and speakest, O Israel, My way is hid from the Lord, and my cause is removed from my God?

40:28 Hast thou not known? Yea, hast thou not heard *that* the everlasting God, the Lord who hath created the foundations of the earth, is not fatigued, neither is weary?" there is no end to His wisdom.

40:29 Who giveth wisdom to the righteous that long for the words of the law; and to those who have no strength, he multiplieth strength.

40:30 And the wicked youths shall be fatigued and shall be weary; and the impious young men shall utterly fall.

40:31 But they that hope for the

40:20 A holm-oak is set apart, he chooseth a tree that will not rot; he seeketh unto him a cunning craftsman to set up an image, that shall not be moved.

40:21 Know ye not? hear ye not? Hath it not been told you from the beginning? Have ye not understood the foundations of the earth?

40:22 It is He that sitteth above the circle of the earth, and the inhabitants thereof are as grasshoppers; that stretcheth out the heavens as a curtain, and spreadeth them out as a tent to dwell in;

40:23 That bringeth princes to nothing; He maketh the judges of the earth as a thing of nought.

40:24 Scarce are they planted, scarce are they sown, scarce hath their stock taken root in the earth; when He bloweth upon them, they wither, and the whirlwind taketh them away as stubble.

40:25 To whom then will ye liken Me, that I should be equal? saith the Holy One.

40:26 Lift up your eyes on high, and see: who hath created these? He that bringeth out their host by number, He calleth them all by name; by the greatness of His might, and for that He is strong in power, not one faileth.

40:27 Why sayest thou, O Jacob, and speakest, O Israel: 'My way is hid from the LORD, and my right is passed over from my God'?

40:28 Hast thou not known? hast thou not heard that the everlasting God, the LORD, the Creator of the ends of the earth, fainteth not, neither is weary? His discernment is past searching out.

40:29 He giveth power to the faint; and to him that hath no might He increaseth strength.

40:30 Even the youths shall faint and be weary, and the young men shall utterly fall;

40:31 But they that wait for the LORD shall renew their strength; they shall mount up with wings as eagles; they shall run, and not be weary; they shall walk, and not faint.

WORLD ENGLISH BIBLE

41:1 "Keep silent before me, islands, and let the peoples renew their strength. Let them come near, then let them speak. Let's meet together for judgment.

41:2 Who has raised up one from the east? Who called him to his foot in righteousness? He hands over nations to him, and makes him rule over kings. He gives them like the dust to his sword, like the driven stubble to his bow.

41:3 He pursues them, and passes by safely, Even by a way that he had not gone with his feet.

41:4 Who has worked and done it, calling the generations from the beginning? I, Yahweh, the first, and with the last, I am he."

41:5 The islands have seen, and fear. The ends of the earth tremble. They approach, and come.

41:6 Everyone helps his neighbor. They say to their brothers, "Be strong!"

41:7 So the carpenter encourages the goldsmith. He who smoothes with the hammer encourages him who strikes the anvil, saying of the soldering, "It is good"; and he fastens it with nails, that it might not totter.

41:8 "But you, Israel, my servant, Jacob whom I have chosen, the seed of Abraham my friend,

41:9 You whom I have taken hold of from the ends of the earth, and called from its corners, and said to you, 'You are my servant, I have chosen you and not cast you away;'

41:10 Don't you be afraid, for I am with you. Don't be dismayed, for I am your God. I will strengthen you. Yes, I will help you. Yes, I will uphold you with the right hand of my righteousness.

TARGUM ISAIAH

salvation of the Lord shall be gathered together from the midst of their captivity, and shall increase their strength, and their youth shall be renewed like the sprout that springeth up: they shall hasten upon the wings of eagles, and not be weary; they shall walk, and not faint.

41:1 Listen unto my word, ye islands, and let the kingdoms increase their strength: let them come nigh, then let them speak; let us approach one another for judgment.

41:2 Who openly brought Abraham from the east? He brought the chosen of the righteous in truth to his place, He delivered up nations before him, and broke in pieces mighty kings, he cast the slain down like the dust before his sword, and he pursued them like stubble before his bow.

41:3 He pursued them, and passed safely by; the roughness of the path shall not affect his feet.

41:4 Who hath promised these things *and* established them? Who hath spoken, and it was done? And *who* hath ranged the generations in their order from the beginning? I, the Lord, I created

TARGUM ISAIAH

JEWISH PUBLICATION SOCIETY 1917

the world from the beginning; yea, ages after ages are mine, and besides me there is no God.

41:5 The isles shall see and be afraid; they that are at the ends of the earth shall tremble; they shall draw nigh, they shall come.

41:6 Let every one help his neighbour, and *every one* say to his brother, Be of good courage.

41:7 Shall they not be confounded in their works? Because the artificer encourageth the silversmith, and he that smiteth with the great hammer him that smiteth with the small: It is time, one saith, for the soldering, it is ready; he fasteneth it with nails, that it may not be moved.

41:8 But thou, Israel, my servant, Jacob, in whom I delight, the seed of Abraham my friend:

41:9 I have brought thee out of the families of the earth, I have chosen thee out of a kingdom: and I have said unto thee, Thou art my servant; I delight in thee, and I will not thrust thee away.

41:10 Fear not, for my WORD shall be thy support; be not dismayed, for I am thy God: I will strengthen thee; yea, I will help thee; yea, I will uphold thee with the

41:1 Keep silence before Me, O islands, and let the peoples renew their strength; let them draw near, then let them speak; let us come near together to judgment.

41:2 Who hath raised up one from the east, at whose steps victory attendeth? He giveth nations before him, and maketh him rule over kings; his sword maketh them as the dust, his bow as the driven stubble.

41:3 He pursueth them, and passeth on safely; the way with his feet he treadeth not.

41:4 Who hath wrought and done it? He that called the generations from the beginning. I, the LORD, who am the first, and with the last am the same.

41:5 The isles saw, and feared; the ends of the earth trembled; they drew near, and came.

41:6 They helped every one his neighbour; and every one said to his brother: 'Be of good courage.'

41:7 So the carpenter encouraged the goldsmith, and he that smootheth with the hammer him that smiteth the anvil, saying of the soldering: 'It is good'; and he fastened it with nails, that it should not be moved.

41:8 But thou, Israel, My servant, Jacob whom I have chosen, the seed of Abraham My friend;

41:9 Thou whom I have taken hold of from the ends of the earth, and called thee from the uttermost parts thereof, and said unto thee: 'Thou art My servant, I have chosen thee and not cast thee away';

41:10 Fear thou not, for I am with thee, be not dismayed, for I am thy God; I strengthen thee, yea, I help thee; yea, I uphold thee with My victorious right hand.

WORLD ENGLISH BIBLE

41:11 Behold, all those who are incensed against you will be disappointed and confounded. Those who strive with you will be like nothing, and shall perish.

41:12 You will seek them, and won't find them, even those who contend with you. Those who war against you will be as nothing, as a non-existent thing.

41:13 For I, Yahweh your God, will hold your right hand, saying to you, 'Don't be afraid. I will help you.'

41:14 Don't be afraid, you worm Jacob, and you men of Israel. I will help you," says Yahweh, "and your Redeemer is the Holy One of Israel.

41:15 Behold, I have made you into a new sharp threshing instrument with teeth. You will thresh the mountains, and beat them small, and will make the hills like chaff.

41:16 You will winnow them, and the wind will carry them away, and the whirlwind will scatter them. You will rejoice in Yahweh. You will glory in the Holy One of Israel.

41:17 The poor and needy seek water, and there is none. Their tongue fails for thirst. I, Yahweh, will answer them. I, the God of Israel, will not forsake them.

41:18 I will open rivers on the bare heights, and springs in the midst of the valleys. I will make the wilderness a pool of water, and the dry land springs of water.

41:19 I will put cedar, acacia, myrtle, and oil trees in the wilderness. I will set fir trees, pine, and box trees together in the desert;

41:20 that they may see, know, consider, and understand together, that the hand of Yahweh has done this, and the Holy One of Israel has created it.

41:21 Produce your cause," says Yahweh. "Bring forth your strong reasons," says the King of Jacob.

41:22 "Let them announce, and declare to us what shall happen. Declare the former things, what they are, that we may consider them, and know the latter end of them; or show us things to come.

TARGUM ISAIAH

right hand of my truth.

41:11 Behold, all the nations that are incensed against thee shall be ashamed and confounded: they shall be as nothing; and they that strive with thee shall perish.

41:12 Thou shalt seek them, and shalt not find them, *even* them that contended with thee: they shall be as nothing; the men that stirred themselves up to make war with thee *shall be* less than nothing.

41:13 For I am the Lord thy God, that will hold thee fast by thy right hand; who saith unto thee, Fear not, my WORD *shall* be thy help.

41:14 Fear ye not, ye tribes of the house of Jacob, ye seed of Israel, my WORD shall be your help, saith the Lord, and your Redeemer, the Holy One of Israel.

41:15 Behold, I will make you a mighty threshing instrument full of sharp edges: thou shalt slay the nations, thou shalt consume the kingdoms, thou shalt make *them* like chaff.

41:16 Thou shalt fan them, and the wind shall carry them away, and my WORD shall scatter them as the whirlwind scattereth the chaff; but as for thee, thou shalt rejoice in the WORD of the Lord, thou shalt glory in the Holy One of Israel.

41:17 The poor and the needy long after instruction, as the thirsty after water, but do not find it; their spirit faints in affliction. I, the Lord, will hear their prayer; I, the God of Israel, will not cast them off.

41:18 I will gather their captives from the midst of the nations, and I will lead them in the right path; and I will open for them rivers in torrent-beds, and fountains in the midst of the valleys: I will make the desert pools of water, and the land that is a thirsty place springs of water.

41:19 I will put cedars, acacias, and myrtles, and oil trees in the wilderness; I will make the fir tree, the elm, and the box tree to grow in the desert together:

41:20 In order that they may see, and know, and put my fear in their heart, and may consider together, that the might of the Lord hath done this, and the Holy One of Israel hath created it.

41:21 Produce your cause, saith the Lord, bring forth your arguments, saith the King of Jacob.

41:22 Let them approach, and show

41:11 Behold, all they that were incensed against thee shall be ashamed and confounded; they that strove with thee shall be as nothing, and shall perish.

41:12 Thou shalt seek them, and shalt not find them, even them that contended with thee; they that warred against thee shall be as nothing, and as a thing of nought.

41:13 For I the LORD thy God hold thy right hand, who say unto thee: 'Fear not, I help thee.'

41:14 Fear not, thou worm Jacob, and ye men of Israel; I help thee, saith the LORD, and thy Redeemer, the Holy One of Israel.

41:15 Behold, I make thee a new threshing-sledge having sharp teeth; thou shalt thresh the mountains, and beat them small, and shalt make the hills as chaff.

41:16 Thou shalt fan them, and the wind shall carry them away, and the whirlwind shall scatter them; and thou shalt rejoice in the LORD, thou shalt glory in the Holy One of Israel.

41:17 The poor and needy seek water and there is none, and their tongue faileth for thirst; I the LORD will answer them, I the God of Israel will not forsake them.

41:18 I will open rivers on the high hills, and fountains in the midst of the valleys; I will make the wilderness a pool of water, and the dry land springs of water.

41:19 I will plant in the wilderness the cedar, the acacia-tree, and the myrtle, and the oil-tree; I will set in the desert the cypress, the plane-tree, and the larch together;

41:20 That they may see, and know, and consider, and understand together, that the hand of the LORD hath done this, and the Holy One of Israel hath created it.

41:21 Produce your cause, saith the LORD; bring forth your reasons, saith the King of Jacob.

41:22 Let them bring them forth, and declare unto us the things that shall happen; the former things, what are they? Declare ye, that we may consider, and know the end of them; or announce to us things to come.

WORLD ENGLISH BIBLE

41:23 Declare the things that are to come hereafter, that we may know that you are gods. Yes, do good, or do evil, that we may be dismayed, and see it together.

41:24 Behold, you are of nothing, and your work is of nothing. He who chooses you is an abomination.

41:25 "I have raised up one from the north, and he has come; from the rising of the sun, one who calls on my name; and he shall come on rulers as on mortar, and as the potter treads clay.

41:26 Who has declared it from the beginning, that we may know? And before, that we may say, 'He is right?' Surely, there is no one who declares. Surely, there is no one who shows. Surely, there is no one who hears your words.

41:27 I am the first to say to Zion, 'Behold, look at them;' and I will give one who brings good news to Jerusalem.

41:28 When I look, there is no man; even among them there is no counselor who, when I ask of them, can answer a word.

41:29 Behold, all of them, their works are vanity and nothing. Their molten images are wind and confusion.

42:1 "Behold, my servant, whom I uphold; my chosen, in whom my soul delights—I have put my Spirit on him. He will bring justice to the nations.

42:2 He will not shout, nor raise his voice, nor cause it to be heard in the street.

42:3 He won't break a bruised reed. He won't quench a dimly burning wick. He will faithfully bring justice.

42:4 He will not fail nor be discouraged, until he has set justice in the earth, and the islands will wait for his law."

TARGUM ISAIAH

us what shall happen unto us; Let them declare the former things what they were, that we may consider and know their event: or declare unto us the things that shall come.

41:23 Declare the things that are to come hereafter, that we may know whether ye worship idols' in which there is any profit, whether they are able to do good, or to do evil; that we may consider and argue together.

41:24 Behold, ye are nothing, and your works are to no purpose; that in which ye delight is an abomination.

41:25 I will certainly bring a king who is mightier than the north wind, and he shall go forth as the going forth of the sun in might from the east: I will strengthen him by my name, and he shall come, and tread the rulers of the nations under foot, as those who tread the dust under foot, as the potter who prepares the clay.

41:26 Who hath declared *this* from the beginning that we should know *it*? and beforetime, that we may say, It is true? Yea, there was none that foretold *it*; yea, none that declared *it*; yea, none that

TARGUM ISAIAH

heard your words.

41:27 The words of consolation which the prophets prophesied from of old concerning Zion, behold, they shall come to pass! and unto Jerusalem I will give one that bringeth good tidings.

41:28 And it was made known to me, that there was no man whose works were good, and of these there was none who would take counsel, that I should ask them, and they would answer a word.

41:29 Behold, all of them are nothing, and their work less than nothing: their thoughts are plunder and destruction.

42:1 Behold, my servant, the Messiah, whom I bring, my chosen in whom *one* delights: *as for* my WORD, I will put my Holy Spirit upon Him; He shall reveal my judgment unto the nations.

42:2 He shall not cry aloud, nor raise a clamour, and He shall not lift up His voice in the street.

42:3 The meek who are like a bruised reed He shall not break, and the poor who are as a glimmering wick with Him, He will not quench: He shall bring forth judgment unto truth.

42:4 He shall not faint nor be wea-

JEWISH PUBLICATION SOCIETY **1917**

41:23 Declare the things that are to come hereafter, that we may know that ye are gods; yea, do good, or do evil, that we may be dismayed, and behold it together.

41:24 Behold, ye are nothing, and your work a thing of nought; an abomination is he that chooseth you.

41:25 I have roused up one from the north, and he is come, from the rising of the sun one that calleth upon My name; and he shall come upon rulers as upon mortar, and as the potter treadeth clay.

41:26 Who hath declared from the beginning, that we may know? and beforetime, that we may say that he is right? Yea, there is none that declareth, yea, there is none that announceth, yea, there is none that heareth your utterances.

41:27 A harbinger unto Zion will I give: 'Behold, behold them', and to Jerusalem a messenger of good tidings.

41:28 And I look, but there is no man; even among them, but there is no counsellor, that, when I ask of them, can give an answer.

41:29 Behold, all of them, their works are vanity and nought; their molten images are wind and confusion.

42:1 Behold My servant, whom I uphold; Mine elect, in whom My soul delighteth; I have put My spirit upon him, he shall make the right to go forth to the nations.

42:2 He shall not cry, nor lift up, nor cause his voice to be heard in the street.

42:3 A bruised reed shall he not break, and the dimly burning wick shall he not quench; he shall make the right to go forth according to the truth.

42:4 He shall not fail nor be crushed, till he have set the right in the earth; and the isles shall wait for his teaching.

WORLD ENGLISH BIBLE

42:5 Thus says God Yahweh, he who created the heavens and stretched them out, he who spread out the earth and that which comes out of it, he who gives breath to its people and spirit to those who walk in it.

42:6 "I, Yahweh, have called you in righteousness, and will hold your hand, and will keep you, and make you a covenant for the people, as a light for the nations;

42:7 to open the blind eyes, to bring the prisoners out of the dungeon, and those who sit in darkness out of the prison.

42:8 "I am Yahweh. That is my name. I will not give my glory to another, nor my praise to engraved images.

42:9 Behold, the former things have happened, and I declare new things. I tell you about them before they come up."

42:10 Sing to Yahweh a new song, and his praise from the end of the earth, you who go down to the sea, and all that is therein, the islands and their inhabitants.

42:11 Let the wilderness and its cities raise their voices, with the villages that Kedar inhabits. Let the inhabitants of Sela sing. Let them shout from the top of the mountains!

42:12 Let them give glory to Yahweh, and declare his praise in the islands.

42:13 Yahweh will go out like a mighty man. He will stir up zeal like a man of war. He will raise a war cry. Yes, he will shout aloud. He will triumph over his enemies.

42:14 "I have been silent a long time. I have been quiet and restrained myself. Now I will cry out like a travailing woman. I will both gasp and pant.

42:15 I will destroy mountains and hills, and dry up all their herbs. I will make the rivers islands, and will dry up the pools.

TARGUM ISAIAH

ry, till He have established judgment in the earth; and the isles shall wait for His law.

42:5 Thus saith the God of eternity, who hath created the heavens and suspended them, *who* hath founded the earth, and hath given breath to its inhabitants, *even* to the people upon it, and spirit to them that walk therein.

42:6 I, the Lord, I will make Thee to grow in truth, and will hold Thine hand, and I will direct Thee, and give Thee for a covenant of the people, for a light of the Gentiles;

42:7 To open the eyes of the house of Israel, who are blind to the law, to bring back their captivity from among the nations, where they are like prisoners, and to redeem them from the servitude of the kingdoms being shut up as those that are bound in darkness.

42:8 I am the Lord: that is my name: and my glory in which I am revealed to you I will not give to another people; nor my praise to the worshippers of images.

42:9 Behold, the former things are come to pass, and new things do I declare: I apprize you of them before they come to pass.

TARGUM ISAIAH

42:10 Sing unto the Lord a new song, proclaim His Praise from the ends of the earth, ye that go down to the sea, and its fullness; the isles, and the inhabitants thereof.

42:11 Let the wilderness praise Him, and the cities that are in it, the villages which inhabit the wilderness of the Arabians; let the dead praise Him, when they go forth from their long abodes; from the tops of the mountains let them lift up their voice.

42:12 Let them ascribe glory unto the Lord, and declare His praise in the islands.

42:13 The Lord shall be seen to do mighty things: He shall reveal Himself in anger to do a mighty work by the word of *His* wrath; He shall reveal Himself to His enemies by His might in an earthquake.

42:14 I have given them prolongation for a long time, if the would but return to my law; but they did not return. My judgment shall be revealed upon them, as pains on a woman in travail; they shall be destroyed, and come to an end together.

42:15 I will make waste mountains

JEWISH PUBLICATION SOCIETY 1917

42:5 Thus saith God the LORD, He that created the heavens, and stretched them forth, He that spread forth the earth and that which cometh out of it, He that giveth breath unto the people upon it, and spirit to them that walk therein:

42:6 I the LORD have called thee in righteousness, and have taken hold of thy hand, and kept thee, and set thee for a covenant of the people, for a light of the nations;

42:7 To open the blind eyes, to bring out the prisoners from the dungeon, and them that sit in darkness out of the prison-house.

42:8 I am the LORD, that is My name; and My glory will I not give to another, neither My praise to graven images.

42:9 Behold, the former things are come to pass, and new things do I declare; before they spring forth I tell you of them.

42:10 Sing unto the LORD a new song, and His praise from the end of the earth; ye that go down to the sea, and all that is therein, the isles, and the inhabitants thereof.

42:11 Let the wilderness and the cities thereof lift up their voice, the villages that Kedar doth inhabit; let the inhabitants of Sela exult, let them shout from the top of the mountains.

42:12 Let them give glory unto the LORD, and declare His praise in the islands.

42:13 The LORD will go forth as a mighty man, He will stir up jealousy like a man of war; He will cry, yea, He will shout aloud, He will prove Himself mighty against His enemies.

42:14 I have long time held My peace, I have been still, and refrained Myself; now will I cry like a travailing woman, gasping and panting at once.

42:15 I will make waste mountains and hills, and dry up all their herbs; and I will make the rivers islands, and will dry up the pools.

WORLD ENGLISH BIBLE

42:16 I will bring the blind by a way that they don't know. I will lead them in paths that they don't know. I will make darkness light before them, and crooked places straight. I will do these things, and I will not forsake them.

42:17 "Those who trust in engraved images, who tell molten images, 'You are our gods' will be turned back. They will be utterly disappointed.

42:18 "Hear, you deaf, and look, you blind, that you may see.

42:19 Who is blind, but my servant? Or who is as deaf as my messenger whom I send? Who is as blind as he who is at peace, and as blind as Yahweh's servant?

42:20 You see many things, but don't observe. His ears are open, but he doesn't listen.

42:21 It pleased Yahweh, for his righteousness' sake, to magnify the law, and make it honorable.

42:22 But this is a robbed and plundered people. All of them are snared in holes, and they are hidden in prisons. They have become a prey, and no one delivers; and a spoil, and no one says, 'Restore them!'

42:23 Who is there among you who will give ear to this? Who will listen and hear for the time to come?

42:24 Who gave Jacob as plunder, and Israel to the robbers? Didn't Yahweh, he against whom we have sinned? For they would not walk in his ways, and they disobeyed his law.

42:25 Therefore he poured the fierceness of his anger on him, and the strength of battle; and it set him on fire all around, but he didn't know; and it burned him, but he didn't take it to heart."

43:1 But now thus says Yahweh who created you, Jacob, and he who formed you, Israel: "Don't be afraid, for I have redeemed you. I have called you by your name. You are mine.

TARGUM ISAIAH

and hills, and dry up all their herbs; and I will make the rivers islands, and I will dry up the pools.

42:16 And I will lead the house of Israel, who are like the blind, in a way which they knew not, in paths they have not learned I will lead them; I will make darkness light before them, and the rugged place a plain. These things will I do for them, and will not forsake them.

42:17 They shall be turned back, they shall be ashamed, that worship images, that say to the molten images, Ye are our gods.

42:18 Ye wicked, (who are like the deaf,) have ye no ears? hear ye! and ye sinners, (who are like the blind,) have ye no eyes?

42:19 Is it not so? if the wicked and the sinners, to whom I have sent my prophets, will repent, they shall be called my servants; but the wicked shall be paid with vengeance for their sins; but if they will repent, they shall be called the servants of the Lord.

42:20 Ye see many things, but ye observe not; having your ears opened, but ye receive not instruction.

TARGUM ISAIAH

42:21 The Lord delights in justifying Israel; He will magnify those that obey His law, yea, He will strengthen them.

42:22 But this is a people robbed, and spoiled, and all their young men are covered with confusion, and shut up in prison-houses: they are for a prey, and there is none who delivereth; for a spoil, and none saith, Restore.

42:23 Who is there among you that will listen to this? *who* will hearken, and consider for the time to come?

42:24 Who delivered Jacob for a spoil, and Israel to the robbers? Was it not the Lord? Because they have sinned against Him; and they would not walk in His righteous paths before Him, neither would they receive the instruction of His law.

42:25 Therefore He hath poured upon them the fury of His anger, and hath brought upon them the strength of His warriors, and hath slain them round about, and they knew *it* not; and they ruled over them, and they did not lay His fear to heart.

43:1 But now thus saith the Lord that created thee, O Jacob, and

JEWISH PUBLICATION SOCIETY 1917

42:16 And I will bring the blind by a way that they knew not, in paths that they knew not will I lead them; I will make darkness light before them, and rugged places plain. These things will I do, and I will not leave them undone.

42:17 They shall be turned back, greatly ashamed, that trust in graven images, that say unto molten images: 'Ye are our gods.'

42:18 Hear, ye deaf, and look, ye blind, that ye may see.

42:19 Who is blind, but My servant? Or deaf, as My messenger that I send? Who is blind as he that is wholehearted, and blind as the LORD'S servant?

42:20 Seeing many things, thou observest not; opening the ears, he heareth not.

42:21 The LORD was pleased, for His righteousness' sake, to make the teaching great and glorious.

42:22 But this is a people robbed and spoiled, they are all of them snared in holes, and they are hid in prison-houses; they are for a prey, and none delivereth, for a spoil, and none saith: 'Restore.'

42:23 Who among you will give ear to this? Who will hearken and hear for the time to come?

42:24 Who gave Jacob for a spoil, and Israel to the robbers? Did not the LORD? He against whom we have sinned, and in whose ways they would not walk, neither were they obedient unto His law.

42:25 Therefore He poured upon him the fury of His anger, and the strength of battle; and it set him on fire round about, yet he knew not, and it burned him, yet he laid it not to heart.

43:1 But now thus saith the LORD that created thee, O Jacob, and He that formed thee, O Israel: Fear not, for I have redeemed thee, I have called thee by thy name, thou art Mine.

WORLD ENGLISH BIBLE

43:2 When you pass through the waters, I will be with you; and through the rivers, they will not overflow you. When you walk through the fire, you will not be burned, and flame will not scorch you.

43:3 For I am Yahweh your God, the Holy One of Israel, your Savior. I have given Egypt as your ransom, Ethiopia and Seba in your place.

43:4 Since you have been precious and honored in my sight, and I have loved you; therefore I will give people in your place, and nations instead of your life.

43:5 Don't be afraid; for I am with you. I will bring your seed from the east, and gather you from the west.

43:6 I will tell the north, 'Give them up!' and tell the south, 'Don't hold them back! Bring my sons from far, and my daughters from the ends of the earth—

43:7 everyone who is called by my name, and whom I have created for my glory, whom I have formed, yes, whom I have made.'"

43:8 Bring out the blind people who have eyes, and the deaf who have ears.

43:9 Let all the nations be gathered together, and let the peoples be assembled. Who among them can declare this, and show us former things? Let them bring their witnesses, that they may be justified; or let them hear, and say, "That is true."

43:10 "You are my witnesses," says Yahweh, "With my servant whom I have chosen; that you may know and believe me, and understand that I am he. Before me there was no God formed, neither will there be after me.

43:11 I myself am Yahweh; and besides me there is no savior.

TARGUM ISAIAH

He that formed thee, O Israel, Fear not, for I have redeemed thee, I have called thee who art mine by thy name.

43:2 For at first when ye did pass the Red sea my WORD was your support. Pharaoh and the Egyptians, who were as many as the waters of the river, did not prevail against you. And again, when ye came amongst nations, who were as mighty as fire, they did not prevail against you; and kingdoms, which were strong as a flame, did not destroy you;

43:3 Because I am the Lord thy God, the Holy One of Israel, thy Saviour: I gave Egypt in exchange for thee, Ethiopia, and Seba, in thy stead.

43:4 Ever since I loved thee, thou wast precious; yea, I loved thee dearly, and I gave nations instead of thee, and kingdoms for thy soul.

43:5 Fear not, for my WORD shall be thy support; I will bring thy children from the east, I will bring together thy captivity from the west.

43:6 I will say to the north, Bring; and to the south, Keep not back: bring my sons from afar, and the

TARGUM ISAIAH

captivity of my people from the ends of the earth.

43:7 All these things *shall come to pass* for the sake of your righteous fathers, upon whom my name was called, yea, for my glory I have created them. I will restore their captivity, yea, I will work wonders for them.

43:8 When I brought forth my people from Egypt, they were like the blind, although they had eyes; and like the deaf, although they had ears.

43:9 Let all the nations be gathered together, let the kingdoms be brought together: who among them can declare this, and give us the joyful tidings of old? Let them bring forth their witnesses, that they may be justified; let them hear, and let them speak the truth.

43:10 Ye are my witnesses, saith the Lord, and my servant, the Messiah, in whom is my delight, in order that ye may know, and that ye may believe in me, and understand that I am He who was from the beginning; yea, ages after ages are mine, and beside me there is no god.

43:11 I, *even* I, am the Lord, and

JEWISH PUBLICATION SOCIETY 1917

43:2 When thou passest through the waters, I will be with thee, and through the rivers, they shall not overflow thee; when thou walkest through the fire, thou shalt not be burned, neither shall the flame kindle upon thee.

43:3 For I am the LORD thy God, The Holy One of Israel, thy Saviour; I have given Egypt as thy ransom, Ethiopia and Seba for thee.

43:4 Since thou art precious in My sight, and honourable, and I have loved thee; therefore will I give men for thee, and peoples for thy life.

43:5 Fear not, for I am with thee; I will bring thy seed from the east, and gather thee from the west;

43:6 I will say to the north: 'Give up,' and to the south: 'Keep not back, bring My sons from far, and My daughters from the end of the earth;

43:7 Every one that is called by My name, and whom I have created for My glory, I have formed him, yea, I have made him.'

43:8 The blind people that have eyes shall be brought forth, and the deaf that have ears.

43:9 All the nations are gathered together, and the peoples are assembled; who among them can declare this, and announce to us former things? Let them bring their witnesses, that they may be justified; and let them hear, and say: 'It is truth.'

43:10 Ye are My witnesses, saith the LORD, and My servant whom I have chosen; that ye may know and believe Me, and understand that I am He; before Me there was no God formed, neither shall any be after Me.

43:11 I, even I, am the LORD; and beside Me there is no saviour.

WORLD ENGLISH BIBLE

43:12 I have declared, I have saved, and I have shown; and there was no strange god among you. Therefore you are my witnesses," says Yahweh, "and I am God.

43:13 Yes, since the day was I am he; and there is no one who can deliver out of my hand. I will work, and who can hinder it?"

43:14 Thus says Yahweh, your Redeemer, the Holy One of Israel: "For your sake, I have sent to Babylon, and I will bring all of them down as fugitives, even the Chaldeans, in the ships of their rejoicing.

43:15 I am Yahweh, your Holy One, the Creator of Israel, your King."

43:16 Thus says Yahweh, who makes a way in the sea, and a path in the mighty waters;

43:17 who brings forth the chariot and horse, the army and the mighty man (they lie down together, they shall not rise; they are extinct, they are quenched like a wick):

43:18 "Don't remember the former things, and don't consider the things of old.

43:19 Behold, I will do a new thing. It springs forth now. Don't you know it? I will even make a way in the wilderness, and rivers in the desert.

43:20 The animals of the field shall honor me, the jackals and the ostriches; because I give water in the wilderness and rivers in the desert, to give drink to my people, my chosen,

43:21 the people which I formed for myself, that they might set forth my praise.

43:22 Yet you have not called on me, Jacob; but you have been weary of me, Israel.

43:23 You have not brought me of your sheep for burnt offerings; neither have you honored me with your sacrifices. I have not burdened you with offerings, nor wearied you with frankincense.

TARGUM ISAIAH

beside me there is no saviour.

43:12 I, I have declared unto Abraham your father what would come to pass; I, I redeemed you out of Egypt, as I swore to him between the pieces; and I, I have made you to hear the doctrine of my law from Sinai, and ye are still alive, when there was no strange god among you; yea, ye are my witnesses, saith the Lord, that I am God.

43:13 Yea, from eternity I am He; and there is none that can deliver out of my hand: I will do it, and who shall turn it back?

43:14 Thus saith the Lord, your Redeemer, the Holy One of Israel, Because of your sins I led you captive to Babylon; but I will prostrate all of them with their oars, yea, the Chaldeans in the ships of which they boast.

43:15 I am the Lord, your Holy One, the Creator of Israel, your King.

43:16 Thus saith the Lord, I am He who prepared a way in the sea, and a path in mighty waters.

43:17 I who brought out the chariots, and horses, *and* a great host, yea, much people; they were swallowed up together, they did not

TARGUM ISAIAH

rise, they were extinguished, they are extinct like the glimmering wick is extinguished.

43:18 Remember not the former things, neither consider the things of old.

43:19 Behold, I make a new thing, and now it shall be revealed: and will ye not know it? I will even make a way in the wilderness, and rivers in the desert.

43:20 They shall honour me, when I make habitable provinces at the desert, and the places where the dragons and the daughters of the ostrich dwell; because I will give water in the wilderness, rivers in the desert, to give drink to the captives of my people, in whom I delight.

43:21 This people have I prepared for my service, they shall declare my praise.

43:22 It hath been said by the prophets, that ye of the house of Jacob have not met together for my worship; but that ye were weary of the doctrine of my law, O Israel.

43:23 Thou hast not brought unto me the lambs of thy burnt offerings, and with thy holy sacrifices thou hast not honoured me. I

43:12 I have declared, and I have saved, and I have announced, and there was no strange god among you; therefore ye are My witnesses, saith the LORD, and I am God.

43:13 Yea, since the day was I am He, and there is none that can deliver out of My hand; I will work, and who can reverse it?

43:14 Thus saith the LORD, your Redeemer, The Holy One of Israel: For your sake I have sent to Babylon, and I will bring down all of them as fugitives, even the Chaldeans, in the ships of their shouting.

43:15 I am the LORD, your Holy One, the Creator of Israel, your King.

43:16 Thus saith the LORD, who maketh a way in the sea, and a path in the mighty waters;

43:17 Who bringeth forth the chariot and horse, the army and the power—they lie down together, they shall not rise, they are extinct, they are quenched as a wick:

43:18 Remember ye not the former things, neither consider the things of old.

43:19 Behold, I will do a new thing; now shall it spring forth; shall ye not know it? I will even make a way in the wilderness, and rivers in the desert.

43:20 The beasts of the field shall honour Me, the jackals and the ostriches; because I give waters in the wilderness, and rivers in the desert, to give drink to My people, Mine elect;

43:21 The people which I formed for Myself, that they might tell of My praise.

43:22 Yet thou hast not called upon Me, O Jacob, neither hast thou wearied thyself about Me, O Israel.

43:23 Thou hast not brought Me the small cattle of thy burnt-offerings; neither hast thou honoured Me with thy sacrifices. I have not burdened thee with a meal-offering, nor wearied thee with frankincense.

WORLD ENGLISH BIBLE

43:24 You have bought me no sweet cane with money, nor have you filled me with the fat of your sacrifices; but you have burdened me with your sins. You have wearied me with your iniquities.

43:25 I, even I, am he who blots out your transgressions for my own sake; and I will not remember your sins.

43:26 Put me in remembrance. Let us plead together. Set forth your case, that you may be justified.

43:27 Your first father sinned, and your teachers have transgressed against me.

43:28 Therefore I will profane the princes of the sanctuary; and I will make Jacob a curse, and Israel an insult."

44:1 Yet listen now, Jacob my servant, and Israel, whom I have chosen.

44:2 This is what Yahweh who made you, and formed you from the womb, who will help you says: "Don't be afraid, Jacob my servant; and you, Jeshurun, whom I have chosen.

44:3 For I will pour water on him who is thirsty, and streams on the dry ground. I will pour my Spirit on your seed, and my blessing on your offspring:

44:4 and they will spring up among the grass, as willows by the watercourses.

44:5 One will say, 'I am Yahweh's;' and another will be called by the name of Jacob; and another will write with his hand 'to Yahweh,' and honor the name of Israel."

44:6 This is what Yahweh, the King of Israel, and his Redeemer, Yahweh of Armies, says: "I am the first, and I am the last; and besides me there is no God.

44:7 Who is like me? Who will call, and will declare it, and set it in order for me, since I established the ancient people? Let them declare the things that are coming, and that will happen.

44:8 Don't fear, neither be afraid. Haven't I declared it to you long ago, and shown it? You are my witnesses. Is there a God besides me? Indeed, there is not. I don't know any other Rock."

TARGUM ISAIAH

have not caused thee to multiply offerings, neither did I burden thee with frankincense.

43:24 Thou hast not bought for me the aromatic reed with silver; with the fat of thy holy sacrifices thou hast not anointed mine altar; but thou hast multiplied thy sins before me; thou hast burdened me with thine iniquities.

43:25 I, *even* I, am He who forgiveth thy sins for the sake of my name, and thy sins shall not be remembered.

43:26 Speak now, we will plead together, declare thou for the purpose, that thou mayest justify thyself, if thou art able to do so.

43:27 Thy first father hath sinned, and thy teachers have rebelled against my WORD.

43:28 Therefore I have profaned the princes of the sanctuary, and I have delivered Jacob to the slaughter, and Israel to reproaches.

44:1 Yet now hear, O Jacob, my servant; and Israel, whom I have chosen:

44:2 Thus saith the Lord, thy Maker; and He that formed thee from the womb, He will help thee; Fear not, O Jacob, my servant, and thou, O Israel, whom I have

TARGUM ISAIAH

chosen.

44:3 For as waters are discharged upon the thirsty land, and are set flowing upon the dry land, so will I give my Holy Spirit unto thy children, and my blessing unto thy children's children.

44:4 The righteous shall grow, and tender and delicate as the flowers of the grass, as a tree that sends forth its roots by the streams of waters.

44:5 This one shall say, I am of them that fear the Lord, and another shall pray in the name of the God of Jacob; this one shall offer his oblation before the Lord, and draw near in the name of Israel.

44:6 Thus saith the King of Israel, and His Redeemer, the Lord of hosts; I am He who was from the beginning, yea, eternities of eternities are mine; and beside me there is no God.

44:7 Who like me shall proclaim this, shall declare it, and set it in order before me, from the time that I appointed the ancient people? and let them declare unto us the things that are coming, and shall come.

44:8 Fear ye not, neither be afraid:

JEWISH PUBLICATION SOCIETY 1917

43:24 Thou hast bought Me no sweet cane with money, neither hast thou satisfied Me with the fat of thy sacrifices; but thou hast burdened Me with thy sins, thou hast wearied Me with thine iniquities.

43:25 I, even I, am He that blotteth out thy transgressions for Mine own sake; and thy sins I will not remember.

43:26 Put Me in remembrance, let us plead together; declare thou, that thou mayest be justified.

43:27 Thy first father sinned, and thine intercessors have transgressed against Me.

43:28 Therefore I have profaned the princes of the sanctuary, and I have given Jacob to condemnation, and Israel to reviling.

44:1 Yet now hear, O Jacob My servant, and Israel, whom I have chosen;

44:2 Thus saith the LORD that made thee, and formed thee from the womb, who will help thee: Fear not, O Jacob My servant, and thou, Jeshurun, whom I have chosen.

44:3 For I will pour water upon the thirsty land, and streams upon the dry ground; I will pour My spirit upon thy seed, and My blessing upon thine offspring;

44:4 And they shall spring up among the grass, as willows by the watercourses.

44:5 One shall say: 'I am the LORD'S'; and another shall call himself by the name of Jacob; and another shall subscribe with his hand unto the LORD, and surname himself by the name of Israel.

44:6 Thus saith the LORD, the King of Israel, and his Redeemer the LORD of hosts: I am the first, and I am the last, and beside Me there is no God.

44:7 And who, as I, can proclaim—let him declare it, and set it in order for Me—since I appointed the ancient people? And the things that are coming, and that shall come to pass, let them declare.

44:8 Fear ye not, neither be afraid; have I not announced unto thee of old, and declared it? And ye are My witnesses. Is there a God beside Me? Yea, there is no Rock; I know not any.

WORLD ENGLISH BIBLE

44:9 Everyone who makes an engraved image is vain. The things that they delight in will not profit. Their own witnesses don't see, nor know, that they may be disappointed.

44:10 Who has fashioned a god, or molds an image that is profitable for nothing?

44:11 Behold, all his fellows will be disappointed; and the workmen are mere men. Let them all be gathered together. Let them stand up. They will fear. They will be put to shame together.

44:12 The blacksmith takes an axe, works in the coals, fashions it with hammers, and works it with his strong arm. He is hungry, and his strength fails; he drinks no water, and is faint.

44:13 The carpenter stretches out a line. He marks it out with a pencil. He shapes it with planes. He marks it out with compasses, and shapes it like the figure of a man, with the beauty of a man, to reside in a house.

44:14 He cuts down cedars for himself, and takes the cypress and the oak, and strengthens for himself one among the trees of the forest. He plants a fir tree, and the rain nourishes it.

44:15 Then it will be for a man to burn; and he takes some of it, and warms himself. Yes, he burns it, and bakes bread. Yes, he makes a god, and worships it; he makes it an engraved image, and falls down to it.

44:16 He burns part of it in the fire. With part of it, he eats meat. He roasts a roast, and is satisfied. Yes, he warms himself, and says, "Aha! I am warm. I have seen the fire."

44:17 The rest of it he makes into a god, even his engraved image. He bows down to it and worships, and prays to it, and says, "Deliver me; for you are my god!"

44:18 They don't know, neither do they consider: for he has shut their eyes, that they can't see; and their hearts, that they can't understand.

TARGUM ISAIAH

have not I told thee from that time, and have declared it? ye also are my witnesses, that there is no God beside me, and there is none strong, except he to whom strength is given from me.

44:9 They that make images *are* all of them vanity, and worship what does not profit them; and they are witnesses against themselves, that they do not see, nor know, that they may be ashamed.

44:10 Whoever maketh a god or a molten image, *it is* for no purpose.

44:11 Behold, all their worshippers shall be ashamed, and the working artificers are workmen of the sons of men; let them all be gathered together, let them stand up; they shall fear and be confounded together.

44:12 The smith maketh an axe out of iron, and bloweth the coals in the fire, and maketh it firm with the hammer, and worketh it with the power of his strength; but when he that worketh it is hungry, and does not eat bread, he hath no strength; and if he is thirsty, and drinketh no water, he fainteth.

44:13 The carpenter stretcheth out the line, he applieth the plummet

TARGUM ISAIAH

to it; he carveth it with a knife, and he dove-taileth it together, and he maketh it after the likeness of a man, according to the beauty of a woman, that it may remain in the house.

44:14 He heweth for himself cedars and taketh the scarlet oak, and the chestnut, and seasons them. He plants the ash amongst the trees of the forest, and the rain nourisheth it.

44:15 That it may *serve* a man to burn: and he taketh thereof, and warmeth himself; yea, he kindleth *it*, and baketh bread; yea, he maketh it a god, and worshippeth *it*; he formeth it an image, and prayeth to it.

44:16 He burneth half thereof in the fire; and by the other half he eateth flesh, he roasteth meat, and is satisfied; he also warmeth himself, and saith, Aha, I am warm, I have seen the fire.

44:17 And the remainder thereof he maketh a god; to the image he boweth down; he becometh servile to it, and prayeth to it, and saith, Deliver me; for thou art my god.

44:18 They know not, neither do they understand; for their eyes

JEWISH PUBLICATION SOCIETY 1917

44:9 They that fashion a graven image are all of them vanity, and their delectable things shall not profit; and their own witnesses see not, nor know; that they may be ashamed.

44:10 Who hath fashioned a god, or molten an image that is profitable for nothing?

44:11 Behold, all the fellows thereof shall be ashamed; and the craftsmen skilled above men; let them all be gathered together, let them stand up; they shall fear, they shall be ashamed together.

44:12 The smith maketh an axe, and worketh in the coals, and fashioneth it with hammers, and worketh it with his strong arm; yea, he is hungry, and his strength faileth; he drinketh no water, and is faint.

44:13 The carpenter stretcheth out a line; he marketh it out with a pencil; he fitteth it with planes, and he marketh it out with the compasses, and maketh it after the figure of a man, according to the beauty of a man, to dwell in the house.

44:14 He heweth him down cedars, and taketh the ilex and the oak, and strengtheneth for himself one among the trees of the forest; he planteth a bay-tree, and the rain doth nourish it.

44:15 Then a man useth it for fuel; and he taketh thereof, and warmeth himself; yea, he kindleth it, and baketh bread; yea, he maketh a god, and worshippeth it; he maketh it a graven image, and falleth down thereto.

44:16 He burneth the half thereof in the fire; with the half thereof he eateth flesh; he roasteth roast, and is satisfied; yea, he warmeth himself, and saith: 'Aha, I am warm, I have seen the fire';

44:17 And the residue thereof he maketh a god, even his graven image; he falleth down unto it and worshippeth, and prayeth unto it, and saith: 'Deliver me, for thou art my god.'

44:18 They know not, neither do they understand; for their eyes are bedaubed, that they cannot see, and their hearts, that they cannot understand.

WORLD ENGLISH BIBLE

44:19 No one thinks, neither is there knowledge nor understanding to say, "I have burned part of it in the fire. Yes, I have also baked bread on its coals. I have roasted meat and eaten it. Shall I make the rest of it into an abomination? Shall I bow down to a tree trunk?"

44:20 He feeds on ashes. A deceived heart has turned him aside; and he can't deliver his soul, nor say, "Isn't there a lie in my right hand?"

44:21 Remember these things, Jacob and Israel; for you are my servant. I have formed you. You are my servant. Israel, you will not be forgotten by me.

44:22 I have blotted out, as a thick cloud, your transgressions, and, as a cloud, your sins. Return to me, for I have redeemed you.

44:23 Sing, you heavens, for Yahweh has done it! Shout, you lower parts of the earth! Break out into singing, you mountains, O forest, all of your trees, for Yahweh has redeemed Jacob, and will glorify himself in Israel.

44:24 Thus says Yahweh, your Redeemer, and he who formed you from the womb: "I am Yahweh, who makes all things; who alone stretches out the heavens; who spreads out the earth by myself;

44:25 who frustrates the signs of the liars, and makes diviners mad; who turns wise men backward, and makes their knowledge foolish;

44:26 who confirms the word of his servant, and performs the counsel of his messengers; who says of Jerusalem, 'She will be inhabited;' and of the cities of Judah, 'They will be built,' and 'I will raise up its waste places;'

44:27 who says to the deep, 'Be dry,' and 'I will dry up your rivers;'

44:28 Who says of Cyrus, 'He is my shepherd, and shall perform all my pleasure,' even saying of Jerusalem, 'She will be built;' and of the temple, 'Your foundation will be laid.'"

TARGUM ISAIAH

are closely shut up, so that they cannot see, and their heart, that they cannot understand.

44:19 And he does not consider in his heart, neither hath he knowledge or understanding to say, Half of it I have burned in the fire; yea, I have baked bread upon the coals thereof; I have roasted flesh and eaten *it*: and shall I make the remnant thereof a god? shall I bow myself down to the stock of a tree?

44:20 Behold his god, part of it is ashes; his undiscerning heart has caused him to err, so that he cannot deliver his soul, nor say, Is it not a lie which I have made with my right hand?

44:21 Remember these things, O Jacob and Israel; for thou art my servant: I have formed thee that thou shouldest serve me, *that* thou, O Israel, shouldest not forget my fear.

44:22 I have blotted out, as a thick cloud, thy transgressions, and as a cloud vanisheth away, all thy sins: return to my worship, for I have redeemed thee.

44:23 Sing, O ye heavens; for the Lord hath wrought redemption for His people: Let the founda-

TARGUM ISAIAH

tions of the earth rejoice; rejoice, O mountains, in praise, O forest, and all the trees therein! for the Lord hath redeemed Jacob, and will glorify Himself in Israel.

44:24 Thus saith the Lord, who hath redeemed thee, and who hath prepared thee from the womb, I am the Lord that maketh all things, I have suspended the heavens by my WORD, I have laid the foundations of the earth by my strength;

44:25 *That* frustrateth the tokens of the liars, and maketh diviners mad; *that* turneth wise men backward, and bringeth their knowledge into contempt.

44:26 That confirmeth the word of His righteous servants, and performeth the counsel of His messengers, that saith to Jerusalem, Thou shalt be inhabited; and concerning the cities of the house of Judah, They shall be built; and her desolated places I will raise up.

44:27 That saith to Babylon, Be desolate, and I will dry up *thy* rivers.

44:28 That promises Cyrus that He will give him a kingdom; and *that* he shall establish all my pleasure,

JEWISH PUBLICATION SOCIETY 1917

44:19 And none considereth in his heart, neither is there knowledge nor understanding to say: 'I have burned the half of it in the fire; yea, also I have baked bread upon the coals thereof; I have roasted flesh and eaten it; and shall I make the residue thereof an abomination? Shall I fall down to the stock of a tree?'

44:20 He striveth after ashes, a deceived heart hath turned him aside, that he cannot deliver his soul, nor say: 'Is there not a lie in my right hand?'

44:21 Remember these things, O Jacob, and Israel, for thou art My servant; I have formed thee, thou art Mine own servant; O Israel, thou shouldest not forget Me.

44:22 I have blotted out, as a thick cloud, thy transgressions, and, as a cloud, thy sins; return unto Me, for I have redeemed thee.

44:23 Sing, O ye heavens, for the LORD hath done it; shout, ye lowest parts of the earth; break forth into singing, ye mountains, O forest, and every tree therein; for the LORD hath redeemed Jacob, and doth glorify Himself in Israel.

44:24 Thus saith the LORD, thy Redeemer, and He that formed thee from the womb: I am the LORD, that maketh all things; that stretched forth the heavens alone; that spread abroad the earth by Myself;

44:25 That frustrateth the tokens of the imposters, and maketh diviners mad; that turneth wise men backward, and maketh their knowledge foolish;

44:26 That confirmeth the word of His servant, and performeth the counsel of His messengers; that saith of Jerusalem: 'She shall be inhabited'; and of the cities of Judah: 'They shall be built, and I will raise up the waste places thereof';

44:27 That saith to the deep: 'Be dry, and I will dry up thy rivers';

44:28 That saith of Cyrus: 'He is My shepherd, and shall perform all My pleasure'; even saying of Jerusalem: 'She shall be built'; and to the temple: 'My foundation shall be laid.'

WORLD ENGLISH BIBLE

45:1 Thus says Yahweh to his anointed, to Cyrus, whose right hand I have held, to subdue nations before him, and strip kings of their armor; to open the doors before him, and the gates shall not be shut:

45:2 "I will go before you, and make the rough places smooth. I will break the doors of brass in pieces, and cut apart the bars of iron.

45:3 I will give you the treasures of darkness, and hidden riches of secret places, that you may know that it is I, Yahweh, who call you by your name, even the God of Israel.

45:4 For Jacob my servant's sake, and Israel my chosen, I have called you by your name. I have surnamed you, though you have not known me.

45:5 I am Yahweh, and there is none else. Besides me, there is no God. I will strengthen you, though you have not known me;

45:6 that they may know from the rising of the sun, and from the west, that there is none besides me. I am Yahweh, and there is no one else.

45:7 I form the light, and create darkness. I make peace, and create calamity. I am Yahweh, who does all these things.

45:8 Distil, you heavens, from above, and let the skies pour down righteousness. Let the earth open, that it may bring forth salvation, and let it cause righteousness to spring up with it. I, Yahweh, have created it.

45:9 Woe to him who strives with his Maker—a clay pot among the clay pots of the earth! Shall the clay ask him who fashions it, 'What are you making?' or your work, 'He has no hands?'

45:10 Woe to him who says to a father, 'What have you become the father of?' or to a mother, 'To what have you given birth?'"

45:11 Thus says Yahweh, the Holy One of Israel, and his Maker: "You ask me about the things that are to come, concerning my sons, and you command me concerning the work of my hands!

TARGUM ISAIAH

even to him that saith to Jerusalem, Thou shalt be built, and the temple shall have its foundation laid.

45:1 Thus saith the Lord to His anointed, to Cyrus, whom I hold firm by his right hand, to deliver the nations unto him; and I will loose the loins of the kings, to open the doors before him, and the gates shall not be shut.

45:2 My WORD shall go before thee, I will have a way in the plains; I will break in pieces the doors of brass, and cut in sunder the bars of iron.

45:3 And I will give thee the treasures of darkness, and hidden treasures, that thou mayest know, that I, the Lord, who called *thee* by thy name, *am* the God of Israel.

45:4 For Jacob my servant's sake, and Israel my elect, yea, I have called thee by thy name; I have guided thee, though thou hast not known that thou shouldest fear me.

45:5 I *am* the Lord, and none else; there is no God beside me: I have supported thee, though thou hast not known that thou shouldest fear me:

TARGUM ISAIAH

45:6 That they may know from the rising of the sun, and from the west; I am the Lord, and *there is* none else:

45:7 Who prepares the light, and creates darkness, makes peace, and creates punishment for evil. I the Lord do all these things.

45:8 Let the heavens drop down from above, and the clouds flow with good, let the earth open itself, and the *dead* live, and let righteousness be revealed together; I the Lord have created them.

45:9 Woe to him who thinks of striving against the words of his Creator, and trusts that the images of a potter shall do him good, which are made out of the dust of the earth. Is it possible, that the clay could say to him that worketh it, Thou hast not made me? or thy work, He hath no hands?

45:10 Woe to him that saith to *his* father, What begettest thou? and to his mother, What hast thou brought forth?

45:11 Thus saith the Lord, the Holy One of Israel, and He that formed him, Ye question me about things concerning my people, which shall come to pass; and will ye com-

JEWISH PUBLICATION SOCIETY 1917

45:1 Thus saith the LORD to His anointed, to Cyrus, whose right hand I have holden, to subdue nations before him, and to loose the loins of kings; to open the doors before him, and that the gates may not be shut:

45:2 I will go before thee, and make the crooked places straight; I will break in pieces the doors of brass, and cut in sunder the bars of iron;

45:3 And I will give thee the treasures of darkness, and hidden riches of secret places, that thou mayest know that I am the LORD, who call thee by thy name, even the God of Israel.

45:4 For the sake of Jacob My servant, and Israel Mine elect, I have called thee by thy name, I have surnamed thee, though thou hast not known Me.

45:5 I am the LORD, and there is none else, beside Me there is no God; I have girded thee, though thou hast not known Me;

45:6 That they may know from the rising of the sun, and from the west, that there is none beside Me; I am the LORD; and there is none else;

45:7 I form the light, and create darkness; I make peace, and create evil; I am the LORD, that doeth all these things.

45:8 Drop down, ye heavens, from above, and let the skies pour down righteousness; let the earth open, that they may bring forth salvation, and let her cause righteousness to spring up together; I the LORD have created it.

45:9 Woe unto him that striveth with his Maker, as a potsherd with the potsherds of the earth! Shall the clay say to him that fashioned it: 'What makest thou?' Or: 'Thy work, it hath no hands'?

45:10 Woe unto him that saith unto his father. 'Wherefore begettest thou?' Or to a woman: 'Wherefore travailest thou?'

45:11 Thus saith the LORD, the Holy One of Israel, and his Maker: Ask Me of the things that are to come; concerning My sons, and concerning the work of My hands, command ye Me.

WORLD ENGLISH BIBLE

45:12 I have made the earth, and created man on it. I, even my hands, have stretched out the heavens; and I have commanded all their army.

45:13 I have raised him up in righteousness, and I will make straight all his ways. He shall build my city, and he shall let my exiles go free, not for price nor reward," says Yahweh of Armies.

45:14 Thus says Yahweh: "The labor of Egypt, and the merchandise of Ethiopia, and the Sabeans, men of stature, shall come over to you, and they shall be yours. They will go after you. They shall come over in chains; and they will bow down to you. They will make supplication to you: 'Surely God is in you; and there is none else. There is no other god.

45:15 Most certainly you are a God who hidden yourself, God of Israel, the Savior.'"

45:16 They will be disappointed, yes, confounded, all of them. Those who are makers of idols will go into confusion together.

45:17 Israel will be saved by Yahweh with an everlasting salvation. You will not be disappointed nor confounded to ages everlasting.

45:18 For thus says Yahweh who created the heavens, the God who formed the earth and made it, who established it and didn't create it a waste, who formed it to be inhabited: "I am Yahweh; and there is no other.

45:19 I have not spoken in secret, in a place of the land of darkness. I didn't say to the seed of Jacob, 'Seek me in vain.' I, Yahweh, speak righteousness. I declare things that are right.

45:20 "Assemble yourselves and come. Draw near together, you who have escaped from the nations. Those have no knowledge who carry the wood of their engraved image, and pray to a god that can't save.

45:21 Declare and present it. Yes, let them take counsel together. Who has shown this from ancient time? Who has declared it of old? Haven't I, Yahweh? There is no other God besides me, a just God and a Savior; There is no one besides me.

TARGUM ISAIAH

mand me concerning the work of my power?

45:12 It is I who have made the earth by my WORD, and I have created man upon it; it is I who have suspended the heavens by my power, and I have laid the foundation of all the hosts of them.

45:13 It is I who will verily bring him forth publicly, and all his paths I will direct: he shall build my city, and he shall let the captives of my people go, not for a price nor for money, saith the Lord of hosts.

45:14 Thus saith the Lord, the wealth of Egypt, and the merchandize of Ethiopia and of the men of the Sabeans, the men of traffic, shall come unto thee, and thine they shall be: they shall walk according to thy command ; they shall pass along in chains; and they shall bow down unto thee, and shall supplicate thee, saying, Verily God *is* in thee, and there is no God whatever besides Him.

45:15 Verily, thou art He, who dost make Thy Shekinah to dwell in the highest heaven, O God of Israel, the Saviour!

45:16 They shall be ashamed and confounded, all of them: the wor-

TARGUM ISAIAH

shippers of images shall walk in confusion.

45:17 Israel shall be saved by the WORD of the Lord with an everlasting salvation: ye shall not be ashamed nor confounded for ever, yea, for ages after ages.

45:18 For thus saith the Lord that created the heavens; He who laid the foundation of the earth and made it, is God; He formed it, He created it not in vain; but He formed it, that the sons of man should multiply upon it. I am the Lord, and *there is* none else.

45:19 I have not spoken in secret, in a dark place of the earth: I said not unto the seed of the house of Jacob, Seek me reverently in vain: I the Lord speak the truth, declaring upright things.

45:20 Assemble yourselves and come; draw near together, *ye* that *are* escaped of the nations: they know nothing that carry about their wooden images, and *who* pray unto a god who shall not save.

45:21 Tell ye, and draw ye near; yea, take counsel together: who hath declared this from ancient time? *who* hath told it from that time? *have* not I the Lord? and

JEWISH PUBLICATION SOCIETY 1917

45:12 I, even I, have made the earth, and created man upon it; I, even My hands, have stretched out the heavens, and all their host have I commanded.

45:13 I have roused him up in victory, and I make level all his ways; he shall build My city, and he shall let Mine exiles go free, not for price nor reward, saith the LORD of hosts.

45:14 Thus saith the LORD: the labour of Egypt, and the merchandise of Ethiopia, and of the Sabeans, men of stature, shall come over unto thee, and they shall be thine; they shall go after thee, in chains they shall come over; and they shall fall down unto thee, they shall make supplication unto thee: Surely God is in thee, and there is none else, there is no other God.

45:15 Verily Thou art a God that hidest Thyself, O God of Israel, the Saviour.

45:16 They shall be ashamed, yea, confounded, all of them; they shall go in confusion together that are makers of idols.

45:17 O Israel, that art saved by the LORD with an everlasting salvation; ye shall not be ashamed nor confounded world without end.

45:18 For thus saith the LORD that created the heavens, He is God; that formed the earth and made it, He established it, He created it not a waste, He formed it to be inhabited: I am the LORD, and there is none else.

45:19 I have not spoken in secret, in a place of the land of darkness; I said not unto the seed of Jacob: 'Seek ye Me in vain'; I the LORD speak righteousness, I declare things that are right.

45:20 Assemble yourselves and come, draw near together, ye that are escaped of the nations; they have no knowledge that carry the wood of their graven image, and pray unto a god that cannot save.

45:21 Declare ye, and bring them near, yea, let them take counsel together: Who hath announced this from ancient time, and declared it of old? Have not I the LORD? And there is no God else beside Me, a just God and a Saviour; there is none beside Me.

WORLD ENGLISH BIBLE

45:22 "Look to me, and be saved, all the ends of the earth; for I am God, and there is no other.

45:23 I have sworn by myself, the word has gone out of my mouth in righteousness, and will not return, that to me every knee shall bow, every tongue shall take an oath.

45:24 They will say of me, 'There is righteousness and strength only in Yahweh.'" Even to him shall men come; and all those who were incensed against him shall be disappointed.

45:25 In Yahweh shall all the seed of Israel be justified, and shall glory.

46:1 Bel bows down, Nebo stoops; their idols are on the animals, and on the livestock: the things that you carried about are made a load, a burden to the weary.

46:2 They stoop, they bow down together; they could not deliver the burden, but themselves have gone into captivity.

46:3 "Listen to me, house of Jacob, and all the remnant of the house of Israel, that have been borne from their birth, that have been carried from the womb;

46:4 and even to old age I am he, and even to gray hairs will I carry you. I have made, and I will bear; yes, I will carry, and will deliver.

46:5 "To whom will you liken me, and make me equal, and compare me, that we may be like?

46:6 Some pour out gold from the bag, and weigh silver in the balance. They hire a goldsmith, and he makes it a god. They fall down—yes, they worship.

46:7 They bear it on the shoulder, they carry it, and set it in its place, and it stands, from its place it shall not move: yes, one may cry to it, yet it can not answer, nor save him out of his trouble.

46:8 "Remember this, and show yourselves men; bring it again to mind, you transgressors.

TARGUM ISAIAH

there is no God whatever besides me; a just God and a Saviour; there is none but I.

45:22 Turn unto my WORD, and be ye saved, all that are at the ends of the earth: for I am the Lord, and there is none else.

45:23 I have sworn by my WORD, the word is gone forth in righteousness from my presence, and shall not fail, That before me every knee shall bow, every tongue shall swear.

45:24 Surely, He has promised to bring me righteousness and strength by the WORD of the Lord. In His WORD they shall offer praise, and all the nations that are incensed against His people shall be ashamed.

45:25 In the WORD of the Lord all the seed of Israel shall be justified and glorified.

46:1 Bel is bowed down, Nebo is cut down. Their images are *in* the likeness of serpents and beasts. The burdens of your idols shall be heavy upon those who carry them; because they be exhausted.

46:2 They are cut off, yea, they are altogether cut to pieces, and they were not able to deliver them that carried them; and their worship-

TARGUM ISAIAH

pers are gone into captivity.

46:3 Hearken unto me, O house of Jacob, and all the remnant of the house of Israel, who are beloved above all nations, yea, beloved above all kingdoms.

46:4 Even unto eternity I am He, and my WORD shall endure for ages after ages. It is I who have created all men, and I have scattered them among the nations, yea, I will forgive their sins, and I will pardon.

46:5 To whom will ye liken me, and equal me, and compare me in truth?

46:6 Behold, the people collect gold out of the bag, and weigh silver in the balance, and hire a goldsmith; and he maketh it a god: they fall down, yea, they do it reverence.

46:7 They bear him upon the shoulder, they carry him and set him in his place, and he abideth; it is not possible for him to move from his place; yea, one supplicates to him; but he does not answer him, nor save him out of his distress.

46:8 Remember this, and be ye strong; and bear *it* in mind, O rebels!

45:22 Look unto Me, and be ye saved, all the ends of the earth; for I am God, and there is none else.

45:23 By Myself have I sworn, the word is gone forth from My mouth in righteousness, and shall not come back, that unto Me every knee shall bow, every tongue shall swear.

45:24 Only in the LORD, shall one say of Me, is victory and strength; even to Him shall men come in confusion, all they that were incensed against Him.

45:25 In the LORD shall all the seed of Israel be justified, and shall glory.

46:1 Bel boweth down, Nebo stoopeth; their idols are upon the beasts, and upon the cattle; the things that ye carried about are made a load, a burden to the weary beast.

46:2 They stoop, they bow down together, they could not deliver the burden; and themselves are gone into captivity.

46:3 Hearken unto Me, O house of Jacob, and all the remnant of the house of Israel, that are borne by Me from the birth, that are carried from the womb:

46:4 Even to old age I am the same, and even to hoar hairs will I carry you; I have made, and I will bear; yea, I will carry, and will deliver.

46:5 To whom will ye liken Me, and make Me equal, and compare Me, that we may be like?

46:6 Ye that lavish gold out of the bag, and weigh silver in the balance; ye that hire a goldsmith, that he make it a god, to fall down thereto, yea, to worship.

46:7 He is borne upon the shoulder, he is carried, and set in his place, and he standeth, from his place he doth not remove; yea, though one cry unto him, he cannot answer, nor save him out of his trouble.

46:8 Remember this, and stand fast; bring it to mind, O ye transgressors.

WORLD ENGLISH BIBLE

46:9 Remember the former things of old: for I am God, and there is none else; I am God, and there is none like me;

46:10 declaring the end from the beginning, and from ancient times things that are not yet done; saying, My counsel shall stand, and I will do all my pleasure;

46:11 calling a ravenous bird from the east, the man of my counsel from a far country; yes, I have spoken, I will also bring it to pass; I have purposed, I will also do it.

46:12 Listen to me, you stout-hearted, who are far from righteousness:

46:13 I bring near my righteousness, it shall not be far off, and my salvation shall not wait; and I will place salvation in Zion for Israel my glory.

47:1 "Come down, and sit in the dust, virgin daughter of Babylon; sit on the ground without a throne, daughter of the Chaldeans: for you shall no more be called tender and delicate.

47:2 Take the millstones, and grind meal; remove your veil, strip off the train, uncover the leg, pass through the rivers.

47:3 Your nakedness shall be uncovered, yes, your shame shall be seen: I will take vengeance, and will spare no man."

47:4 Our Redeemer, Yahweh of Armies is his name, the Holy One of Israel.

47:5 "Sit in silence, and go into darkness, daughter of the Chaldeans; for you shall no more be called the mistress of kingdoms.

47:6 I was angry with my people, I profaned my inheritance, and gave them into your hand: you showed them no mercy; on the aged you have very heavily laid your yoke.

47:7 You said, 'I shall be a mistress forever;' so that you did not lay these things to your heart, nor did you remember the latter end of it.

47:8 "Now therefore hear this, you who are given to pleasures, who sit securely, who say in your heart, 'I am, and there is none else besides me; I shall not sit as a widow, neither shall I know the loss of children:'

TARGUM ISAIAH

46:9 Remember the former things of old; for I am God, and there is no God whatever besides me,

46:10 Declaring the end from the beginning, and from ancient times the things that are not *yet* done, saying, My counsel shall stand, and I will do all my pleasure:

46:11 Who hath promised to gather together the captivity from the East, to bring openly, as a swift bird, the sons of Abraham, my chosen, from a distant land; yea, I have promised *it*; yea, I will bring it to pass; I have ordained it; yea, I will do it.

46:12 Hearken unto my WORD, ye stout-hearted, that are far from righteousness.

46:13 My righteousness is nigh, it is not far off, and my salvation shall not tarry: and I will place salvation in Zion, and my glory in Israel.

47:1 Descend and sit in the dust, O kingdom of the congregation of Babylon; sit on the ground, there is no throne of glory, O kingdom of the Chaldeans; for thou shalt no more be called tender and delicate.

47:2 Receive this calamity and go into servitude; put away the glory

TARGUM ISAIAH

of thy kingdom, thy princes are overthrown, the people of thy armies are scattered, they have vanished away like waters of the river.

47:3 Thy nakedness shall be uncovered, thy shame shall be seen; I will take full vengeance, on thee and I will change thy judgment from the children of men.

47:4 As for our Redeemer, the Lord of hosts is His name, the Holy One of Israel.

47:5 Sit thou silent, and get thee into darkness, O glory of the kingdom of Chaldeans; thou shalt no more be called, The mighty one of the kingdoms.

47:6 I was angry with my people, I have polluted mine inheritance, and given them into thine hand: thou hast not had compassion upon them, thou didst make thy dominion over the ancient very cruel.

47:7 And thou saidst, I shall be the mighty one of kingdoms, so that thou didst not lay these things to thy heart, neither didst remember the end *of them.*

47:8 Therefore, hear now this, O voluptuous one, that dwellest in security, that saith in her heart,

JEWISH PUBLICATION SOCIETY 1917

46:9 Remember the former things of old: that I am God, and there is none else; I am God, and there is none like Me;

46:10 Declaring the end from the beginning, and from ancient times things that are not yet done; saying: 'My counsel shall stand, and all My pleasure will I do';

46:11 Calling a bird of prey from the east, the man of My counsel from a far country; yea, I have spoken, I will also bring it to pass, I have purposed, I will also do it.

46:12 Hearken unto Me, ye stout-hearted, that are far from righteousness:

46:13 I bring near My righteousness, it shall not be far off, and My salvation shall not tarry; and I will place salvation in Zion for Israel My glory.

47:1 Come down, and sit in the dust, O virgin daughter of Babylon, sit on the ground without a throne, O daughter of the Chaldeans; for thou shalt no more be called tender and delicate.

47:2 Take the millstones, and grind meal; remove thy veil, strip off the train, uncover the leg, pass through the rivers.

47:3 Thy nakedness shall be uncovered, yea, thy shame shall be seen; I will take vengeance, and will let no man intercede.

47:4 Our Redeemer, the LORD of hosts is His name, The Holy One of Israel.

47:5 Sit thou silent, and get thee into darkness, O daughter of the Chaldeans; for thou shalt no more be called the mistress of kingdoms.

47:6 I was wroth with My people, I profaned Mine inheritance, and gave them into thy hand; thou didst show them no mercy; upon the aged hast thou very heavily laid thy yoke.

47:7 And thou saidst: 'For ever shall I be mistress'; so that thou didst not lay these things to thy heart, neither didst remember the end thereof.

47:8 Now therefore hear this, thou that art given to pleasures, that sittest securely, that sayest in thy heart: 'I am, and there is none else beside me; I shall not sit as a widow, neither shall I know the loss of children';

WORLD ENGLISH BIBLE

47:9 but these two things shall come to you in a moment in one day, the loss of children, and widowhood; in their full measure shall they come on you, in the multitude of your sorceries, and the great abundance of your enchantments.

47:10 For you have trusted in your wickedness; you have said, No one sees me; your wisdom and your knowledge, it has perverted you, and you have said in your heart, I am, and there is none else besides me.

47:11 Therefore evil will come on you; you won't know when it dawns: and mischief will fall on you; you will not be able to put it away: and desolation shall come on you suddenly, which you don't know.

47:12 "Stand now with your enchantments, and with the multitude of your sorceries, in which you have labored from your youth; if so be you shall be able to profit, if so be you may prevail.

47:13 You are wearied in the multitude of your counsels: let now the astrologers, the stargazers, the monthly prognosticators, stand up, and save you from the things that shall come on you.

47:14 Behold, they shall be as stubble; the fire shall burn them; they shall not deliver themselves from the power of the flame: it shall not be a coal to warm at, nor a fire to sit before.

47:15 Thus shall the things be to you in which you have labored: those who have trafficked with you from your youth shall wander everyone to his quarter; there shall be none to save you.

48:1 "Hear this, house of Jacob, you who are called by the name of Israel, and have come forth out of the waters of Judah; who swear by the name of Yahweh, and make mention of the God of Israel, but not in truth, nor in righteousness

TARGUM ISAIAH

I am, and there is none else besides me; I shall not sit a widow, neither shall I know the loss of children:

47:9 But these two things shall come to thee, in an appointed time, in one day, loss of children, and widowhood: they shall come upon thee in their perfection: notwithstanding the multitude of thy sorceries, notwithstanding the great strength of thine enchantments.

47:10 For thou hast trusted in thy wickedness: thou hast said, None seeth thee. Thy wisdom and thy knowledge have corrupted thee; thou hast said in thine heart, I am, and there is none else besides me.

47:11 Therefore shall evil come upon thee: thou shalt not know how to deprecate it; distress shall fall upon thee, and thou shalt not be able to remove it; a tumult shall come upon thee suddenly, unawares.

47:12 Persist now in thine enchantments; and in the multitude of thy sorceries, in which thou wast occupied from thy youth; if so be thou shalt be able to prevail.

47:13 Thou art wearied in the multitude of thy counsels. Let them

TARGUM ISAIAH

now rise up, and save thee, who are familiar with the Zodiac of the heavens, who look at the stars, who make known appointed seasons: deceiving thee, saying, Thus it shall happen unto thee each month.

47:14 Behold, they shall be weak as stubble. The nations which are as strong as fire shall consume them, they shall not deliver themselves from the hand of the slayers: there shall be no remnant nor escaped of them, yea, not a place, in which one might deliver himself.

47:15 Thus shall the workers of thy lies be in thee, with whom thou wast occupied from thy youth; the princes of thy power, shall go into captivity; each one straight before his face, none shall save thee.

48:1 Hear ye this, O house of Jacob, who are called by the name of Israel, and are come forth from the stock of Judah, with whom he hath made a covenant in the name of the Lord, the God of Israel, that the remembrance of them shall not cease. Shall not His WORD stand in truth and righteousness?

47:9 But these two things shall come to thee in a moment in one day, the loss of children, and widow-hood; in their full measure shall they come upon thee, for the multitude of thy sorceries, and the great abundance of thine enchantments.

47:10 And thou hast been secure in thy wickedness, thou hast said: 'None seeth me'; thy wisdom and thy knowledge, it hath perverted thee; and thou hast said in thy heart. 'I am, and there is none else beside me.'

47:11 Yet shall evil came upon thee; thou shalt not know how to charm it away; and calamity shall fall upon thee; thou shalt not be able to put it away; and ruin shall come upon thee suddenly, before thou knowest.

47:12 Stand now with thine enchantments, and with the multitude of thy sorceries, wherein thou hast laboured from thy youth; if so be thou shalt be able to profit, if so be thou mayest prevail.

47:13 Thou art wearied in the multitude of thy counsels; let now the astrologers, the stargazers, the monthly prognosticators, stand up, and save thee from the things that shall come upon thee.

47:14 Behold, they shall be as stubble; the fire shall burn them; they shall not deliver themselves from the power of the flame; it shall not be a coal to warm at, nor a fire to sit before.

47:15 Thus shall they be unto thee with whom thou hast laboured; they that have trafficked with thee from thy youth shall wander every one to his quarter; there shall be none to save thee.

48:1 Hear ye this, O house of Jacob, who are called by the name of Israel, and are come forth out of the fountain of Judah; who swear by the name of the LORD, and make mention of the God of Israel, but not in truth, nor in righteousness.

WORLD ENGLISH BIBLE

48:2 (for they call themselves of the holy city, and stay themselves on the God of Israel; Yahweh of Armies is his name):

48:3 I have declared the former things from of old; yes, they went forth out of my mouth, and I showed them: suddenly I did them, and they happened.

48:4 Because I knew that you are obstinate, and your neck is an iron sinew, and your brow brass;

48:5 therefore I have declared it to you from of old; before it came to pass I showed it to you; lest you should say, 'My idol has done them, and my engraved image, and my molten image, has commanded them.'

48:6 You have heard it; see all this; and you, will you not declare it? "I have shown you new things from this time, even hidden things, which you have not known.

48:7 They are created now, and not from of old; and before this day you didn't hear them; lest you should say, 'Behold, I knew them.'

48:8 Yes, you didn't hear; yes, you didn't know; yes, from of old your ear was not opened: for I knew that you dealt very treacherously, and was called a transgressor from the womb.

48:9 For my name's sake will I defer my anger, and for my praise will I refrain for you, that I not cut you off.

48:10 Behold, I have refined you, but not as silver; I have chosen you in the furnace of affliction.

48:11 For my own sake, for my own sake, will I do it; for how should my name be profaned? I will not give my glory to another.

48:12 "Listen to me, O Jacob, and Israel my called: I am he; I am the first, I also am the last.

48:13 Yes, my hand has laid the foundation of the earth, and my right hand has spread out the heavens: when I call to them, they stand up together.

TARGUM ISAIAH

48:2 For their portion is in the holy city, and their confidence is in the God of Israel; The Lord of hosts is His name.

48:3 I have declared the former things from the beginning; and they have gone forth from my WORD, and I announced them; suddenly I will do them, and they shall come to pass.

48:4 I knew that thou wouldest be a rebel, and thy neck would be as hard iron, and thy brow strong as brass.

48:5 Therefore I have declared *these things* to thee from the beginning; before they came to pass I announced them unto thee: lest thou shouldest say, Mine idol hath done them, and my molten image hath prepared them.

48:6 Hast thou heard whether that was revealed to any people which was revealed unto thee? and as for you, will ye not declare *it*? I have shewed thee new things from this time, and hidden things, and thou didst not know them.

48:7 They are created now, and not of old; yea, I have not announced them before the day of their coming to pass, lest thou shouldest say, Behold, I have known them.

TARGUM ISAIAH

48:8 Yea, thou didst not listen to the words of the prophets; yea, thou didst not accept the instruction of the law; yea, thou didst not incline thine ear to receive the words of the blessings and curses of my covenant which I made with you in Horeb; for it was manifest to me that thou wouldest altogether deal falsely, and be called a rebel from the womb.

48:9 For my name's sake, I will defer mine anger, and for my praise I will preserve thee, so as not to destroy thee.

48:10 Behold, I have reined thee, but not in the crucible of silver; I tried thee in the distress of poverty.

48:11 For my name's sake, for the sake of my WORD, that it may not be profaned, I will do *it*, and my glory *in* which I have revealed myself unto you, I will not give to another people.

48:12 Hearken unto my WORD, ye who *are* of the house of Jacob and Israel, my called, I *am* He, who *was* of old, yea, ages after ages are mine, and besides me there is no God.

48:13 Yea, by my WORD I have laid the foundation of the earth, and

JEWISH PUBLICATION SOCIETY 1917

48:2 For they call themselves of the holy city, and stay themselves upon the God of Israel, the LORD of hosts is His name.

48:3 I have declared the former things from of old; yea, they went forth out of My mouth, and I announced them; suddenly I did them, and they came to pass.

48:4 Because I knew that thou art obstinate, and thy neck is an iron sinew, and thy brow brass;

48:5 Therefore I have declared it to thee from of old; before it came to pass I announced it to thee; lest thou shouldest say: 'Mine idol hath done them, and my graven image, and my molten image, hath commanded them.'

48:6 Thou hast heard, see, all this; and ye, will ye not declare it? I have announced unto thee new things from this time, even hidden things, which thou hast not known.

48:7 They are created now, and not from of old, and before this day thou heardest them not; lest thou shouldest say: 'Behold, I knew them.'

48:8 Yea, thou heardest not; yea, thou knewest not; yea, from of old thine ear was not opened; for I knew that thou wouldest deal very treacherously, and wast called a transgressor from the womb.

48:9 For My name's sake will I defer Mine anger, and for My praise will I refrain for thee, that I cut thee not off.

48:10 Behold, I have refined thee, but not as silver; I have tried thee in the furnace of affliction.

48:11 For Mine own sake, for Mine own sake, will I do it; for how should it be profaned? And My glory will I not give to another.

48:12 Hearken unto Me, O Jacob, and Israel My called: I am He; I am the first, I also am the last.

48:13 Yea, My hand hath laid the foundation of the earth, and My right hand hath spread out the heavens; when I call unto them, they stand up together.

WORLD ENGLISH BIBLE

48:14 "Assemble yourselves, all you, and hear; who among them has declared these things? He whom Yahweh loves shall perform his pleasure on Babylon, and his arm shall be on the Chaldeans.

48:15 I, even I, have spoken; yes, I have called him; I have brought him, and he shall make his way prosperous.

48:16 "Come near to me and hear this: "From the beginning I have not spoken in secret; from the time that it was, there am I." Now the Lord Yahweh has sent me, with his Spirit.

48:17 Thus says Yahweh, your Redeemer, the Holy One of Israel: I am Yahweh your God, who teaches you to profit, who leads you by the way that you should go.

48:18 Oh that you had listened to my commandments! then your peace would have been like a river, and your righteousness like the waves of the sea:

48:19 your seed also had been as the sand, and the offspring of your body like its grains: his name would not be cut off nor destroyed from before me.

48:20 Go forth from Babylon, flee from the Chaldeans; with a voice of singing declare, tell this, utter it even to the end of the earth: say, Yahweh has redeemed his servant Jacob.

48:21 They didn't thirst when he led them through the deserts; he caused the waters to flow out of the rock for them; he split the rock also, and the waters gushed out.

48:22 "There is no peace," says Yahweh, "for the wicked."

49:1 Listen, islands, to me; and listen, you peoples, from far: Yahweh has called me from the womb; from the bowels of my mother has he made mention of my name:

TARGUM ISAIAH

by my might I have suspended the heavens: *when* I call unto them, they stand up together.

48:14 All ye, assemble yourselves, and hear: who among them hath declared these *things* ever since the Lord loved Israel? He will do His pleasure on Babylon, and He will reveal the strength of His arm on the Chaldeans.

48:15 I by my WORD have made a covenant with Abraham your father; yea, I have called him, I have brought him into the land of the place of my Shekinah, and I prospered his way.

48:16 Come ye near to my WORD; hear ye this; I have not spoken in secret from the beginning; at the time when the nations separated themselves from fearing me, at that time I brought Abraham your father to my service. The prophet saith: And now the Lord God, and His WORD, hath sent me.

48:17 Thus saith the Lord, thy Redeemer, the Holy One of Israel; I *am* the Lord thy God, *who* teacheth thee what will profit thee, *who* sheweth the way wherein thou shouldest walk.

48:18 If thou hadst hearkened to

my commandments, thy peace would certainly have been as the overflowing of the river Euphrates, and thy righteousness as the waves of the sea.

48:19 Thy seed had certainly been as numerous as the sand; and thy children's children as the gravel thereof: the name of Israel should not have ceased nor have been destroyed from before me for ever.

48:20 Go ye forth from Babylon, flee ye from the province of the land of the Chaldeans, declare ye with a voice of singing, bring the joyful tidings of this, bring it to the ends of the earth, say ye, The Lord hath redeemed His servants of the house of Jacob.

48:21 He will not suffer them to thirst in the desert; He will guide them; He will cause water to flow for them from the rock: yea, He will cleave the rock, and the waters shall gush out.

48:22 There is no peace, saith the Lord, unto the wicked.

49:1 Listen, O isles, unto my WORD, and hearken, O kingdoms, from afar; the Lord called me before I was; He hath made mention of my name from the bowels of my

48:14 Assemble yourselves, all ye, and hear; which among them hath declared these things? He whom the LORD loveth shall perform His pleasure on Babylon, and show His arm on the Chaldeans.

48:15 I, even I, have spoken, yea, I have called him; I have brought him, and he shall make his way prosperous.

48:16 Come ye near unto Me, hear ye this: From the beginning I have not spoken in secret; from the time that it was, there am I; and now the Lord GOD hath sent me, and His spirit.

48:17 Thus saith the LORD, thy Redeemer, the Holy One of Israel: I am the LORD thy God, who teacheth thee for thy profit, who leadeth thee by the way that thou shouldest go.

48:18 Oh that thou wouldest hearken to My commandments! then would thy peace be as a river, and thy righteousness as the waves of the sea;

48:19 Thy seed also would be as the sand, and the offspring of thy body like the grains thereof; his name would not be cut off nor destroyed from before Me.

48:20 Go ye forth from Babylon, flee ye from the Chaldeans; with a voice of singing declare ye, tell this, utter it even to the end of the earth; say ye: 'The LORD hath redeemed His servant Jacob.

48:21 And they thirsted not when He led them through the deserts; He caused the waters to flow out of the rock for them; He cleaved the rock also, and the waters gushed out.'

48:22 There is no peace, saith the LORD concerning the wicked.

49:1 Listen, O isles, unto me, and hearken, ye peoples, from far: the LORD hath called me from the womb, from the bowels of my mother hath He made mention of my name;

WORLD ENGLISH BIBLE

49:2 and he has made my mouth like a sharp sword; in the shadow of his hand, he has hidden me: and he has made me a polished shaft; in his quiver has he kept me close:

49:3 and he said to me, "You are my servant; Israel, in whom I will be glorified."

49:4 But I said, "I have labored in vain, I have spent my strength for nothing and vanity; yet surely the justice due to me is with Yahweh, and my reward with my God."

49:5 Now says Yahweh who formed me from the womb to be his servant, to bring Jacob again to him, and that Israel be gathered to him (for I am honorable in the eyes of Yahweh, and my God has become my strength);

49:6 yes, he says, "It is too light a thing that you should be my servant to raise up the tribes of Jacob, and to restore the preserved of Israel: I will also give you for a light to the nations, that you may be my salvation to the end of the earth."

49:7 Thus says Yahweh, the Redeemer of Israel, and his Holy One, to him whom man despises, to him whom the nation abhors, to a servant of rulers: "Kings shall see and arise; princes, and they shall worship; because of Yahweh who is faithful, even the Holy One of Israel, who has chosen you."

49:8 Thus says Yahweh, "In an acceptable time have I answered you, and in a day of salvation have I helped you; and I will preserve you, and give you for a covenant of the people, to raise up the land, to make them inherit the desolate heritage:

49:9 saying to those who are bound, 'Come out!'; to those who are in darkness, 'Show yourselves!' "They shall feed in the ways, and on all bare heights shall be their pasture.

49:10 They shall not hunger nor thirst; neither shall the heat nor sun strike them: for he who has mercy on them will lead them, even by springs of water he will guide them.

TARGUM ISAIAH

mother.

49:2 And he hath put His words in my mouth like a sharp sword; in the shadow of His power hath He protected me, and He hath made me like a choice arrow, which is hidden in the quiver.

49:3 And said unto me, Thou art my servant, O Israel, in whom I will be glorified.

49:4 And as for me, I said, I have laboured in vain, I have spent my strength for naught, and in vain; but my cause is known to the Lord, and the reward of my work is before my God.

49:5 And now, saith the Lord, that formed me from the womb to be a perfect servant before Him, to make the house of Jacob to return to His service, and Israel shall be brought to fear Him and we shall be glorious before the Lord; and the WORD of my God shall be my support.

49:6 And He said, Is it too little for you that ye should be called my servants, to raise up the tribes of Jacob, and to bring back the captivity of Israel? Yea, I will give thee for a light to the nations, to be my salvation unto the ends of the earth.

TARGUM ISAIAH

49:7 Thus saith the Lord, the Redeemer of Israel, *and* His Holy One, to them that are despised among the nations, to them that are scattered among the kingdoms, to them that are the servants to rulers: Kings shall look at them; and princes shall rise and fall prostrate, because of the Lord that is faithful, *and* the Holy One of Israel, and He shall delight in thee.

49:8 Thus saith the Lord, at the time when ye do my will, I hear your prayer, and in the day of distress I uphold you with salvation and support; for I will maintain thee, and I will give thee for a covenant with the people, to raise up the righteous that lie in the dust, to cause to inherit the desolate heritages;

49:9 Saying to them who *are* prisoners among the nations, Go forth to them who are kept back in darkness among the kingdoms; shew yourselves to the light; they shall dwell in all the paths, and by all the rivers *shall be* the place of their dwelling.

49:10 They shall not hunger nor thirst, neither shall the heat nor the sun smite them: for He that

JEWISH PUBLICATION SOCIETY 1917

49:2 And He hath made my mouth like a sharp sword, in the shadow of His hand hath He hid me; and He hath made me a polished shaft, in His quiver hath He concealed me;

49:3 And He said unto me: 'Thou art My servant, Israel, in whom I will be glorified.'

49:4 But I said: 'I have laboured in vain, I have spent my strength for nought and vanity; yet surely my right is with the LORD, and my recompense with my God.'

49:5 And now saith the LORD that formed me from the womb to be His servant, to bring Jacob back to Him, and that Israel be gathered unto Him—for I am honourable in the eyes of the LORD, and my God is become my strength—

49:6 Yea, He saith: 'It is too light a thing that thou shouldest be My servant to raise up the tribes of Jacob, and to restore the offspring of Israel; I will also give thee for a light of the nations, that My salvation may be unto the end of the earth.'

49:7 Thus saith the LORD, the Redeemer of Israel, his Holy One, to him who is despised of men, to him who is abhorred of nations, to a servant of rulers: kings shall see and arise, princes, and they shall prostrate themselves; because of the LORD that is faithful, even the Holy One of Israel, who hath chosen thee.

49:8 Thus saith the LORD: in an acceptable time have I answered thee, and in a day of salvation have I helped thee; and I will preserve thee, and give thee for a covenant of the people, to raise up the land, to cause to inherit the desolate heritages;

49:9 Saying to the prisoners: 'Go forth'; to them that are in darkness: 'Show yourselves'; they shall feed in the ways, and in all high hills shall be their pasture;

49:10 They shall not hunger nor thirst, neither shall the heat nor sun smite them; for He that hath compassion on them will lead them, even by the springs of water will He guide them.

WORLD ENGLISH BIBLE

49:11 I will make all my mountains a way, and my highways shall be exalted.

49:12 Behold, these shall come from far; and behold, these from the north and from the west; and these from the land of Sinim."

49:13 Sing, heavens; and be joyful, earth; and break forth into singing, mountains: for Yahweh has comforted his people, and will have compassion on his afflicted.

49:14 But Zion said, "Yahweh has forsaken me, and the Lord has forgotten me."

49:15 "Can a woman forget her nursing child, that she should not have compassion on the son of her womb? Yes, these may forget, yet I will not forget you!

49:16 Behold, I have engraved you on the palms of my hands; your walls are continually before me.

49:17 Your children make haste; your destroyers and those who made you waste shall go forth from you.

49:18 Lift up your eyes all around, and see: all these gather themselves together, and come to you. As I live," says Yahweh, "you shall surely clothe yourself with them all as with an ornament, and dress yourself with them, like a bride.

49:19 "For, as for your waste and your desolate places, and your land that has been destroyed, surely now you shall be too small for the inhabitants, and those who swallowed you up shall be far away.

49:20 The children of your bereavement shall yet say in your ears, The place is too small for me; give place to me that I may dwell.

49:21 Then you will say in your heart, 'Who has conceived these for me, since I have been bereaved of my children, and am solitary, an exile, and wandering back and forth? Who has brought up these? Behold, I was left alone; these, where were they?'"

TARGUM ISAIAH

shall have mercy on them shall guide them, and He shall cause them to dwell by the springs of water.

49:11 And I will make all the mountains trodden paths like a way before them, and the footpaths shall be cast up.

49:12 Behold, these shall come from far: and, lo, these from the North and from the West, and these from the land of the South.

49:13 Sing, O heavens; and be joyful, O earth; and be glad, O mountains, with praise, for the Lord will comfort His people, and will have mercy upon His afflicted.

49:14 But Zion said, The Lord hath taken His Shekinah from me, and the Lord hath cast me away.

49:15 Is it possible that a mother can forget her child, that she should not have compassion on the son of her womb? The congregation of Israel answered and said: If there is no forgetfulness with Him, perhaps He will not forget that I have made a calf of gold? The prophet said to her, Yea, these things shall be forgotten. And she said to him, If there is forgetfulness with Him, perhaps it will be forgotten that I said on

TARGUM ISAIAH

Sinai: We will do and obey? He answered and said to her: My WORD shall not cast you off.

49:16 Behold, as upon the hands thou art engraven before me; thy walls *are* continually before me.

49:17 Those that shall build thy desolate places shall make haste, thy destroyers and they that made thee waste, shall go forth of thee.

49:18 Lift up thine eyes round about, O Jerusalem, and see; all the children of the people of thy captivity are gathered together and come unto thee. As I live, saith the Lord, all these shall be unto thee as a vesture of glory, and their works in the midst of thee as the ornament of a bride.

49:19 For thy waste and desolate places, and the land of thy destruction, surely now shall be too strait by reason of the inhabitants, and they that swallowed thee up shall be far away.

49:20 Henceforth shall each of the children of thy captivity in the midst of thee say: The place is too strait for me: make room for me that I may dwell.

49:21 Then thou shalt say in thine heart, Who hath nourished up these for me, seeing I have lost

JEWISH PUBLICATION SOCIETY 1917

49:11 And I will make all My mountains a way, and My highways shall be raised on high.

49:12 Behold, these shall come from far; and, lo, these from the north and from the west, and these from the land of Sinim.

49:13 Sing, O heavens, and be joyful, O earth, and break forth into singing, O mountains; for the LORD hath comforted His people, and hath compassion upon His afflicted.

49:14 But Zion said: 'The LORD hath forsaken me, and the Lord hath forgotten me.'

49:15 Can a woman forget her sucking child, that she should not have compassion on the son of her womb? Yea, these may forget, yet will not I forget thee.

49:16 Behold, I have graven thee upon the palms of My hands; thy walls are continually before Me.

49:17 Thy children make haste; thy destroyers and they that made thee waste shall go forth from thee.

49:18 Lift up thine eyes round about, and behold: all these gather themselves together, and come to thee. As I live, saith the LORD, thou shalt surely clothe thee with them all as with an ornament, and gird thyself with them, like a bride.

49:19 For thy waste and thy desolate places and thy land that hath been destroyed—surely now shalt thou be too strait for the inhabitants, and they that swallowed thee up shall be far away.

49:20 The children of thy bereavement shall yet say in thine ears: 'The place is too strait for me; give place to me that I may dwell.'

49:21 Then shalt thou say in thy heart: 'Who hath begotten me these, seeing I have been bereaved of my children, and am solitary, an exile, and wandering to and fro? And who hath brought up these? Behold, I was left alone; these, where were they?'

WORLD ENGLISH BIBLE

49:22 Thus says the Lord Yahweh, "Behold, I will lift up my hand to the nations, and set up my banner to the peoples; and they shall bring your sons in their bosom, and your daughters shall be carried on their shoulders.

49:23 Kings shall be your nursing fathers, and their queens your nursing mothers: they shall bow down to you with their faces to the earth, and lick the dust of your feet; and you shall know that I am Yahweh; and those who wait for me shall not be disappointed."

49:24 Shall the prey be taken from the mighty, or the lawful captives be delivered?

49:25 But thus says Yahweh, "Even the captives of the mighty shall be taken away, and the prey of the terrible shall be delivered; for I will contend with him who contends with you, and I will save your children.

49:26 I will feed those who oppress you with their own flesh; and they shall be drunken with their own blood, as with sweet wine: and all flesh shall know that I, Yahweh, am your Savior, and your Redeemer, the Mighty One of Jacob."

50:1 Thus says Yahweh, "Where is the bill of your mother's divorce, with which I have put her away? or which of my creditors is it to whom I have sold you? Behold, for your iniquities were you sold, and for your transgressions was your mother put away.

TARGUM ISAIAH

my children, and have been solitary; an exile, and an outcast; who then hath brought up these? Lo! I was left alone; these, where were they?

49:22 Thus saith the Lord God, Behold, I will reveal my power among the Gentiles, and unto the kingdoms I will raise my standard, and thy children shall come in palanquins, and thy daughters shall be carried upon the shoulders.

49:23 And kings shall be thy nursing fathers, and their queens shall minister unto thee; they shall prostrate themselves with their faces to the earth to supplicate to thee, and lick the dust of thy feet; and thou shalt know that I *am* the Lord; because the righteous that hope for my salvation shall not be ashamed.

49:24 Shall the spoil be taken from the mighty, and shall that which the just have taken captive be delivered? [ANOTHER PARAPHRASE. Jerusalem says, Is it possible, that the prey shall be taken from Esau the wicked, which he took from me? concerning whom it was said, By thy sword thou shalt live. Or the captive whom Ishmael led captive, concerning whom it has been

TARGUM ISAIAH

said, That which belongeth to the righteous shall he deliver?]

49:25 For thus saith the Lord, I will surely restore the captivity of the mighty, and I will deliver the prey of the terrible: Surely the captivity of the mighty I will restore, and the prey of the terrible I will deliver, and I will take vengeance for thee, and I will save thy children. [ANOTHER PARAPHRASE. -For thus saith the Lord: Yea, the prey, which the mighty Esau hath taken of thee, shall be taken from him, and the captivity, which the proud Ishmael led captive (concerning whom it has been said: He shall be a conqueror among men) be delivered? and I will save thy children.]

49:26 And I will give the flesh of them who oppress thee for food to every fowl of the heavens, and as they are drunken with new wine, so the beasts of the field shall be drunk with their blood, and all flesh shall know, that I, the Lord, am thy Saviour and thy Redeemer, the mighty One of Jacob.

50:1 Thus saith the Lord, Where is the bill of divorcement, which I gave to your congregation, that

JEWISH PUBLICATION SOCIETY 1917

49:22 Thus saith the Lord GOD: Behold, I will lift up My hand to the nations, and set up Mine ensign to the peoples, and they shall bring thy sons in their bosom, and thy daughters shall be carried upon their shoulders.

49:23 And kings shall be thy foster-fathers, and their queens thy nursing mothers; they shall bow down to thee with their face to the earth, and lick the dust of thy feet; and thou shalt know that I am the LORD, for they shall not be ashamed that wait for Me.

49:24 Shall the prey be taken from the mighty, or the captives of the victorious be delivered?

49:25 But thus saith the LORD: even the captives of the mighty shall be taken away, and the prey of the terrible shall be delivered; and I will contend with him that contendeth with thee, and I will save thy children.

49:26 And I will feed them that oppress thee with their own flesh; and they shall be drunken with their own blood, as with sweet wine; and all flesh shall know that I the LORD am thy Saviour, and thy Redeemer, the Mighty One of Jacob.

50:1 Thus saith the LORD: Where is the bill of your mother's divorcement, wherewith I have put her away? Or which of My creditors is it to whom I have sold you? Behold, for your iniquities were ye sold, and for your transgressions was your mother put away.

WORLD ENGLISH BIBLE

50:2 Why, when I came, was there no man? when I called, was there none to answer? Is my hand shortened at all, that it can't redeem? or have I no power to deliver? Behold, at my rebuke I dry up the sea, I make the rivers a wilderness: their fish stink, because there is no water, and die for thirst.

50:3 I clothe the heavens with blackness, and I make sackcloth their covering."

50:4 The Lord Yahweh has given me the tongue of those who are taught, that I may know how to sustain with words him who is weary: he wakens morning by morning, he wakens my ear to hear as those who are taught.

50:5 The Lord Yahweh has opened my ear, and I was not rebellious, neither turned away backward.

50:6 I gave my back to the strikers, and my cheeks to those who plucked off the hair; I didn't hide my face from shame and spitting.

50:7 For the Lord Yahweh will help me; therefore I have not been confounded: therefore have I set my face like a flint, and I know that I shall not be disappointed.

50:8 He is near who justifies me; who will bring charges against me? Let us stand up together: who is my adversary? Let him come near to me.

50:9 Behold, the Lord Yahweh will help me; who is he who shall condemn me? Behold, all they shall wax old as a garment, the moth shall eat them up.

50:10 Who is among you who fears Yahweh, who obeys the voice of his servant? He who walks in darkness, and has no light, let him trust in the name of Yahweh, and rely on his God.

50:11 Behold, all you who kindle a fire, who adorn yourselves with torches around yourselves; walk in the flame of your fire, and among the brands that you have kindled. You shall have this of my hand; you shall lie down in sorrow.

TARGUM ISAIAH

she is cast off? Or who is the man, who has a debt against me, unto whom I sold you? Behold, for your sins ye were sold, and for your rebellion your congregation was put away.

50:2 Wherefore have I sent my prophets, and they have not repented? They prophesied, but they obeyed not. Is my power altogether deficient, so that I cannot save? Behold, at my rebuke I dry up the sea, I make the rivers a wilderness: their fish stinketh, because there is no water, and dieth for thirst.

50:3 I cover the heavens as with blackness, and as with sackcloth I make their covering.

50:4 The Lord God hath given me a tongue to teach, to give knowledge, *and* to instruct the righteous with wisdom, who weary themselves with the words of the law; each morning rising up early to send His prophets, that perhaps the ears of the sinners might be opened, and they might receive instruction.

50:5 The Lord God hath sent me to prophesy, and I did not refuse, neither turned away back.

50:6 I gave my back to the smiters,

TARGUM ISAIAH

and my cheeks to them that plucked off the hair: I hid not my face from shame and spitting. **50:7** The Lord God is my helper, therefore shall I not be confounded: therefore have I set my face strong as a rock, and I know that I shall not be confounded.

50:8 My righteousness is near; who is he that will contend with me? Let us stand forth together: who is my adversary? let him come near me.

50:9 Behold, the Lord God is my helper; who is he that shall condemn me? lo, they all shall be as a garment that waxeth old, yea, as when the moth eateth it.

50:10 The prophet said: The Holy One, blessed be He, shall say to all the nations: Who is among you that feareth the Lord, that obeyeth the voice of His servant the prophet, who keepeth the law, being in distress, as a man that walketh in darkness and has no light, he trusting in the name of the Lord, will stay upon the salvation of his God?

50:11 The nations answered and said to him: O our Lord! it is not possible for us to occupy ourselves with the law; because we

JEWISH PUBLICATION SOCIETY 1917

50:2 Wherefore, when I came, was there no man? when I called, was there none to answer? Is My hand shortened at all, that it cannot redeem? Or have I no power to deliver? Behold, at My rebuke I dry up the sea, I make the rivers a wilderness; their fish become foul, because there is no water, and die for thirst.

50:3 I clothe the heavens with blackness, and I make sackcloth their covering.

50:4 The Lord GOD hath given me the tongue of them that are taught, that I should know how to sustain with words him that is weary; He wakeneth morning by morning, He wakeneth mine ear to hear as they that are taught.

50:5 The Lord GOD hath opened mine ear, and I was not rebellious, neither turned away backward.

50:6 I gave my back to the smiters, and my checks to them that plucked off the hair; I hid not my face from shame and spitting.

50:7 For the Lord GOD will help me; therefore have I not been confounded; therefore have I set my face like a flint, and I know that I shall not be ashamed.

50:8 He is near that justifieth me; who will contend with me? let us stand up together; who is mine adversary? let him come near to me.

50:9 Behold, the Lord GOD will help me; who is he that shall condemn me? Behold, they all shall wax old as a garment, the moth shall eat them up.

50:10 Who is among you that feareth the LORD, that obeyeth the voice of His servant? though he walketh in darkness, and hath no light, let him trust in the name of the LORD, and stay upon his God.

50:11 Behold, all ye that kindle a fire, that gird yourselves with firebrands, begone in the flame of your fire, and among the brands that ye have kindled. This shall ye have of My hand; ye shall lie down in sorrow.

WORLD ENGLISH BIBLE

51:1 "Listen to me, you who follow after righteousness, you who seek Yahweh: look to the rock you were cut from, and to the hold of the pit you were dug from.

51:2 Look to Abraham your father, and to Sarah who bore you; for when he was but one I called him, and I blessed him, and made him many.

51:3 For Yahweh has comforted Zion; he has comforted all her waste places, and has made her wilderness like Eden, and her desert like the garden of Yahweh; joy and gladness shall be found therein, thanksgiving, and the voice of melody.

51:4 "Attend to me, my people; and give ear to me, my nation: for a law shall go forth from me, and I will establish my justice for a light of the peoples.

51:5 My righteousness is near, my salvation is gone forth, and my arms shall judge the peoples; the islands shall wait for me, and on my arm shall they trust.

51:6 Lift up your eyes to the heavens, and look on the earth beneath; for the heavens shall vanish away like smoke, and the earth shall wax old like a garment; and those who dwell therein shall die in the same way: but my salvation shall be forever, and my righteousness shall not be abolished.

51:7 "Listen to me, you who know righteousness, the people in whose heart is my law; don't fear the reproach of men, neither be dismayed at their insults.

TARGUM ISAIAH

continually wage war against each other, and when we gain the victory one over the other, we burn their houses with fire, and bring their children and their treasures into captivity, and in this manner our days are spent; thus it is impossible for us to occupy ourselves with the law. The Holy One, blessed be He, answered and said unto them: Behold, all of you who stir up a fire, and lay hold on the sword; go ye, fall into the fire which ye have stirred up, and by the sword, which ye have laid hold on. This shall be unto you from my WORD, ye shall turn to your destruction.

51:1 Hearken to my WORD, ye that follow after truth, who seek instruction from the Lord; consider that ye were cut out like a stone hewn from a rock, that ye were cut out like a mass hewn out of a hollow cistern.

51:2 Consider Abraham your father, and Sarah who conceived you: for Abraham was one alone in the world, and I brought him to my service, I also blessed him, and multiplied him.

51:3 For the Lord will comfort Zion, He will comfort all her waste plac-

TARGUM ISAIAH

es, and He will make her wilderness like Eden, and her desert like the garden of the Lord; joy and gladness shall be found therein, they that offer thanksgiving, and the voice of them that praise.

51:4 Listen to my WORD, O my people, and give ear, O my congregation, to my service; for the law shall go forth from me, and my judgment like a light; the nations which I led into captivity shall praise it.

51:5 My righteousness is near; my salvation is gone forth, and the nations shall be judged by the strength of the arm of my might; the isles shall hope for my WORD, and they shall wait for the strength of the arm of my might.

51:6 Lift up your eyes to the heavens, and consider the earth beneath: for the heavens shall vanish away like smoke, and the earth that waxeth old like a garment, so shall it wax old, and its inhabitants, also, they shall die; but my salvation shall be for ever, and my righteousness shall not tarry.

51:7 Hearken unto my WORD, ye that know the truth, the people in whose heart is the instruction of my law; be ye not afraid of the

JEWISH PUBLICATION SOCIETY 1917

51:1 Hearken to Me, ye that follow after righteousness, ye that seek the LORD; look unto the rock whence ye were hewn, and to the hole of the pit whence ye were digged.

51:2 Look unto Abraham your father, and unto Sarah that bore you; for when he was but one I called him, and I blessed him, and made him many.

51:3 For the LORD hath comforted Zion; He hath comforted all her waste places, and hath made her wilderness like Eden, and her desert like the garden of the LORD; joy and gladness shall be found therein, thanksgiving, and the voice of melody.

51:4 Attend unto Me, O My people, and give ear unto Me, O My nation; for instruction shall go forth from Me, and My right on a sudden for a light of the peoples.

51:5 My favour is near, My salvation is gone forth, and Mine arms shall judge the peoples; the isles shall wait for Me, and on Mine arm shall they trust.

51:6 Lift up your eyes to the heavens, and look upon the earth beneath; for the heavens shall vanish away like smoke, and the earth shall wax old like a garment, and they that dwell therein shall die in like manner; but My salvation shall be for ever, and My favour shall not be abolished.

51:7 Hearken unto Me, ye that know righteousness, the people in whose heart is My law; fear ye not the taunt of men, neither be ye dismayed at their revilings.

WORLD ENGLISH BIBLE

51:8 For the moth shall eat them up like a garment, and the worm shall eat them like wool; but my righteousness shall be forever, and my salvation to all generations."

51:9 Awake, awake, put on strength, arm of Yahweh; awake, as in the days of old, the generations of ancient times. Isn't it you who cut Rahab in pieces, who pierced the monster?

51:10 Isn't it you who dried up the sea, the waters of the great deep; who made the depths of the sea a way for the redeemed to pass over?

51:11 The ransomed of Yahweh shall return, and come with singing to Zion; and everlasting joy shall be on their heads. They shall obtain gladness and joy. Sorrow and sighing shall flee away.

51:12 "I, even I, am he who comforts you: who are you, that you are afraid of man who shall die, and of the son of man who shall be made as grass;

51:13 and have forgotten Yahweh your Maker, who stretched forth the heavens, and laid the foundations of the earth; and fear continually all the day because of the fury of the oppressor, when he makes ready to destroy? and where is the fury of the oppressor?

51:14 The captive exile shall speedily be freed; and he shall not die and go down into the pit, neither shall his bread fail.

51:15 For I am Yahweh your God, who stirs up the sea, so that its waves roar: Yahweh of Armies is his name.

51:16 I have put my words in your mouth, and have covered you in the shadow of my hand, that I may plant the heavens, and lay the foundations of the earth, and tell Zion, 'You are my people.'"

TARGUM ISAIAH

reproaches of the sons of men, neither be terrified on account of their grandeur.

51:8 For they vanish like a garment, which the moth eateth, and like wool, which rottenness seizeth; but my righteousness shall be for ever, and my salvation from generation to generation.

51:9 Reveal thyself, reveal thyself, put on the strength of might from the Lord; reveal thyself as in the days of old, *in* the generations which were at the beginning: was it not for thy sake, O congregation of Israel, that I broke the mighty, *that* I destroyed Pharaoh and his host, who were strong as a dragon?

51:10 Was it not for thy sake, O congregation of Israel, that I dried up the sea, the water of the great deep, I made the depth of the sea a way for the ransomed to pass over?

51:11 Thus the redeemed of the Lord shall be gathered together out of their captivity, and come to Zion with singing; and everlasting joy shall be theirs, which shall not cease: and a cloud of glory shall shadow over their heads; they shall find joy and gladness,

TARGUM ISAIAH

and there shall be an end of sorrow and sighing for the house of Israel.

51:12 I, *even* I, *am* He that comforteth you: of whom are ye afraid? of a mortal man? or of a son of man, who is counted like grass?

51:13 And that thou shouldest forget the worship of the Lord thy maker, who hath suspended the heavens and founded the earth; and shouldest fear continually all the day because of the fury of the oppressor, as if he were ready to destroy; and where is now the fury of the oppressor?

51:14 Vengeance hasteneth to be revealed, and the righteous shall not die in the pit, nor be in want of their food.

51:15 For I am the Lord thy God, who rebuketh the sea, though its waves roar; the Lord of hosts is His name.

51:16 I have put the words of my prophecy in thy mouth, and with the shadow of my power have I protected thee, to raise up the nation, concerning which it hath been promised that they shall be as many as the stars of heaven, and to establish the congregation it has been promised concerning

51:8 For the moth shall eat them up like a garment, and the worm shall eat them like wool; but My favour shall be for ever, and My salvation unto all generations.

51:9 Awake, awake, put on strength, O arm of the LORD; awake, as in the days of old, the generations of ancient times. Art thou not it that hewed Rahab in pieces, that pierced the dragon?

51:10 Art thou not it that dried up the sea, the waters of the great deep; that made the depths of the sea a way for the redeemed to pass over?

51:11 And the ransomed of the LORD shall return, and come with singing unto Zion, and everlasting joy shall be upon their heads; they shall obtain gladness and joy, and sorrow and sighing shall flee away.

51:12 I, even I, am He that comforteth you: who art thou, that thou art afraid of man that shall die, and of the son of man that shall be made as grass;

51:13 And hast forgotten the LORD thy Maker, that stretched forth the heavens, and laid the foundations of the earth; and fearest continually all the day because of the fury of the oppressor, as he maketh ready to destroy? And where is the fury of the oppressor?

51:14 He that is bent down shall speedily be loosed; and he shall not go down dying into the pit, neither shall his bread fail.

51:15 For I am the LORD thy God, who stirreth up the sea, that the waves thereof roar; the LORD of hosts is His name.

51:16 And I have put My words in thy mouth, and have covered thee in the shadow of My hand, that I may plant the heavens, and lay the foundations of the earth, and say unto Zion: 'Thou art My people.'

WORLD ENGLISH BIBLE

51:17 Awake, awake, stand up, Jerusalem, that have drunk at the hand of Yahweh the cup of his wrath; you have drunken the bowl of the cup of staggering, and drained it.

51:18 There is none to guide her among all the sons whom she has brought forth; neither is there any who takes her by the hand among all the sons who she has brought up.

51:19 These two things have happened to you. Who will bemoan you? Desolation and destruction, and the famine and the sword; how shall I comfort you?

51:20 Your sons have fainted, they lie at the head of all the streets, as an antelope in a net; they are full of the wrath of Yahweh, the rebuke of your God.

51:21 Therefore hear now this, you afflicted, and drunken, but not with wine:

51:22 Thus says your Lord Yahweh, and your God who pleads the cause of his people, "Behold, I have taken out of your hand the cup of staggering, even the bowl of the cup of my wrath; you shall no more drink it again:

51:23 and I will put it into the hand of those who afflict you, who have said to your soul, 'Bow down, that we may walk over you;' and you have laid your back as the ground, and as the street, to those who walk over."

52:1 Awake, awake, put on your strength, Zion; put on your beautiful garments, Jerusalem, the holy city: for henceforth there shall no more come into you the uncircumcised and the unclean.

52:2 Shake yourself from the dust! Arise, sit up, Jerusalem! Release yourself from the bonds of your neck, captive daughter of Zion!

52:3 For thus says Yahweh, "You were sold for nothing; and you shall be redeemed without money."

52:4 For thus says the Lord Yahweh, "My people went down at the first into Egypt to live there: and the Assyrian has oppressed them without cause.

TARGUM ISAIAH

them, that they shall multiply like the dust of the earth, and to say to the inhabitants of Zion, Ye are my people.

51:17 Magnify thyself, magnify thyself; arise, O Jerusalem! who hast received from the Lord the cup of His wrath; the vial of the cup of cursing thou hast drunk, and thou hast removed it.

51:18 There is none to comfort thee, of all the sons which she hath brought forth; neither is there one to lay hold on her hand, of all the sons she hath nourished.

51:19 Two tribulations have come upon thee, O Jerusalem, thou art not able to arise; when four shall come upon thee, spoiling, and destruction, and famine, and sword, there shall be none to comfort thee beside me.

51:20 Thy children shall be torn in pieces, they *shall* be cast at the head of all the streets as broken vials: they are full of the fury of the Lord, and of the rebuke of thy God

51:21 Therefore hear now this, thou who art cast out, drunk with tribulation and not with wine:

51:22 Thus saith thy Lord, the Lord, even thy God will take vengeance

TARGUM ISAIAH

of judgment for His people, behold, I have taken away the cup of cursing, the vial of the cup of my fury; thou shalt no more drink it again.

51:23 But I will deliver it into the hand of them that afflict thee: which have said to thee, Bow down that we may go over; and thou hast humbled thy glory as the ground, and thou becamest like the street to them that passed by.

52:1 Reveal thyself, reveal thyself, put on thy strength, O Zion; put on thy beautiful garments, O Jerusalem, the city of holiness: for the uncircumcised and the polluted shall pass no more through thee.

52:2 Shake thyself from the dust; arise, *and* sit upon the throne of glory, O Jerusalem; the chains of thy neck are broken, O captive congregation of Zion.

52:3 For thus saith the Lord, Ye were sold for nought; and ye shall be redeemed without money.

52:4 For thus saith the Lord God, My people went down aforetime into Egypt to sojourn there; and the Assyrian oppressed them without cause.

JEWISH PUBLICATION SOCIETY 1917

51:17 Awake, awake, stand up, O Jerusalem, that hast drunk at the hand of the LORD the cup of His fury; thou hast drunken the beaker, even the cup of staggering, and drained it.

51:18 There is none to guide her among all the sons whom she hath brought forth; neither is there any that taketh her by the hand of all the sons that she hath brought up.

51:19 These two things are befallen thee; who shall bemoan thee? desolation and destruction, and the famine and the sword; how shall I comfort thee?

51:20 Thy sons have fainted, they lie at the head of all the streets, as an antelope in a net; they are full of the fury of the LORD, the rebuke of thy God.

51:21 Therefore hear now this, thou afflicted, and drunken, but not with wine;

51:22 Thus saith thy Lord the LORD, and thy God that pleadeth the cause of His people: behold, I have taken out of thy hand the cup of staggering; the beaker, even the cup of My fury, thou shalt no more drink it again;

51:23 And I will put it into the hand of them that afflict thee; that have said to thy soul: 'Bow down, that we may go over'; and thou hast laid thy back as the ground, and as the street, to them that go over.

52:1 Awake, awake, put on thy strength, O Zion; put on thy beautiful garments, O Jerusalem, the holy city; for henceforth there shall no more come into thee the uncircumcised and the unclean.

52:2 Shake thyself from the dust; arise, and sit down, O Jerusalem; loose thyself from the bands of thy neck, O captive daughter of Zion.

52:3 For thus saith the LORD: ye were sold for nought; and ye shall be redeemed without money.

52:4 For thus saith the Lord GOD: My people went down aforetime into Egypt to sojourn there; and the Assyrian oppressed them without cause.

WORLD ENGLISH BIBLE

52:5 "Now therefore, what do I do here," says Yahweh, "seeing that my people are taken away for nothing? Those who rule over them mock," says Yahweh, "and my name continually all the day is blasphemed.

52:6 Therefore my people shall know my name. Therefore they shall know in that day that I am he who speaks; behold, it is I."

52:7 How beautiful on the mountains are the feet of him who brings good news, who publishes peace, who brings good news of good, who publishes salvation, who says to Zion, "Your God reigns!"

52:8 The voice of your watchmen! they lift up the voice, together do they sing; for they shall see eye to eye, when Yahweh returns to Zion.

52:9 Break forth into joy, sing together, you waste places of Jerusalem; for Yahweh has comforted his people, he has redeemed Jerusalem.

52:10 Yahweh has made bare his holy arm in the eyes of all the nations; and all the ends of the earth have seen the salvation of our God.

52:11 Depart, depart, go out from there, touch no unclean thing! Go out of the midst of her! Cleanse yourselves, you who bear the vessels of Yahweh.

52:12 For you shall not go out in haste, neither shall you go by flight: for Yahweh will go before you; and the God of Israel will be your rear guard.

52:13 Behold, my servant shall deal wisely, he shall be exalted and lifted up, and shall be very high.

52:14 Like as many were astonished at you (his appearance was marred more than any man, and his form more than the sons of men),

52:15 so shall he sprinkle many nations; kings shall shut their mouths at him: for that which had not been told them shall they see; and that which they had not heard shall they understand.

TARGUM ISAIAH

52:5 Therefore now I am ready to redeem *them*, saith the Lord; for my people was sold for nought; the nations that ruled over them boasted, saith the Lord; and they continually, all the day, provoke *them* to anger, because of the worship of my name.

52:6 Therefore my name shall be magnified among the nations: therefore at that time ye shall know, that I *am* He that hath spoken: and my WORD shall abide.

52:7 How beautiful upon the mountains of the land of Israel are the feet of him that bringeth good tidings, that publisheth peace, that publisheth salvation, saying to the congregation of Zion, The kingdom of thy God is revealed.

52:8 The voice of thy rulers! They are lifting up their voice, together they offer praise; because with their eyes they see the mighty works which the Lord shall do, when He shall return His Shekinah to Zion.

52:9 Rejoice and shout together, ye desolate places of Jerusalem, for the Lord shall comfort His people, Jerusalem shall be redeemed.

52:10 The Lord hath revealed His holy arm in the eyes of all the na-

TARGUM ISAIAH

tions; and all that are in the ends of the earth shall see the salvation of our God.

52:11 Separate yourselves, separate yourselves, go ye out from thence, do not come near the unclean; come forth from the midst of her: those that carry the vessels of the house of the sanctuary of the Lord have been chosen.

52:12 For ye shall not go forth in haste from among the nations, nor be carried in flight to your land: for your guide is the Lord, and He that shall gather your captivity is the God of Israel.

52:13 Behold, my servant the Messiah shall prosper, He shall be exalted and extolled, and He shall be very strong.

52:14 As the house of Israel *anxiously* hoped for Him many days, (which was poor among the nations; their appearance and their brightness being worse than that of the sons of men:)

52:15 Thus shall He scatter many nations; before Him kings shall keep silence: they shall put their hands upon their mouths, for that which had not been told them shall they see: and *that* which they had not heard shall they consider.

JEWISH PUBLICATION SOCIETY 1917

52:5 Now therefore, what do I here, saith the LORD, seeing that My people is taken away for nought? They that rule over them do howl, saith the LORD, and My name continually all the day is blasphemed.

52:6 Therefore My people shall know My name; therefore they shall know in that day that I, even He that spoke, behold, here I am.

52:7 How beautiful upon the mountains are the feet of the messenger of good tidings, that announceth peace, the harbinger of good tidings, that announceth salvation; that saith unto Zion: 'Thy God reigneth!'

52:8 Hark, thy watchmen! they lift up the voice, together do they sing; for they shall see, eye to eye, the LORD returning to Zion.

52:9 Break forth into joy, sing together, ye waste places of Jerusalem; for the LORD hath comforted His people, He hath redeemed Jerusalem.

52:10 The LORD hath made bare His holy arm in the eyes of all the nations; and all the ends of the earth shall see the salvation of our God.

52:11 Depart ye, depart ye, go ye out from thence, touch no unclean thing; go ye out of the midst of her; be ye clean, ye that bear the vessels of the LORD.

52:12 For ye shall not go out in haste, neither shall ye go by flight; for the LORD will go before you, and the God of Israel will be your rearward.

52:13 Behold, My servant shall prosper, he shall be exalted and lifted up, and shall be very high.

52:14 According as many were appalled at thee—so marred was his visage unlike that of a man, and his form unlike that of the sons of men—

52:15 So shall he startle many nations, kings shall shut their mouths because of him; for that which had not been told them shall they see, and that which they had not heard shall they perceive.

WORLD ENGLISH BIBLE

53:1 Who has believed our message? To whom has the arm of Yahweh been revealed?

53:2 For he grew up before him as a tender plant, and as a root out of dry ground. He has no good looks or majesty. When we see him, there is no beauty that we should desire him.

53:3 He was despised, and rejected by men; a man of suffering, and acquainted with disease. He was despised as one from whom men hide their face; and we didn't respect him.

53:4 Surely he has borne our sickness, and carried our suffering; yet we considered him plagued, struck by God, and afflicted.

53:5 But he was pierced for our transgressions. He was crushed for our iniquities. The punishment that brought our peace was on him; and by his wounds we are healed.

53:6 All we like sheep have gone astray. Everyone has turned to his own way; and Yahweh has laid on him the iniquity of us all.

53:7 He was oppressed, yet when he was afflicted he didn't open his mouth. As a lamb that is led to the slaughter, and as a sheep that before its shearers is mute, so he didn't open his mouth.

53:8 He was taken away by oppression and judgment; and as for his generation, who considered that he was cut off out of the land of the living and stricken for the disobedience of my people?

53:9 They made his grave with the wicked, and with a rich man in his death; although he had done no violence, neither was any deceit in his mouth.

53:10 Yet it pleased Yahweh to bruise him. He has caused him to suffer. When you make his soul an offering for sin, he shall see his seed. He shall prolong his days, and the pleasure of Yahweh shall prosper in his hand.

TARGUM ISAIAH

53:1 Who hath believed this our report? and to whom is now the power of the arm of the Lord revealed?

53:2 The righteous shall be great before Him, behold, like branches that bud; and like a tree which sends forth its roots by the streams of water, thus shall the generation of the just multiply in the land, which hath need of Him.

53:3 His visage shall not be the visage of a common person, neither His fear the fear of a plebeian; but a holy brightness shall be His brightness, that every one who seeth Him shall contemplate Him.

53:4 Although He shall be in contempt; yet He shall cut off the glory of all the wicked, they shall be weak and wretched. Lo, we are in contempt and not esteemed, as a man of pain and appointed to sickness, and as if He had removed the face of His Shekinah from us.

53:5 Therefore He shall pray for our sins, and our iniquities for His sake shall be forgiven us; for we are considered crushed, smitten of the Lord, and afflicted.

53:6 He shall build the house of the sanctuary, which has been

TARGUM ISAIAH

profaned on account of our sins; He was delivered over on account of our iniquities, and through His doctrine peace shall be multiplied upon us, and through the teaching of His words our sins shall be forgiven us.

53:7 All we like sheep have been scattered, every one of us has turned to his own way; it pleased the Lord to forgive the sins of all of us for His sake.

53:8 He shall pray and He shall be answered, yea, before He shall open His mouth, He shall be heard; He shall deliver over the mighty of the nations as a lamb to the slaughter, and like a sheep before her shearers is dumb, none shall in His presence open his mouth, or speak a word.

53:9 He shall gather our captives from affliction and pain, and who shall be able to narrate the wonderful works which shall be done for us in His days? He shall remove the rule of the nations from the land of Israel, the sins which my people have committed have come upon them.

53:10 And He shall deliver the wicked into hell, and the riches of treasures which they got by

JEWISH PUBLICATION SOCIETY 1917

53:1 'Who would have believed our report? And to whom hath the arm of the LORD been revealed?

53:2 For he shot up right forth as a sapling, and as a root out of a dry ground; he had no form nor comeliness, that we should look upon him, nor beauty that we should delight in him.

53:3 He was despised, and forsaken of men, a man of pains, and acquainted with disease, and as one from whom men hide their face: he was despised, and we esteemed him not.

53:4 Surely our diseases he did bear, and our pains he carried; whereas we did esteem him stricken, smitten of God, and afflicted.

53:5 But he was wounded because of our transgressions, he was crushed because of our iniquities: the chastisement of our welfare was upon him, and with his stripes we were healed.

53:6 All we like sheep did go astray, we turned every one to his own way; and the LORD hath made to light on him the iniquity of us all.

53:7 He was oppressed, though he humbled himself and opened not his mouth; as a lamb that is led to the slaughter, and as a sheep that before her shearers is dumb; yea, he opened not his mouth.

53:8 By oppression and judgment he was taken away, and with his generation who did reason? for he was cut off out of the land of the living, for the transgression of my people to whom the stroke was due.

53:9 And they made his grave with the wicked, and with the rich his tomb; although he had done no violence, neither was any deceit in his mouth.'

53:10 Yet it pleased the LORD to crush him by disease; to see if his soul would offer itself in restitution, that he might see his seed, prolong his days, and that the purpose of the LORD might prosper by his hand:

WORLD ENGLISH BIBLE

53:11 After the suffering of his soul, he will see the light and be satisfied. My righteous servant will justify many by the knowledge of himself; and he will bear their iniquities.

53:12 Therefore will I divide him a portion with the great, and he shall divide the spoil with the strong; because he poured out his soul to death, and was numbered with the transgressors; yet he bore the sin of many, and made intercession for the transgressors.

54:1 "Sing, barren, you who didn't bear; break forth into singing, and cry aloud, you who did not travail with child: for more are the children of the desolate than the children of the married wife," says Yahweh.

54:2 "Enlarge the place of your tent, and let them stretch forth the curtains of your habitations; don't spare: lengthen your cords, and strengthen your stakes.

54:3 For you shall spread out on the right hand and on the left; and your seed shall possess the nations, and make the desolate cities to be inhabited.

54:4 "Don't be afraid; for you shall not be ashamed: neither be confounded; for you shall not be disappointed: for you shall forget the shame of your youth; and the reproach of your widowhood you shall remember no more.

54:5 For your Maker is your husband; Yahweh of Armies is his name: and the Holy One of Israel is your Redeemer; the God of the whole earth shall he be called.

TARGUM ISAIAH

violence unto the death of Abaddon, that they who commit sin shall not remain, and that they should not speak folly with their mouth.

53:11 And it was the pleasure of the Lord to refine and to purify the remnant of His people, in order to cleanse their souls from sin, that they might see the kingdom of their Messiah, that their sons and daughters might multiply, and prolong *their* days, and those that keep the law of the Lord shall prosper through His pleasure.

53:12 He shall deliver their souls from the servitude of the nations, they shall see the vengeance upon their enemies; they shall be satisfied with the spoil of their kings. By His wisdom He shall justify the righteous, in order to make many to keep the law, and He shall pray for their sin.

53:13 Therefore, I will divide to Him the spoil of many people, and the treasures of strong fortifications; He shall divide the spoil; because He has delivered His life unto death, and He shall make the rebellious to keep the law; He shall pray for the sins of many,

TARGUM ISAIAH

and as for the transgressors, each shall be pardoned for His sake.

54:1 Sing, O Jerusalem, who was like a barren woman that beareth not; rejoice with praise and be glad, who was like a woman that conceiveth not: for more shall be the children of Jerusalem that was laid desolate, than of the inhabited city, saith the Lord.

54:2 Enlarge the place of the house of thy dwelling, and from the cities of the land do not keep back the inhabitants; multiply the people of the camp, and increase the number of thy governors.

54:3 For thou shalt spread abroad to the south and to the north, and they children shall inherit the nations, and make the desolate cities to be inhabited.

54:4 Fear not, for thou shalt not be ashamed; neither be thou confounded, for thou shalt not be put to shame: for thou shalt forget the shame of thy youth, and shalt not remember the reproaches of thy widowhood any more.

54:5 For thy husband, who is thy Maker, the Lord of hosts is His name, and thy Redeemer *is* the Holy One of Israel; the God of the whole earth shall He be called.

JEWISH PUBLICATION SOCIETY 1917

53:11 Of the travail of his soul he shall see to the full, even My servant, who by his knowledge did justify the Righteous One to the many, and their iniquities he did bear.

53:12 Therefore will I divide him a portion among the great, and he shall divide the spoil with the mighty; because he bared his soul unto death, and was numbered with the transgressors; yet he bore the sin of many, and made intercession for the transgressors.

54:1 Sing, O barren, thou that didst not bear, break forth into singing, and cry aloud, thou that didst not travail; for more are the children of the desolate than the children of the married wife, saith the LORD.

54:2 Enlarge the place of thy tent, and let them stretch forth the curtains of thy habitations, spare not; lengthen thy cords, and strengthen thy stakes.

54:3 For thou shalt spread abroad on the right hand and on the left; and thy seed shall possess the nations, and make the desolate cities to be inhabited.

54:4 Fear not, for thou shalt not be ashamed. Neither be thou confounded, for thou shalt not be put to shame; for thou shalt forget the shame of thy youth, and the reproach of thy widowhood shalt thou remember no more.

54:5 For thy Maker is thy husband, the LORD of hosts is His name; and the Holy One of Israel is thy Redeemer, the God of the whole earth shall He be called.

WORLD ENGLISH BIBLE

54:6 For Yahweh has called you as a wife forsaken and grieved in spirit, even a wife of youth, when she is cast off," says your God.

54:7 "For a small moment have I forsaken you; but with great mercies will I gather you.

54:8 In overflowing wrath I hid my face from you for a moment; but with everlasting loving kindness will I have mercy on you," says Yahweh your Redeemer.

54:9 "For this is like the waters of Noah to me; for as I have sworn that the waters of Noah shall no more go over the earth, so have I sworn that I will not be angry with you, nor rebuke you.

54:10 For the mountains may depart, and the hills be removed; but my loving kindness shall not depart from you, neither shall my covenant of peace be removed," says Yahweh who has mercy on you.

54:11 "You afflicted, tossed with storms, and not comforted, behold, I will set your stones in beautiful colors, and lay your foundations with sapphires.

54:12 I will make your pinnacles of rubies, and your gates of sparkling jewels, and all your walls of precious stones.

54:13 All your children shall be taught of Yahweh; and great shall be the peace of your children.

54:14 In righteousness you shall be established: you shall be far from oppression, for you shall not be afraid; and from terror, for it shall not come near you.

54:15 Behold, they may gather together, but not by me: whoever shall gather together against you shall fall because of you.

54:16 "Behold, I have created the smith who blows the fire of coals, and brings forth a weapon for his work; and I have created the waster to destroy.

54:17 No weapon that is formed against you will prevail; and you will condemn every tongue that rises against you in judgment. This is the heritage of the servants of Yahweh, and their righteousness which is of me," says Yahweh.

TARGUM ISAIAH

54:6 For as a woman forsaken, and afflicted in spirit, the Shekinah, the Lord, met thee, like a woman of youth which was forsaken, saith thy God.

54:7 In a little anger have I forsaken thee; but with great mercies will I bring together thy captivity.

54:8 For a little moment I removed the presence of my Shekinah, *yea*, for a short time from thee, but with everlasting kindness, which shall not cease, will I have mercy on thee, saith the Lord thy Redeemer.

54:9 This shall be before me as the days of Noah, when I swore by my WORD, that the waters of the deluge, which were in the days of Noah, shall no more pass over the earth; thus I swear by my WORD, that my anger shall not be hurled upon thee, neither will I reprove thee.

54:10 For the mountains shall depart, and the hills shall be rent; but my kindness shall not depart from thee, O Jerusalem, neither shall the covenant of my peace be removed, saith the Lord, that will have mercy on thee.

54:11 O distressed city that receiveth affliction, concerning her the na-

TARGUM ISAIAH

tions say, She shall not be comforted: behold, I lay the stones of thy pavement with Mosaic, and thy foundations with costly stones.

54:12 And I will place thy timber with gems, and thy gates shall be of carbuncles, and all thy borders with precious stones.

54:13 And all thy children shall learn the law of the Lord; and great shall be the peace of thy children.

54:14 In righteousness shalt thou be established: thou shalt be far removed from oppression, for thou shalt not fear *it*: and from terror; for it shall not come upon thee,

54:15 Behold, the captivity of thy people shall surely be gathered unto thee: in the end, the kings of the nations, who are gathered together to oppress thee, O Jerusalem, shall be cast down in the midst of thee.

54:16 Behold, I have created the smith that bloweth the coals in the fire, and that bringeth forth an instrument for his use; and I have created the destroyer to destroy.

54:17 No weapon that is formed against thee, O Jerusalem, shall

JEWISH PUBLICATION SOCIETY 1917

54:6 For the LORD hath called thee as a wife forsaken and grieved in spirit; and a wife of youth, can she be rejected? saith thy God.

54:7 For a small moment have I forsaken thee; but with great compassion will I gather thee.

54:8 In a little wrath I hid My face from thee for a moment; but with everlasting kindness will I have compassion on thee, saith the LORD thy Redeemer.

54:9 For this is as the waters of Noah unto Me; for as I have sworn that the waters of Noah should no more go over the earth, so have I sworn that I would not be wroth with thee, nor rebuke thee.

54:10 For the mountains may depart, and the hills be removed; but My kindness shall not depart from thee, neither shall My covenant of peace be removed, saith the LORD that hath compassion on thee.

54:11 O thou afflicted, tossed with tempest, and not comforted, behold, I will set thy stones in fair colours, and lay thy foundations with sapphires.

54:12 And I will make thy pinnacles of rubies, and thy gates of carbuncles, and all thy border of precious stones.

54:13 And all thy children shall be taught of the LORD; and great shall be the peace of thy children.

54:14 In righteousness shalt thou be established; be thou far from oppression, for thou shalt not fear, and from ruin, for it shall not come near thee.

54:15 Behold, they may gather together, but not by Me; whosoever shall gather together against thee shall fall because of thee.

54:16 Behold, I have created the smith that bloweth the fire of coals, and bringeth forth a weapon for his work; and I have created the waster to destroy.

54:17 No weapon that is formed against thee shall prosper; and every tongue that shall rise against thee in judgment thou shalt condemn. This is the heritage of the servants of the LORD, and their due reward from Me, saith the LORD.

WORLD ENGLISH BIBLE

55:1 "Come, everyone who thirsts, to the waters! Come, he who has no money, buy, and eat! Yes, come, buy wine and milk without money and without price.

55:2 Why do you spend money for that which is not bread? and your labor for that which doesn't satisfy? listen diligently to me, and eat you that which is good, and let your soul delight itself in fatness.

55:3 Turn your ear, and come to me; hear, and your soul shall live: and I will make an everlasting covenant with you, even the sure mercies of David.

55:4 Behold, I have given him for a witness to the peoples, a leader and commander to the peoples.

55:5 Behold, you shall call a nation that you don't know; and a nation that didn't know you shall run to you, because of Yahweh your God, and for the Holy One of Israel; for he has glorified you."

55:6 Seek Yahweh while he may be found; call you on him while he is near:

55:7 let the wicked forsake his way, and the unrighteous man his thoughts; and let him return to Yahweh, and he will have mercy on him; and to our God, for he will abundantly pardon.

55:8 "For my thoughts are not your thoughts, neither are your ways my ways," says Yahweh.

55:9 "For as the heavens are higher than the earth, so are my ways higher than your ways, and my thoughts than your thoughts.

55:10 For as the rain comes down and the snow from the sky, and doesn't return there, but waters the earth, and makes it bring forth and bud, and gives seed to the sower and bread to the eater;

TARGUM ISAIAH

prosper; and every tongue that shall rise against thee in judgment thou shalt condemn. This is the heritage of the servants of the Lord, and their righteousness is from me, saith the Lord.

55:1 Ho, every one that is willing to learn, let him come and learn, and he that hath no silver, come, hear and learn; come, hear and learn, without price and money, doctrine that is better than wine and milk.

55:2 Wherefore do ye weigh out your silver for that which is not food? and your wealth for that which satisfieth not? Hearken diligently to my WORD, and ye shall eat that which *is* good, and let your soul delight itself in fatness.

55:3 Incline your ear and receive *instruction of my law*, obey my WORD and your soul shall be quickened, and I will make an everlasting covenant with you, even the mercies of David, which are sure.

55:4 Behold, I have appointed him a prince, a king, and a ruler over all the kingdoms.

55:5 Behold, a people which thou knowest not shall serve thee, and a people which hath not known thee shall run to offer tribute

TARGUM ISAIAH

unto thee, because of the Lord thy God, and for the Holy One of Israel; for He hath glorified thee.

55:6 Seek ye the fear of the Lord whilst ye are alive, supplicate before His presence whilst ye remain.

55:7 Let the wicked forsake his way of wickedness, and the man of violence his thoughts, and let him return to the worship of the Lord, and He will have mercy upon him; and unto the fear of our God, for He will abundantly pardon.

55:8 For your thoughts are not as my thoughts, and your ways are not right, as the ways of my goodness, saith the Lord.

55:9 For as the heavens are higher than the earth, thus are my ways better than your ways, and my thoughts better than your thoughts.

55:10 For as the rain cometh down, and the snow from heaven, and it is impossible that it should return thither, but watereth the earth, and maketh it to sprout, and to be fruitful, that it may give sufficient grain of seed to the sower, and food sufficient to the eater:

JEWISH PUBLICATION SOCIETY 1917

55:1 Ho, every one that thirsteth, come ye for water, and he that hath no money; come ye, buy, and eat; yea, come, buy wine and milk without money and without price.

55:2 Wherefore do ye spend money for that which is not bread? and your gain for that which satisfieth not? Hearken diligently unto Me, and eat ye that which is good, and let your soul delight itself in fatness.

55:3 Incline your ear, and come unto Me; hear, and your soul shall live; and I will make an everlasting covenant with you, even the sure mercies of David.

55:4 Behold, I have given him for a witness to the peoples, a prince and commander to the peoples.

55:5 Behold, thou shalt call a nation that thou knowest not, and a nation that knew not thee shall run unto thee; because of the LORD thy God, and for the Holy One of Israel, for He hath glorified thee.

55:6 Seek ye the LORD while He may be found, call ye upon Him while He is near;

55:7 Let the wicked forsake his way, and the man of iniquity his thoughts; and let him return unto the LORD, and He will have compassion upon him, and to our God, for He will abundantly pardon

55:8 For My thoughts are not your thoughts, neither are your ways My ways, saith the LORD.

55:9 For as the heavens are higher than the earth, so are My ways higher than your ways, and My thoughts than your thoughts.

55:10 For as the rain cometh down and the snow from heaven, and returneth not thither, except it water the earth, and make it bring forth and bud, and give seed to the sower and bread to the eater;

WORLD ENGLISH BIBLE

55:11 so shall my word be that goes forth out of my mouth: it shall not return to me void, but it shall accomplish that which I please, and it shall prosper in the thing I sent it to do.

55:12 For you shall go out with joy, and be led forth with peace: the mountains and the hills shall break forth before you into singing; and all the trees of the fields shall clap their hands.

55:13 Instead of the thorn shall come up the fir tree; and instead of the brier shall come up the myrtle tree: and it shall be to Yahweh for a name, for an everlasting sign that shall not be cut off."

56:1 Thus says Yahweh, "Keep justice, and do righteousness; for my salvation is near to come, and my righteousness to be revealed.

56:2 Blessed is the man who does this, and the son of man who holds it fast; who keeps the Sabbath from profaning it, and keeps his hand from doing any evil."

56:3 Neither let the foreigner, who has joined himself to Yahweh, speak, saying, "Yahweh will surely separate me from his people"; neither let the eunuch say, "Behold, I am a dry tree."

56:4 For thus says Yahweh, "To the eunuchs who keep my Sabbaths, and choose the things that please me, and hold fast my covenant:

56:5 to them I will give in my house and within my walls a memorial and a name better than of sons and of daughters; I will give them an everlasting name, that shall not be cut off.

56:6 Also the foreigners who join themselves to Yahweh, to minister to him, and to love the name of Yahweh, to be his servants, everyone who keeps the Sabbath from profaning it, and holds fast my covenant;

56:7 even them will I bring to my holy mountain, and make them joyful in my house of prayer: their burnt offerings and their sacrifices shall be accepted on my altar; for my house shall be called a house of prayer for all peoples."

TARGUM ISAIAH

55:11 Thus shall be the word of my kindness, which proceeds from my presence, it is not possible that it shall return to my presence void, but it shall accomplish that which I please, and shall prosper *in* the thing whereto I sent it.

55:12 For ye shall go out with joy from among the nations, and with peace ye shall be carried to your land: the mountains and the hills shall rejoice before you with praise, and all the trees of the field shall clap with their branches.

55:13 Instead of the wicked the righteous shall rise up, and instead of sinners shall rise up those that fear sin: and it shall be before the Lord for a name, for an everlasting sign, that shall not cease.

56:1 Thus saith the Lord, keep ye judgment, and do justice: for my salvation *is* near to come, and my righteousness to be revealed.

56:2 Blessed is the man that doeth this, and the son of man that layeth hold on it; every one that shall keep the Sabbath from polluting it, and shall keep his hand from doing any evil.

56:3 Neither let the son of the heathen, that is joined to the people of the Lord, say, The Lord hath

TARGUM ISAIAH

utterly separated me from His people: neither let the eunuch say, Behold, I am considered a dry tree.

56:4 For thus saith the Lord unto the eunuchs that keep my Sabbath days, and delight in what I desire, and take hold on my covenant:

56:5 Even unto them will I give in the house of my sanctuary, and in the land of the house of my Shekinah a place, and a name that is better than that of sons and of daughters: I will give them an everlasting name that shall not be cut off.

56:6 And the sons of the Gentiles, that are joined unto the people of the Lord, to serve Him, and to love the name of the Lord, to be His servants, every one that keepeth the Sabbath from polluting it, and taketh hold of my covenant;

56:7 Even them will I bring to my holy mountain, and make them joyful in my house of prayer: their burnt offerings and their holy sacrifices shall be offered up with acceptance upon mine altar; for the house of my sanctuary shall be called an house of prayer for all people.

55:11 So shall My word be that goeth forth out of My mouth: it shall not return unto Me void, except it accomplish that which I please, and make the thing whereto I sent it prosper.

55:12 For ye shall go out with joy, and be led forth with peace; the mountains and the hills shall break forth before you into singing, and all the trees of the field shall clap their hands.

55:13 Instead of the thorn shall come up the cypress, and instead of the brier shall come up the myrtle; and it shall be to the LORD for a memorial, for an everlasting sign that shall not be cut off.

56:1 Thus saith the LORD: Keep ye justice, and do righteousness; for My salvation is near to come, and My favour to be revealed.

56:2 Happy is the man that doeth this, and the son of man that holdeth fast by it: that keepeth the sabbath from profaning it, and keepeth his hand from doing any evil.

56:3 Neither let the alien, that hath joined himself to the LORD, speak, saying: 'The LORD will surely separate me from His people'; neither let the eunuch say: 'Behold, I am a dry tree.'

56:4 For thus saith the LORD concerning the eunuchs that keep My sabbaths, and choose the things that please Me, and hold fast by My covenant:

56:5 Even unto them will I give in My house and within My walls a monument and a memorial better than sons and daughters; I will give them an everlasting memorial, that shall not be cut off.

56:6 Also the aliens, that join themselves to the LORD, to minister unto Him, and to love the name of the LORD, to be His servants, every one that keepeth the sabbath from profaning it, and holdeth fast by My covenant:

56:7 Even them will I bring to My holy mountain, and make them joyful in My house of prayer; their burnt-offerings and their sacrifices shall be acceptable upon Mine altar; for My house shall be called a house of prayer for all peoples.

WORLD ENGLISH BIBLE

56:8 The Lord Yahweh, who gathers the outcasts of Israel, says, "Yet will I gather others to him, besides his own who are gathered."

56:9 All you animals of the field, come to devour, all you animals in the forest.

56:10 His watchmen are blind, they are all without knowledge; they are all mute dogs, they can't bark; dreaming, lying down, loving to slumber.

56:11 Yes, the dogs are greedy, they can never have enough; and these are shepherds who can't understand: they have all turned to their own way, each one to his gain, from every quarter.

56:12 "Come," say they, "I will get wine, and we will fill ourselves with strong drink; and tomorrow shall be as this day, great beyond measure."

57:1 The righteous perishes, and no man lays it to heart; and merciful men are taken away, none considering that the righteous is taken away from the evil.

57:2 He enters into peace; they rest in their beds, each one who walks in his uprightness.

57:3 "But draw near here, you sons of the sorceress, the seed of the adulterer and the prostitute.

57:4 Against whom do you sport yourselves? Against whom do you make a wide mouth, and stick out your tongue? Aren't you children of disobedience, a seed of falsehood,

57:5 you who inflame yourselves among the oaks, under every green tree; who kill the children in the valleys, under the clefts of the rocks?

57:6 Among the smooth stones of the valley is your portion; they, they are your lot; you have even poured a drink offering to them. You have offered an offering. Shall I be appeased for these things?

57:7 On a high and lofty mountain you have set your bed; there also you went up to offer sacrifice.

57:8 Behind the doors and the posts you have set up your memorial: for you have uncovered to someone besides me, and have gone up; you have enlarged your bed, and made you a covenant with them: you loved their bed where you saw it.

TARGUM ISAIAH

56:8 The Lord God, who will gather together the scattered ones of Israel, saith, I will again gather their captivity, by collecting them together.

56:9 All the kings of the nations, who are assembled together to oppress thee, O Jerusalem, shall be cast down in the midst of thee; they shall be for food to the beasts of the field, the beasts of the forest shall be satisfied with them.

56:10 Their watchmen are blind: they know nothing, all of them are dumb dogs, they are not able to bark, *they are* slumbering, they lie down, they love to sleep,

56:11 Yea, they are greedy dogs, they know not *how* to be satisfied; they are evildoers, they know not *how* to become wise: all of them go their own way, to rob the treasures of Israel.

56:12 Come ye, *say they*, We will fetch wine, and we will be inebriated with old wine, and tomorrow our banquet shall be better than today, great, very great.

57:1 The righteous die, and no man layeth my fear to heart; and the men who shew mercy are taken away, and they consider not that the righteous are taken away on

TARGUM ISAIAH

account of the evil which shall come.

57:2 They shall enter into peace; they shall rest in the place of their beds, those that do His law.

57:3 But ye, come nigh hither, O people of a generation whose works are evil, whose plant *was* of a holy plant; but they *are* adulterers, and fornicators.

57:4 Of whom do ye make your sport? and before whom do ye open your mouth? do ye continue speaking great things? are ye not rebellious children, a lying seed?

57:5 Who worship idols beneath every green tree, *who* sacrifice the children in the valleys under the clifts of the rocks.

57:6 Among the smooth stones of the valley is thy portion; yea, there they shall be thy lot, even to them thou hast poured out drink-offerings, thou hast offered sacrifices; ah! on account of these things my WORD shall retribute.

57:7 Upon a lofty and high mountain hast thou set the place of the house of thy dwelling, even thither didst thou go up to sacrifice.

57:8 Behind the doors and the posts hast thou set up the re-

JEWISH PUBLICATION SOCIETY 1917

56:8 Saith the Lord GOD who gathereth the dispersed of Israel: yet I will gather others to him, beside those of him that are gathered.

56:9 All ye beasts of the field, come to devour, yea, all ye beasts in the forest.

56:10 His watchmen are all blind, without knowledge; they are all dumb dogs, they cannot bark; raving, lying down, loving to slumber.

56:11 Yea, the dogs are greedy, they know not when they have enough; and these are shepherds that cannot understand; they all turn to their own way, each one to his gain, one and all.

56:12 'Come ye, I will fetch wine, and we will fill ourselves with strong drink; and to-morrow shall be as this day, and much more abundant.'

57:1 The righteous perisheth, and no man layeth it to heart, and godly men are taken away, none considering that the righteous is taken away from the evil to come.

57:2 He entereth into peace, they rest in their beds, each one that walketh in his uprightness.

57:3 But draw near hither, ye sons of the sorceress, the seed of the adulterer and the harlot.

57:4 Against whom do ye sport yourselves? Against whom make ye a wide mouth, and draw out the tongue? Are ye not children of transgression, a seed of falsehood,

57:5 Ye that inflame yourselves among the terebinths, under every leafy tree; that slay the children in the valleys, under the clefts of the rocks?

57:6 Among the smooth stones of the valley is thy portion; they, they are thy lot; even to them hast thou poured a drink-offering, thou hast offered a meal-offering. Should I pacify Myself for these things?

57:7 Upon a high and lofty mountain hast thou set thy bed; thither also wentest thou up to offer sacrifice.

57:8 And behind the doors and the posts hast thou set up thy symbol; for thou hast uncovered, and art gone up from Me, thou hast enlarged thy bed, and chosen thee of them whose bed thou lovedst, whose hand thou sawest.

WORLD ENGLISH BIBLE

57:9 You went to the king with oil, and increased your perfumes, and sent your ambassadors far off, and debased yourself even to Sheol.

57:10 You were wearied with the length of your way; yet you didn't say, 'It is in vain.' You found a reviving of your strength; therefore you weren't faint.

57:11 "Of whom have you been afraid and in fear, that you lie, and have not remembered me, nor laid it to your heart? Haven't I held my peace even of long time, and you don't fear me?

57:12 I will declare your righteousness; and as for your works, they shall not profit you.

57:13 When you cry, let those who you have gathered deliver you; but the wind shall take them, a breath shall carry them all away: but he who takes refuge in me shall possess the land, and shall inherit my holy mountain."

57:14 He will say, "Cast up, cast up, prepare the way, take up the stumbling-block out of the way of my people."

57:15 For thus says the high and lofty One who inhabits eternity, whose name is Holy: "I dwell in the high and holy place, with him also who is of a contrite and humble spirit, to revive the spirit of the humble, and to revive the heart of the contrite.

57:16 For I will not contend forever, neither will I be always angry; for the spirit would faint before me, and the souls who I have made.

TARGUM ISAIAH

membrance of thy idols; thou hast been like a woman who is beloved by her husband, but goeth astray after strangers; thou hast enlarged thy bed: thou hast made a covenant with some of them, thou lovedst the place, the place of their beds, the place thou hast chosen.

57:9 When thou didst keep the law, thou didst prosper in the kingdom; and when thou didst multiply for thyself good works, thy camp was enlarged, and thou didst send thy messengers to a distant land; and thou didst humble mighty nations unto hades.

57:10 Thou hast wearied thyself in the greatness of thy way; *yet* thou didst not think to return the many treasures thou hast multiplied, wherefore thou thoughtest not to repent.

57:11 And of whom hast thou been afraid? and on account of whom hast thou feared? Thou hast surely multiplied speaking lies, and thou hast not remembered my service, and hast not had my fear in thine heart: I would have given you the ends of the world, if you had returned to my law; but thou hast not returned to me.

TARGUM ISAIAH

57:12 I have shewn thee those good works, which would have been thy righteousness; but thou hast multiplied evil works which did not profit thee.

57:13 Proclaim aloud, whether thy deceitful works will save thee, in which thou hast been occupied from thy youth? the wind shall carry away all of them, they shall be as nothing: but he that putteth his trust in my WORD shall possess the earth, and shall inherit my holy mountain.

57:14 And he shall say, Teach and admonish, turn the heart of this people to the right way; remove the stumbling-block of the wicked out of the way of the congregation of my people.

57:15 For thus saith the high and lofty One, that dwelleth in the heavens, and whose name is Holy, who inhabits the height—yea, His holy Shekinah hath promised to save the contrite of heart, and the humble of spirit, to revive the spirit of the humble, and to support the heart of the contrite.

57:16 For I will not take vengeance of judgment for ever, neither shall my wrath be eternal: for I will revive the spirits of the dead, and

JEWISH PUBLICATION SOCIETY 1917

57:9 And thou wentest to the king with ointment, and didst increase thy perfumes, and didst send thine ambassadors far off, even down to the nether-world.

57:10 Thou wast wearied with the length of thy way; yet saidst thou not: 'There is no hope'; thou didst find a renewal of thy strength, therefore thou wast not affected.

57:11 And of whom hast thou been afraid and in fear, that thou wouldest fail? And as for Me, thou hast not remembered Me, nor laid it to thy heart. Have not I held My peace even of long time? Therefore thou fearest Me not.

57:12 I will declare thy righteousness; thy works also—they shall not profit thee.

57:13 When thou criest, let them that thou hast gathered deliver thee; but the wind shall carry them all away, a breath shall bear them off; but he that taketh refuge in Me shall possess the land, and shall inherit My holy mountain.

57:14 And He will say: cast ye up, cast ye up, clear the way, take up the stumblingblock out of the way of My people.

57:15 For thus saith the High and Lofty One that inhabiteth eternity, whose name is Holy: I dwell in the high and holy place, with him also that is of a contrite and humble spirit, to revive the spirit of the humble, and to revive the heart of the contrite ones.

57:16 For I will not contend for ever, neither will I be always wroth; for the spirit that enwrappeth itself is from Me, and the souls which I have made.

WORLD ENGLISH BIBLE

57:17 For the iniquity of his covetousness was I angry, and struck him; I hid myself and was angry; and he went on backsliding in the way of his heart.

57:18 I have seen his ways, and will heal him: I will lead him also, and restore comforts to him and to his mourners.

57:19 I create the fruit of the lips: Peace, peace, to him who is far off and to him who is near," says Yahweh; "and I will heal them."

57:20 But the wicked are like the troubled sea; for it can't rest, and its waters cast up mire and dirt.

57:21 "There is no peace," says my God, "for the wicked."

58:1 "Cry aloud, don't spare, lift up your voice like a trumpet, and declare to my people their disobedience, and to the house of Jacob their sins.

58:2 Yet they seek me daily, and delight to know my ways: as a nation that did righteousness, and didn't forsake the ordinance of their God, they ask of me righteous judgments; they delight to draw near to God.

58:3 'Why have we fasted,' say they, 'and you don't see? Why have we afflicted our soul, and you take no knowledge?' "Behold, in the day of your fast you find pleasure, and exact all your labors.

58:4 Behold, you fast for strife and contention, and to strike with the fist of wickedness: you don't fast this day so as to make your voice to be heard on high.

58:5 Is such the fast that I have chosen? the day for a man to afflict his soul? Is it to bow down his head as a rush, and to spread sackcloth and ashes under him? Will you call this a fast, and an acceptable day to Yahweh?

58:6 "Isn't this the fast that I have chosen: to release the bonds of wickedness, to undo the bands of the yoke, and to let the oppressed go free, and that you break every yoke?

TARGUM ISAIAH

the souls I have created.

57:17 My wrath is upon them on account of their robbed riches, and I smote them; I removed my Shekinah from them, and cast them out; I scattered their captives, because they went astray after the imagination of their hearts.

57:18 The way of their repentance is revealed before me, and I will forgive them, and I will have compassion upon them, and requite consolations to them and to those that mourn with them.

57:19 The prophet saith: He that creates the speech in the lips of every man, peace shall be wrought for the righteous, who have kept my law of old, and peace shall be wrought out for the penitent, who return to my law. It is at hand that I will pardon them, saith the Lord.

57:20 But the wicked are like the troubled sea, that seeketh to rest, but cannot, and its waters bring forth mire and dirt.

57:21 There is no peace, saith my God, to the wicked.

58:1 Cry aloud, O prophet, spare not, lift up thy voice like the voice of a trumpet, and shew unto my people their rebellion, and unto

TARGUM ISAIAH

the house of Jacob their sins.

58:2 And they seek daily instruction from me, as if to know the ways which are right before me, finding delight in my presence as a people that doeth righteousness, and have not forsaken the judgment of their God: they ask of me judgment and truth, as if they delighted to draw nigh to the fear of the Lord.

58:3 They say, Wherefore do we fast, as it is revealed before Thee? wherefore have we afflicted ourselves, as known unto Thee? The prophet said unto them, Behold, in the day of your fast ye seek your extortions, and ye bring near all your stumbling-blocks.

58:4 Behold, ye fast for provocation and strife, and to smite with the fist of wickedness; ye shall not fast a fast as if to make your voice to be heard on high.

58:5 Is this the fast which I delight in? a day to afflict oneself? Is it to have his head bent down as a bulrush, and passing the night in sackcloth and ashes? Will ye call this a fast before the presence of the Lord, and a day in which I delight?

58:6 Is not this the fast which I

JEWISH PUBLICATION SOCIETY 1917

57:17 For the iniquity of his covetousness was I wroth and smote him, I hid Me and was wroth; and he went on frowardly in the way of his heart.
57:18 I have seen his ways, and will heal him; I will lead him also, and requite with comforts him and his mourners.
57:19 Peace, peace, to him that is far off and to him that is near, saith the LORD that createth the fruit of the lips; and I will heal him.
57:20 But the wicked are like the troubled sea; for it cannot rest, and its waters cast up mire and dirt.
57:21 There is no peace, saith my God concerning the wicked.
58:1 Cry aloud, spare not, lift up thy voice like a horn, and declare unto My people their transgression, and to the house of Jacob their sins.
58:2 Yet they seek Me daily, and delight to know My ways; as a nation that did righteousness, and forsook not the ordinance of their God, they ask of Me righteous ordinances, they delight to draw near unto God.
58:3 'Wherefore have we fasted, and Thou seest not? Wherefore have we afflicted our soul, and Thou takest no knowledge?'— Behold, in the day of your fast ye pursue your business, and exact all your labours.
58:4 Behold, ye fast for strife and contention, and to smite with the fist of wickedness; ye fast not this day so as to make your voice to be heard on high.
58:5 Is such the fast that I have chosen? the day for a man to afflict his soul? Is it to bow down his head as a bulrush, and to spread sackcloth and ashes under him? Wilt thou call this a fast, and an acceptable day to the LORD?
58:6 Is not this the fast that I have chosen? to loose the fetters of wickedness, to undo the bands of the yoke, and to let the oppressed go free, and that ye break every yoke?

WORLD ENGLISH BIBLE

58:7 Isn't it to distribute your bread to the hungry, and that you bring the poor who are cast out to your house? When you see the naked, that you cover him; and that you not hide yourself from your own flesh?

58:8 Then your light shall break forth as the morning, and your healing shall spring forth speedily; and your righteousness shall go before you; the glory of Yahweh shall be your rear guard.

58:9 Then you shall call, and Yahweh will answer; you shall cry, and he will say, 'Here I am.' "If you take away from the midst of you the yoke, the putting forth of the finger, and speaking wickedly;

58:10 and if you draw out your soul to the hungry, and satisfy the afflicted soul: then your light shall rise in darkness, and your obscurity be as the noonday;

58:11 and Yahweh will guide you continually, and satisfy your soul in dry places, and make strong your bones; and you shall be like a watered garden, and like a spring of water, whose waters don't fail.

58:12 Those who shall be of you shall build the old waste places; you shall raise up the foundations of many generations; and you shall be called The repairer of the breach, The restorer of paths to dwell in.

58:13 "If you turn away your foot from the Sabbath, from doing your pleasure on my holy day; and call the Sabbath a delight, and the holy of Yahweh honorable; and shall honor it, not doing your own ways, nor finding your own pleasure, nor speaking your own words:

58:14 then you shall delight yourself in Yahweh; and I will make you to ride on the high places of the earth; and I will feed you with the heritage of Jacob your father:" for the mouth of Yahweh has spoken it.

TARGUM ISAIAH

have chosen? to scatter the assembly of wickedness, to loose the fetters of a decree of perverted judgment, to set at liberty the sons of the freeborn, who have suffered violence, and to remove all perverted judgment?

58:7 Shouldest not thou sustain the hungry with thy bread, and bring the poor that are cast out, into the midst of thy house? When thou seest the naked, that thou cover him, and shouldest not hide thine eyes from the kindred who is thy flesh?

58:8 Then shall thy light be revealed like the early dawn, and the healing of thy wound shall appear quickly; thy great righteousness shall go before thee, and thou shalt be gathered to the glory, which is in the presence of the Lord.

58:9 Then thou shalt pray, and the Lord shall hear thy prayer; thou shalt supplicate before Him, and He shall grant thy supplication, if thou put away from the midst of thee perverted judgment, the pointing of the finger, and the speaking of violent words;

58:10 And if thou breathest out thy soul before the hungry and satis-

TARGUM ISAIAH

fiest the afflicted soul, then shall thy light rise in obscurity, and thy darkness be as the noonday:

58:11 And the Lord shall guide thee continually, and satisfy thy soul in the years of drought, and He shall quicken thy body with eternal life, and thy soul shall be full with delicacies like a watered garden, well irrigated, and like a spring of water, whose waters fail not.

58:12 Thy offspring shall build the old waste places: thou shalt raise up the foundations of many generations, and they shall call thee, The restorer of the right way; The converter of the wicked to the law.

58:13 If thou turn away thy foot from the Sabbath from following thine employment on my holy day, and dost meet the Sabbath with great delight to sanctify the Lord, and honour Him, not doing thine own ways, nor making thy wants ample, nor speaking violent words:

58:14 Then shalt thou delight thyself in the Lord; and He shall cause thee to dwell in the strong places of the earth, and feed thee with the heritage of Jacob thy fa-

JEWISH PUBLICATION SOCIETY 1917

58:7 Is it not to deal thy bread to the hungry, and that thou bring the poor that are cast out to thy house? when thou seest the naked, that thou cover him, and that thou hide not thyself from thine own flesh?

58:8 Then shall thy light break forth as the morning, and thy healing shall spring forth speedily; and thy righteousness shall go before thee, the glory of the LORD shall be thy rearward.

58:9 Then shalt thou call, and the LORD will answer; thou shalt cry, and He will say: 'Here I am.' If thou take away from the midst of thee the yoke, the putting forth of the finger, and speaking wickedness;

58:10 And if thou draw out thy soul to the hungry, and satisfy the afflicted soul; then shall thy light rise in darkness, and thy gloom be as the noonday;

58:11 And the LORD will guide thee continually, and satisfy thy soul in drought, and make strong thy bones; and thou shalt be like a watered garden, and like a spring of water, whose waters fail not.

58:12 And they that shall be of thee shall build the old waste places, thou shalt raise up the foundations of many generations; and thou shalt be called The repairer of the breach, the restorer of paths to dwell in.

58:13 If thou turn away thy foot because of the sabbath, from pursuing thy business on My holy day; and call the sabbath a delight, and the holy of the LORD honourable; and shalt honour it, not doing thy wonted ways, nor pursuing thy business, nor speaking thereof;

58:14 Then shalt thou delight thyself in the LORD, and I will make thee to ride upon the high places of the earth, and I will feed thee with the heritage of Jacob thy father; for the mouth of the LORD hath spoken it.

WORLD ENGLISH BIBLE

59:1 Behold, Yahweh's hand is not shortened, that it can't save; neither his ear heavy, that it can't hear:

59:2 but your iniquities have separated between you and your God, and your sins have hidden his face from you, so that he will not hear.

59:3 For your hands are defiled with blood, and your fingers with iniquity; your lips have spoken lies, your tongue mutters wickedness.

59:4 None sues in righteousness, and none pleads in truth: they trust in vanity, and speak lies; they conceive mischief, and bring forth iniquity.

59:5 They hatch adders' eggs, and weave the spider's web: he who eats of their eggs dies; and that which is crushed breaks out into a viper.

59:6 Their webs shall not become garments, neither shall they cover themselves with their works: their works are works of iniquity, and the act of violence is in their hands.

59:7 Their feet run to evil, and they make haste to shed innocent blood: their thoughts are thoughts of iniquity; desolation and destruction are in their paths.

59:8 The way of peace they don't know; and there is no justice in their goings: they have made them crooked paths; whoever goes therein does not know peace.

59:9 Therefore is justice far from us, neither does righteousness overtake us: we look for light, but, behold, darkness; for brightness, but we walk in obscurity.

59:10 We grope for the wall like the blind; yes, we grope as those who have no eyes: we stumble at noonday as in the twilight; among those who are lusty we are as dead men.

59:11 We roar all like bears, and moan bitterly like doves: we look for justice, but there is none; for salvation, but it is far off from us.

TARGUM ISAIAH

ther; for thus it is decreed by the Word of the Lord.

59:1 Behold, it is not on account of *any* deficiency in the power of the Lord that ye are not saved; nor because it is too difficult for Him to hear, that your prayer is not received:

59:2 But your iniquities separate between you and your God, and your sins have caused *Him* to take away the favour of His Shekinah from you, not to receive your prayer.

59:3 For your hands are associated with innocent blood, and your fingers with iniquity; your lips speak lies, your tongue muttereth deceit.

59:4 There is none that truly prayeth, nor *any* that pleadeth for faithfulness: they trust in vanity, and speak lies; *they* hasten, and bring forth words of violence out of their heart.

59:5 Behold, they hatch as it were eggs of a basilisk; they are like the threads which the spiders weave: he that eateth of their eggs dieth; and when they are hatched, they bring forth the flying serpents.

59:6 Behold, like a spider's web, with which no one can be covered, thus there is no profit from

TARGUM ISAIAH

the works of the wicked; their works are the works of violence, and the work of a lie is in their hands.

59:7 Their feet run to do that which is evil, and they make haste to shed innocent blood: their thoughts *are* thoughts of violence, plunder and destruction are in their paths.

59:8 The way of peace they know not; and there is no justice in their ways, they have perverted their ways: whoever goeth therein shall not know peace.

59:9 Therefore is judgment removed far from us, and *the least* righteousness does not meet us: we wait for light, but behold, darkness; for brightness, but behold, we are walking in obscurity.

59:10 We grope for the wall like the blind, and we grope as if we had no eyes: we stumble at noonday as those that stumble in the dark; it is shut up before us, as the graves are shut up before the dead.

59:11 We all roar like bears by reason of our enemies, who are gathered against us, and mourn like doves: we hoped for judgment, but there is none; for salvation,

JEWISH PUBLICATION SOCIETY **1917**

59:1 Behold, the LORD'S hand is not shortened, that it cannot save, neither His ear heavy, that it cannot hear;

59:2 But your iniquities have separated between you and your God, and your sins have hid His face from you, that He will not hear.

59:3 For your hands are defiled with blood, and your fingers with iniquity; your lips have spoken lies, your tongue muttereth wickedness.

59:4 None sueth in righteousness, and none pleadeth in truth; they trust in vanity, and speak lies, they conceive mischief, and bring forth iniquity.

59:5 They hatch basilisks' eggs, and weave the spider's web; he that eateth of their eggs dieth, and that which is crushed breaketh out into a viper.

59:6 Their webs shall not become garments, neither shall men cover themselves with their works; their works are works of iniquity, and the act of violence is in their hands.

59:7 Their feet run to evil, and they make haste to shed innocent blood; their thoughts are thoughts of iniquity, desolation and destruction are in their paths.

59:8 The way of peace they know not, and there is no right in their goings; they have made them crooked paths, whosoever goeth therein doth not know peace.

59:9 Therefore is justice far from us, neither doth righteousness overtake us; we look for light, but behold darkness, for brightness, but we walk in gloom.

59:10 We grope for the wall like the blind, yea, as they that have no eyes do we grope; we stumble at noonday as in the twilight; we are in dark places like the dead.

59:11 We all growl like bears, and mourn sore like doves; we look for right, but there is none; for salvation, but it is far off from us.

WORLD ENGLISH BIBLE

59:12 For our transgressions are multiplied before you, and our sins testify against us; for our transgressions are with us, and as for our iniquities, we know them:

59:13 transgressing and denying Yahweh, and turning away from following our God, speaking oppression and revolt, conceiving and uttering from the heart words of falsehood.

59:14 Justice is turned away backward, and righteousness stands afar off; for truth is fallen in the street, and uprightness can't enter.

59:15 Yes, truth is lacking; and he who departs from evil makes himself a prey. Yahweh saw it, and it displeased him that there was no justice.

59:16 He saw that there was no man, and wondered that there was no intercessor: therefore his own arm brought salvation to him; and his righteousness, it upheld him.

59:17 He put on righteousness as a breastplate, and a helmet of salvation on his head; and he put on garments of vengeance for clothing, and was clad with zeal as a mantle.

59:18 According to their deeds, accordingly he will repay, wrath to his adversaries, recompense to his enemies; to the islands he will repay recompense.

59:19 So shall they fear the name of Yahweh from the west, and his glory from the rising of the sun; for he will come as a rushing stream, which the breath of Yahweh drives.

59:20 "A Redeemer will come to Zion, and to those who turn from disobedience in Jacob," says Yahweh.

59:21 "As for me, this is my covenant with them," says Yahweh. "My Spirit who is on you, and my words which I have put in your mouth, shall not depart out of your mouth, nor out of the mouth of your seed, nor out of the mouth of your seed's seed," says Yahweh, "from henceforth and forever."

TARGUM ISAIAH

but it is far removed from us.

59:12 Because our iniquities are multiplied before Thee, and our sins testify against us: for our iniquities are revealed unto us, and our crimes we know them.

59:13 We have rebelled, and acted falsely against the WORD of the Lord; we have turned backward from following after the worship of our God; we have spoken falsehood and apostasy, hastening and bringing forth from their hearts lying words.

59:14 And justice is turned away backward, and righteousness standeth afar off: for they that follow truth stumble in the street; and they that follow faithfulness cannot shew themselves.

59:15 And they that follow truth are hidden, and those that depart from evil become a prey. It is revealed before the Lord, that there is no justice, which is evil in His sight

59:16 And it is revealed in His sight that there is no man who hath good works, and it is known to Him that there is no man, who would arise and seek after them: therefore He will redeem them by the arm of His strength, and by

TARGUM ISAIAH

the WORD of His delight He will help them.

59:17 It is revealed, that He will work a great salvation for His people, yea, He will render vengeance to His enemies.

59:18 He is the Lord of retributions, He shall render recompense: vengeance to His enemies, retribution to His adversaries; He shall render recompense to the islands.

59:19 They shall fear the name of the Lord from the west, and His glory from the rising of the sun. When the oppressors shall come in like an inundation of the river Euphrates, they shall be broken by the WORD of the Lord.

59:20 And the Redeemer shall come to Zion, and turn the transgressors of the house of Jacob to the law, saith the Lord.

59:21 And as for me, this shall be my covenant with them, saith the Lord; My Holy Spirit that is upon thee, and the words of my prophecy which I have put in thy mouth, shall not depart out of thy mouth, nor out of the mouth of thy children, nor out of the mouth of thy children's children, saith the Lord, from henceforth

JEWISH PUBLICATION SOCIETY 1917

59:12 For our transgressions are multiplied before Thee, and our sins testify against us; for our transgressions are present to us, and as for our iniquities, we know them:

59:13 Transgressing and denying the LORD, and turning away from following our God, speaking oppression and perverseness, conceiving and uttering from the heart words of falsehood.

59:14 And justice is turned away backward, and righteousness standeth afar off; for truth hath stumbled in the broad place, and uprightness cannot enter.

59:15 And truth is lacking, and he that departeth from evil maketh himself a prey. And the LORD saw it, and it displeased Him that there was no justice;

59:16 And He saw that there was no man, and was astonished that there was no intercessor; therefore His own arm brought salvation unto Him; and His righteousness, it sustained Him;

59:17 And He put on righteousness as a coat of mail, and a helmet of salvation upon His head, and He put on garments of vengeance for clothing, and was clad with zeal as a cloak.

59:18 According to their deeds, accordingly He will repay, fury to His adversaries, recompense to His enemies; to the islands He will repay recompense.

59:19 So shall they fear the name of the LORD from the west, and His glory from the rising of the sun; for distress will come in like a flood, which the breath of the LORD driveth.

59:20 And a redeemer will come to Zion, and unto them that turn from transgression in Jacob, saith the LORD.

59:21 And as for Me, this is My covenant with them, saith the LORD; My spirit that is upon thee, and My words which I have put in thy mouth, shall not depart out of thy mouth, nor out of the mouth of thy seed, nor out of the mouth of thy seed's seed, saith the LORD, from henceforth and for ever.

WORLD ENGLISH BIBLE

60:1 "Arise, shine; for your light has come, and the glory of Yahweh is risen on you.

60:2 For, behold, darkness shall cover the earth, and gross darkness the peoples; but Yahweh will arise on you, and his glory shall be seen on you.

60:3 Nations shall come to your light, and kings to the brightness of your rising.

60:4 "Lift up your eyes all around, and see: they all gather themselves together, they come to you; your sons shall come from far, and your daughters shall be carried in the arms.

60:5 Then you shall see and be radiant, and your heart shall thrill and be enlarged; because the abundance of the sea shall be turned to you, the wealth of the nations shall come to you.

60:6 The multitude of camels shall cover you, the dromedaries of Midian and Ephah; all they from Sheba shall come; they shall bring gold and frankincense, and shall proclaim the praises of Yahweh.

60:7 All the flocks of Kedar shall be gathered together to you, the rams of Nebaioth shall minister to you; they shall come up with acceptance on my altar; and I will glorify the house of my glory.

60:8 "Who are these who fly as a cloud, and as the doves to their windows?

60:9 Surely the islands shall wait for me, and the ships of Tarshish first, to bring your sons from far, their silver and their gold with them, for the name of Yahweh your God, and for the Holy One of Israel, because he has glorified you.

60:10 "Foreigners shall build up your walls, and their kings shall minister to you: for in my wrath I struck you, but in my favor have I had mercy on you.

TARGUM ISAIAH

and for ever.

60:1 Arise, shine, O Jerusalem, for the time of thy redemption is come, and the glory of the Lord is revealed upon thee.

60:2 For, behold, the darkness shall cover the earth, and gross darkness the kingdoms: but in thee the Shekinah of the Lord shall dwell, and His glory shall be revealed upon thee.

60:3 And the Gentiles shall come to thy light, and kings to thy brightness.

60:4 Lift up thine eyes, O Jerusalem, round about, and see all the children of the people of thy captivity, who are gathered together: thy sons shall come from far into thy midst, and thy daughters shall be carried upon the arms.

60:5 Then thou shalt see and be enlightened, and thou shalt be struck with awe, and thine heart shall be enlarged on account of the terror of sinners, for the riches of the west shall be transferred unto thee; the treasures of the nations shall be brought unto thee.

60:6 A multitude of Arabians shall cover thee round about, the dromedaries of Midian and Holad, all of them from Sheba shall come:

TARGUM ISAIAH

they shall be laden with gold and frankincense, and those that are coming with them, shall shew forth the praises of the Lord.

60:7 All the sheep of the Arabians shall be gathered unto thee, the rams of Nebaioth shall minister unto thee: they shall be offered up with acceptance upon mine altar, and I will glorify the house of my glory.

60:8 Who are these that are coming openly like swift clouds, and tarry not? the captives of Israel, who are gathered together, come to their land, lo, as doves which return to their dove-houses.

60:9 Surely, the isles shall wait for my WORD, and those that embark in the ships of the sea, the hand that stretcheth out their sails shall be first, to bring thy sons from far, their silver and their gold with them, unto the name of the Lord thy God, and to the Holy One of Israel, because He hath glorified thee.

60:10 And the sons of the nations shall build up thy walls, and their kings shall minister unto thee: for in my wrath I smote thee, but in my favour have I had mercy on thee.

JEWISH PUBLICATION SOCIETY 1917

60:1 Arise, shine, for thy light is come, and the glory of the LORD is risen upon thee.

60:2 For, behold, darkness shall cover the earth, and gross darkness the peoples; but upon thee the LORD will arise, and His glory shall be seen upon thee.

60:3 And nations shall walk at thy light, and kings at the brightness of thy rising.

60:4 Lift Up thine eyes round about, and see: they all are gathered together, and come to thee; thy sons come from far, and thy daughters are borne on the side.

60:5 Then thou shalt see and be radiant, and thy heart shall throb and be enlarged; because the abundance of the sea shall be turned unto thee, the wealth of the nations shall come unto thee.

60:6 The caravan of camels shall cover thee, and of the young camels of Midian and Ephah, all coming from Sheba; they shall bring gold and incense, and shall proclaim the praises of the LORD.

60:7 All the flocks of Kedar shall be gathered together unto thee, the rams of Nebaioth shall minister unto thee; they shall come up with acceptance on Mine altar, and I will glorify My glorious house.

60:8 Who are these that fly as a cloud, and as the doves to their cotes?

60:9 Surely the isles shall wait for Me, and the ships of Tarshish first, to bring thy sons from far, their silver and their gold with them, for the name of the LORD thy God, and for the Holy One of Israel, because He hath glorified thee.

60:10 And aliens shall build up thy walls, And their kings shall minister unto thee; for in My wrath I smote thee, but in My favour have I had compassion on thee.

WORLD ENGLISH BIBLE

60:11 Your gates also shall be open continually; they shall not be shut day nor night; that men may bring to you the wealth of the nations, and their kings led captive.

60:12 For that nation and kingdom that will not serve you shall perish; yes, those nations shall be utterly wasted.

60:13 "The glory of Lebanon shall come to you, the fir tree, the pine, and the box tree together, to beautify the place of my sanctuary; and I will make the place of my feet glorious.

60:14 The sons of those who afflicted you shall come bending to you; and all those who despised you shall bow themselves down at the soles of your feet; and they shall call you The city of Yahweh, The Zion of the Holy One of Israel.

60:15 "Whereas you have been forsaken and hated, so that no man passed through you, I will make you an eternal excellency, a joy of many generations.

60:16 You shall also drink the milk of the nations, and shall nurse from royal breasts; and you shall know that I, Yahweh, am your Savior, and your Redeemer, the Mighty One of Jacob.

60:17 For brass I will bring gold, and for iron I will bring silver, and for wood brass, and for stones iron. I will also make your officers peace, and righteousness your ruler.

60:18 Violence shall no more be heard in your land, desolation nor destruction within your borders; but you shall call your walls Salvation, and your gates Praise.

60:19 The sun shall be no more your light by day; neither for brightness shall the moon give light to you: but Yahweh will be to you an everlasting light, and your God your glory.

60:20 Your sun shall no more go down, neither shall your moon withdraw itself; for Yahweh will be your everlasting light, and the days of your mourning shall be ended.

60:21 Your people also shall be all righteous; they shall inherit the land forever, the branch of my planting, the work of my hands, that I may be glorified.

TARGUM ISAIAH

60:11 Thy gates shall be open continually; they shall not be shut day nor night; that *men* may bring unto thee the treasures of the nations, and their kings *in* chains.

60:12 For the nation and kingdom that will not serve thee, O Jerusalem, shall perish; yea, *those* nations shall be utterly destroyed.

60:13 The glory of Lebanon shall be brought unto thee, the fir-tree, the elm, and the box together, to beautify the place of the house of my sanctuary; and I will make the place of the dwelling of my Shekinah glorious.

60:14 The sons of them that enslaved thee shall come and bow down to thee, and all that provoked thee to anger shall prostrate themselves at the soles of thy feet to make supplication unto thee; and they shall call thee, The city of the Lord, *The* Zion in which the Holy One of Israel delights.

60:15 Whereas thou hast been forsaken, and an outcast, so that none went through *thee*, I will make thee an eternal glory, the house of joy for generation and generation.

60:16 And thou shalt be satisfied with the riches of the nations, and

TARGUM ISAIAH

in the spoil of their kings thou shalt delight thyself; and thou shalt know that I am the Lord, thy Saviour and thy Redeemer, the mighty One of Jacob.

60:17 For the brass which they spoiled thee of, O Jerusalem, I will bring gold, and for the iron I will bring silver, and for the wood brass, and for the stones iron: I will also make thy pastors peace, and thy rulers righteousness.

60:18 Violence shall no more be heard in thy land, spoil nor destruction within thy borders; but they shall proclaim salvation on thy walls, and on thy gates there shall be those that praise.

60:19 Thou shalt need no more the sun for a light by day, neither for brightness the moon by night: but the Lord shall be unto thee an everlasting light, and thy God thy glory.

60:20 Thy kingdom shall cease no more, and thy glory shall not be removed: for the Lord shall be thine everlasting light, and the days of thy mourning shall be ended.

60:21 Thy people shall be all righteous: for ever shall they inherit

JEWISH PUBLICATION SOCIETY 1917

60:11 Thy gates also shall be open continually, day and night, they shall not be shut; that men may bring unto thee the wealth of the nations, and their kings in procession.

60:12 For that nation and kingdom that will not serve thee shall perish; yea, those nations shall be utterly wasted.

60:13 The glory of Lebanon shall come unto thee, the cypress, the plane-tree and the larch together; to beautify the place of My sanctuary, and I will make the place of My feet glorious.

60:14 And the sons of them that afflicted thee shall come bending unto thee, and all they that despised thee shall bow down at the soles of thy feet; and they shall call thee The city of the LORD, the Zion of the Holy One of Israel.

60:15 Whereas thou hast been forsaken and hated, so that no man passed through thee, I will make thee an eternal excellency, a joy of many generations.

60:16 Thou shalt also suck the milk of the nations, and shalt suck the breast of kings; and thou shalt know that I the LORD am thy Saviour, and I, the Mighty One of Jacob, thy Redeemer.

60:17 For brass I will bring gold, and for iron I will bring silver, and for wood brass, and for stones iron; I will also make thy officers peace, and righteousness thy magistrates.

60:18 Violence shall no more be heard in thy land, desolation nor destruction within thy borders; but thou shalt call thy walls Salvation, and thy gates Praise.

60:19 The sun shall be no more thy light by day, neither for brightness shall the moon give light unto thee; but the LORD shall be unto thee an everlasting light, and thy God thy glory.

60:20 Thy sun shall no more go down, Neither shall thy moon withdraw itself; for the LORD shall be thine everlasting light, and the days of thy mourning shall be ended.

60:21 Thy people also shall be all righteous, they shall inherit the land for ever; the branch of My planting, the work of My hands, wherein I glory.

WORLD ENGLISH BIBLE

60:22 The little one shall become a thousand, and the small one a strong nation; I, Yahweh, will hasten it in its time."

61:1 The Spirit of the Lord Yahweh is on me; because Yahweh has anointed me to preach good news to the humble. He has sent me to bind up the brokenhearted, to proclaim liberty to the captives, and release to those who are bound;

61:2 to proclaim the year of Yahweh's favor, and the day of vengeance of our God; to comfort all who mourn;

61:3 to appoint to those who mourn in Zion, to give to them a garland for ashes, the oil of joy for mourning, the garment of praise for the spirit of heaviness; that they may be called trees of righteousness, the planting of Yahweh, that he may be glorified.

61:4 They shall build the old wastes, they shall raise up the former desolations, and they shall repair the waste cities, the desolations of many generations.

61:5 Strangers shall stand and feed your flocks, and foreigners shall be your plowmen and your vinedressers.

61:6 But you shall be named the priests of Yahweh; men will call you the ministers of our God: you will eat the wealth of the nations, and you will boast in their glory.

61:7 Instead of your shame you shall have double; and instead of dishonor they shall rejoice in their portion: therefore in their land they shall possess double; everlasting joy shall be to them.

61:8 "For I, Yahweh, love justice, I hate robbery with iniquity; and I will give them their recompense in truth, and I will make an everlasting covenant with them.

61:9 Their seed shall be known among the nations, and their offspring among the peoples; all who see them shall acknowledge them, that they are the seed which Yahweh has blessed."

TARGUM ISAIAH

the land, the plant of my delight, the work of my might, that I may *assuredly* be glorified.

60:22 He that is little amongst them shall become a thousand, and he that is weak *shall become* a strong nation: I the Lord will bring it to pass in its time.

61:1 The prophet said, the spirit of prophecy from before the presence of the Lord God is upon me; because that the Lord hath anointed me to preach good tidings to the meek; He hath sent me to strengthen the brokenhearted, to proclaim liberty to the captives, and to the prisoners! Appear in light!

61:2 To proclaim the acceptable year of the Lord, and the day of vengeance of our God; to comfort all that mourn.

61:3 To appoint unto them that mourn in Zion, that unto them be given a crown for ashes, the oil of joy for mourning, the spirit of praise for their spirit which is faint; they shall be called princes of truth, the people of the Lord, that He may *assuredly* be glorified.

61:4 And they shall build the old wastes, they shall raise up the former desolations, and they shall re-

TARGUM ISAIAH

pair the cities which were wastes, the desolations of many generations.

61:5 And strangers shall stand and feed your flocks, and the sons of the Gentiles shall be your plowmen, and they shall dress your vineyards.

61:6 But ye shall be called the Priests of the Lord: it shall be said of you *that ye are those* who minister before our God: ye shall eat the riches of the Gentiles, and in their glory ye shall delight yourselves.

61:7 Instead of your having suffered shame, and confusion, I will bring unto you double mercies, which I have promised you; and the Gentiles who glory in their portion shall be confounded: therefore in their own land they shall possess double: everlasting joy shall be unto them.

61:8 For I, the Lord, love justice; lying and violence are an abomination in my presence; and I will render the reward of their work in truth, and I will make an everlasting covenant with them.

61:9 And their sons shall be magnified amongst the nations, and their sons' sons amongst the king-

JEWISH PUBLICATION SOCIETY 1917

60:22 The smallest shall become a thousand, and the least a mighty nation; I the LORD will hasten it in its time.

61:1 The spirit of the Lord GOD is upon me; because the LORD hath anointed me to bring good tidings unto the humble; He hath sent me to bind up the brokenhearted, to proclaim liberty to the captives, and the opening of the eyes to them that are bound;

61:2 To proclaim the year of the LORD'S good pleasure, and the day of vengeance of our God; to comfort all that mourn;

61:3 To appoint unto them that mourn in Zion, to give unto them a garland for ashes, the oil of joy for mourning, the mantle of praise for the spirit of heaviness; that they might be called terebinths of righteousness, the planting of the LORD, wherein He might glory.

61:4 And they shall build the old wastes, they shall raise up the former desolations, and they shall renew the waste cities, the desolations of many generations.

61:5 And strangers shall stand and feed your flocks, and aliens shall be your plowmen and your vinedressers.

61:6 But ye shall be named the priests of the LORD, men shall call you the ministers of our God; ye shall eat the wealth of the nations, and in their splendour shall ye revel.

61:7 For your shame which was double, and for that they rejoiced: 'Confusion is their portion'; therefore in their land they shall possess double, everlasting joy shall be unto them.

61:8 For I the LORD love justice, I hate robbery with iniquity; and I will give them their recompense in truth, and I will make an everlasting covenant with them.

61:9 And their seed shall be known among the nations, and their offspring among the peoples; all that see them shall acknowledge them, that they are the seed which the LORD hath blessed.

WORLD ENGLISH BIBLE

61:10 I will greatly rejoice in Yahweh, my soul shall be joyful in my God; for he has clothed me with the garments of salvation, he has covered me with the robe of righteousness, as a bridegroom decks himself with a garland, and as a bride adorns herself with her jewels.

61:11 For as the earth brings forth its bud, and as the garden causes the things that are sown in it to spring forth; so the Lord Yahweh will cause righteousness and praise to spring forth before all the nations.

62:1 For Zion's sake will I not hold my peace, and for Jerusalem's sake I will not rest, until her righteousness go forth as brightness, and her salvation as a lamp that burns.

62:2 The nations shall see your righteousness, and all kings your glory, and you shall be called by a new name, which the mouth of Yahweh shall name.

62:3 You shall also be a crown of beauty in the hand of Yahweh, and a royal diadem in the hand of your God.

62:4 You shall no more be termed Forsaken; neither shall your land any more be termed Desolate: but you shall be called Hephzibah, and your land Beulah; for Yahweh delights in you, and your land shall be married.

62:5 For as a young man marries a virgin, so your sons shall marry you; and as the bridegroom rejoices over the bride, so your God will rejoice over you.

62:6 I have set watchmen on your walls, Jerusalem; they shall never hold their peace day nor night: you who call on Yahweh, take no rest,

62:7 and give him no rest, until he establishes, and until he makes Jerusalem a praise in the earth.

62:8 Yahweh has sworn by his right hand, and by the arm of his strength, "Surely I will no more give your grain to be food for your enemies; and foreigners shall not drink your new wine, for which you have labored:

TARGUM ISAIAH

doms: all that see them shall acknowledge them, that they are the seed which the Lord has blessed.

61:10 Jerusalem shall say, I will greatly rejoice in the WORD of the Lord, my soul shall be joyful in the salvation of my God; for He hath clothed me with the garments of salvation, He hath covered me with the upper garment of righteousness, like a bridegroom who is happy in his bridechamber, and like the high priest who decketh *himself* with his robes, and like a bride who is adorned with her jewels.

61:11 For as the earth bringeth forth her shoots, and as a watered garden causeth the things that are sown in it to grow, thus the Lord God shall reveal the righteousness and the praise of Jerusalem before all the nations.

62:1 Till I work salvation for Zion, I will give no rest to the nations, until I bring consolation to Jerusalem, I will give no rest to the kingdoms, till her light be revealed as the early dawn, and her salvation shall burn as a lamp.

62:2 And the Gentiles shall see thy righteousness, and all kings thy glory: and they shall call thee by

TARGUM ISAIAH

JEWISH PUBLICATION SOCIETY 1917

a new name, which the WORD of the Lord shall declare.

62:3 Ye shall be a crown of joy before the Lord, and a diadem of glory before thy God.

62:4 Thou shalt no more be termed Forsaken; neither shall thy land any more be termed Desolate: but thou shalt be called Abĕday Rĕoothee Bahh, and thy land Inhabited: for the Lord shall delight in thee, and thy land shall be inhabited.

62:5 For as a young man dwelleth with a virgin, thus thy sons shall dwell in thee: and as the bridegroom rejoiceth over the bride, *so* shall thy God rejoice over thee.

62:6 Behold, the works of thy righteous fathers, O city of Jerusalem, are right, and kept by me all the day and all the night, continually; the remembrance of thine excellencies is declared before the Lord, it shall not fail you.

62:7 Their remembrance shall not cease from before Him, till He establish and make Jerusalem a praise in the earth.

62:8 The Lord hath sworn by His right hand, and by the arm of His strength, I will no more give thy corn *to be* food for thy ene-

61:10 I will greatly rejoice in the LORD, my soul shall be joyful in my God; for He hath clothed me with the garments of salvation, He hath covered me with the robe of victory, as a bridegroom putteth on a priestly diadem, and as a bride adorneth herself with her jewels.

61:11 For as the earth bringeth forth her growth, and as the garden causeth the things that are sown in it to spring forth; so the Lord GOD will cause victory and glory to spring forth before all the nations.

62:1 For Zion's sake will I not hold My peace, and for Jerusalem's sake I will not rest, until her triumph go forth as brightness, and her salvation as a torch that burneth.

62:2 And the nations shall see thy triumph, and all kings thy glory; and thou shalt be called by a new name, which the mouth of the LORD shall mark out.

62:3 Thou shalt also be a crown of beauty in the hand of the LORD, and a royal diadem in the open hand of thy God.

62:4 Thou shalt no more be termed Forsaken, neither shall thy land any more be termed Desolate; but thou shalt be called, My delight is in her, and thy land, Espoused; for the LORD delighteth in thee, and thy land shall be espoused.

62:5 For as a young man espouseth a virgin, so shall thy sons espouse thee; and as the bridegroom rejoiceth over the bride, so shall thy God rejoice over thee.

62:6 I have set watchmen upon thy walls, O Jerusalem, they shall never hold their peace day nor night: 'Ye that are the LORD'S remembrancers, take ye no rest,

62:7 And give Him no rest, till He establish, and till He make Jerusalem a praise in the earth.'

62:8 The LORD hath sworn by His right hand, and by the arm of His strength: Surely I will no more give thy corn to be food for thine enemies; and strangers shall not drink thy wine, for which thou hast laboured;

WORLD ENGLISH BIBLE

62:9 but those who have garnered it shall eat it, and praise Yahweh; and those who have gathered it shall drink it in the courts of my sanctuary."

62:10 Go through, go through the gates! Prepare the way of the people! Cast up, cast up the highway! Gather out the stones! Lift up a banner for the peoples.

62:11 Behold, Yahweh has proclaimed to the end of the earth, "Say to the daughter of Zion, Behold, your salvation comes. Behold, his reward is with him, and his recompense before him.'"

62:12 They shall call them The holy people, The redeemed of Yahweh: and you shall be called Sought out, A city not forsaken.

63:1 Who is this who comes from Edom, with dyed garments from Bozrah? this who is glorious in his clothing, marching in the greatness of his strength? "It is I who speak in righteousness, mighty to save."

63:2 Why are you red in your clothing, and your garments like him who treads in the wine vat?

63:3 "I have trodden the winepress alone; and of the peoples there was no man with me: yes, I trod them in my anger, and trampled them in my wrath; and their lifeblood is sprinkled on my garments, and I have stained all my clothing.

63:4 For the day of vengeance was in my heart, and the year of my redeemed has come.

63:5 I looked, and there was none to help; and I wondered that there was none to uphold: therefore my own arm brought salvation to me; and my wrath, it upheld me.

TARGUM ISAIAH

mies; and the sons of the Gentiles shall not drink thy wine, for the which thou hast laboured.

62:9 But they that gather the corn, they shall eat it, and offer praise before the Lord; and they that tread out the wine, they shall drink it in the courts of my holiness.

62:10 O prophets, pass through and return through the gates; turn the heart of the people into the right way; bring good tidings of good things, and consolations to the righteous, who remove the thoughts of *an evil* imagination, which are like a stone of stumbling; lift up a standard for the people.

62:11 Behold, the Lord hath proclaimed unto the ends of the world, Say ye to the congregation of Zion, Behold, thy Redeemer shall be revealed; Behold, the reward for them that do His word is with Him: and all their works are manifest before Him.

62:12 And they shall call them, The holy people, The redeemed of the Lord: and thou shalt be called Teviātha, A city not forsaken.

63:1 Who hath spoken these things? He who shall bring the blow upon

TARGUM ISAIAH

Persia, the mighty vengeance upon Bozrah, to execute vengeance of judgment of His people, as He hath sworn unto them by His WORD. He hath said, Behold, I shall reveal myself as I have spoken in righteousness, great is my power to save.

63:2 Wherefore are the mountains red from the blood of the slain? yea, the valleys shall flow as the wine from the winepress.

63:3 Behold, as the grapes are trodden in the vat, thus He shall increase the slaughter in the camps of the nations; they shall have no strength before me: yea, I will slay them in my anger, and tread them down in my fury; and I will break the strength of their mighty ones before me, and all their wise men will I consume.

63:4 For the day of vengeance is before me, and the year of the salvation of my people hath come.

63:5 And it is revealed before me, that there is no man whose works are good, and it is known to me, that there is no man who will stand up and pray in behalf of them; yea, I will redeem them by the arm of my strength, and by the WORD of my delight I will

JEWISH PUBLICATION SOCIETY 1917

62:9 But they that have garnered it shall eat it, and praise the LORD, and they that have gathered it shall drink it in the courts of My sanctuary.

62:10 Go through, go through the gates, clear ye the way of the people; cast up, cast up the highway, gather out the stones; lift up an ensign over the peoples.

62:11 Behold, the LORD hath proclaimed unto the end of the earth: say ye to the daughter of Zion: 'Behold, thy salvation cometh; behold, His reward is with Him, and His recompense before Him.'

62:12 And they shall call them The holy people, the redeemed of the LORD; and thou shalt be called Sought out, a city not forsaken.

63:1 'Who is this that cometh from Edom, with crimsoned garments from Bozrah? This that is glorious in his apparel, stately in the greatness of his strength?'—' I that speak in victory, mighty to save.'—

63:2 'Wherefore is Thine apparel red, and Thy garments like his that treadeth in the winevat?'—

63:3 'I have trodden the winepress alone, and of the peoples there was no man with Me; yea, I trod them in Mine anger, and trampled them in My fury; and their lifeblood is dashed against My garments, and I have stained all My raiment.

63:4 For the day of vengeance that was in My heart, and My year of redemption are come.

63:5 And I looked, and there was none to help, and I beheld in astonishment, and there was none to uphold; therefore Mine own arm brought salvation unto Me, and My fury, it upheld Me.

WORLD ENGLISH BIBLE

63:6 I trod down the peoples in my anger, and made them drunk in my wrath, and I poured out their lifeblood on the earth."

63:7 I will make mention of the loving kindnesses of Yahweh and the praises of Yahweh, according to all that Yahweh has bestowed on us, and the great goodness toward the house of Israel, which he has bestowed on them according to his mercies, and according to the multitude of his loving kindnesses.

63:8 For he said, "Surely, they are my people, children who will not deal falsely:" so he was their Savior.

63:9 In all their affliction he was afflicted, and the angel of his presence saved them: in his love and in his pity he redeemed them; and he bore them, and carried them all the days of old.

63:10 But they rebelled, and grieved his holy Spirit: therefore he was turned to be their enemy, and he himself fought against them.

63:11 Then he remembered the days of old, Moses and his people, saying, Where is he who brought them up out of the sea with the shepherds of his flock? where is he who put his holy Spirit in their midst?

63:12 who caused his glorious arm to go at the right hand of Moses? who divided the waters before them, to make himself an everlasting name?

63:13 who led them through the depths, as a horse in the wilderness, so that they didn't stumble?

63:14 As the livestock that go down into the valley, the Spirit of Yahweh caused them to rest; so you led your people, to make yourself a glorious name.

63:15 Look down from heaven, and see from the habitation of your holiness and of your glory: where are your zeal and your mighty acts? the yearning of your heart and your compassion is restrained toward me.

TARGUM ISAIAH

help them.

63:6 And I will slay the nations in my anger, and I will tread them down in my fury, and I will cast the slain of their mighty ones into the lowest *parts* of the earth.

63:7 The prophet said, I will mention the loving-kindness of the Lord; the praise of the Lord according to all that the Lord hath dealt bountifully with us, and His great goodness toward the house of Israel which He hath bestowed upon them according to His mercies, and according to the multitude of His loving-kindnesses.

63:8 And He said, Surely, they *are* my people, children that will not lie: and His WORD became their salvation.

63:9 Whenever they sinned against Him, that He might have brought upon them distress, He did not distress them; but an angel was sent from Him, who in His mercy redeemed them; and in His compassion, behold, He delivered them; and He bare them, and carried them all the days of old.

63:10 But they rebelled against the word of His holy prophets, and blasphemed, and His WORD became their enemy, and He waged war

TARGUM ISAIAH

against them.

63:11 And He had compassion for the glory of His name, because of the remembrance of His goodness of old, the mighty works which He did by the hands of Moses for His people; lest the Gentiles should say, Where is He that brought them up out of the sea? Where is He that led them through the wilderness, as a shepherd his flock? Where is He that made the word of His holy prophets to dwell amongst them?

63:12 That led *them* by the right hand of Moses, the arm of His glory, dividing the waters of the Red Sea before them, to make Himself an everlasting name?

63:13 That led them through the depths, as a horse that stumbleth not in the plain? thus also they stumbled not.

63:14 As a beast is led in a plain, the WORD of the Lord led them; so didst Thou lead Thy people to make Thyself a glorious name.

63:15 Look down from heaven, and reveal Thyself from the habitation of Thy holiness and of Thy glory: where is Thy vengeance, and Thy great might? the multitude of Thy mercies and Thy compas-

JEWISH PUBLICATION SOCIETY 1917

63:6 And I trod down the peoples in Mine anger, and made them drunk with My fury, and I poured out their lifeblood on the earth.'

63:7 I will make mention of the mercies of the LORD, and the praises of the LORD, according to all that the LORD hath bestowed on us; and the great goodness toward the house of Israel, which He hath bestowed on them according to His compassions, and according to the multitude of His mercies.

63:8 For He said: 'Surely, they are My people, children that will not deal falsely'; so He was their Saviour.

63:9 In all their affliction He was afflicted, and the angel of His presence saved them; in His love and in His pity He redeemed them; and He bore them, and carried them all the days of old.

63:10 But they rebelled, and grieved His holy spirit; therefore He was turned to be their enemy, Himself fought against them.

63:11 Then His people remembered the days of old, the days of Moses: 'Where is He that brought them up out of the sea with the shepherds of His flock? Where is He that put His holy spirit in the midst of them?

63:12 That caused His glorious arm to go at the right hand of Moses? that divided the water before them, to make Himself an everlasting name?

63:13 That led them through the deep, as a horse in the wilderness, without stumbling?

63:14 As the cattle that go down into the valley, the spirit of the LORD caused them to rest; so didst Thou lead Thy people, to make Thyself a glorious name.'

63:15 Look down from heaven, and see, even from Thy holy and glorious habitation; where is Thy zeal and Thy mighty acts, the yearning of Thy heart and Thy compassions, now restrained toward me?

WORLD ENGLISH BIBLE

63:16 For you are our Father, though Abraham doesn't know us, and Israel does not acknowledge us: you, Yahweh, are our Father; our Redeemer from everlasting is your name.

63:17 O Yahweh, why do you make us to err from your ways, and harden our heart from your fear? Return for your servants' sake, the tribes of your inheritance.

63:18 Your holy people possessed it but a little while: our adversaries have trodden down your sanctuary.

63:19 We have become as they over whom you never bear rule, as those who were not called by your name.

64:1 Oh that you would tear the heavens, that you would come down, that the mountains might quake at your presence,

64:2 as when fire kindles the brushwood, and the fire causes the waters to boil; to make your name known to your adversaries, that the nations may tremble at your presence!

64:3 When you did awesome things which we didn't look for, you came down, the mountains quaked at your presence.

64:4 For from of old men have not heard, nor perceived by the ear, neither has the eye seen a God besides you, who works for him who waits for him.

TARGUM ISAIAH

sion towards me are restrained.

63:16 For Thou art He, whose mercies towards us are as many as a father's towards *his* children: for Abraham hath not brought us up out of Egypt, and Israel hath not wrought for us wonderful works in the wilderness; Thou art the Lord; Thy mercies towards us are many, like a father's towards *his* children, O, our Redeemer; Thy name is from everlasting.

63:17 Why hast Thou cast us off, O Lord, that *we* should go astray from the paths which are right in Thy sight, as the nations which have no part in the instruction of Thy law? Our heart is not turned away from Thy fear: return Thy Shekinah unto Thy people, for the sake of Thy righteous servants, unto whom Thou hast sworn by Thy WORD to make the tribes amongst them Thine inheritance.

63:18 The people of Thy holiness have possessed *Thy sanctuary* but a little time, our adversaries have trodden *it* down.

63:19 We are Thy people that were of old: not unto the Gentiles hast Thou given the doctrine of Thy law, neither is Thy name invoked upon them; not unto them hast

TARGUM ISAIAH

Thou inclined the heavens *and* revealed Thyself; the mountains quaked before Thee.

64:1 When Thou didst send forth Thine anger like fire in the days of Elijah, the sea was melted, the waters were flames of fire, to make Thy name known to the enemies of Thy people, *that* the nations may tremble at Thy presence.

64:2 When Thou didst wonderful things, which we expected not, Thou didst reveal Thyself; the mountains trembled at Thy presence.

64:3 And since the world was, ear hath not heard the report of such mighty deeds, nor hearkened to the speech of rapture, nor hath eye seen, what Thy people saw, the Shekinah of Thy glory, O Lord; for there is none besides Thee, who will do such things for Thy righteous people, who were of old; who hope for Thy salvation.

64:4 The works of our righteous fathers were acceptable in Thy sight, who rejoiced to do Thy will in truth and in righteousness: in the way of Thy goodness and mercy they remembered Thy fear

JEWISH PUBLICATION SOCIETY 1917

63:16 For Thou art our Father; for Abraham knoweth us not, and Israel doth not acknowledge us; Thou, O LORD, art our Father, our Redeemer from everlasting is Thy name.

63:17 O LORD, why dost Thou make us to err from Thy ways, and hardenest our heart from Thy fear? Return for Thy servants' sake, the tribes of Thine inheritance.

63:18 Thy holy people they have well nigh driven out, our adversaries have trodden down Thy sanctuary.

63:19 We are become as they over whom Thou never borest rule, as they that were not called by Thy name.

64:1 (63:19) Oh, that Thou wouldest rend the heavens, that Thou wouldest come down, that the mountains might quake at Thy presence,

64:2 (64:1) As when fire kindleth the brush-wood, and the fire causeth the waters to boil; to make Thy name known to Thine adversaries, that the nations might tremble at Thy presence,

64:3 (64:2) When Thou didst tremendous things which we looked not for— Oh that Thou wouldest come down, that the mountains might quake at Thy presence!—

64:4 (64:3) And whereof from of old men have not heard, nor perceived by the ear, neither hath the eye seen a God beside Thee, who worketh for him that waiteth for Him.

64:5 (64:4) Thou didst take away him that joyfully worked righteousness, those that remembered Thee in Thy ways—behold, Thou wast wroth, and we sinned—upon them have we stayed of old, that we might be saved.

WORLD ENGLISH BIBLE

64:5 You meet him who rejoices and works righteousness, those who remember you in your ways. Behold, you were angry, and we sinned. We have been in sin for a long time; and shall we be saved?

64:6 For we have all become as one who is unclean, and all our righteousness is as a polluted garment: and we all fade as a leaf; and our iniquities, like the wind, take us away.

64:7 There is none who calls on your name, who stirs up himself to take hold of you; for you have hidden your face from us, and have consumed us by means of our iniquities.

64:8 But now, Yahweh, you are our Father; we are the clay, and you our potter; and we all are the work of your hand.

64:9 Don't be furious, Yahweh, neither remember iniquity forever: see, look, we beg you, we are all your people.

64:10 Your holy cities are become a wilderness, Zion has become a wilderness, Jerusalem a desolation.

64:11 Our holy and our beautiful house, where our fathers praised you, is burned with fire; and all our pleasant places are laid waste.

64:12 Will you refrain yourself for these things, Yahweh? Will you hold your peace, and afflict us very severely?

65:1 "I am inquired of by those who didn't ask; I am found by those who didn't seek me: I said, See me, see me, to a nation that was not called by my name.

65:2 I have spread out my hands all the day to a rebellious people, who walk in a way that is not good, after their own thoughts;

65:3 a people who provoke me to my face continually, sacrificing in gardens, and burning incense on bricks;

65:4 who sit among the graves, and lodge in the secret places; who eat pig's flesh, and broth of abominable things is in their vessels;

TARGUM ISAIAH

whenever Thy wrath from Thy presence was upon us, because we had sinned: on account of the works of our righteous fathers, we have been saved.

64:5 But we are all as an unclean *thing*; all our righteousnesses are as an abominable garment, and we all do fade as the fading of a leaf; and because of our sins, we are taken away as by the wind.

64:6 And there is none that prayeth in Thy name willing to lay hold on Thy fear; because Thou hast taken away the fear of Thy Shekinah from us, and Thou hast delivered us to the power of our sins.

64:7 And Thy mercies, O Lord, have been as many upon us as a father's upon *his* children; we are the clay, and Thou hast formed us, and we all are the work of Thy hand.

64:8 Let there not be, O Lord, very sore wrath from Thee against us, neither remember iniquities for ever: behold, it is revealed before Thee, that we *are* all Thy people.

64:9 Thy holy cities have become a wilderness, Zion is a wilderness, Jerusalem has become a desolation.

TARGUM ISAIAH

64:10 The house of our holiness and of our glory, where our fathers worshipped Thee, is burned up with fire: and every place of our desire hath become a waste.
64:11 Wilt Thou refrain Thyself for these *things*, O Lord? and wilt Thou give prosperity for ever to the wicked, who make us servile?
65:1 I am asked concerning my WORD of them that have not asked after me; I am inquired of for instruction in my law, of them who have not sought my fear: I will say, Behold, I am inquired after continually, all the day, of a people that hath not prayed in my name.
65:2 I have sent my prophets every day unto a rebellious people, which walketh in a way which was not good, after their own thoughts;
65:3 A people that provoketh my WORD to anger continually to my face; that sacrificeth in gardens to idols, and offereth aromatic spices upon bricks;
65:4 Who dwell in houses, which are built of the dust of graves, with the dead bodies of the sons of men they dwell, which eat swine's flesh, and broth of abomi-

JEWISH PUBLICATION SOCIETY 1917

64:6 (64:5) And we are all become as one that is unclean, and all our righteousnesses are as a polluted garment; and we all do fade as a leaf, and our iniquities, like the wind, take us away.
64:7 (64:6) And there is none that calleth upon Thy name, that stirreth up himself to take hold of Thee; for Thou hast hid Thy face from us, and hast consumed us by means of our iniquities.
64:8 (64:7) But now, O LORD, Thou art our Father; we are the clay, and Thou our potter, and we all are the work of Thy hand.
64:9 (64:8) Be not wroth very sore, O LORD, neither remember iniquity for ever; behold, look, we beseech Thee, we are all Thy people.
64:10 (64:9) Thy holy cities are become a wilderness, Zion is become a wilderness, Jerusalem a desolation.
64:11 (64:10) Our holy and our beautiful house, where our fathers praised Thee, is burned with fire; and all our pleasant things are laid waste.
64:12 (64:11) Wilt Thou refrain Thyself for these things, O LORD? Wilt Thou hold Thy peace, and afflict us very sore?
65:1 I gave access to them that asked not for Me, I was at hand to them that sought Me not; I said: 'Behold Me, behold Me', unto a nation that was not called by My name.
65:2 I have spread out My hands all the day unto a rebellious people, that walk in a way that is not good, after their own thoughts;
65:3 A people that provoke Me to My face continually, that sacrifice in gardens, and burn incense upon bricks;
65:4 That sit among the graves, and lodge in the vaults; that eat swine's flesh, and broth of abominable things is in their vessels;

WORLD ENGLISH BIBLE

65:5 who say, Stand by yourself, don't come near to me, for I am holier than you. These are a smoke in my nose, a fire that burns all the day.

65:6 "Behold, it is written before me: I will not keep silence, but will recompense, yes, I will recompense into their bosom,

65:7 your own iniquities, and the iniquities of your fathers together," says Yahweh, "who have burned incense on the mountains, and blasphemed me on the hills; therefore will I first measure their work into their bosom."

65:8 Thus says Yahweh, "As the new wine is found in the cluster, and one says, 'Don't destroy it, for a blessing is in it:' so will I do for my servants' sake, that I may not destroy them all.

65:9 I will bring forth a seed out of Jacob, and out of Judah an inheritor of my mountains; and my chosen shall inherit it, and my servants shall dwell there.

65:10 Sharon shall be a fold of flocks, and the valley of Achor a place for herds to lie down in, for my people who have sought me.

65:11 "But you who forsake Yahweh, who forget my holy mountain, who prepare a table for Fortune, and who fill up mixed wine to Destiny;

65:12 I will destine you to the sword, and you shall all bow down to the slaughter; because when I called, you didn't answer; when I spoke, you didn't listen; but you did that which was evil in my eyes, and chose that in which I didn't delight."

65:13 Therefore thus says the Lord Yahweh, "Behold, my servants shall eat, but you shall be hungry; behold, my servants shall drink, but you shall be thirsty; behold, my servants shall rejoice, but you shall be disappointed;

65:14 behold, my servants shall sing for joy of heart, but you shall cry for sorrow of heart, and shall wail for anguish of spirit.

TARGUM ISAIAH

nable things *is* in their vessels;

65:5 Who say, Stand by thyself, come not near to me; because I am purer than thou. These their provocations *are* as smoke before me: their recompense shall be in hell, where the fire burneth all the day.

65:6 Behold, it is written before me: I will not give unto them prolongation in this life; but I will recompense unto them the wages for their sins, and deliver their bodies to the second death.

65:7 Your sins and the sins of your fathers together are revealed before me, saith the Lord, which have offered incense upon the mountains, and blasphemed me upon the hills: therefore will I give the reward of their former works into their bosom.

65:8 Thus saith the Lord, As Noah was found righteous in the generation of the deluge, and I said that I would not destroy him, for the purpose that I might raise up the world by him; so will I do for my righteous servants' sakes, in order that I may not destroy them all.

65:9 And I will bring forth a seed out of Jacob, and out of Judah an

TARGUM ISAIAH

inheritor of my mountains: and mine elect shall inherit it, and my righteous servants shall dwell there.

65:10 And Sharon shall be a fold of flocks, and the valley of Achor a place for the crouching down of the herds of oxen, for my people which have sought my fear.

65:11 But ye, O house of Israel, ye have forsaken the worship of the Lord, ye have forgotten the worship of my holy mountain, that prepare tables for the idols, and mix goblets for their gods.

65:12 Therefore will I deliver them to the sword, yea, all of you shall be delivered to the slaughter; because I sent my prophets, and ye repented not; they prophesied, and ye did not receive them; but did evil before me, and delighted yourselves in that I would not.

65:13 Therefore thus saith the Lord God, Behold, my righteous servants shall eat, but ye, O wicked, shall be hungry: behold, my righteous servants shall drink, but ye, O wicked, shall be thirsty: behold, my righteous servants shall rejoice, but ye, O wicked, shall be ashamed:

65:14 Behold, my righteous servants

65:5 That say: 'Stand by thyself, come not near to me, for I am holier than thou'; these are a smoke in My nose, a fire that burneth all the day.

65:6 Behold, it is written before Me; I will not keep silence, except I have requited, yea, I will requite into their bosom,

65:7 Your own iniquities, and the iniquities of your fathers together, saith the LORD, that have offered upon the mountains, and blasphemed Me upon the hills; therefore will I first measure their wage into their bosom.

65:8 Thus saith the LORD: as, when wine is found in the cluster, one saith: 'Destroy it not, for a blessing is in it'; so will I do for My servants' sakes, that I may not destroy all.

65:9 And I will bring forth a seed out of Jacob, and out of Judah an inheritor of My mountains; and Mine elect shall inherit it, and My servants shall dwell there.

65:10 And Sharon shall be a fold of flocks, and the valley of Achor a place for herds to lie down in, for My people that have sought Me;

65:11 But ye that forsake the LORD, that forget My holy mountain, that prepare a table for Fortune, and that offer mingled wine in full measure unto Destiny,

65:12 I will destine you to the sword, and ye shall all bow down to the slaughter; because when I called, ye did not answer, when I spoke, ye did not hear; but ye did that which was evil in Mine eyes, and chose that wherein I delighted not.

65:13 Therefore thus saith the Lord GOD: Behold, My servants shall eat, but ye shall be hungry; behold, My servants shall drink, but ye shall be thirsty; behold, My servants shall rejoice, but ye shall be ashamed;

65:14 Behold, My servants shall sing for joy of heart, but ye shall cry for sorrow of heart, and shall wail for vexation of spirit.

WORLD ENGLISH BIBLE

65:15 You shall leave your name for a curse to my chosen; and the Lord Yahweh will kill you; and he will call his servants by another name:

65:16 so that he who blesses himself in the earth shall bless himself in the God of truth; and he who swears in the earth shall swear by the God of truth; because the former troubles are forgotten, and because they are hidden from my eyes.

65:17 "For, behold, I create new heavens and a new earth; and the former things shall not be remembered, nor come into mind.

65:18 But be you glad and rejoice forever in that which I create; for, behold, I create Jerusalem a rejoicing, and her people a joy.

65:19 I will rejoice in Jerusalem, and joy in my people; and there shall be heard in her no more the voice of weeping and the voice of crying.

65:20 "There shall be no more there an infant of days, nor an old man who has not filled his days; for the child shall die one hundred years old, and the sinner being one hundred years old shall be accursed.

65:21 They shall build houses, and inhabit them; and they shall plant vineyards, and eat their fruit.

65:22 They shall not build, and another inhabit; they shall not plant, and another eat: for as the days of a tree shall be the days of my people, and my chosen shall long enjoy the work of their hands.

65:23 They shall not labor in vain, nor bring forth for calamity; for they are the seed of the blessed of Yahweh, and their offspring with them.

65:24 It shall happen that, before they call, I will answer; and while they are yet speaking, I will hear.

65:25 The wolf and the lamb shall feed together, and the lion shall eat straw like the ox; and dust shall be the serpent's food. They shall not hurt nor destroy in all my holy mountain," says Yahweh.

66:1 Thus says Yahweh, "Heaven is my throne, and the earth is my footstool: what kind of house will you build to me? and what place shall be my rest?

TARGUM ISAIAH

shall sing for joy of heart, but ye shall cry for sorrow of heart, and ye shall howl for vexation of spirit.

65:15 And ye shall leave your name for a curse to my chosen: for the Lord God shall slay you with the second death, and call His righteous servants by another name:

65:16 That he who blesseth in the earth shall bless by the God of the covenant, and he that sweareth in the earth shall swear by the God of the covenant; because, the former troubles shall be forgotten, and because they shall be hidden from before me.

65:17 For, behold, I create new heavens and a new earth: and the former shall not be remembered, neither shall they come into mind.

65:18 But be ye glad and rejoice in the world of worlds, which I create; for behold, I create Jerusalem a rejoicing, and her people a joy.

65:19 And I will rejoice in Jerusalem, and my people shall be glad in her: and the voice of weeping shall be no more heard in her, nor the voice of those that cry.

65:20 There shall be no more thence a suckling of days, or an old man that shall not accomplish his days, for *even* the child that sinneth shall

TARGUM ISAIAH

die an hundred years old; but he that is a sinner *being* an hundred years old shall be thrust out.

65:21 And they shall build houses, and inhabit *them*; and they shall plant vineyards, and eat the fruit of them.

65:22 They shall not build, and others inhabit; they shall not plant, and others eat: for as the days of the tree of life *are* the days of my people, and mine elect shall wear out the work of their hands.

65:23 They shall not labour in vain, neither shall they rear up children for death, for they shall be the seed which the Lord has blessed, and the children of their children with them.

65:24 And it shall come to pass, before they shall pray before me, that I will hear their prayer; and before they supplicate before me, I will grant their request.

65:25 The wolf and the lamb shall feed together, and the lion shall eat straw like the bullock: and as for the serpent, dust shall be its food. They shall not hurt nor destroy in all my holy mountain, saith the Lord.

66:1 Thus saith the Lord, the heavens are the throne of my

JEWISH PUBLICATION SOCIETY 1917

65:15 And ye shall leave your name for a curse unto Mine elect: 'So may the Lord GOD slay thee'; but He shall call His servants by another name;

65:16 So that he who blesseth himself in the earth shall bless himself by the God of truth; and he that sweareth in the earth shall swear by the God of truth; because the former troubles are forgotten, and because they are hid from Mine eyes.

65:17 For, behold, I create new heavens and a new earth; and the former things shall not be remembered, nor come into mind.

65:18 But be ye glad and rejoice for ever in that which I create; for, behold, I create Jerusalem a rejoicing, and her people a joy.

65:19 And I will rejoice in Jerusalem, and joy in My people; and the voice of weeping shall be no more heard in her, nor the voice of crying.

65:20 There shall be no more thence an infant of days, nor an old man, that hath not filled his days; for the youngest shall die a hundred years old, and the sinner being a hundred years old shall be accursed.

65:21 And they shall build houses, and inhabit them; and they shall plant vineyards, and eat the fruit of them.

65:22 They shall not build, and another inhabit, they shall not plant, and another eat; for as the days of a tree shall be the days of My people, and Mine elect shall long enjoy the work of their hands.

65:23 They shall not labour in vain, nor bring forth for terror; for they are the seed blessed of the LORD, and their offspring with them.

65:24 And it shall come to pass that, before they call, I will answer, and while they are yet speaking, I will hear.

65:25 The wolf and the lamb shall feed together, and the lion shall eat straw like the ox; and dust shall be the serpent's food. They shall not hurt nor destroy in all My holy mountain, saith the LORD.

66:1 Thus saith the LORD: the heaven is My throne, and the earth is My footstool; where is the house that ye may build unto Me? And where is the place that may be My resting-place?

WORLD ENGLISH BIBLE

66:2 For all these things has my hand made, and so all these things came to be," says Yahweh:
"but to this man will I look, even to him who is poor and of a contrite spirit, and who trembles at my word.
66:3 He who kills an ox is as he who kills a man; he who sacrifices a lamb, as he who breaks a dog's neck; he who offers an offering, as he who offers pig's blood; he who burns frankincense, as he who blesses an idol. Yes, they have chosen their own ways, and their soul delights in their abominations:
66:4 I also will choose their delusions, and will bring their fears on them; because when I called, no one answered; when I spoke, they didn't listen; but they did that which was evil in my eyes, and chose that in which I didn't delight."
66:5 Hear the word of Yahweh, you who tremble at his word: "Your brothers who hate you, who cast you out for my name's sake, have said, 'Let Yahweh be glorified, that we may see your joy;' but it is those who shall be disappointed.
66:6 A voice of tumult from the city, a voice from the temple, a voice of Yahweh that renders recompense to his enemies.
66:7 "Before she travailed, she brought forth; before her pain came, she delivered a son.
66:8 Who has heard such a thing? who has seen such things? Shall a land be born in one day? shall a nation be brought forth at once? for as soon as Zion travailed, she brought forth her children.
66:9 Shall I bring to the birth, and not cause to bring forth?" says Yahweh: "shall I who cause to bring forth shut the womb?" says your God.
66:10 "Rejoice with Jerusalem, and be glad for her, all you who love her: rejoice for joy with her, all you who mourn over her;

TARGUM ISAIAH

glory, and the earth is a footstool before me: where is the house that ye build unto me? and where is the place of the dwelling of my Shekinah?

66:2 For all these things my power hath made, and have not all these things been? saith the Lord: but it shall be my delight to consider the man, *even him*, who is of an humble and a contrite spirit, and trembleth on account of my word.

66:3 He that killeth an ox is as if he slew a man; he that sacrificeth a lamb, as if he cut off a dog's neck; he that offereth an oblation, *as if he offered* swine's blood; the offering of their gifts is the gift of violence. Yea, they delight in their paths, and their soul findeth pleasure in their abominations.

66:4 I also will desire their destruction, and they shall not be delivered from that which they dread; because, when I sent my prophets, yea, they did not repent; they prophesied, but they obeyed not: but they did evil before me, and they delighted in that I desired not.

66:5 Hear the word of the Lord, O *ye* righteous! who tremble on account of the words of His will;

TARGUM ISAIAH

your brethren that hate you, that cast you out for my name's sake, say "Let the glory of the Lord be magnified, that we may see your joy;" but they shall be confounded.

66:6 A voice of a tumult from the city of Jerusalem, a voice from the temple, a voice of the WORD of the Lord, who rendereth recompense to His enemies.

66:7 Before distress cometh upon her, she shall be redeemed; and before trembling cometh upon her, like the pains upon a woman in child-bearing, her King shall be revealed.

66:8 Who hath heard such a thing? who hath seen such things? Is it possible that a country be made in one day, and a nation be created at once? but Zion shall be comforted, and shall be filled with the people of the captivity of her captivity.

66:9 I am God; I have created the world from the beginning, saith the Lord; I, even I have created all men; I, even I have scattered them among the nations, also I will gather thy captivity, saith thy God.

66:10 Rejoice ye on account of

JEWISH PUBLICATION SOCIETY 1917

66:2 For all these things hath My hand made, and so all these things came to be, saith the LORD; but on this man will I look, even on him that is poor and of a contrite spirit, and trembleth at My word.

66:3 He that killeth an ox is as if he slew a man; he that sacrificeth a lamb, as if he broke a dog's neck; he that offereth a meal-offering, as if he offered swine's blood; he that maketh a memorial-offering of frankincense, as if he blessed an idol; according as they have chosen their own ways, and their soul delighteth in their abominations;

66:4 Even so I will choose their mockings, and will bring their fears upon them; because when I called, none did answer; when I spoke, they did not hear, but they did that which was evil in Mine eyes, and chose that in which I delighted not.

66:5 Hear the word of the LORD, ye that tremble at His word: your brethren that hate you, that cast you out for My name's sake, have said: 'Let the LORD be glorified, that we may gaze upon your joy', but they shall be ashamed.

66:6 Hark! an uproar from the city, Hark! it cometh from the temple, Hark! the LORD rendereth recompense to His enemies.

66:7 Before she travailed, she brought forth; before her pain came, she was delivered of a man-child.

66:8 Who hath heard such a thing? Who hath seen such things? Is a land born in one day? Is a nation brought forth at once? For as soon as Zion travailed, she brought forth her children.

66:9 Shall I bring to the birth, and not cause to bring forth? saith the LORD; shall I that cause to bring forth shut the womb? saith thy God.

66:10 Rejoice ye with Jerusalem, and be glad with her, all ye that love her; rejoice for joy with her, all ye that mourn for her;

WORLD ENGLISH BIBLE

66:11 that you may nurse and be satisfied at the comforting breasts; that you may drink deeply, and be delighted with the abundance of her glory."

66:12 For thus says Yahweh, "Behold, I will extend peace to her like a river, and the glory of the nations like an overflowing stream: and you will nurse. You will be carried on her side, and will be dandled on her knees.

66:13 As one whom his mother comforts, so will I comfort you; and you will be comforted in Jerusalem."

66:14 You will see it, and your heart shall rejoice, and your bones shall flourish like the tender grass: and the hand of Yahweh shall be known toward his servants; and he will have indignation against his enemies.

66:15 For, behold, Yahweh will come with fire, and his chariots shall be like the whirlwind; to render his anger with fierceness, and his rebuke with flames of fire.

66:16 For by fire will Yahweh execute judgment, and by his sword, on all flesh; and the slain of Yahweh shall be many.

66:17 "Those who sanctify themselves and purify themselves to go to the gardens, behind one in the midst, eating pig's flesh, and the abomination, and the mouse, they shall come to an end together," says Yahweh.

66:18 "For I know their works and their thoughts: the time comes, that I will gather all nations and languages; and they shall come, and shall see my glory.

66:19 "I will set a sign among them, and I will send such as escape of them to the nations, to Tarshish, Pul, and Lud, who draw the bow, to Tubal and Javan, to the islands afar off, who have not heard my fame, neither have seen my glory; and they shall declare my glory among the nations.

66:20 They shall bring all your brothers out of all the nations for an offering to Yahweh, on horses, and in chariots, and in litters, and on mules, and on dromedaries, to my holy mountain Jerusalem, says Yahweh, as the children of Israel bring their offering in a clean vessel into the house of Yahweh.

TARGUM ISAIAH

Jerusalem, and be ye glad on account of her, all ye that love her: rejoice greatly with her, all ye that mourn for her:

66:11 In order that ye may delight yourselves and be satisfied with the food of her consolations, in order that ye may drink and overflow with the wine of her glory.

66:12 For thus saith the Lord, behold, I bring unto her peace, as the floods of the river Euphrates, and the glory of the nations, as an overwhelming stream, and ye shall delight yourselves: ye shall be borne upon the sides, and ye shall be nourished upon the knees.

66:13 As a man whom his mother comforts, so my WORD shall comfort you; and ye shall be comforted in Jerusalem.

66:14 And when ye see this, your heart shall rejoice, and your bodies shall flourish like grass; and the power of the Lord shall be revealed to do good to His righteous servants; but a curse shall come upon His enemies.

66:15 For, behold, the Lord shall be revealed with fire, and His chariots as a whirlwind, to render His anger with fury, and His rebuke with flames of fire.

TARGUM ISAIAH

66:16 For by fire and by His sword will the Lord judge all flesh, and the slain shall be many before the Lord.

66:17 They who prepare and purify themselves in the gardens of idols, multitude after multitude, eating swines' flesh, and the abomination, and the mouse, shall be consumed together, saith the Lord.

66:18 Their works and their thoughts are revealed before me: I will gather all people, nations and tongues; and they shall come and see my glory.

66:19 And I will set a sign among them, and I will send those that escape of them among the nations to the province of the sea, Pul and Lud, that draw the bow, and smite *with it,* to the province of Tubal, and Javan, *the* isles that are afar off, that have not heard the fame of my might, neither have seen my glory; but they shall declare my glory among the nations.

66:20 And they shall bring all your brethren out of all nations an offering before the Lord upon horses, and in chariots, and litters, and upon mules, yea, with songs unto my holy mountain in

JEWISH PUBLICATION SOCIETY 1917

66:11 That ye may suck, and be satisfied with the breast of her consolations; that ye may drink deeply with delight of the abundance of her glory.

66:12 For thus saith the LORD: Behold, I will extend peace to her like a river, and the wealth of the nations like an overflowing stream, and ye shall suck thereof: ye shall be borne upon the side, and shall be dandled upon the knees.

66:13 As one whom his mother comforteth, so will I comfort you; and ye shall be comforted in Jerusalem.

66:14 And when ye see this, your heart shall rejoice, and your bones shall flourish like young grass; and the hand of the LORD shall be known toward His servants, and He will have indignation against His enemies.

66:15 For, behold, the LORD will come in fire, and His chariots shall be like the whirlwind; to render His anger with fury, and His rebuke with flames of fire.

66:16 For by fire will the LORD contend, and by His sword with all flesh; and the slain of the LORD shall be many.

66:17 They that sanctify themselves and purify themselves to go unto the gardens, behind one in the midst, eating swine's flesh, and the detestable thing, and the mouse, shall be consumed together, saith the LORD.

66:18 For I know their works and their thoughts; the time cometh, that I will gather all nations and tongues; and they shall come, and shall see My glory.

66:19 And I will work a sign among them, and I will send such as escape of them unto the nations, to Tarshish, Pul and Lud, that draw the bow, to Tubal and Javan, to the isles afar off, that have not heard My fame, neither have seen My glory; and they shall declare My glory among the nations.

66:20 And they shall bring all your brethren out of all the nations for an offer-

WORLD ENGLISH BIBLE

66:21 Of them also will I take for priests and for Levites," says Yahweh.

66:22 "For as the new heavens and the new earth, which I will make, shall remain before me," says Yahweh, "so your seed and your name shall remain.

66:23 It shall happen, that from one new moon to another, and from one Sabbath to another, shall all flesh come to worship before me," says Yahweh.

66:24 "They shall go forth, and look on the dead bodies of the men who have transgressed against me: for their worm shall not die, neither shall their fire be quenched; and they will be loathsome to all mankind."

TARGUM ISAIAH

Jerusalem, saith the Lord, as the children of Israel bring an offering in a clean vessel into the house of the sanctuary of the Lord.

66:21 And I will also take of them to be priests and Levites, saith the Lord.

66:22 For as the new heavens and the new earth, which I will make, shall remain before me, saith the Lord, thus shall your seed and your name be made to remain.

66:23 And it shall come to pass at the time of the beginning of each month, and at the time of each Sabbath, that all flesh shall come to worship before me, saith the Lord.

66:24 And they shall go forth, and look upon the carcases of the men, the sinners, who have rebelled against my WORD: for their souls shall not die, and their fire shall not be quenched; and the wicked shall be judged in hell, till the righteous shall say concerning them, we have seen enough.

ing unto the LORD, upon horses, and in chariots, and in fitters, and upon mules, and upon swift beasts, to My holy mountain Jerusalem, saith the LORD, as the children of Israel bring their offering in a clean vessel into the house of the LORD.

66:21 And of them also will I take for the priests and for the Levites, saith the LORD.

66:22 For as the new heavens and the new earth, which I will make, shall remain before Me, saith the LORD, so shall your seed and your name remain.

66:23 And it shall come to pass, that from one new moon to another, and from one sabbath to another, shall all flesh come to worship before Me, saith the LORD.

66:24 And they shall go forth, and look upon the carcasses of the men that have rebelled against Me; for their worm shall not die, neither shall their fire be quenched; and they shall be an abhorring unto all flesh.

About The Author

Eliyahu ben David resides in Texas and reaches out globally from there. Eliyahu is known by his listeners and readers as an anointed researcher and teacher of the Scriptures. His unique Hebraic teaching has thrilled many for over three decades. His ministry experience includes a wide range of venues such as: personal ministry on four continents, establishing and teaching home and group fellowships, ministering to congregations and groups of varied persuasions, and public speaking at conventions, meetings, seminars and other events. Eliyahu is best known, however, for his global radio outreach, which broadcasts on AM, FM, Satellite, Shortwave, Internet Radio and Podcasting. Eliyahu also writes books and articles, ministers via his websites and publishes a weekly newsletter, and more.

Eliyahu ben David is the founder and director of Tsiyon Radio, on the web at www.tsiyon.org. Eliyahu offers a free Messianic Scripture training program to all listeners at the Tsiyon website. Tsiyon Radio also publishes a news site from Israel at www.tsiyon.co.il. and other related websites. *On The Road To Tsiyon*, a weekly radio program heard in over 100 countries, is produced and hosted by Eliyahu, with the capable and pleasant assistance of his co-host, Dawn. The radio ministry has produced well over 300 hours of unique programming, all available from the Tsiyon Radio archive. In 2009 Eliyahu released one of his more unique creations, a skekel of .999 fine silver, of his own beautiful and meaningful design.

Eliyahu ben David is a best-selling author and is currently credited with three Zarach Publishing titles. These include Holy Order Restored, ISBN 0967947111, a best-seller in its category and rated 5 stars at Amazon. Eliyahu is in the midst of writing an in-depth seven volume series of books which interprets Revelation from a unique Hebraic perspective. The series is entitled, The Messianic Revelation Series and Volume 1, Announcing: Judgment Day, ISBN 9780967947136, has been a best-seller in its category at Amazon since its release early in 2009. Eliyahu's latest release, also available at Amazon, is titled: Tsiyon Edition Targum Isaiah In English With Parallel Jewish and Christian Texts, ISBN 9780967947129, which is abbreviated as Tsiyon Targum Isaiah (TTI). Eliyahu also authors e-books and articles which are offered from his website.

For three decades Eliyahu has had something to say, and he has been saying it in multiple ways. By reading Eliyahu's books and listening to his radio programs, led by the Holy Spirit (Heb. Ruach HaKodesh), you will discover truth from a Hebraic point of view that many of his listeners and readers say sets Eliyahu ben David apart from all other teachers.

Also Available by Eliyahu ben David

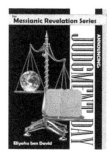

The Messianic Revelation Series: Volume 1
Announcing: Judgment Day

Thousands of books have been written on Revelation, most from one of only a handful of theological schemes. Finally, one book has been written that offers a truly unique perspective on Revelation. The author plainly demonstrates in these pages, complete with illustrations, that the prophetic message of Revelation speaks to the very time and situation which grips the world today. ISBN **9780967947136**

Holy Order Restored

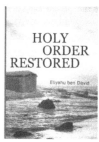

What this book does is more important than what it is about. What it does is get you back in touch with the fundamentals of what it means to be a man or a woman. That may sound too simple to be of benefit. Actually, exactly the opposite is true. The age in which we live is far removed from God's original purpose in creating men and women. Most of us really do not know why we were created or how we were intended to function or even what our true inheritance is in this earth. This book can help with that!   ISBN **9780967947112**

Tsiyon Edition Targum Isaiah in English
With Parallel Jewish and Christian Texts

Tzvi Nassi, son of an Orthodox Jewish Rabbi, made an astounding discovery, in *Targum Isaiah*, an ancient Jewish text credited to Jonathan Ben Uzziel from over 2000 years ago. According to the *Jewish Encyclopedia* Jonathan ben Uzziel was "Hillel's most distinguished pupil". (Suk. 28a; B. B. 134a) That discovery: Targum Isaiah reveals a Divine Messiah!
ISBN **9780967947129**

Holy Time
Join Your Creator Walking in Holy Time with HIM!

Holy Time is set-apart time, sanctified time. Holy Time belongs to Him but it is created for us, His holy people, so that we can meet Him and live our lives with Him there. Holy Time will give you a more Biblically correct understanding of Yah's Appointed Times which He has set. Absolutely know without doubt the right time for Sabbath and other Holy Days! Learn to live in Holy Time everyday with Him! Available exclusively at www.Tsiyon.org

Talmidim Training Program
Join the Tsiyon Dischipleship Program

The Tsiyon Talmidim training program is easy to participate in, stimulating, fun and is sure to help you walk in the Way of Y'shua the Messiah as one of His Talmidim (disciples). This program will give you an unsurpassed Messianic education in one hour per week. You may also progress at your own pace. Available exclusively at www.Tsiyon.org

On The Road To Tsiyon With Eliyahu ben David
Listen to the Radio Programs and Audio CDs

Listen to On The Road to Tsiyon programming through internet radio, AM/FM radio, short wave, cell phone, online, or satellite radio, or join the Tsiyon Radio weekly audio CD club. Please inquire as to the quantity of CDs you would like to receive weekly.

WWW.TSIYON.ORG

ISAIAH TARGUM AUDIO CD SERIES

Author, Eliyahu ben David, hosts the weekly hour-long syndicated radio program *On The Road To Tsiyon with Eliyahu ben David*. Now you can order the accompanying teaching CD set with Eliyahu's in-depth teaching exploring Targum Isaiah, Elohim, the Memra, prophecy, and more. The series includes the following programs:

> Copy this page then check the CDs you want.
>
> Send per instructions below.
>
> Please include phone

- ☐ The Mystery of God in Genesis
- ☐ The WORD: Greek or Jewish?
- ☐ Isaiah Targum Reveals the WORD
- ☐ Immanuel in Q
- ☐ Who is Mahershalalhashbaz?
- ☐ Right on Targum
- ☐ Sealed Among My Talmidim

Order for a suggested Tsiyon Ministry donation of $12 US per CD
Or order the entire set for a suggested donation of $45 US.

Send your order with
your return address
and donation to:

Tsiyon (Payable to "Tsiyon")
1511 S Texas Ave #297
College Station, TX, USA, 77840

Kingdom Silver Shekel and Shekelim
Restoring Purity and Weight

Survive the global economic crisis outlined in Revelation Unsealed. Obtain your Shekel today to have the Holy-Half Shekel needed for the second Exodus. Write to Tsiyon Ministry, 1511 S Texas Ave #297, College Station TX 77840 or contact Tsiyon online at www.Tsiyon.org for more details.

*The prophet said to the house of David,
"For unto us a Child is born, unto us a Son is given,
and He has taken the law upon Himself to keep it.*

*His name is called from eternity, Wonderful,
The mighty God, who liveth to eternity, the Messiah,
whose peace shall be great upon us in His days.*

*The greatness of those who do the law
shall be magnified,
and to those, that preserve peace.*

*There shall be no end to the throne of David,
and of his kingdom, to establish it and to build it
in judgment and in righteousness from henceforth,
even for ever.*

*By the WORD of the Lord of hosts
this shall be done.*

Jonathan ben Uzziel
"Hillel's most distinguished pupil"
Isaiah 9:6 & 7 (TTI)
Targum Isaiah

30 BCE